CHILTON'S

REPAIR MANUAL

CHEVY S-10 GMC S-15 PICK-UPS 1982-91

All U.S and Canadian models of Chevrolet S-10 and GMC S-15 Pick-Ups • gasoline and diesel engines • 2 and 4 wheel drive

President GARY R. INGERSOLL
Senior Vice President, Book Publishing and Research RONALD A. HOXTER
Publisher KERRY A. FREEMAN
Editor-in-Chief DEAN F. MORGANTINI S.A.E.
Senior Editor RICHARD J. RIVELE S.A.E.

CHILTON BOOK COMPANY
ONE OF THE ABC PUBLISHING COMPANIES,
A PART OF CAPITAL CITIES/ABC INC.
Radnor, Pennsylvania 19089

CONTENTS

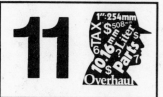

SAFETY NOTICE

Proper service and repair procedures are vital to the safe, reliable operation of all motor vehicles, as well as the safety of those performing repairs. This book outlines procedures for servicing and repairing vehicles using safe effective methods. The procedures contain many NOTES, CAUTIONS and WARNINGS which should be followed along with standard safety procedures to eliminate the possibility of personal injury or improper service which could damage the vehicle or compromise its safety.

It is important to note that repair procedures and techniques, tools and parts for servicing motor vehicles, as well as the skill and experience of the individual performing the work vary widely. It is not possible to anticipate all of the conceivable ways or conditions under which vehicles may be serviced, or to provide cautions as to all of the possible hazards that may result. Standard and accepted safety precautions and equipment should be used during cutting, grinding, chiseling, prying, or any other process that can cause material removal or projectiles.

Some procedures require the use of tools specially designed for a specific purpose. Before substituting another tool or procedure, you must be completely satisfied that neither your personal safety, nor the performance of the vehicle will be endangered.

Although the information in this guide is based on industry sources and is as complete as possible at the time of publication, the possibility exists that the manufacturer made later changes which could not be included here. While striving for total accuracy, Chilton Book Company cannot assume responsibilty for any errors, changes, or omissions that may occur in the compilation of this data.

PART NUMBERS

Part numbers listed in the reference are not recommendations by Chilton for any product by brand name. They are references that can be used with interchange manuals and aftermarket supplier catalogs to locate each brand supplier's discrete part number.

SPECIAL TOOLS

Special tools are recommended by the vehicle manufacturer to perform their specific job. Use has been kept to a minimum, but where absolutely necessary, they are referred to in the text by the part number of the tool manufacturer. These tools can be purchased, under the appropiate part number, from the Service Tool Division, Kent-Moore Corporation, 29784 Little Mac, Roseville MI. or an equivalent tool can be purchased locally from a tool supplier or parts outlet. Before substituting any tool for the one recommended, read the SAFETY NOTICE at the top of this page.

ACKNOWLEDGEMENTS

Chilton Book Company expresses appreciation to Chevrolet Motor Division, General Motors Corporation, Detroit, Michigan 48202; and GMC Truck and Coach Division, General Motors Corporation, Pontiac, Michigan 48053 for their generous assistance

629.287
CHI   2/92

Manufactured in the United States of America
1234567890   0987654321

Chilton's Repair Manual: Chevrolet S-10 and GMC S-15 Pick-Ups 1982–91
ISBN 0–8019–8142–5 pbk.
Library of Congress Catalog Card No. 90–056132

General Information and Maintenance

HOW TO USE THIS BOOK

Chilton's Repair Manual for the S-10/S-15 Pickups is intended to help you learn more about the inner working of your truck and save you money in it's upkeep and operation.

The first two Chapters will be the most used, since they contain maintenance and tune-up information and procedures. Studies have shown that a properly tuned and maintained truck can get at least 10% better gas mileage than an out-of-tune truck. Other Chapters deal with the more complex systems of your truck. Operating systems from engine through brakes are covered. This book will give you detailed instructions to help you perform minor to major repairs on your truck that in turn will save you money, give you personal satisfaction and help you avoid expensive repair bills.

A secondary purpose of this book is a reference for owners who want to understand their truck and/or their mechanics better. In this case, no tools at all are required.

Before removing any bolts, read through the entire procedure. This will give you the overall view of what tools and supplies will be required. There is nothing more frustrating than having to walk to the bus stop on Monday morning because you were short one bolt on Sunday afternoon. So read ahead and plan ahead. Each operation should be approached logically and all procedures thoroughly understood before attempting any work.

All Chapters contain adjustments, maintenance, removal/installation and repair or overhaul procedures. When repair is not considered practical, we tell you how to remove the part and then how to install the new or rebuilt replacement. In this way, you at least save the labor costs. Backyard repair of some components is just not practical.

Two basic mechanic's rules should be mentioned: One, the left-side of the truck or engine is the driver's side of the truck. Conversely, the right-side of the truck means the passenger's side. Secondly, most screws and bolts are removed by turning them counterclockwise and tightened by turning them clockwise.

Safety is always the most important rule. Constantly be aware of the dangers involved in working on a truck and take the proper precautions. (See the section in this Chapter, Servicing Your Vehicle Safely and the SAFETY NOTICE on the acknowledgment page).

Pay attention to the instructions provided. There are 3 common mistakes in mechanical work:

1. Incorrect order of assembly, disassembly or adjustment: When taking something apart or putting it together, doing things in the wrong order usually costs extra time, however, it CAN break something. Read the entire procedure before beginning disassembly. Do everything in the order in which the instructions say you should do it, even if you can't immediately see a reason for it. When you're taking something apart that is very intricate (for example, a carburetor), you might want to draw (or take) a picture of how it looks when assembled at one point, in order to make sure you get everything back in its proper position. (We will supply exploded views whenever possible). When making adjustments, especially tune-up adjustments, do them in order. Often, one adjustment affects another and you cannot expect satisfactory results unless each adjustment is made only when it cannot be changed by any other.

2. Overtorquing (or undertorquing): While it is more common for overtorquing to cause

damage, undertorquing can cause a fastener to vibrate loose causing serious damage. Especially, when dealing with aluminum parts, pay attention to torque specifications and utilize a torque wrench in assembly. If a torque figure is not available, remember that if you are using the right tool to do the job, you will probably not have to strain yourself to get a fastener tight enough. The pitch of most threads is so slight that the tension you put on the wrench will be multiplied many times (in actual force) on the fastener you are tightening. A good example of how critical torque is can be seen in the case of spark plug installation, especially where you are putting the plug into an aluminum cylinder head. Too little torque can fail to crush the gasket, causing leakage of combustion gases and consequent overheating of the plug and engine parts. Too much torque can damage the threads or distort the plug, which changes the spark gap.

NOTE: *There are many commercial products available for ensuring that fasteners won't come loose, even if they are not torqued just right (a very common brand is Loctite®). If you're worried about getting something together tight enough to hold but loose enough to avoid mechanical damage during assembly, one of these products might offer substantial insurance. Read the label on the package and make sure the product is compatible with the components involved before choosing one.*

3. Crossthreading: Crossthreading occurs when a part such as a bolt is screwed into a nut or casting at the wrong angle. It is more likely to occur if access is difficult. To help prevent crossthreading, clean and lubricate the fasteners, then start threading with the part to be installed going straight in. Start the bolt or spark plug with your fingers. If you encounter resistance, unscrew the part and start over again at a different angle until it can be inserted and turned several turns without much effort. Keep in mind that many parts, especially spark plugs, use tapered threads so that gentle turning will automatically bring the part you're threading to the proper angle if you don't force it or resist a change in angle. Don't put a wrench on the part until it's been turned a couple of turns by hand. If you suddenly encounter resistance, and the part has not been fully seated, don't force it. Pull it back out and make sure it's clean and threading properly.

NOTE: *Always take your time and be patient. Once you have some experience working on your truck, it will become an enjoyable hobby.*

TOOLS AND EQUIPMENT

Naturally, without the proper tools and equipment, it is impossible to properly service your truck. It would be impossible to catalog each tool that you would need to perform each and every operation in this book. It would also be unwise for the amateur to rush out and buy an expensive set of tools on the theory that he may need one or more of them at sometime.

The best approach is to proceed slowly, gathering a good quality set of tools that are used most frequently. Don't be misled by the low cost of bargain tools. It is far better to spend a little more for better quality. Forged wrenches, 6 or 12 point sockets and fine tooth ratchets are by far preferable to their less expensive counterparts. As any good mechanic can tell you, there are few worse experiences than trying to work on a truck with bad tools. Your monetary savings will be far outweighed by frustration and mangled knuckles.

Begin accumulating tools that are used most frequently; those associated with routine maintenance and tune-up.

In addition to the normal assortment of screwdrivers and pliers you should have the following tools for routine maintenance jobs:

1. SAE and Metric wrenches and sockets in sizes from $1/8-3/4$ in. (6–19mm) and a spark plug socket ($13/16$ in. or $5/8$ in. depending on plug type).

NOTE: *If possible, buy various length socket drive extensions. One break in this department is that the metric sockets available in the U.S. will all fit the ratchet handles and extensions you may already have ($1/4$ in., $3/8$ in. and $1/2$ in. drive).*

2. Jackstands, for support
3. Oil filter wrench
4. Oil filler spout, for pouring oil
5. Grease gun, for chassis lubrication
6. Hydrometer, for checking the battery
7. A container for draining oil
8. Many rags for wiping up inevitable spills.
9. A quality floor jack.

In addition to the above items there are several others that are not absolutely necessary but handy to have around. These include oil dry (kitty litter is a good substitute), a transmission funnel and the usual supply of lubricants, antifreeze and fluids, although these can be purchased as needed. This is a basic list for routine maintenance but only your personal needs and desires can accurately determine your list of tools.

The second list of tools is for tune-ups. While the tools involved here are slightly more sophisticated, they need not be outrageously expen-

FROM TOP: BATTERY TERMINAL TOOL; FEELER GAUGES; OIL SPOUT; FILTER WRENCH

ALLEN WRENCHES

JACKSTAND

BEAM-TYPE TORQUE WRENCH

DWELL/TACHOMETER

VACUUM GAUGE

COMPRESSION GAUGE

TIMING LIGHT

This basic collection of tools and test instruments is all you need for most maintenance on your truck.

sive. There are several inexpensive tach/dwell meters on the market that are every bit as good for the average mechanic as an expensive professional model. Just be sure that the meter reads 1,200–1,500 rpm on the tach scale and that it works on 4- and 6-cylinder engines. A basic list of tune-up equipment should include:

1. Tach/dwell meter.
2. Spark plug wrench.
3. Timing light (a DC light that works from the truck's battery is best, although an AC light that plugs into 110V house current will suffice at some sacrifice in brightness).
4. Wire spark plug gauge/adjusting tools.
5. Set of feeler gauges.

Here again, be guided by your own needs. A feeler gauge will set the points as easily as a dwell meter will read dwell, but slightly less accurately. Since you will need a tachometer anyway ... well, make your own decision.

There are several other tools that, in time, you will find you can't live without. These include:

1. A compression gauge. The screw-in type is slower to use but eliminates the possibility of a faulty reading due to escaping pressure.
2. A manifold vacuum gauge.
3. A test light, volt/ohm meter.
4. An induction meter. This is used for determining whether or not there is current in a wire. These are handy for use if a wire is broken somewhere in a wiring harness.

As a final note, you will find a torque wrench necessary for all but the most basic work. The beam type models are perfectly adequate, although the newer click type are more precise.

NOTE: *Special tools are occasionally necessary to perform a specific job or are recommended to make a job easier. Their use has been kept to a minimum. When a special tool is indicated, it will be referred to by manufacturer's part number, and, where possible, an illustration of the tool will be provided so that an equivalent tool may be used. Special tools may be purchased through your local Chevrolet dealer or directly from the tool manufacturers. A list of tool manufacturers and their addresses follows:*

In the United States, contact:
Service Tool Division
Kent-Moore Corporation
29784 Little Mack
Roseville, MI 48066-2298
In Canada, contact:
Kent-Moore of Canada, Ltd.
2395 Cawthra Mississauga
Ontario, Canada L5A 3P2.

SERVICING YOUR VEHICLE SAFELY

It is virtually impossible to anticipate all of the hazards involved with automotive maintenance and service but care and common sense will prevent most accidents.

The rules of safety for mechanics range from "don't smoke around gasoline," to "use the proper tool for the job." The trick to avoiding injuries is to develop safe work habits and take every possible precaution.

Do's

• Do keep a fire extinguisher and first aid kit within easy reach.
• Do wear safety glasses or goggles when cutting, drilling, grinding or prying, even if you have 20/20 vision. If you wear glasses for the sake of vision, then they should be made of hardened glass that can serve also as safety glasses or wear safety goggles over your regular glasses.
• Do shield your eyes whenever you work around the battery. Batteries contain sulphuric acid. In case of contact with the eyes or skin, flush the area with water or a mixture of water and baking soda, then get medical attention immediately.
• Do use safety stands for any under truck service. Jacks are for raising the truck. Safety stands are for making sure the truck stays raised until you want it to come down. Whenever the truck is raised, block the wheels remaining on the ground and set the parking brake.
• Do use adequate ventilation when working with any chemicals. Like carbon monoxide, the asbestos dust resulting from brake lining wear can be poisonous in sufficient quantities.
• Do disconnect the negative battery cable when working on the electrical system. The primary ignition system can contain up to 40,000 volts.
• Do follow the manufacturer's instructions when working with potentially hazardous materials. Both brake fluid and antifreeze are poisonous if taken internally.
• Do properly maintain your tools. Loose hammer heads, mushroomed punches/chisels, frayed or poorly grounded electrical cords, excessively worn screwdrivers, spread wrenches (open end), cracked sockets, slipping ratchets and/or faulty droplight sockets cause accidents.
• Do use the proper size and type of tool for the job being done.
• Do pull on a wrench handle rather than push on it and adjust your stance to prevent a fall.
• Do be sure that adjustable wrenches are

tightly adjusted on the nut or bolt and pulled so that the face is on the side of the fixed jaw.

• Do select a wrench or socket that fits the nut or bolt. The wrench or socket should sit straight, not cocked.

• Do strike squarely with a hammer—avoid glancing blows.

• Do set the parking brake and block the drive wheels if the work requires that the engine be running.

Dont's

• Don't run an engine in a garage or anywhere else without proper ventilation—EVER! Carbon monoxide is poisonous. It takes a long time to leave the body and can build up a deadly supply of it in your system by simply breathing in a little every day. You may not realize you are slowly poisoning yourself. Always use power vents, windows, fans or open the garage doors.

• Don't work around moving parts while wearing a necktie or other loose clothing. Short sleeves are much safer than long, loose sleeves and hard-toed shoes with neoprene soles protect your toes and give a better grip on slippery surfaces. Jewelry such as watches, fancy belt buckles, beads or body adornment or any kind

When using an open end wrench, make sure it is the correct size

Vehicle Identification Plate

Keep screwdrivers in good shape. They should fit the slot as shown 'A'. If they look like those in 'B', they need grinding or replacing.

is not safe working around a truck. Long hair should be hidden under a hat or cap.

• Don't use pockets for tool boxes. A fall or bump can drive a screwdriver deep into your body. Even a wiping cloth hanging from the back pocket can wrap around a spinning shaft or fan.

• Don't smoke when working around gasoline, cleaning solvent or other flammable material.

• Don't smoke when working around the

When using electric tools, make sure they are properly grounded.

PREVENTIVE MAINTENANCE SCHEDULE

Model/Interval	Item	Service
Gasoline Engine Models		
Every 6 months or 6,000 miles	Crankcase	change oil & filter
	Cooling system	change coolant
	Idle speed and TSP-off speed	adjust
	Ignition timing	adjust
	Decel throttle control system	check
	Chassis fittings	lubricate
	Clutch linkage	inspect and oil
	Exhaust system heat shields	inspect
	Transmission, automatic	adjust bands, check level
Every 15 months or 15,000 miles	Spark plugs	replace
	Exhaust control valve	check & lubricate
	Drive belts	check and adjust
	Air cleaner temperature control	check
	Choke system	check
	Thermactor system	check
	Crankcase breathe cap	clean
	EGR system	clean and inspect
	PCV system	clean and inspect
Every 30 months or 30,000 miles	PCV valve	replace
	Air cleaner element	replace
	Air cleaner crankcase filter	replace
	Fuel vapor system	replace
	Brake master cylinder	check
	Brakes	inspect
	Rear wheel bearings, Dana axles	clean and repack
Diesel Engine Models		
Every 6 months or 5,000 miles	Crankcase	change oil and filter
	Idle speed	check and adjust
	Throttle linkage	check operation
	Fuel/water separator	drain water
	U-joints	lubricate
	Front axle spindles	lubricate
Every 6 months or 15,000 miles	Fuel filter	replace
	Drive belts	check/adjust
	Steering linkage	lubricate
Every year	Coolant	check condition/replace
	Cooling hoses, clamps	check condition/replace

ENGINE IDENTIFICATION CHART

Year	V.I.N. Code	Number of Cylinders Displacement in Liters	cu. in.	Engine Manufacturer	Fuel System
1982–85	A	4–1.9	118.9	Isuzu	2-bbl
	B	6–2.8	173	Chevrolet	2-bbl
1983–84	Y	4–2.0	121	Chevrolet	2-bbl
1983–85	S	4–2.2	136.6	Isuzu	Diesel
1985–91	E	4–2.5	151	Pontiac	TBI
1986–91	R	6–2.8	173	Chevrolet	TBI
1988–91	Z	6–4.3	262	Chevrolet	TBI

TBI—Throttle Body Injection

battery. When the battery is being charged, it gives off explosive hydrogen gas.

• Don't use gasoline to wash your hands. There are excellent soaps available. Gasoline may contain lead, and lead can enter the body through a cut, accumulating in the body until you are very ill. Gasoline also removes all the natural oils from the skin so that bone dry hands will suck up oil and grease.

• Don't service the air conditioning system unless you are equipped with the necessary tools and training. The refrigerant, R-12, is extremely cold and when exposed to the air, will instantly freeze any surface it comes in contact with, including your eyes. Although the re-

1. VIN
2. Wheel Base
3. Model Number
4. Order Number
5. RPO/SEO Codes
6. Exterior Color WA Number
7. Paint System

Service parts identification label

Certification label

Location of the Vehicle Identification Number (VIN)

frigerant is normally non-toxic, R-12 becomes a deadly poisonous gas in the presence of an open flame. One good whiff of the vapors from burning refrigerant can be fatal.

• Don't release refrigerant into the atmosphere. In most states it is now illegal to discharge refrigerant into the atmosphere due to the harmful effects Freon (R-12) has on the ozone layer. Check with local authorities about the laws in your state.

IDENTIFICATION

Models

Three separate models of the S10/S15 pickup are offered—the regular cab, the extended cab, and the chassis cab. The chassis cab comes without a cargo bed so that a specialized aftermarket bed may be added after purchase.

Four wheel drive versions of the S-10/S-15 were introduced in 1983. Model reference indicates "S" as a two wheel drive vehicle, and "T" as a four wheel drive vehicle.

Service Parts Identification Label

The service parts identification label is located on the inside of the glove box door. The label lists the VIN, wheelbase, paint informa-

Explanation of the Vehicle Identification Number (VIN)

Engine identification number location — 1.9L engine

tion and all production options or special equipment on the truck when it was shipped from the factory. Always refer to this information when ordering parts.

Certification Label

The certification label shows the Gross Vehicle Weight Rating (GVWR), the front and rear Gross Axle Weight Rating (GAWR) and the Payload Rating.

Gross Vehicle Weight (GVW) is the weight of the originally equipped truck and all items added to it after leaving the factory. The GVW must not exceed the Gross Vehicle Weight Rating (GVWR) of your truck.

The Payload Rating shown on the label is the maximum allowable cargo load (including the weight of the occupants) that the truck can carry. The payload rating is decreased if any accessories or other equipment is added to the truck after delivery from the factory. Deduct the weight of any added accessories from the original payload rating to determine the new payload rating.

Engine identification number location — 2.0L engine

Serial Number

Vehicle

The Vehicle Identification Number (VIN) is on a plate attached to the left hand top of the instrument panel, visible through the windshield. See the illustration for an explanation of the coding.

Engine

1.9L Engine

The engine identification number is on a machined flat surface, on the lower left-side of the block, near the flywheel.

2.0L Engine

The engine identification number is stamped on a flat, machined surface, facing forward, on the front of the engine block, just below the head.

Engine identification number location — 2.5L engine

1. Engine I.D.
2. Engine I.D. (optional location)

Engine identification number location — 2.2L diesel engine

TRANSMISSION I.D.
NAMEPLATE
LOCATION

HYDRA-MATIC 3L30 TRANSMISSION I.D. NAMEPLATE

TRANSMISSION I.D.
LOCATION

HYDRA-MATIC 4L60/THM 700-R4 TRANSMISSION
IDENTIFICATION INFORMATION

180C and 700-R4 automatic transmission identification numbers

2.2L Diesel Engine

The engine identification number is stamped on a flat, machined surface, facing forward, on the left-front of the engine block, just below the water pump.

2.5L Engine

The engine identification number is stamped on a flat, machined surface, on the left rear-side of the engine block, near the flywheel.

2.8L Engine

The engine identification code is stamped either on an upward facing, machined surface on the right-front of the block, just below the head, or on the left front of the block just above the water pump.

4.3L Engine

The engine identification number is stamped either on a flat, machined surface, on the right-front of the engine block, just above the water

Location of the 220C automatic transmission identification numbers

pump, or on the left-rear side of the engine block, where the transmission is joined to the engine.

Transmission

Manual

The transmission identification number is stamped on a metal plate which is attached to the extension housing case bolt, on the left-side.

Automatic

• The identification number for the 180C is located on a metal tag attached to the left-front of the transmission case.
• The identification number, for the 200C (3-spd), is stamped on the right rear-side of the transmission case, behind the modulator.
• The identification number, for the 700-R4, is stamped on the right or left rear-side of the transmission pan rail.

Location and explanation of the rear axle identification number

1. Air cleaner assembly	15. Carburetor gasket
2. Body assembly	16. Clip
3. Cover assembly	17. Cap
4. Vacuum control	18. Clamp
5. Thermo sensor assembly	19. Wing nut
6. Seal	20. Washer
7. Vacuum hose	21. Bracket
8. Element	22. Screw
9. Hot idle compensator	23. Stud
10. Element gasket	24. Screw
11. Cover gasket	25. Hose
12. Hose tee	26. Clamp
13. Vacuum hose	27. Flex hose
14. Vacuum hose	

1.9L Thermostatic Air Cleaner (TAC) assembly—others similar

FILL PLUG

IDENTIFICATION TAG

DRAIN PLUG

Location of the Model 207 and 231 transfer case identification tag

Drive Axle

On rear axles, the identification number is stamped on the right-front side of the axle tube, next to the differential. On front axles, the ID number is stamped on a tag, attached to the differential cover by a cover bolt.

Transfer Case

The model 207 and 231 transfer cases are equipped with an identification tag which is attached to the rear half of the case; the tag gives the model number, the low range reduction ratio and the assembly part number. If for some reason it becomes dislodged or removed, reattach it with an adhesive sealant.

ROUTINE MAINTENANCE

Air Cleaner

The air cleaner element is a paper cartridge type, it should be replaced every year or 30,000 miles; if the truck is operated in heavy traffic or under dusty conditions, replace the element at more frequent intervals.

REMOVAL AND INSTALLATION

1. Remove the top of the air cleaner.
2. Remove and discard the paper element.
3. Using a new element, reverse the removal procedures.

Gasoline Fuel Filter

The fuel filter should be serviced every 15,000 miles; if operated under severe conditions, change it more often. Three types of fuel filters are used, a pleated-paper element type (with a internal check valve), an in-line type and an in-tank type.

NOTE: *If an in-line fuel filter is used on an engine which has a filter installed in the carburetor body, be sure to change both at the same time.*

CAUTION: *Filter replacement should not be attempted when the engine is HOT. Additionally, it is a good idea to place some absorbent rags under the fuel fittings to absorb any gasoline which will spill out when the lines are loosened.*

FUEL PRESSURE RELEASE TBI FUEL SYSTEMS ONLY

TBI Model 700 (2.5L engine)

1. Place the transmission selector in park (neutral on manual transmissions) set the parking brake and block the drive wheels.

2. Loosen the fuel filler cap to relieve tank pressure.
3. Disconnect the three terminal electrical connectors at the fuel tank.
4. Start the engine and allow to run until it stops due to lack of fuel.
5. Engage the starter (turn key to start) for three seconds to release pressure in the fuel lines.
6. Disconnect the negative battery cable to prevent accidental fuel spillage.
7. When fuel service is finished, reconnect the connector at the fuel tank, tighten the fuel filler cap and connect the negative battery cable.

TBI Model 220 (2.8L and 4.3L engines)

1. Disconnect the negative battery cable.
2. Loosen fuel filler cap to relieve fuel tank pressure.
3. The internal constant bleed feature of the Model 220 TBI unit relieves fuel pump system pressure when the engine is turned OFF. Therefore, no further action is required.
4. When fuel service is finished, tighten the fuel filler cap and connect the negative battery cable.

REMOVAL AND INSTALLATION

There are three types of fuel filters: Internal (in the carburetor fitting), inline (in the fuel line) and in-tank (the sock on the fuel pickup tube).

Internal Filter

1. Disconnect the fuel line connection at the fuel inlet filter nut on the carburetor.
2. Remove the fuel inlet filter nut from the carburetor.
3. Remove the filter and the spring.

NOTE: *If a check valve is not present with the filter, install one when the filter is replaced.*

4. Install the spring, filter and check valve (must face the fuel line), then reverse the removal procedures. Torque the filter nut-to-car-

A. Front
1. Upper fuel line fitting
2. Lower fuel line fitting
3. Bracket
5. Bolt

2.5L in-line fuel filter

2-bbl carburetor internal fuel filter; check valve facing the fuel inlet nut

1	LEFT FRAME SIDE MEMBER
2	BOLT – TIGHTEN 16 N·m (24 lb. ft.)
3	CLAMP
4	REAR FUEL FEED PIPE TIGHTEN 26 N·m (20 lb. ft.)
5	INTERMEDIATE FUEL FEED PIPE TIGHTEN 26 N·m (20 lb. ft.)
6	IN – LINE FUEL FILTER

2.8L in-line fuel filter

10. Liquid-vapor separator
11. Return tube
12. Fuel tube
13. Coupler and sound insulator
14. Fuel level sender
15. Electric fuel pump
16. Filter strainer

Fuel injected engine in-tank fuel filter

buretor to 25 ft. lbs. and the fuel line-to-connector to 18 ft. lbs.; DO NOT overtighten.

5. Start the engine and check for leaks.

Inline Filter

CAUTION: *Before disconnecting any component of the fuel system, refer to the "Fuel Pressure Release" procedures in this Chapter and release the fuel pressure.*

1. Remove the fuel filler cap to relieve the pressure in the fuel tank.

2. Disconnect the fuel lines from the filter.

3. Remove the fuel filter from the retainer or mounting bolt.

NOTE: *The filter has an arrow (fuel flow direction) on the side of the case, be sure to install it correctly in the system, with the arrow facing away from the fuel tank.*

4. To install, reverse the removal procedures. Start the engine and check for leaks.

In-Tank Filter

To service the in-tank fuel filter, refer to the "Electric Fuel Pump Removal and Installation" procedures in Chapter 5.

Diesel Fuel Filter

REMOVAL AND INSTALLATION

Filter Element

1. Disconnect the negative battery terminal.

2. Disconnect the water sensor wire connector from the filter assembly.

3. Disconnect the water sensor-to-main body hose.

4. Using a filter band wrench, remove the fuel filter element by turning the cartridge counterclockwise, while being careful not to spill diesel fuel from the element.

5. Drain the fuel from the element into a container and discard it. Take precautions to avoid the risk of fire during replacement procedures.

Exploded view of the diesel fuel filter assembly

2.2L diesel fuel heater controller

Diesel fuel filter installation

6. Remove the water and heater sensor from the bottom of the used filter element.

7. Apply a thin coat of diesel fuel to the water sensor O-ring, then install the water and heater sensor on the bottom of the replacement filter element and tighten.

8. Wipe all filter sealing surfaces clean before installing the new filter and apply a thin coat of diesel fuel to the gasket on the new fuel filter element.

9. Install the new filter element by turning it clockwise until the gasket contacts the sealing surfaces on the main filter body. Hand tighten another 2/3 of a turn after the gasket contacts the sealing surface; DO NOT overtighten.

10. Reconnect the water sensor wiring connector, then disconnect the fuel outlet hose

from the injection pump and place the end in a clean container.

11. Operate the priming pump handle on the injection pump several times to fill the new filter with fuel, until fuel flows from the outlet hose. Reconnect the outlet hose to the injection pump when priming is complete.

NOTE: *It is very important to prime the new filter element before starting the engine, as the shock of the diesel engine's high operating fuel pressure hitting a dry element can tear small pieces of debris away and allow them to pass into the injection pump and injectors, possibly causing injection pump or injector damage.*

12. Start the engine and check for leaks.

Filter Assembly

1. Disconnect the negative battery terminal.

1	PCV VALVE
2	GROMMET
3	TUBE ASSEMBLY
4	TBI UNIT · PORT "C"
5	AIR CLEANER FITTING ·
6	MAP SENSOR

2.0L PCV system

PCV flow through the engine

CRANKCASE VENTILATION VALVE

PCV CONTROL VALVE

⇨ CLEAN AIR

→ VOLATILE OIL FUMES

- - → MIXTURE OF AIR AND FUMES

1	TUBE ASSEMBLY
2	PCV VALVE
3	GROMMET
4	BOLT—TIGHTEN TO 25 N·m (18 LBS. FT.)
5	CONNECTOR
6	HOSE

2.5L PCV system

2. Disconnect the water sensor electrical connector.

3. Disconnect the fuel hoses from the filter assembly.

4. Remove the filter assembly-to-bracket screws and the filter main body, element and sensors as an assembly.

5. To install, reverse the removal procedures. Refer to the "Draining the Water Separator" procedures in this Chapter and prime the fuel system.

Draining the Water Separator

1. Turn the engine Off and allow it to cool.

2. Open the hood and place a 2 quart con-

tainer under the end of the drain hose attached to the separator.

3. Turn the wing nut about four turns **counterclockwise** to open the drain plug, then operate the priming pump lever until all of the water is drained and ONLY clean diesel fuel flows from the water separator.

4. Tighten the drain plug wing nut **clockwise** until securely closed; DO NOT overtighten. Again operate the priming pump handle until resistance is felt, indicating that the fuel filter is properly primed.

5. Start the engine and check for fuel leaks from the separator and fuel lines. Make sure the "Water In Fuel" light is Off; if the light remains On, the fuel tank must be purged of water with a siphon hose and hand pump fed into the tank through the fuel filter.

CAUTION: *DO NOT attempt to siphon any fuel tank contents by using mouth suction to start the siphon effect. Diesel fuel is poisonous and is by far the worst tasting stuff you can imagine. Use a hand siphon pump or power drill attachment to pull the water from the fuel tank.*

Positive Crankcase Ventilation (PCV)

The PCV valve is attached to the valve cover by a rubber grommet and connected to the intake manifold through a ventilation hose. Inspect the PCV system and replace the PCV valve and filter (located in the air cleaner) every 30,000 miles.

1	PCV	4	GROMMET
2	TBI UNIT PORT "C"	5	TUBE ASSEMBLY
3	HOSE	6	AIR CLEANER EXTENSION

2.8L PCV system

4.3L PCV system

Cross section of a PCV valve

FUNCTIONAL CHECK

If the engine is idling rough, check for a clogged PCV valve, dirty vent filter or air cleaner element, or plugged hose. Test the system using the following procedure and replace components as necessary.

1. Remove the PCV valve from the rocker cover.

2. Run the engine at idle and place your thumb over the end of the valve to check for vacuum.

3. If no vacuum exists, check for plugged hoses, manifold port vacuum at the carburetor or TBI unit, or a defective PCV valve.

4. To check PCV valve, remove the valve from the hose and shake it. If a rattling noise is heard, the valve is good. If no noise is heard, the valve is plugged and replacement is necessary.

REMOVAL AND INSTALLATION

1. Pull the PCV from the valve cover grommet and disconnect it from the ventilation hose(s).

2. Inspect the valve for operation: (1) Shake it to see if the valve is free; (2) Blow through it (air will pass in one direction only).

NOTE: *When replacing the PCV valve, it is recommended to use a new one.*

3. To install, reverse the removal procedures.

Evaporative Canister

This system is designed to limit gasoline vapor, which normally escapes from the fuel tank and the intake manifold, from discharge into the atmosphere. Vapor absorption is accomplished through the use of the charcoal canister. The canister absorbs fuel vapors and stores them until they can be removed and burned in the combustion process. Removal of the vapors from the canister to the engine is accomplished through: a canister mounted purge valve, the throttle valve position, a thermostatic vacuum (TVS) switch or a computer controlled canister purge solenoid.

In addition to the canister, the fuel tank requires a non-vented gas cap. This cap does not allow fuel vapor to discharge into the atmosphere. All fuel vapor travels through a vent line, inserted high into the domed fuel tank, directly to the canister.

SERVICING

Every 30,000 miles or 24 months, check all fuel, vapor lines and hoses for proper hookup, routing and condition. If equipped, check that the bowl vent and purge valves work properly. Remove the canister and check for cracks or damage and replace (if necessary).

FUNCTIONAL TEST

1. Apply a short length of hose to the lower tube of the purge valve and attempt to blow through it. Little or no air should pass into the canister.

2. With a hand vacuum pump, apply a vacuum of 15 in. Hg to the control valve tube (upper tube). If the diaphragm does not hold vacuum for at least 20 seconds, the diaphragm is leaking and the canister must be replaced.

3. If the diaphragm holds vacuum, again try to blow through the hose connected to the lower tube while vacuum is still being applied. An increased flow of air should be observed. If not, the canister must be replaced.

REMOVAL AND INSTALLATION

1. Label and disconnect the charcoal canister vent hoses.

2. Remove the canister-to-bracket bolt.

4-cylinder evaporative canister and hoses

CANISTER

PURPLE STRIPE

WHITE STRIPE

ORANGE STRIPE

FRT

FRT

6-cylinder engine evaporative canister and hoses

3. Lift the canister from the bracket.

4. To install, reverse the removal procedures.

Battery

All S-10/S-15 Pickups have a Maintenance Free battery as standard equipment, eliminating the need for fluid level checks and the possibility of specific gravity tests. Nevertheless, the battery does require some attention.

At least once a year, the battery terminals and the cable clamps should be cleaned. Remove the side terminal bolts and the cables, negative cable first. Clean the cable clamps and the battery terminals with a wire brush until all corrosion, grease, etc. is removed and the metal is shiny. It is especially important to clean the inside of the clamp thoroughly. A small deposit of foreign material or oxidation will prevent a sound electrical connection and inhibit either starting or charging. Special tools are available for cleaning side terminal clamps and terminals.

Before installing the cables, loosen the battery holddown clamp, remove the battery and check the battery tray. Clear it of any debris and check it for soundness. Rust should be wire brushed away and the metal given a coat of anti-rust paint. Replace the battery and tighten the holddown clamp securely but be careful not to overtighten, which will crack the battery case.

NOTE: *Surface coatings on battery cases can actually conduct electricity which will cause a slight voltage drain, so make sure the*

BATTERY

FRT

FRT

FENDER

WELD NUTS (FENDER INNER)

VIEW A

Battery tray installation

The specific gravity of the battery can be checked with a simple float-type hydrometer

Special tools are also available for cleaning the posts and clamps on side terminal batteries

battery case is clean. Batteries can be cleaned using a paste made from mixture of baking soda and water. Spread the paste on any corrosion, wait a few minutes, and rinse with water. Finish the job by cleaning metal parts with a wire brush.

After the clamps and terminals are clean, reinstall the cables, negative cable last. Give the clamps and terminals a thin external coat of nonmetallic grease after installation, to retard corrosion.

Check the cables at the same time that the terminals are cleaned. If the cable insulation is cracked, broken or the ends are frayed, the cable should be replaced with a new one of the same length and gauge.

CAUTION: *Keep flames or sparks away from the battery. It gives off explosive hydrogen gas. The battery electrolyte contains sulphuric acid. If you should get any on your skin or in your eyes, flush the affected areas with plenty of clear water. If it lands in your eyes, seek medical help immediately.*

Testing the Maintenance Free Battery

Maintenance free batteries, do not require normal attention as far as fluid level checks are concerned. However, the terminals require periodic cleaning, which should be performed at least once a year.

The sealed top battery cannot be checked for charge in the normal manner, since there is no provision for access to the electrolyte. To check the condition of the battery:

1. If the indicator eye on top of the battery is dark, the battery has enough fluid. If the eye is lit, the electrolyte fluid is too low and the battery must be replaced.

2. If a green dot appears in the middle of the eye, the battery is sufficiently charged. Proceed to Step 4. If no green dot is visible, go to Step 3.

3. Charge the battery.

NOTE: *DO NOT charge the battery for more than 50 amp-hours. If the green dot appears or if the electrolyte squirts out of the vent hole, stop the charge and proceed to Step 4.*

It may be necessary to tip the battery from side-to-side to get the green dot to appear after charging.

Charging Rate Amps	Time
75	40 min
50	1 hr
25	2 hr
10	5 hr

Battery charging rates chart

Temperature (°F)	Minimum Voltage
70 or above	9.6
60	9.5
50	9.4
40	9.3
30	9.1
20	8.9
10	8.7
0	8.5

Battery minimum voltage chart

Battery	Test Load (Amps)
83–50	150
83-60	180
85A-60	170
87A-60	230
89A-60	270
1981103	200
1981104	250
1981105	270
1981577	260

Battery test load specifications chart

BATTERY TOP	BATTERY TOP	BATTERY TOP
DARKENED INDICATOR (WITH GREEN DOT)	DARKENED INDICATOR (NO GREEN DOT)	LIGHT YELLOW OR BRIGHT INDICATOR
MAY BE JUMP STARTED	MAY BE JUMP STARTED	DO NOT JUMP START

Maintenance-free batteries contain their own built in hydrometer

CAUTION: *When charging the battery, the electrical system and control unit can be quickly damaged by improper connections, high output battery chargers or incorrect service procedures.*

4. Connect a battery load tester and a voltmeter across the battery terminals (the battery cables should be disconnected from the battery). Apply a 300 amp load to the battery for 15 seconds to remove the surface charge. Remove the load.

5. Wait 15 seconds to allow the battery to recover. Apply the appropriate test load, as specified in the chart.

Apply the load for 15 seconds while reading the voltage. Disconnect the load.

6. Check the results against the chart. If the battery voltage is at or above the specified voltage for the temperature listed, the battery is good. It the voltage falls below what's listed, the battery should be replaced.

Early Fuel Evaporation (EFE) Heater

The EFE heating system is used on all carbureted engines. The purpose of the heating unit is to further vaporize the fuel droplets as they enter the intake manifold; vaporization of the air/fuel mixture ensures complete combustion which provides the maximum power and minimum emissions output for the fuel used.

REMOVAL AND INSTALLATION

Heater Unit

The EFE heater unit is located directly under the carburetor and is electrically operated.

1. Disconnect the negative battery terminal. Remove the air cleaner.

2. From the carburetor, disconnect the vacuum hoses, electrical connectors and fuel hoses. Disconnect the EFE Heater electrical connector from the wiring harness.

3. Remove the carburetor-to-intake manifold nuts and the carburetor from the manifold. Lift the EFE Heater from the intake manifold.

4. Using a putty knife, clean the gasket mounting surfaces.

5. To install, use new gaskets and reverse the removal procedures. Torque the carburetor-to-intake manifold nuts to 13 ft. lbs.

Heater Switch

The heater switch is located near the thermostat housing (2.8L carbureted engine), on the bottom rear-side of the intake manifold (2.0L carbureted engine) or on the top right-side of the engine (1.9L carbureted engine).

1. Using a drain pan, position it under the radiator, then open the drain cock and drain the coolant to a level below the heater switch.

CAUTION: *When draining the coolant, keep in mind that cats and dogs are attracted by the ethylene glycol antifreeze, and are quite likely to drink any that is left in an uncovered container or in puddles on the ground. This will prove fatal in sufficient quantity. Always drain the coolant into a sealable container. Coolant should be reused unless it is contaminated or several years old.*

2. Disconnect the wiring harness connector from the EFE heater switch.

1.9L EFE heater and heater switch

Carbureted 2.8L EFE heater assembly

2.8L EFE heater switch

1. Carburetor
2. EFE heater switch

EFE heater switch relay on the 2.0L engine

3. Remove the EFE heater switch (turn it counterclockwise) from the intake manifold.

4. To install the new EFE heater switch, coat the threads with a soft setting sealant and torque it to 10 ft. lbs. Reconnect the wiring harness connector to the EFE heater switch. Refill the cooling system.

NOTE: *When applying sealant to the EFE heater, be careful not to coat the sensor and/or the switch.*

Heater Switch Relay

The heater switch relay is located on the left-fender.

1. Disconnect the negative battery terminal.

2. Disconnect the wiring harness connector(s) from the heater switch relay.

3. Remove the heater switch relay-to-bracket screw and the relay from the truck.

4. To install, use a new relay and reverse the removal procedures.

TESTING

1. Disconnect the wiring harness connector from the EFE heater switch, located near the thermostat housing (2.8L carbureted engine), on the bottom rear-side of the intake manifold (2.0L carbureted engine) or on the top right-side of the engine (1.9L carbureted engine).

NOTE: *To perform the following inspection, the engine temperature must be below 140°F (60°C).*

2. Using a 12V test lamp, connect it across the EFE wiring harness connector terminals. Turn the ignition switch On (the engine is Off), the lamp should glow; if the lamp glows, the EFE heater is good.

3. If the lamp does not glow, reconnect the wiring harness connector to the EFE heater switch.

4. Using a DC voltmeter, place it on the 0–15V scale, insert the test probes into the rear of the wiring harness connector body (the black wire is to be grounded) and measure the voltage; it should read 11–13V.

5. If the voltage is not 11–13V, insure that the black wire is grounded; if the voltage is not 0V, the black (grounded) wire is an Open circuit, repair it.

6. If the voltage is 0V, check for voltage-to-ground at each heater switch terminal—the voltage at each switch terminal should be 11–13V.

7. If one terminal measures 11–13V and the other is low or 0V, check the connector for deformed terminals and repair, as necessary.

8. If the electrical connector is making proper contact, replace the EFE heater switch.

9. If the voltage is not 11–13V at each switch terminal, check the wiring harness circuit between the heater switch and the ignition switch, then repair as necessary.

10. Start the engine, allow it to warm to 170°F (76.7°C), then check the voltage across the EFE heater terminals; it should be 0V. If

1. EFE relay
2. Manifold differential pressure sensor
3. W.O.T. relay

1984–85 EFE heater switch relay

2.8L EFE heater and heater switch relay

the voltage is not 0V, replace the EFE heater switch.

Accessory Drive Belts

INSPECTION

Check the drive belt(s) every 15,000 miles/12 months (heavy usage) or 30,000 miles/24 months (light usage) for evidence of wear such as cracking, fraying and incorrect tension. Determine the belt tension at a point halfway between the pulleys by pressing on the belt with moderate thumb pressure. The belt should deflect about 1/4 in. (6mm) over a 7–10 in. (178–254mm) span, or 1/2 in. (12.7mm) over a 13–16 in. (330–406mm) span. If the deflection is found to be too much or too little, perform the tension adjustments.

ADJUSTING TENSION

When adjusting belt tension note the following:

• A used belt is one that has been rotated at least one complete revolution on the pulleys. This begins the belt seating process and it must never be tensioned to the new belt specifications.

• It is better to have belts too loose than too tight, because overly tight belts will lead to bearing failure, particularly in the water pump and alternator. However, loose belts place an extremely high impact load on the driven components due to the whipping action of the belt.

• A GM Belt Tension Gauge No. BT-33-95-ACBN (regular V-belts), BT-33-97M (poly V-belts) or equivalent is required for tensioning accessory drive belts on 1982–86 trucks.

V-Belt tensioning (1982–86)

1. If the belt is cold, operate the engine (at idle speed) for 15 minutes; the belt will seat itself in the pulleys allowing the belt fibers to relax or stretch. If the belt is hot, allow it to cool, until it is warm to the touch.

2. Loosen the component-to-mounting bracket bolts.

3. Using a GM Belt Tension Gauge No. BT-33-95-ACBN (standard V-belts), BT-33-97M (poly V-belts) or equivalent, place the tension

1.9L V-belt and pulley diagram

2.5 L ENGINE

2.8 L ENGINE

21. Belt
22. Idler Pulley
23. Air Conditioning Compressor
24. Water Pump
25. Crankshaft

26. Tensioner
27. Generator
28. Power Steering
29. AIR Pump

2.5L and 2.8L serpentine drive belt routing

1	AC COMPRESSOR
2	GENERATOR BELT
3	GENERATOR
4	WATER PUMP PULLEY
5	AC BELT
6	P/S PUMP
7	P/S BELT
8	CRANKSHAFT PULLEY

W/AC, PS   W/PS

1	AC COMPRESSOR
2	GENERATOR BELT
3	GENERATOR
4	WATER PUMP PULLEY
5	AC BELT
6	CRANKSHAFT PULLEY

W/AC   BASE

2.5L V-Belt and pulley diagram

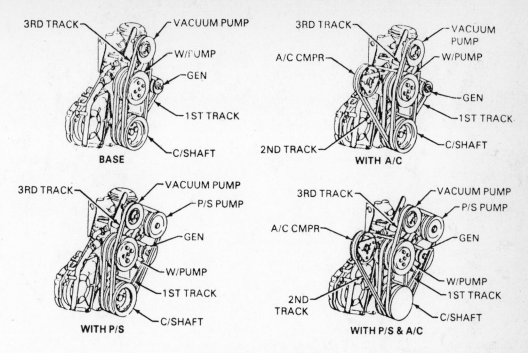

2.2L V-Belt and pulley diagram

2.0L V-Belt and pulley diagram

21. Belt
22. Idler Pulley
23. Air Conditioning Compressor
24. Water Pump
25. Crankshaft
26. Tensioner
27. Generator
28. Power Steering
29. AIR Pump

WITHOUT AIR CONDITIONING

WITH AIR CONDITIONING

4.3L serpentine belt routing

2.8L V-Belt and pulley diagram

gauge at the center of the belt between the longest span.

4. Applying belt tension pressure on the component, adjust the drive belt tension to the correct specifications.

5. While holding the correct tension on the component, tighten the component-to-mounting bracket bolt.

6. When the belt tension is correct, remove the tension gauge.

Serpentine Belt Tensioning (1987–91)

1987–91 trucks are equipped with an automatic tensioner. No belt tensioning is necessary as the tensioner adjusts by spring action.

REMOVAL AND INSTALLATION

V-Belt

1. Loosen the component-to-mounting bracket bolts.

2. Rotate the component to relieve the tension on the drive belt.

3. Slip the drive belt from the component pulley and remove it from the engine.

NOTE: *If the engine uses more than one belt, it may be necessary to remove other belts that are in front of the one being removed.*

4. Installation is the reverse of removal. Adjust the component drive belt tension to specifications.

HOW TO SPOT WORN V-BELTS

V-Belts are vital to efficient engine operation—they drive the fan, water pump and other accessories. They require little maintenance (occasional tightening) but they will not last forever. Slipping or failure of the V-belt will lead to overheating. If your V-belt looks like any of these, it should be replaced.

Cracking or weathering

This belt has deep cracks, which cause it to flex. Too much flexing leads to heat build-up and premature failure. These cracks can be caused by using the belt on a pulley that is too small. Notched belts are available for small diameter pulleys.

Softening (grease and oil)

Oil and grease on a belt can cause the belt's rubber compounds to soften and separate from the reinforcing cords that hold the belt together. The belt will first slip, then finally fail altogether.

Glazing

Glazing is caused by a belt that is slipping. A slipping belt can cause a run-down battery, erratic power steering, overheating or poor accessory performance. The more the belt slips, the more glazing will be built up on the surface of the belt. The more the belt is glazed, the more it will slip. If the glazing is light, tighten the belt.

Worn cover

The cover of this belt is worn off and is peeling away. The reinforcing cords will begin to wear and the belt will shortly break. When the belt cover wears in spots or has a rough jagged appearance, check the pulley grooves for roughness.

Separation

This belt is on the verge of breaking and leaving you stranded. The layers of the belt are separating and the reinforcing cords are exposed. It's just a matter of time before it breaks completely.

HOW TO SPOT BAD HOSES

Both the upper and lower radiator hoses are called upon to perform difficult jobs in an inhospitable enviorment. They are subject to nearly 18 psi at under hood temperature often over 280F., and must circulate an hour-3 good reasons to have good hoses.

Swollen hose

A good test for any hose is to feel it for soft or spongy spots. Frequently these will appear as swollen areas of the hose. The most likely cause is oil soaking. This hose could burst at any time, when hot or under pressure.

Cracked hose

Cracked hoses can usually be seen but feel the hoses to be sure they have not hardened; a prime cause of cracking. This hose has cracked down to the reinforcing cords and could split at any of the cracks.

Frayed hose end (due to weak clamp)

Weakened clamps frequently are the cause of hose and cooling system failure. The connection between the pipe and hose has deteriorated enough to allow coolant to escape when the engine is hot.

Debris in cooling system

Debris, rust and scale in the cooling system can cause the inside of a hose to weaken. This can usually be felt on the outside of the hose as soft or thinner areas.

Serpentine Belt

1. Place a wrench over the tensioner pulley axis bolt and rotate the tensioner counterclockwise.

2. While holding the tensioner in this position, remove the accessory drive belt.

3. Installation is the reverse of removal. No belt tensioning is necessary as the automatic tensioner is spring loaded.

Hoses

The upper/lower radiator hoses and all heater hoses should be checked for deterioration, leaks and loose hose clamps every 15,000 miles or 12 months.

REMOVAL AND INSTALLATION

1. Drain the cooling system.

CAUTION: *When draining the coolant, keep in mind that cats and dogs are attracted by the ethylene glycol antifreeze, and are quite likely to drink any that is left in an uncovered container or in puddles on the ground. This will prove fatal in sufficient quantity. Always drain the coolant into a sealable container. Coolant should be reused unless it is contaminated or several years old.*

2. Loosen the hose clamps at each end of the hose.

3. Working the hose back and forth, slide it off it's connection and then install a new hose, if necessary.

NOTE: *When replacing the heater hoses, maintain a 1 1/2 in. (38mm) clearance between the hose clip-to-upper control arm and between the rear overhead heater core lines-to-exhaust pipe.*

4. To install, reverse the removal procedures. Refill the cooling system.

NOTE: *Draw the hoses tight to prevent sagging or rubbing against other components; route the hoses through the clamps as installed originally. Always make sure that the hose clamps are beyond the component bead and placed in the center of the clamping surface before tightening them.*

Air Conditioning

NOTE: *This book contains simple testing procedures for your trucks's air conditioning system. More comprehensive testing, diagnosis and service procedures may be found in CHILTON'S GUIDE TO AIR CONDITIONING SERVICE AND REPAIR, available at your local retailer.*

SAFETY WARNINGS

Because of the importance of the necessary safety precautions that must be exercised when working with air conditioning systems and R-12 refrigerant, a recap of the safety precautions are outlined.

• Avoid contact with a charged refrigeration system, even when working on another part of the air conditioning system or truck. If a heavy tool comes into contact with a section of copper tubing or a heat exchanger, it can easily cause the relatively soft material to rupture.

• When it is necessary to apply force to a

PRESSURE CYCLING SYSTEM

"HPV" — HIGH PRESSURE VAPOR LEAVING COMPRESSOR.

"HPL" — VAPOR IS COOLED DOWN BY CONDENSER AIR FLOW AND LEAVES AS HIGH PRESSURE LIQUID.

"LPL" — ORIFICE METERS THE LIQUID R-12, INTO EVAPORATOR, REDUCING ITS PRESSURE, AND WARM BLOWER AIR ACROSS EVAPORATOR CORE CAUSES BOILING OFF OF LIQUID INTO VAPOR.

"LPV" — LEAVES EVAPORATOR AS LOW PRESSURE VAPOR AND RETURNS WITH THE SMALL AMOUNT OF . . .

"lpl" — . . . LOW PRESSURE LIQUID THAT DIDN'T BOIL OFF COMPLETELY BACK TO THE COMPRESSOR TO BE COMPRESSED AGAIN.

Air conditioning system schematic

fitting which contains refrigerant, as when checking that all system couplings are securely tightened, use a wrench on both parts of the fitting involved, if possible. This will avoid putting torque on the refrigerant tubing. It is recommended that tube or line wrenches be used when tightening these flare nut fittings.

• Avoid applying heat to any refrigerant line or storage vessel. Charging may be aided by using water heated to less than 125° to warm the refrigerant container. Never allow a refrigerant storage container to sit out in the sun or near any other heat source, such as a radiator.

• Always wear goggles when working on a system to protect the eyes. If refrigerant contacts the eyes, it is advisable in all cases to see a physician as soon as possible.

• Frostbite from liquid refrigerant should be treated by first gradually warming the area with cool water and then gently applying petroleum jelly. A physician should be consulted.

• Always keep the refrigerant can fittings capped when not in use. Avoid any sudden shock to the can, which might occur from dropping it or from banging a heavy tool against it. Never carry a can in the passenger compartment of a truck.

• Always have the system completely discharged before painting the truck (if the paint is to be baked on), or before welding anywhere near the refrigerant lines.

NOTE: *Any repair work to an air conditioning system should be left to a professional. DO NOT, under any circumstances, attempt to loosen or tighten any fittings or perform any work other than that outlined here.*

SYSTEM INSPECTIONS

NOTE: *The Cycling Clutch Orifice Tube (CCOT) A/C system does not use a sight glass.*

Checking For Oil Leaks

Refrigerant leaks show up as oily areas on the various components because the compressor oil is transported around the entire system along with the refrigerant. Look for oily spots on all the hoses and lines, especially on the hose and tubing connections. If there are oily deposits, the system may have a leak, have it checked by a qualified repairman.

NOTE: *A small area of oil on the front of the compressor is normal and no cause for alarm.*

Keep The Condenser Clear

Periodically inspect the front of the condenser for bent fins or foreign material (dirt, buts, leaves, etc.). If any cooling fins are bent, straighten them carefully with needlenose

F. Inlet
G. Outlet (to evaporator)
H. Dent on tube (retains the expansion tube)
20. Outlet Screen
21. Expansion tube
22. Inlet screen
23. Seal

Sectional view of the air conditioning system orifice tube

pliers. You can remove any debris with a stiff bristle brush or hose.

Operate The A/C System Periodically

A lot of A/C problems can be avoided by simply running the air conditioner at least once a week regardless of the season. Simply let the system run for at least 5 minutes a week (even in the winter) and you'll keep the internal parts lubricated as well as preventing the hoses from hardening.

Leak Testing the System

There are several methods of detecting leaks in an air conditioning system; among them, the two most popular are (1) halide leak detection or the open flame method and (2) electronic leak detector.

The Halide Leak Detection tool No. J-6084 or equivalent, is a torch like device which produces a yellow-green color when refrigerant is introduced into the flame at the burner. A purple or violet color indicates the presence of large amounts of refrigerant at the burner.

An Autobalance Refrigerant Leak Detector tool No. J-29547 or equivalent, is a small portable electronic device with an extended probe. With the unit activated, the probe is passed along those components of the system which contain refrigerant. If a leak is detected, the unit will sound an alarm signal or activate a display signal depending on the manufacturer's design. It is advisable to follow the manufacturer's instructions as the design and function of the detection may vary significantly.

CAUTION: *Care should be taken to operate either type of detector in well ventilated areas, so as to reduce the chance of personal injury, which may result from coming in contact with poisonous gases produced when R-12 is exposed to flame or electric spark.*

GAUGE SETS (USE)

Most of the service work performed in air conditioning requires the use of a two gauge set.

The gauges on the set monitor the high (head) pressure side and the low (suction) side of the system.

The low side gauge records both pressure and vacuum. Vacuum readings are calibrated from 0–30 in. Hg, and the pressure graduations read from 0–60 psi. The high side gauge measures pressure from 0–600 psi.

Both gauges are threaded into a manifold that contains two hand shut-off valves. Proper manipulation of these valves and the use of the attached test hoses allow the user to perform the following services:

- Test high and low side pressures.
- Charge the system with refrigerant.

The manifold valves are designed so they have no direct effect on the gauge readings but serve only to provide for or cut off the flow of refrigerant through the manifold. During all testing and hook-up operations, the valves are kept in a closed position to avoid disturbing the refrigeration system. The valves are opened ONLY to purge the system of refrigerant or to charge it.

When purging the system, the center hose is uncapped at the lower end and both valves are cracked (opened) slightly. This allows the refrigerant pressure to force the entire contents of the system out through the center hose. During charging, the valve on the high side of the manifold is closed and the valve on the low

5. Accumulator
15. Electrical connector
16. Pressure cycling switch adjusting screw
17. "Schrader" type valve

A/C accumulator with Schrader valve

side is cracked (opened). Under these conditions, the low pressure in the evaporator will draw refrigerant from the relatively warm refrigerant storage container into the system.

Service Valves

For the user to diagnose an air conditioning system he or she must gain entrance to the system in order to observe the pressures; the type of terminal for this purpose is the familiar Schrader valve.

The Schrader valve is similar to a tire valve stem and the process of connecting the test hoses is the same as threading a hand pump outlet hose to a bicycle tire. As the test hose is

J-6271-01
J-6272-02

J-23575-01

J-23390

80. Low side valve
81. High side valve
82. Vacuum pump
83. 12 or 30 Lb. drum
84. Disposable cans
4. Accumulator

Air conditioning charging system with gauges

threaded to the service port the valve core is depressed, allowing the refrigerant to enter the test hose outlet. Removal of the test hose automatically closes the system.

Extreme caution must be observed when removing test hoses from the Schrader valves as some refrigerant will normally escape.

Using The Manifold Gauges

The following are step-by-step procedures to guide the user in the correct usage of the gauge set:

CAUTION: *Wear goggles or face shield during all testing operations. Backseat hand shut-off type service valves.*

1. Remove the caps from the high and low side service ports. Make sure both gauge valves are closed.
2. Connect the low side test hose to the service valve that leads to the evaporator (located between the evaporator outlet and the compressor).
3. Attach the high side test hose to the service valve that leads to the condenser.
4. Mid-position the hand shutoff type service valves.
5. Start the engine and allow it to warm-up. All testing and charging of the system should be done after the engine and system has reached normal operating temperatures (except when using certain charging stations).
6. Adjust the air conditioner controls to MAX-COLD.
7. Observe the gauge readings.

When the gauges are not being used it is a good idea to:

  a. Keep both hand valves in the closed position.
  b. Attach both ends of the high and low service hoses to the manifold, if extra outlets are present on the manifold or plug them (if not).
  c. Keep the center charging hose attached to an empty refrigerant can. This extra precaution will reduce the possibility of moisture entering the gauges. If the air and moisture have gotten into the gauges, purge the hoses by supplying refrigerant under pressure to the center hose with both gauge valves open and all openings unplugged.

CHARGING

CAUTION: *Never attempt to charge the system by opening the high pressure gauge control while the compressor is operating. The compressor accumulating pressure can burst the refrigerant container, causing severe personal injury.*

1. Start the engine, operate it with the choke Open and normal idle speed, then position the A/C control lever on the Off.
2. Using drum or 14 oz. cans of refrigerant, in the inverted position, allow about 1 lb. of refrigerant to enter the system through the low side service fitting on the accumulator.
3. After 1 lb. of refrigerant enters the system, position the control lever on Norm (the compressor will engage) and the blower motor on Hi speed; this operation will draw the remainder of the refrigerant into the system.

NOTE: *To speed up the operation, position a fan in front of the condenser; the lowering of the condenser temperature will allow refrigerant to enter the system faster.*

4. When the system is charged, turn Off the refrigerant source and allow the engine to run for 30 seconds to clear the lines and gauges.
5. With the engine running, remove the hose adapter from the accumulator service fitting (unscrew the hose quickly to prevent refrigerant from escaping).

CAUTION: *Never remove the gauge line from the adapter when the line is connected to the system; always remove the line adapter from the service fitting first.*

6. Replace the accumulator protective caps and turn the engine Off.
7. Using a leak detector, inspect the A/C system for leaks. If a leak is present, repair it.

Windshield Wipers

For maximum effectiveness and longest element life, the windshield and wiper blades should be kept clean. Dirt, tree sap, road tar and so on will cause streaking, smearing and blade deterioration if left on the glass. It is advisable to wash the windshield carefully with a commercial glass cleaner at least once a month. Wipe off the rubber blades with the wet rag, afterwards.

If the blades are found to be cracked, broken or torn, they should be replaced immediately. Replacement intervals will vary with usage, although ozone deterioration usually limits blade life to about one year. If the wiper pattern is smeared, streaked or if the blade chatters across the glass, the elements should be replaced. It is easiest and most sensible to replace the elements in pairs.

Typical windshield wiper assembly

BLADE REPLACEMENT

1. Lift the wiper arm assembly from the windshield.

2. Depress the wiper arm-to-blade assembly pin to disconnect the blade assembly from the wiper arm.

3. To install, use new 16 in. blade assemblies and reverse the removal procedures.

Tires and Wheels

TIRE ROTATION

Tire wear can be equalized by switching the position of the tire about every 6,000 miles. Including a conventional spare in the rotation pattern can give up to 20% more tire life.

CAUTION: *DO NOT include the new Space Saver® or temporary spare tires in the rotation pattern.*

There are certain exceptions to tire rotation, however. Studded snow tires should not be rotated and radials should be kept on the same side of the truck (maintain the same direction of rotation). The belts on radial tires get set in a pattern. If the direction of rotation is reversed, it can cause rough ride and vibration.

NOTE: *When radials or studded snows are taken off the truck, mark them, so you can maintain the same direction of rotation.*

TIRE TYPES

For maximum satisfaction, tires should be used in sets of five. Mixing of different types (radial, bias-belted, fiberglass belted) should be avoided. Conventional bias tires are constructed so that the cords run bead-to-bead at an angle. This type of construction gives rigidity to both tread and sidewall. Bias-belted tires are similar in construction to conventional bias ply tires. Belts run at an angle and also at a 90° angle to the bead, as in the radial tire. Tread life is improved considerably over the conventional bias tire. The radial tire differs in construction, but instead of the carcass plies running are an angle of 90° to each other, they run at an angle of 90° to the bead. This gives the tread a great deal of rigidity and the sidewall a great deal of flexibility and accounts for the characteristic bulge associated with radial tires.

Chevrolet and GMC trucks are capable of using radial tires and they are recommended. If they are used, tire sizes and wheel diameters should be selected to maintain ground clearance and tire load capacity equivalent to the minimum specified tire. Radial tires should always be used in sets of five, but in an emergency, radial tires can be used with caution on the rear axle only. If this is done, both tires on the rear should be of radial design.

CAUTION: *Radial tires should never be used on ONLY the front axle.*

Snow tires should not be operated at sustained speeds over 70 mph.

On four wheel drive trucks, all tires must be of the same size, type, and tread pattern, to provide even traction on loose surfaces, to prevent driveline bind when conventional four wheel drive is used, and to prevent excessive wear on

Tire rotation patterns

the center differential with full time four wheel drive.

TREAD DEPTH

All tires have 8 built-in tread wear indicator bars that show up as ½ in. (12.7mm) wide smooth bands across the tire when 1/16 in. (1.5mm) of tread remains. The appearance of tread wear indicators means that the tires should be replaced. In fact, many states have laws prohibiting the use of tires with less than 1/16 in. (1.5mm) tread.

You can check your own tread depth with an inexpensive gauge or by using a Lincoln head penny. Slip the Lincoln penny into several tread grooves. If you can see the top of Lincoln's head in 2 adjacent grooves, the tires have less than 1/16 in. (1.5mm) tread left and should be replaced. You can measure snow tires in the same manner by using the tails side of the Lincoln penny. If you can see the top of the Lincoln memorial, it's time to replace the snow tires.

An quicker way to check tread depth is with a penny. If all of Lincoln's head is visible in two or more adjacent grooves, the tire should be replaced

Tread wear indicators appear when the tire needs replacement

TIRE STORAGE

Store the tires at proper inflation pressures if they are mounted on wheels. All tires should be kept in a cool, dry place. If they are stored in the garage or basement, DO NOT let them stand on a concrete floor, set them on strips of wood.

ALUMINUM WHEELS

CAUTION: *If your truck has aluminum wheels, be very careful when using any type of cleaner on either the wheels or the tires. Read the label on the package of the cleaner to make sure that it will not damage aluminum.*

TIRE INFLATION

The inflation is the most ignored item of auto maintenance. Gasoline mileage can drop as much as 0.8% for every 1 pound/square inch (psi) of under inflation.

Two items should be a permanent fixture in every glove compartment: a tire pressure gauge and a tread depth gauge. Check the tire air pressure (including the spare) regularly with a pocket type gauge. Kicking the tires won't tell you a thing and the gauge on the service station air hose is notoriously inaccurate.

The tire pressures recommended for your truck are usually found on the glove box door or in the owner's manual. Ideally, inflation pressure should be checked when the tires are cool. When the air becomes heated it expands and the pressure increases. Every 10° rise (or drop) in temperature means a difference of 1 psi, which also explains why the tire appears to lose air on a very cold night. When it is impossible to check the tires cold, allow for pressure build-up due to heat. If the hot pressure exceeds the cold pressure by more than 15 psi, reduce your speed, load or both. Otherwise internal heat is created in the tire. When the heat approaches the temperature at which the tire was cured during manufacture, the tread can separate from the body.

Tread wear can be accurately measured with a tread depth gauge

CAUTION: *Never counteract excessive pressure build-up by bleeding off air pressure (letting some air out). This will only further raise the tire operating temperature.*

Before starting a long trip with lots of luggage, you can add about 2–4 psi to the tires to make them run cooler, but never exceed the maximum inflation pressure on the side of the tire.

Factory installed wheels and tires are designed to handle loads up to and including their rated load capacity when inflated to the recommended inflation pressures. Correct tire pressures and driving techniques have an important influence on tire life. Heavy cornering, excessively rapid acceleration and unnecessary braking increase tire wear. Under inflated tires can cause handling problems, poor fuel economy, shortened tire life and tire overloading.

Maximum axle load must never exceed the value shown on the side of the tire. The inflation pressure should never exceed 35 psi (standard tires) or 60 psi (compact tire).

FLUID AND LUBRICANTS

Engine Oil and Fuel Recommendations

ENGINE OIL

Use ONLY SG or SG/CE rated oils of the recommended viscosity.

Under the classification system developed by the American Petroleum Institute, the SG rating designates the highest quality oil for use in passenger vehicles. In addition, Chevrolet recommends the use of an SG/Energy Conserving oil. Oils labeled Energy Conserving (or Saving), Fuel (Gas or Gasoline) Saving, etc. are recommended due to their superior lubricating qualities (less friction—easier engine operation) and fuel saving characteristics.

Pick oil viscosity with regard to the anticipated temperatures during the period before your next oil change. Using the accompanying chart, choose the oil viscosity for the lowest expected temperature. You will be assured of easy cold starting and sufficient engine protection.

FUEL

Gasoline

NOTE: *Some fuel additives contain chemicals that can damage the catalytic converter and/or oxygen sensor. Read all of the labels carefully before using any additive in the engine or fuel system.*

Fuel should be selected for the brand and octane which performs best with your engine. Judge a gasoline by its ability to prevent pinging, it's engine starting capabilities (cold and hot) and general all weather performance.

As far as the octane rating is concerned, refer to the General Engine Specifications chart in Chapter 3 to find your engine and its compression ratio. If the compression ratio is 9.0:1 or lower, in most cases a regular unleaded grade of gasoline can be used. If the compression ratio is 9.0:1–9.3:1, use a premium grade of unleaded fuel.

NOTE: *Your truck's engine fuel requirement can change with time, due to carbon buildup, which changes the compression ratio. If your truck's engine knocks, pings or runs on, switch to a higher grade of fuel (if possible) and check the ignition timing. Sometimes changing brands of gasoline will cure*

NOTE: Fluids and lubricants identified below by name, part number or specification may be obtained from your GM Truck Dealer.

USAGE	FLUID/LUBRICANT
Engine Oil	GM Goodwrench Motor Oil or equivalent for API Service SG or SG/CE of the recommended viscosity
Engine Coolant	Mixture of water and a good quality ethylene glycol base antifreeze conforming to GM-6038-M (GM Part No. 1052103).
Hydraulic Clutch System	Hydraulic Clutch Fluid (GM Part No 12345347) or DOT-3 brake fluid
Hydraulic Brake Systems	Delco Supreme 11 brake fluid (GM Part No. 1052535 or DOT-3)
Parking Brake Cables	Chassis grease meeting requirements of GM-6031-M (GM Part No. 1052497)
Power Steering System	GM Power Steering Fluid (GM Part No 1050017) or equivalent conforming to GM spec 9985010.
Manual Steering Gear	GM Lubricant (GM Part No 1052182) or equivalent
Automatic Transmission	DEXRON* II Automatic Transmission Fluid (GM Part No. 1051855).
Manual Transmission:	
4-Speed (RPO MC9, MF2)	DEXRON* II Automatic Transmission Fluid (GM Part No. 1051855).
4-Speed (RPO M20)	SAE-80W-90 gear lubricant (GM Part No 12345577).
4-Speed Overdrive (RPO MY6)	DEXRON* II Automatic Transmission Fluid (GM Part No. 1051855).
5-Speed (RPO ML2, ML3 and MH3)	DEXRON* II Automatic Transmission Fluid (GM Part No. 1051855).
5-Speed (RPO MG5)	Manual Transmission Fluid (GM Part No 1052931).
Differential:	
Standard - Front and Rear Axle	SAE-80W-90 GL-5 gear lubricant (GM Part No. 1052271).
Locking	SAE-80W-90 gear lubricant (GM Part No 1052271)
Transfer Case	Dexron* II Automatic Transmission Fluid (GM Part No 1051855)

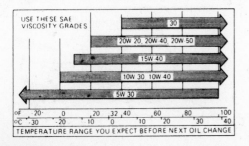

USE THESE SAE VISCOSITY GRADES

30	
20W 20, 20W 40, 20W 50	
15W 40	
10W 30, 10W 40	
5W 30	

°F -20 0 20 32 40 60 80 100
°C -30 -20 -10 0 10 20 30 40

TEMPERATURE RANGE YOU EXPECT BEFORE NEXT OIL CHANGE

Gasoline engine oil viscosity recommedations

Recommended fluids and lubricants

Diesel engine oil viscosity recommendation

the problem. If it is necessary to retard the timing from specifications, don't change it more than a few degrees. Retarded timing will reduce the power output and the fuel mileage, plus it will increase the engine temperature.

Diesel

Diesel-engine pick-ups require the use of diesel fuel. Two grades are manufactured, #1 and #2 – although #2 grade is generally the only grade available. Better fuel economy results from the use of #2 grade fuel.

In some northern parts of the USA, and in most parts of Canada, #1 grade fuel is available in winter, or a winterized blend of #2 grade is supplied in winter months. If #1 grade is available, it should be used whenever temperatures fall below 20°F (–7°C). Winterized #2 grade may also be used at these temperatures. However, unwinterized #2 grade should not be used below 20°F (–7°C). Cold temperatures cause unwinterized #2 grade to thicken (it actually gels), blocking the fuel lines and preventing the engine from running.

CAUTION: *DO NOT use home heating oil or gasoline in the diesel truck. DO NOT attempt to "thin" unwinterized #2 diesel fuel with gasoline. Gasoline or home heating oil will damage the engine and void the manu-*

The oil level is checked with the dipstick. When checking engine oil level, note the color and smell of the oil. Oil that is black or has a gas smell indicates a need for engine service

facturer's warranty. A mixture of gasoline and diesel fuel produces an extremely potent explosive that is more volatile than gasoline alone.

Engine

OIL CHECK LEVEL

The engine oil should be checked on a regular basis, ideally at each fuel stop. If the truck is used for trailer towing or for heavy-duty use, it is recommended to check the oil more frequently.

When checking the oil level, it is best that the oil be at operating temperature. Checking the level immediately after stopping will give a false reading due to oil left in the upper part of the engine. Be sure that the truck is resting on a level surface, allowing time for the oil to drain back into the crankcase.

1. Open the hood and locate the dipstick. Remove it from the tube (The oil dipstick is located on the driver's side).

2. Wipe the dipstick with a clean rag.

3. Insert the dipstick fully into the tube and remove it again.

4. Hold the dipstick horizontally and read the oil level. The level should be between the FULL and ADD marks.

5. If the oil level is at or below the ADD mark, oil should be added as necessary. Oil is added through the capped opening on the valve cover(s) on gasoline engines. Diesel engines have a capped oil fill tube at the front of the engine. Refer to the "Engine Oil and Fuel Recommendations" in this Chapter for the proper viscosity oil to use.

6. Replace the dipstick and check the level after adding oil. Be careful not to overfill the crankcase. Approximately one quart of oil will raise the level from ADD to FULL.

OIL AND FILTER CHANGE

Engine oil should be changed every 3,000 miles on gasoline engines and every 3,000 miles on diesel engines. The oil change and filter replacement interval should be cut in half under conditions such as:

- Driving in dusty conditions.
- Continuous trailer pulling or RV use.

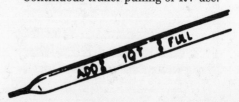

The full level should be between the "add" and "full" marks on the dipstick

• Extensive or prolonged idling.

• Extensive short trip operation in freezing temperatures (when the engine is not thoroughly warmed-up).

• Frequent long runs at high speed and high ambient temperatures.

• Stop-and-go service such as delivery trucks.

Operation of the engine in severe conditions such as a dust storm may require an immediate oil and filter change.

Chevrolet and GMC recommend changing both the oil and filter during the first oil change and the filter every other oil change thereafter. For the small price of an oil filter, it's cheap insurance to replace the filter at every oil change. One of the larger filter manufacturers points out in its advertisements that not changing the filter leaves one quart of dirty oil in the engine. This claim is true and should be kept in mind when changing your oil.

NOTE: *The oil filter on the diesel engine must be changed every oil change.*

To change the oil, the truck should be on a level surface and the engine should be at operating temperature. This is to ensure that the foreign matter will be drained away along with the oil and not left in the engine to form sludge. You should have available a container that will hold a minimum of 8 quarts of liquid, a wrench to fit the old drain plug, a spout for pouring in new oil and a rag or two, which you will always

1. *Warm the car up before changing your oil. Raise the front end of the car and support it on drive-on ramps or jackstands.*

2. *Locate the drain plug on the bottom of the oil pan and slide a low flat pan of sufficient capacity under the engine to catch the oil. Loosen the plug with a wrench and turn it out the last few turns by hand. Keep a steady inward pressure on the plug to avoid hot oil from running down your arm.*

3. *Remove the oil filter with a filter wrench. The filter can hold more than a quart of oil, which will be hot. Be sure the gasket comes off with the filter and clean the mounting base on the engine.*

4. *Lubricate the gasket on the new filter with clean engine oil. A dry gasket may not make a good seal and will allow the filter to leak.*

5. *Position a new filter on the mounting base and spin it on by hand. Do not use a wrench. When the gasket contacts the engine, tighten it another ½–1 turn by hand.*

6. *Using a rag, clean the drain plug and the area around the drain hole in the oil pan.*

7. *Install the drain plug and tighten it finger-tight. If you feel resistance, stop and be sure you are not cross-threading the plug. Finally, tighten the plug with a wrench.*

8. *Locate the oil cap on the valve cover. An oil spout is the easiest way to add oil, but a funnel will do just as well.*

9. *Start the engine and check for leaks. The oil pressure warning light will remain on for a few seconds; when it goes out, stop the engine and check the level on the dipstick.*

need. If the filter is being replaced, you will also need a band wrench or filter wrench to fit the end of the filter.

NOTE: *If the engine is equipped with an oil cooler, this will also have to be drained, using the drain plug. Be sure to add enough oil to fill the cooler in addition to the engine.*

1. Position the truck on a level surface and set the parking brake or block the wheels. Slide a drain pan under the oil drain plug.

2. From under the truck, loosen, but do not remove the oil drain plug. Cover your hand with a rag or glove and slowly unscrew the drain plug.

CAUTION: *The engine oil will be HOT. Keep your arms, face and hands clear of the oil as it drains out.*

3. Remove the plug and let the oil drain into the pan. Do not drop the plug into the drain pan.

4. When all of the oil has drained, clean off the drain plug and reinstall it into pan. Torque the drain plug to 20 ft. lbs. (gasoline) or 30 ft. lbs. (diesel) engines.

5. Using an oil filter wrench, loosen the oil filter. On most Chevrolet engines, especially the V6s, the oil filter is next to the exhaust pipes. Stay clear of these, since even a passing contact will result in a painful burn.

NOTE: *On trucks equipped with catalytic converters, stay clear of the converter. The outside temperature of a hot catalytic converter can approach 1200°F.*

6. Cover your hand with a rag and spin the filter off by hand; turn it slowly.

7. Coat the rubber gasket on a new filter with a light film of clean engine oil. Screw the filter onto the mounting stud and tighten it according to the directions on the filter (usually hand-tight one turn past the point where the gasket contacts the mounting base); DO NOT over tighten the filter.

8. Refill the engine with the specified amount of clean engine oil.

9. Run the engine for several minutes, checking for leaks. Check the level of the oil and add oil if necessary.

When you have finished this job, you will notice that you now possess four or five quarts of dirty oil. The best thing to do with it is to pour it into plastic jugs, such as milk or antifreeze containers. Then, locate a service station where you can pour it into their used oil tank for recycling.

CAUTION: *Pouring used motor oil into a storm drain not only pollutes the environment, it violates Federal law. Dispose of waste oil properly.*

Manual Transmission

FLUID RECOMMENDATIONS

S-10/S-15 trucks equipped with manual transmissions may use either Dexron® II automatic transmission fluid or SAE 80W-90 gear oil. Check the Recommended Fluids and Lubricants Chart to determine which type of lubricant your transmission uses.

LEVEL CHECK

Remove the filler plug from the passenger's-side of the transmission (the upper plug if the transmission has two plugs). The oil should be level with the bottom edge of the filler hole. This should be checked at least once every 6,000 miles or more often if any leakage or seepage is observed.

DRAIN AND REFILL

Under normal conditions, the transmission fluid should not be changed. However, if the truck is driven in deep water, replace the fluid.

1. Raise and support the vehicle on jackstands.

2. Place a fluid catch pan under the transmission.

3. Remove the bottom plug and drain the fluid.

4. Install the bottom plug and refill the transmission housing.

Automatic Transmission

FLUID RECOMMENDATIONS

When adding fluid or refilling the transmission, use Dexron® II automatic transmission fluid.

LEVEL CHECK

Before checking the fluid level of the transmission, drive the truck for at least 15 miles to warm the fluid.

1. Place the truck on a level surface, apply the parking brake and block the front wheels.

2. Start the engine and move the selector through each range, then place it in Park.

NOTE: *When moving the selector through each range, DO NOT race the engine.*

3. With the engine running at a low idle, remove the transmission's dipstick to check the fluid level.

4. The level should be at the Full Hot mark of the dipstick. If not, add fluid.

CAUTION: *DO NOT overfill the transmission, damage to the seals could occur. Use Dexron® II automatic transmission fluid. One pint raises the level from Add to Full.*

Automatic transmission fluid dipstick. When checking transmission oil, note the color and smell of the oil. Oil that is brown or has a burnt smell indicates a need for transmission service

DRAIN AND REFILL

The truck should be driven 15 miles to warm the transmission fluid before the pan is removed.

NOTE: *The fluid should be drained while the transmission is warm.*

1. Raise and support the front of vehicle on jackstands.
2. Place a drain pan under the transmission pan.
3. Remove the pan bolts from the front and the sides, then loosen the rear bolts 4 turns.
4. Using a small pry bar, pry the pan from the transmission. This will allow the pan to partially drain. Remove the remaining pan bolts and lower the pan from the transmission.

NOTE: *If the transmission fluid is dark or has a burnt smell, transmission damage is indicated. Have the transmission checked professionally.*

5. Empty the pan, remove the gasket material and clean with a solvent.
6. Using a putty knife, clean gasket mounting surfaces.
7. To install the oil pan, use a new gasket and sealant, then reverse the removal procedures. Torque the pan bolts to 8 ft. lbs. in a criss-cross pattern.
8. Using Dexron® II automatic transmission fluid, add it through the filler tube. See the Capacities Chart to determine the proper amount of fluid to be added.

Adding automatic transmission fluid

CAUTION: *DO NOT OVERFILL the transmission. Foaming of the fluid and subsequent transmission damage due to slippage will result.*

9. With the gearshift lever in PARK, start the engine and let it idle. DO NOT race the engine.
10. Apply the parking brake and move the gearshift lever through each position. Return the lever to Park and check the fluid level with the engine idling. The level should be between the two dimples on the dipstick, about 1/4 in. (6mm) below the ADD mark. Add fluid, if necessary.
11. Check the fluid level after the truck has been driven enough to thoroughly warm the transmission.

PAN AND FILTER SERVICE

1. Refer to the Drain and Refill procedures in this Chapter and remove the oil pan.
2. Remove the screen and the filter from the valve body.
3. Install a new filter using a new gasket or O-ring.

NOTE: *If the transmission uses a filter having a fully exposed screen, it may be cleaned and reused.*

4. To install the oil pan, use a new gasket and sealant, then reverse the removal procedures. Torque the pan bolts to 8 ft. lbs. in a criss-cross pattern. Refill the transmission.

Transfer Case

FLUID RECOMMENDATIONS

When adding fluid or refilling the transfer case, use Dexron® II automatic transmission fluid.

LEVEL CHECK

1. Raise and support the vehicle (level) on jackstands.
2. At the rear-side of the transfer case, remove the filler plug.
3. Using your finger, check the fluid level, it should be level with the bottom of the filler hole.
4. If the fluid level is low, use Dexron® II automatic transmission fluid to bring the fluid up to the proper level.
5. Install the filler plug and torque it to 30–40 ft. lbs.

DRAIN AND REFILL

1. Raise and support the front of the vehicle on jackstands.
2. Position drain pan under transfer case.
3. Remove drain and fill plugs, then drain the lubricant into the drain pan.

4. Install drain plug. Torque the plug to 30–40 ft. lbs.

5. Remove the drain pan and dump the fluid into a used oil storage tank, for recycling purposes.

6. Using Dexron® II automatic transmission fluid, fill transfer case to edge of fill plug opening.

7. Install fill plug and torque it to 30–40 ft. lbs.

8. Lower vehicle and check the operation of the transfer case.

Drive Axles

If the truck is equipped with a front drive axle, perform the same procedures as for the standard rear drive axle. Replace the fluid at the first oil change. If the truck is operated in dusty areas or used in trailer towing applications, replace the fluid every 15,000 miles. Check fluid and add as needed to maintain a Full fluid level of $3/8$ in. below the filler plug hole every oil change.

FLUID RECOMMENDATIONS

Standard Axle

Always use SAE-80W or SAE 80W-90 GL5.

Locking Axle

CAUTION: *Never use standard differential lubricant in a positraction differential.*
Always use GM Rear Axle Fluid No. 1052271. Before refilling the rear axle, add 4 ounces of GM Fluid No. 1052358.

LEVEL CHECK

The lubricant level should be checked at each oil change and maintained at $3/8$ in. below the bottom of the filler plug hole.

1. Raise and support the vehicle on jackstands; be sure that the vehicle is level.

2. Remove the filler plug, located at the side of the differential carrier.

3. Check the fluid level, it should be $3/8$ in. below the bottom of the filler plug hole, add fluid (if necessary).

4. Replace the filler plug.

DRAIN AND REFILL

Refer to Fluid Recommendations in this Chapter for information on when to change the fluid.

1. Run the vehicle until the lubricant reaches operating temperature.

2. Raise and support the vehicle on jackstands; be sure that the vehicle is level.

3. Using a floor jack, support the drive axle. Position a drain pan under the rear axle.

4. Remove the cover from the rear of the drive axle and drain the lubricant.

5. Using a putty knife, clean the gasket mounting surfaces.

6. To install, use a new gasket, sealant and reverse the removal procedures.

7. Torque the cover-to-rear axle bolts in a criss-cross pattern to 20 ft. lbs. Using a suction gun or a squeeze bulb, install the fluid through the filler plug hole. Install the filler plug.

Cooling System

At least once every 2 years or 30,000 miles, the engine cooling system should be inspected, flushed and refilled with fresh coolant. If the coolant is left in the system too long, it loses its ability to prevent rust and corrosion. If the coolant has too much water, it won't protect against freezing.

FLUID RECOMMENDATIONS

Using a good quality of ethylene glycol antifreeze (one that will not effect aluminum), mix it with water until a 50–50 antifreeze solution is attained.

LEVEL CHECK

NOTE: *When checking the coolant level, the radiator cap need not be removed, simply check the coolant tank.*
Check the coolant recovery bottle (see through plastic bottle). With the engine Cold, the coolant should be at the ADD mark (recovery tank $1/4$ full). With the engine warm, the coolant should be at the FULL mark (recovery tank $1/2$ full). If necessary, add fluid to the recovery bottle.

DRAIN AND REFILL

CAUTION: *To avoid injuries from scalding fluid and steam, DO NOT remove the radiator cap while the engine and radiator are still HOT.*

1. When the engine is cool, remove the radiator cap using the following procedures.

Coolant recovery system see-through bottle

The coolant system should be pressure checked at least once a year

Coolant protection can be checked with a simple float-type tester

a. Slowly rotate the cap counterclockwise to the detent.

b. If any residual pressure is present, WAIT until the hissing noise stops.

c. After the hissing noise has ceased, press down on the cap and continue rotating it counterclockwise to remove it.

2. Place a fluid catch pan under the radiator, open the radiator drain valve and the engine drain plugs, then drain the coolant.

CAUTION: *When draining the coolant, keep in mind that cats and dogs are attracted by the ethylene glycol antifreeze, and are quite likely to drink any that is left in an uncovered container or in puddles on the ground. This will prove fatal in sufficient quantity. Always drain the coolant into a sealable container. Coolant should be reused unless it is contaminated or several years old.*

3. Close the drain valve and install the engine drain plugs.

4. Empty the coolant reservoir and flush it.

5. Using the correct mixture of antifreeze, fill the radiator to the bottom of the filler neck and the coolant tank to the FULL mark.

6. Install the radiator cap (make sure that the arrows align with the overflow tube).

7. Run the engine until it reaches the operating temperatures, allow it to cool, then check the fluid level and add fluid (if necessary).

FLUSHING AND CLEANING THE SYSTEM

1. Refer to the Drain and Refill procedures in this Chapter, then drain the cooling system.

CAUTION: *When draining the coolant, keep in mind that cats and dogs are attracted by the ethylene glycol antifreeze, and are quite likely to drink any that is left in an uncovered container or in puddles on the ground. This will prove fatal in sufficient quantity.*

Always drain the coolant into a sealable container. Coolant should be reused unless it is contaminated or several years old.

2. Close the drain valve and install the engine drain plugs, then add sufficient water to the cooling system.

CAUTION: *When draining the coolant, keep in mind that cats and dogs are attracted by the ethylene glycol antifreeze, and are quite likely to drink any that is left in an uncovered container or in puddles on the ground. This will prove fatal in sufficient quantity. Always drain the coolant into a sealable container. Coolant should be reused unless it is contaminated or several years old.*

3. Run the engine, then drain and refill the system. Perform this procedure several times, until the fluid (drained from the system) is clear.

4. Empty the coolant reservoir and flush it.

5. Using the correct mixture of antifreeze, fill the radiator to the bottom of the filler neck and the coolant tank to the FULL mark.

6. Install the radiator cap (make sure that the arrows align with the overflow tube).

Master Cylinder

NOTE: *Refer to Anti-Lock Brake System in Chapter 8 for special service procedures.*

Chevrolet and GMC trucks are equipped with a dual braking system, allowing a truck to be brought to a safe stop in the event of failure in either the front or rear brakes. The dual master cylinder has two separate reservoirs, one connected to the front brakes and the other connected to the rear brakes. In the event of

Master cylinder reservoir showing the minimum fluid level line

failure in either portion, the remaining portion is unaffected.

FLUID RECOMMENDATIONS

Use only heavy-duty Delco Supreme 11 or DOT-3 brake fluid.

CAUTION: *Brake fluid damages paint. It also absorbs moisture from the air; never leave a container or the master cylinder uncovered any longer than necessary. All parts in contact with the brake fluid (master cylinder, hoses, plunger assemblies and etc.) must be kept clean, since any contamination of the brake fluid will adversely affect braking performance.*

LEVEL CHECK

The brake fluid level should be inspected every 6 months.

1. Remove the master cylinder reservoir cap.

Power steering fluid dipstick

NOTE: *If equipped with a see through reservoir, it is not necessary to remove the reservoir cap unless you are adding fluid.*

2. The fluid should be $1/4$ in. (6mm) from top of the reservoir, if necessary, add fluid.

3. Replace the reservoir caps.

Hydraulic Clutch

NOTE: *The clutch master cylinder is mounted on the firewall next to the brake master cylinder.*

FLUID RECOMMENDATIONS

Use only heavy duty Delco Supreme 11 or DOT-3 brake fluid.

LEVEL CHECK

The hydraulic clutch reservoir should be checked at least every 6 months. Fill to the line on the reservoir.

Power Steering Pump

The power steering pump reservoir is located at the front left-side of the engine.

FLUID RECOMMENDATIONS

Use GM Power Steering Fluid No. 1050017 or equivalent.

NOTE: *Avoid using automatic transmission fluid in the power steering unit, except in an emergency.*

LEVEL CHECK

The power steering fluid should be checked at least every 6 months. There is a Cold and a Hot mark on the dipstick. The fluid should be checked when the engine is warm and turned OFF. If necessary, add fluid to the power steering pump reservoir.

NOTE: *On models equipped with a remote reservoir, the fluid level should be $1/2$–1 in. (25.4mm) from the top when the wheels are turned to the extreme left position.*

Manual Steering Gear

The steering gear is factory-filled with a lubricant which does not require seasonal change. The housing should not be drained; no lubrication is required for the life of the gear.

FLUID RECOMMENDATIONS

Use GM steering gear lubricant No. 1052182 or equivalent.

LEVEL CHECK

The steering lubricant should be checked every 6 months or 7,500 miles. The gear should be inspected for seal leakage when specified in the Maintenance Interval chart. Look for solid grease, not an oily film. If a seal is replaced or the gear overhauled, it should be refilled with lubricant.

Chassis Greasing

Chassis greasing should be performed every 6 months or 7,500 miles, it can be performed with a commercial pressurized grease gun or at home by using a hand operated grease gun. Wipe the grease fittings clean before greasing in order to prevent the possibility of forcing any dirt into the component.

The four wheel drive front driveshaft requires special attention for lubrication. The large constant velocity joint at the front of the transfer case has a special grease fitting in the centering ball. A special needle nose adapter for a flush type fitting is required, as well as a special lubricant (GM part No. 1050679). You can only get at this fitting when it is facing up toward the floorboard, so you need a flexible hose, too.

Water resistant EP chassis lubricant (grease) conforming to GM specification 6031-M should be used for all chassis grease points.

Body Lubrication

HOOD LATCH AND HINGES

Clean the latch surfaces and apply white grease to the latch pilot bolts and the spring anchor. Use the engine oil to lubricate the hood hinges as well. Use a chassis grease to lubricate all the pivot points in the latch release mechanism.

DOOR HINGES

The gas tank filler door, the front doors and rear door hinges should be wiped clean and lubricated with white grease. The door lock cylinders can be lubricated easily with a shot of GM silicone spray No. 1052276 or one of the many dry penetrating lubricants commercially available.

PARKING BRAKE LINKAGE

Use chassis grease on the parking brake cable where it contacts the guides, links, levers and pulleys. The grease should be a water resistant for durability under the truck.

ACCELERATOR LINKAGE

Lubricate the throttle body lever, the cable and the accelerator pedal lever (at the support inside the truck) with white grease.

TRANSMISSION SHIFT LINKAGE

Lubricate the shift linkage with water resistant chassis grease which meets GM specification No. 6031M or equivalent.

Front Wheel Bearings—2WD Only

Once every 30,000 miles, clean and repack wheel bearings with a GM Wheel Bearing Grease No. 1051344 or equivalent. Use only enough grease to completely coat the rollers. Remove any excess grease from the exposed surface of the hub and seal.

REMOVAL, PACKING AND INSTALLATION

NOTE: *The following procedures require the use of GM tools No. J-29117, J-8092, J-8850, J-8457, J-9746-02 or equivalent.*

1. Raise and support the front of the vehicle on jackstands.
2. Remove the tire/wheel assembly.
3. Remove the caliper-to-steering knuckle bolts and the caliper from the steering knuckle. Using a wire, support the caliper from the vehicle; DO NOT disconnect the brake line.
4. From the hub/disc assembly, remove the dust cap, the cotter pin, the spindle nut, the thrust washer and the outer bearing.
5. Grasping the hub/disc assembly firmly, pull the assembly from the axle spindle.
6. Using a small pry bar, pry the grease seal from the rear of the hub/disc assembly, then remove the inner bearing.

NOTE: *DO NOT remove the bearing races from the hub, unless they show signs of damage.*

7. If it is necessary to remove the wheel bearing races, use the GM front bearing race removal tool No. J-29117 or equivalent, to drive the races from the hub/disc assembly.
8. Using solvent, clean the grease from all of the parts, then wipe dry with a clean cloth. Blowing bearing dry with compressed air may damage them
9. Inspect all of the parts for scoring, pitting or cracking and replace if necessary.
10. If the bearing races were removed, place the replacement races in the freezer for a few minutes and then perform the following procedures to the install the them:

   a. Using grease, lightly lubricate the inside of the hub/disc assembly.

   b. Using the GM seal installation tools No. J-8092 and J-8850 or equivalent, drive the inner bearing race into the hub/disc assembly until it seats.

J-8092
WITH
J-8457

OUTER
BEARING
RACE

J-29117

Installing the outer bearing race — 2WD

Removing the bearing race — 2WD

NOTE: *When installing the bearing races, be sure to support the hub/disc assembly with GM tool No. J-9746-02 or equivalent.*

c. Using the GM seal installation tools No. J-8092 and J-8457 or equivalent, drive the outer race into the hub/disc assembly until it seats.

11. Using wheel bearing grease, lubricate the bearings, the races and the spindle; be sure to place a gob of grease (inside the hub/disc assembly) between the races to provide an ample supply of lubricant.

NOTE: *To lubricate each bearing, place a gob of grease in the palm of the hand, then roll the bearing through the grease until it is well lubricated.*

12. Place the inner wheel bearing into the hub/disc assembly. Using a flat plate, drive the new grease seal into the rear of the hub/disc assembly until it is flush with the outer surface.

13. Onto the spindle, install the hub/disc as-

sembly, the thrust washer and the hub nut. While turning the wheel, torque the hub nut to 16 ft. lbs. until the bearings seat. Loosen the nut, retighten it and back it off until the nearest nut slot aligns with a spindle hole (not more than a $\frac{1}{2}$ turn).

14. Install a new cotter pin through the nut and the spindle, then bend the ends and cut off the excess pin. Install the grease cap.

15. If necessary, use a dial indicator to the check the rotor endplay. The endplay should be 0.001–0.005 in. (0.025–0.127mm); if not, readjust the hub/disc assembly.

16. Install the caliper onto the steering knuckle and torque the bolts to 37 ft. lbs. Road test the vehicle.

STEERING KNUCKLE   SHIELD   DISC   COTTER PIN

WASHER

GASKET   SEAL   RACE   RACE   NUT   CAP

BEARING

INNER BEARING

Exploded view of the front wheel bearing assembly — 2WD

Installing the inner bearing race — 2WD

TRAILER TOWING

Trucks are popular as trailer towing vehicles. Their strong construction and variety of power train combinations make them ideal for towing campers, boat and utility trailers.

Factory trailer towing packages are available on most trucks. However, if you are installing a trailer hitch and wiring on your truck, there are a few things you ought to know.

General Recommendations

Wiring

Wiring the truck for towing is fairly easy. There are a number of good wiring kits available and these should be used, rather than trying to design your own. All trailers will need brake lights, turn signals, tail lights and side marker lights. Most states require extra marker lights for overly wide trailers. Also, most states have recently required back-up lights for trailers, and most trailer manufacturers have been building trailers with back-up lights for several years.

Additionally, some Class I, most Class II and all Class III trailers will have electric brakes.

Add to this number an accessories wire, to operate the trailer internal equipment or to charge the trailer's battery, and you can have as many as seven wires in the harness.

Determine the equipment on your trailer and buy the wiring kit necessary. The kit will contain all the wires needed, plus a plug adapter set which included the female plug, mounted on the bumper or hitch, and the male plug, wired into, or plugged into the trailer harness.

When installing the kit, follow the manufacturer's instructions. The color coding of the wires is standard throughout the industry.

One point to note: some domestic vehicles and most imported vehicles, have separate turn signals. On most domestic vehicles, the brake lights and rear turn signals operate with the same bulb. For those vehicles with separate turn signals, you can purchase an isolation unit so that the brake lights won't blink whenever the turn signals are operated, or, you can go to your local electronics supply house and buy four diodes to wire in series with the brake and turn signal bulbs. Diodes will isolate the brake and turn signals. The choice is yours. The isolation units are simple and quick to install, but far more expensive than the diodes. The diodes, however, require more work to install properly, since they require the cutting of each bulb's wire and soldering in place of the diode.

One, final point, the best kits are those with a spring loaded cover on the vehicle mounted socket. This cover prevents dirt and moisture from corroding the terminals. Never let the vehicle socket hang loosely; always mount it securely to the bumper or hitch.

Cooling

ENGINE

The most common problem associated with trailer towing is engine overheating.

With factory installed trailer towing packages, a heavy duty cooling system is usually included. Heavy duty cooling systems are available as optional equipment on most trucks, with or without a trailer package. If you have one of these extra capacity systems, you shouldn't have overheating problems.

If you have a standard cooling system, without an expansion tank, you'll definitely need to get an aftermarket expansion tank kit, preferably one with at least a 2 quart capacity. These kits are easily installed on the radiator's overflow hose, and come with a pressure cap designed for expansion tanks.

Another helpful accessory is a Flex Fan. These fan are large diameter units are designed to provide more air flow at low speeds, with blades that have deeply cupped surfaces. The blades then flex, or flatten out, at high speed, when less cooling air is needed. These fans are far lighter in weight than stock fans, requiring less horsepower to drive them. Also, they are far quieter than stock fans.

If you do decide to replace your stock fan with a flex fan, note that if your truck has a fan clutch, a spacer between the flex fan and water pump hub will be needed.

Aftermarket engine oil coolers are helpful for prolonging engine oil life and reducing overall engine temperatures. Both of these factors increase engine life. While not absolutely necessary in towing Class I and some Class II trailers, they are recommended for heavier Class II and all Class III towing.

Engine oil cooler systems consist of an adapter, screwed on in place of the oil filter, a remote filter mounting and a multi-tube, a finned heat exchanger, which is mounted in front of the radiator or air conditioning condenser.

TRANSMISSION

An automatic transmission is usually recommended for trailer towing. The increased load of trailer towing causes increase in the temperature of the automatic transmission fluid—heat is the worst enemy of an automatic transmission. As the temperature of the fluid increases, the life of the fluid decreases. It is essential, therefore, that you install an automatic transmission cooler.

The cooler, which consists of a multi-tube, finned heat exchanger, is usually installed in front of the radiator or air conditioning compressor, and hooked inline with the transmission cooler tank inlet line. Follow the cooler manufacturer's installation instructions and select a cooler of at least adequate capacity, based upon the combined gross weights of the truck and trailer.

Cooler manufacturers recommend that you use an aftermarket cooler in addition to, and not instead of, the present cooling tank in your trucks radiator. If you do want to use it in place of the radiator cooling tank, get a cooler at least two sizes larger than normally necessary.

One note: A transmission cooler can, sometimes, cause slow or harsh shifting in the transmission until the fluid has a chance to come up to normal operating temperature. This condition is usually more pronounced in the Winter months. Some coolers can be purchased or retrofitted with a temperature bypass valve which will allow fluid flow through the cooler only when the fluid has reached operating temperature, or above.

Trailer and Hitch Weight Limits

Trailer Weight

Trailer weight is the first, and most important factor in determining whether or not your truck is suitable for towing the trailer you have in mind. To determine if your truck is capable of towing a given trailer, calculate the horsepower-to-weight ratio. The basic standard is a ratio of 35:1. That is, 35 lbs. of GVW for every horsepower.

To calculate this ratio, multiply you engine's rated horsepower by 35, then subtract the weight of the truck, including passengers and luggage. The resulting figure is the ideal maximum trailer weight that you can tow. One point to consider: a numerically higher axle ratio can offset what appears to be a low trailer weight. If the weight of the trailer that you have in mind is somewhat higher than the weight you just calculated, you might consider changing your rear axle ratio to compensate.

Hitch Weight

There are three kinds of hitches: bumper mounted, frame mounted and load equalizing.

Bumper mounted hitches are those which attach solely to the truck's bumper. Many states prohibit towing with this type of hitch, when it attaches to the truck's stock bumper, since it subjects the bumper to stresses for which it was not designed. Aftermarket rear step bumpers, designed for trailer towing, are acceptable for use with bumper mounted hitches.

Frame mounted hitches can be of the type which bolts to two or more points on the frame, plus the bumper, or just to several points on the frame. Frame mounted hitches can also be of the tongue type, for Class I towing, or, of the receiver type, for classes II and III.

Load equalizing hitches are usually used for large trailers. Most equalizing hitches are welded in place, they use equalizing bars and chains to level the truck after the trailer is connected.

Check the gross weight rating of your trailer. Tongue weight is usually figured as 10% of gross trailer weight. Therefore, a trailer with a maximum gross weight of 2,000 lbs. will have a maximum tongue weight of 200 lbs. Class I trailers fall into this category. Class II trailers are those with a gross weight rating of 2,000–3,500 lbs., while Class III trailers fall into the 3,500–6,000 lbs. category. Class IV trailers are those over 6,000 lbs. and are for use with fifth wheel trucks, only.

When you've determined the hitch that you'll need, follow the manufacturer's installation instructions exactly, especially when it comes to fastener torques. The hitch will subjected to a lot of stress and good hitches come with hardened bolts. Never substitute an inferior bolt for a hardened bolt.

PUSHING AND TOWING

CAUTION: *Pushing or towing your truck to start it may result in unusually high catalytic converter and exhaust system temperatures, which under extreme conditions may ignite the interior floor covering material above the converter.*

Pushing

Chevrolet and GMC trucks with manual transmissions can be push started. To push start, make sure that both bumpers are in reasonable alignment. Turn the ignition switch ON and engage High gear. Depress the clutch pedal. When a speed of about 10 mph is reached, slightly depress the gas pedal and slowly release the clutch. The engine should start.

NOTE: *Automatic transmission equipped trucks cannot be started by pushing.*

Towing

Chevrolet and GMC trucks can be towed on all four wheels (flat towed) at speeds of less than 35 mph for distances less than 50 miles, providing that the axle, driveline and engine/transmission are operable. The transmission should be in Neutral, the engine should be Off, the steering column unlocked, and the parking brake released.

Do not attach chains to the bumpers or bracketing. All attachments must be made to the structural members. Safety chains should be used. it should also be remembered that power steering and brake assists will not be working with the engine off.

The rear wheels must be raised off the ground or the driveshaft disconnected when the transmission is not operating properly, or when speeds or over 35 mph will be used or when towing more than 50 miles.

CAUTION: *If a truck is towed on its front wheels only, the steering wheel must be secured with the wheels in a straight ahead position.*

JUMP STARTING

The following procedure is recommended by the manufacturer. Be sure that the booster battery is 12 volt with negative ground. Follow this procedure exactly to avoid possible damage to the electrical system, especially on models equipped with computerized engine controls.

CAUTION: *DO NOT attempt this procedure on a frozen battery—it will probably explode.*

DO NOT *attempt it on a sealed Delco Freedom battery showing a light color in the charge indicator. Be certain to observe correct polarity connections. Failure to do so will result in almost immediate computer, alternator and regulator destruction. Never allow the jumper cable ends to touch each other.*

1. Position the vehicles so that they are not touching. Set the parking brake and place automatic transmission in Park and manual transmission in Neutral. Turn Off the lights, heater and other electrical loads. Turn both ignition switches Off.
2. Remove the vent caps from both the booster and discharged battery. Lay a cloth over the open vent cells of each battery. This isn't necessary on batteries equipped with sponge type flame arrestor caps, and it isn't possible on sealed batteries.
3. Attach one cable to the positive terminal of the booster battery and the other end to the positive terminal of the discharged battery.

NOTE: *If you are attempting to start a Chevrolet or GMC pick-up with the diesel engine, it is suggested that this connection be made to the battery on the driver's side of the truck, because this battery is closer to the starter, and thus the resistance of the electrical cables is lower. From this point on, ignore the other battery in the truck.*

CAUTION: *DO NOT attempt to jump start the truck with a 24 volt power source.*

4. Attach one end of the remaining cable to the negative terminal of the booster battery and the other end to a good ground. Do not attach to the negative terminal of discharged batteries. Do not lean over the battery when making this last connection.
5. Start the engine of the truck with the booster battery. Start the engine of the truck with the discharged battery. If the engine will not start, disconnect the batteries as soon as possible. If this is not done, the two batteries will soon reach a state of equilibrium, with both too weak to start an engine. This will not be a problem of the engine of the booster truck is kept running fast enough. Lengthy cranking can also overheat and damage the starter.
6. Reverse the above steps to disconnect the booster and discharge batteries. Be certain to remove negative connections first.
7. Reinstall the vent caps. Dispose of the cloths; they may have battery acid on them.

CAUTION: *The use of any "hot shot" type of jumper system in excess of 12 volts can damage the electronic control units or cause the discharged battery to explode.*

JUMP STARTING A DEAD BATTERY

The chemical reaction in a battery produces explosive hydrogen gas. This is the safe way to jump start a dead battery, reducing the chances of an accidental spark that could cause an explosion.

Jump Starting Precautions

1. Be sure both batteries are of the same voltage.
2. Be sure both batteries are of the same polarity (have the same grounded terminal).
3. Be sure the vehicles are not touching.
4. Be sure the vent cap holes are not obstructed.
5. Do not smoke or allow sparks around the battery.
6. In cold weather, check for frozen electrolyte in the battery. Do not jump start a frozen battery.
7. Do not allow electrolyte on your skin or clothing.
8. Be sure the electrolyte is not frozen.
CAUTION: *Make certain that the ignition key, in the vehicle with the dead battery, is in the OFF position. Connecting cables to vehicles with on-board computers will result in computer destruction if the key is not in the OFF position.*

Jump Starting Procedure

1. Determine voltages of the two batteries; they must be the same.
2. Bring the starting vehicle close (they must not touch) so that the batteries can be reached easily.
3. Turn off all accessories and both engines. Put both cars in Neutral or Park and set the handbrake.
4. Cover the cell caps with a rag—do not cover terminals.
5. If the terminals on the run-down battery are heavily corroded, clean them.
6. Identify the positive and negative posts on both batteries and connect the cables in the order shown.
7. Start the engine of the starting vehicle and run it at fast idle. Try to start the car with the dead battery. Crank it for no more than 10 seconds at a time and let it cool off for 20 seconds in between tries.
8. If it doesn't start in 3 tries, there is something else wrong.
9. Disconnect the cables in the reverse order.
10. Replace the cell covers and dispose of the rags.

Side terminal batteries occasionally pose a problem when connecting jumper cables. There frequently isn't enough room to clamp the cables without touching sheet metal .Side terminal adaptors are available to alleviate this problem and should be removed after use.

Make sure vehicles do not touch

This hook–up for negative ground cars only

Schedule II ②

Item No.	To Be Serviced	When to Perform Miles or Months, Whichever Occurs First Miles (000)	The services shown in this schedule up to 60,000 miles are to be performed after 60,000 miles at the same intervals							
			7.5	15	22.5	30	37.5	45	52.5	60
1	Engine Oil Change	Every 7,500 Miles or 12 Months	•	•	•	•	•	•	•	•
	Oil Filter Change	At First and Every Other Oil Change or 12 Months	•		•		•		•	
2	Chassis Lubrication	Every oil change	•	•	•	•	•	•	•	•
3	Carburetor Choke and Hoses Inspection	At 6 Months or 7,500 Miles and at 60,000 Miles	•							•
4	Carburetor or T.B.I. Mounting Bolt Torque Check	At 6 Months or 7,500 Miles and at 60,000 Miles	•							•
5	Engine Idle Speed Adjustment	At 6 Months or 7,500 Miles and at 60,000 Miles	•							•
6	Engine Accessory Drive Belts Inspection	Every 24 Months or 30,000 Miles					•			•
7	Cooling System Service	Every 24 Months or 30,000 Miles					•			•
8	Front Wheel Bearing Repack	Every 30,000 Miles					•			•
9	Transmission Service	30,000 miles					•			•
10	Vacuum Advance System Inspection	Check at 6 Months or 7,500 Miles, then at 30,000 Miles, and then at 15,000 Mile intervals.	•				•		•	•
11	Spark Plugs and Wire Service	Every 30,000 Miles					•			•
12	PCV System Inspection	Every 30,000 Miles					•			•
13	ERG System Check	Every 30,000 Miles					•			•
14	Air Cleaner and PCV Filter Replacement	Every 30,000 Miles					•			•
15	Engine Timing Check	Every 30,000 Miles					•			•
16	Fuel Tank, Cap and Lines Inspection	Every 24 Months 30,000 Miles					•			•
17	Early Fuel Evaporation System Inspection	At 7,500 Miles and at 30,000 Miles than at 30,000 Mile intervals.	•				•			•
18	Evaporative Control System Inspection	Every 30,000 Miles					•			•
19	Fuel Filter Replacement	Every 30,000 Miles					•			•
20	Valve Lash Adjustment	Every 15,000 Miles		•				•		•
21	Thermostatically Controlled Air Cleaner Inspection	Every 30,000 Miles					•			•

① Severe service
② Normal service

Maintenance Intervals Schedule I ①

Item No.	To Be Serviced	When to Perform Miles of Months, Whichever Occurs First Miles (000)	The services shown in this schedule up to 48,000 miles are to be performed after 48,000 miles at the same intervals														
			3	6	9	12	15	18	21	24	27	30	33	36	39	42	45	48
1	Every Oil and Oil filter Change	Every 3,000 Miles or 3 Months	•	•	•	•	•	•	•	•	•	•	•	•	•	•	•	•
2	Chassis Lubrication	Every oil change	•	•	•	•	•	•	•	•	•	•	•	•	•	•	•	•
3	Carburetor Choke and Hose Inspection	At 6,000 Miles, then at 30,000 Miles		•								•				•		
4	Carburetor or T.B.I. Mounting Bolt Torque Check			•								•						
5	Engine Idle Speed Adjustment			•								•						
6	Engine Accessory Drive Belts Inspection	Every 12 Months or 15,000 Miles					•					•				•		
7	Cooling System Service	Every 24 Months or 30,000 Miles										•						
8	Front Wheel Bearing Repack	Every 15,000 Miles					•					•				•		
9	Transmission Service	15,000 Miles					•					•						
10	Vacuum Advance System Inspection	Check at 6,000 Miles at 30,000 Miles, and at 45,000 Miles		•								•					•	
11	Spark Plugs and Wire Service	Every 30,000 Miles										•						
12	PCV System Inspection	Every 30,000 Miles										•						
13	EGR System Check	Every 30,000 Miles										•						
14	Air Cleaner and PCV Filter Replacement	Every 30,000 Miles										•						
15	Engine Timing Check	Every 30,000 Miles										•						
16	Fuel Tank, Cap and Lines Inspection	Every 12 Months or 15,000 Miles					•					•				•		
17	Early Fuel Evaporation System Inspection	At 6,000 Miles then at 30,000 Miles					•											
18	Evaporative Control System Inspection	At 30,000 Miles										•						
19	Fuel Filter Replacement	Every 15,000 Miles					•					•				•		
20	Valve Lash Adjustment	Every 15,000 Miles					•					•				•		
21	Thermostatically Controlled Air Cleaner Inspection	Every 30,000 Miles										•						

JACKING AND HOISTING

The jack supplied with the truck is meant for changing tires. It was not meant to support the truck while you crawl under it and work. Whenever it is necessary to get under a truck to perform service operations, always be sure that it is adequately supported, by jackstands at the proper points. Always block the wheels when changing tires.

If your truck is equipped with a Positraction rear axle, do not run the engine for any reason with one rear wheel off the ground. Power will be transmitted through the rear wheel remaining on the ground, possibly causing the truck to drive itself off the jack.

Some of the service operations in this book require that one or both ends of the truck be raised and supported safely. The best arrangement for this, of course, is a grease pit or a vehicle lift, but these items are seldom found in the home garage. Hydraulic jacks and jackstands are next best thing to a vehicle lift. Spend a little extra time to make sure that your truck is lifted and supported safely. Remember! the truck you are laying under weighs $1/2$ ton.

CAUTION: *Concrete blocks are not recommended for supporting a vehicle; they may crumble if the load is not evenly distributed. Boxes and milk crates of any description must not be used. Shake the truck a few times to make sure the jackstands are securely supporting the weight before crawling under.*

CAPACITIES

Year	Engine No. Cyl. cc. (Cu. In.) Displacement	Engine Crankcase (qts.)	Transmission Pts. To Refill After Draining			Transfer Case (pts.)	Rear Drive Axle (pts.)	Front Drive Axle (pts.)	Gasoline Tank (gals.)	Cooling System (qts.)	
			Manual								
			4-Speed	5-Speed	Automatic					With Heater	With A/C
1982–85	4-1.9 (118.9)	4.0	3.0	3.0	7.0② ③	5.2	3.5	2.6	13.0①	9.4	9.5
	6-2.8 (173)	4.0	3.0	3.0	7.0② ③	5.2	3.5	2.6	13.0①	12.0	12.0
1983–84	4-2.0 (121)	4.0	3.0	3.0	7.0② ③	5.2	3.5	2.6	13.0①	9.6	9.6
1983–85	4-2.2 (136.6)	5.0	3.0	3.0	7.0② ③	5.2	3.5	2.6	13.0①	10.0	10.0
1985–91	4-2.5 (151)	3.0	3.0	3.0	7.0② ③	5.2	3.5	2.6	13.0①	10.5	10.5
1986–91	6-2.8 (173)	4.0	3.0	3.0	7.0② ③	5.2	3.5	2.6	13.0①	11.6	11.6
1988–91	6-4.3 (262)	4.0	3.0	3.0	7.0② ③	5.2	3.5	2.6	13.0①	12.1	12.1

① Optional: 20.0 gal.
② Figure shown is for pan removal only. Total overhaul is 19.0 pts.
③ If equipped with a 700-R4: Pan removal 10 pts. Overhaul 23 pts.

Engine Performance and Tune-Up

2

TUNE-UP PROCEDURES

In order to extract the full measure of performance and economy from your engine it is essential that it is properly tuned at regular intervals. A regular tune-up will keep your truck's engine running smoothly and will prevent the annoying breakdowns and poor performance associated with an untuned engine.

A complete tune-up should be performed every 30,000 miles. This interval should be halved if the vehicle is operated under severe conditions such as trailer towing, prolonged idling, start-and-stop driving, or if starting or running problems are noticed. It is assumed that the routine maintenance described in Chapter 1 has been kept up, as this will have a de-

cided effect on the results of a tune-up. All of the applicable steps of a tune-up should be followed in order, as the result is a cumulative one.

NOTE: *Diesel engines do not require tune-ups per se, as they do not have an ignition system.*

If the specifications on the underhood tune-up sticker in the engine compartment disagree with the Tune-Up Specifications chart in this Chapter, the figures on the sticker must be used. The sticker often reflects changes made during the production run.

Spark Plugs

Normally, a set of spark plugs requires replacement about every 20,000–30,000 miles, on

GASOLINE ENGINE TUNE-UP SPECIFICATIONS

Year	V.I.N. Code	Eng. No. Cyl. Disp. Liters (Cu. in.)	Eng. Mfg.	hp	Spark Plugs Orig. Type	Gap (in.)	Ignition Timing (deg.) Man. Trans.	Auto. Trans.	Intake Valve Opens (deg.)	Fuel Pump Pressure (psi)	Idle Speed (rpm) Man. Trans.	Auto. Trans.
1982–85	A	4-1.9 (118.9)	Isuzu	84	R42LXS	0.040	6B	6B	21B	3.0	800	900
	B	6-2.8 (173)	Chev.	110	R42TS	0.040	6B	10B	7B	7.0	1000	750
1983–84	Y	4-2.0 (121)	Chev.	83	R42CTS	0.035	12B	12B	30B	5.0	750	700
1985–91	E	4-2.5 (151)	Pontiac	98	R43CTS6	①	②	②	—	9–13	②	②
1986–91	R	6-2.8 (173)	Chev.	125	R43CTS	①	②	②	—	9–13	②	②
1988–91	Z	6-4.3 (262)	Chev.	125	R45TS	①	②	②	—	9–13	②	②

① Refer to the information on the underhood sticker.
② This function is controlled by the emissions computer; no adjustment is necessary.

DIESEL ENGINE TUNE-UP SPECIFICATIONS

Year	VIN	Eng. No. Cyl. Displ. cc (Cu. In.)	Injection Timing (deg.)	Intake Valve Opens (deg.)	Low Idle (rpm)	Compression Pressure (psi)	Valve Clearance (In.)		Firing Order
							Intake	Exhaust	
1983–85	S	4-2238 (136.6)	15B	16B	750	441①	0.016C	0.016C	1-3-4-2

NOTE: The underhood specifications sticker often reflects tune-up specification changes made in production. Sticker figures must be used if they disagree with those in this chart.
① @ 200 rpm

vehicles equipped with an High Energy Ignition (HEI) system. Any vehicle which is subjected to severe conditions will need more frequent plug replacement.

Under normal operation, the plug gap increases about 0.001 in. (0.0254mm) for every 1,000–2,000 miles. As the gap increases, the plug's voltage requirement also increases. It requires a greater voltage to jump the wider gap and about 2–3 times as much voltage to fire a plug at high speeds than at idle.

When you are removing the spark plugs, work on one at a time. Don't start by removing the plug wires all at once, for unless you number them, they may become mixed up. Take a minute before you begin and number the wires with tape. The best location for numbering the wires is near the distributor cap.

REMOVAL

When removing the spark plugs, work on one at a time. Don't start by removing the plug wires all at once because unless you number them, they're going to get mixed up. On some models, it will be more convenient for you to remove all of the wires before you start to work on the plugs. If this is necessary, take a minute

before you begin and number the wires with tape before you take them off. The time you spend here will pay off later on.

1. Twist the spark plug boot ½ turn and remove the boot from the plug. You may also use a plug wire removal tool designed especially for this purpose. DO NOT pull on the wire itself. When the wire has been removed, take a wire brush and clean the area around the plug. Make sure that all the grime is removed so that none will enter the cylinder after the plug has been removed.

2. Remove the plug using the proper size socket, extensions and universals as necessary.

3. If removing the plug is difficult, drip some penetrating oil (Liquid Wrench®, WD-40®) on the plug threads, allow it to work, then remove the plug. Also, be sure that the socket is straight on the plug—especially on those hard to reach plugs.

INSPECTION

Check the plugs for deposits and wear. If they are not going to be replaced, clean the plugs thoroughly. Remember that any kind of deposit will decrease the efficiency of the plug. Plugs can be cleaned on a spark plug cleaning machine or with a stiff brush.

After the plugs are cleaned, the electrodes must be filed flat. Use an ignition points file, not an emery board or the like, which will leave deposits. The electrodes must be filed perfectly

PORCELAIN INSULATOR

INSULATOR CRACKS OFTEN OCCUR HERE

SHELL

ADJUST FOR PROPER GAP

SIDE ELECTRODE (BEND TO ADJUST GAP)

CENTER ELECTRODE; FILE FLAT WHEN ADJUSTING GAP DO NOT BEND!

Cross section of a spark plug

THE SHORTER THE PATH, THE FASTER THE HEAT IS DISSIPATED AND THE COOLER THE PLUG

THE LONGER THE PATH, THE SLOWER THE HEAT IS DISSIPATED AND THE HOTTER THE PLUG

HEAVY LOADS, HIGH SPEEDS

SHORT Insulator Tip
Fast Heat Transfer
LOWER Heat Range
COLD PLUG

SHORT TRIP STOP-AND-GO

LONG Insulator Tip
Slow Heat Transfer
HIGHER Heat Range
HOT PLUG

Spark plug heat range

Always use a wire gauge to check the electrode gap; a flat feeler gauge may not give the proper reading.

Adjust the electrode gap by bending the electrode

Filing an electrode square with an ignition points file

flat with sharp edges; rounded edges reduce the spark plug voltage by as much as 50%.

Check the spark plug gap before installation. The ground electrode (the L-shaped wire connected to the body of the plug) must be parallel to the center electrode and the specified size wire gauge (see Tune-Up Specifications) should pass through the gap with a slight drag. Always check the gap on the new plugs, they are not always set correctly at the factory. DO NOT use a flat feeler gauge when measuring the gap, because the reading will be inaccurate.

Wire gapping tools usually have a bending tool attached. Use that to adjust the side electrode until the proper distance is obtained. Absolutely, never bend the center electrode. Also, be careful not to bend the side electrode too far or too often; it may weaken and break off within the engine, requiring removal of the cylinder head to retrieve it.

Heat range is a term used to describe the cooling characteristics of spark plugs. Plugs with longer nosed insulators take a longer time to dissipate heat than plugs with shorter nosed insulators. These are termed "hot" or "cold" plugs, respectively. It is generally advisable to use the factory recommended plugs. However,

in conditions of extremely hard use (cross-country driving in summer) going to the next cooler heat range may be advisable. If most driving is done in the city or over short distances, go to the next hotter heat range plug to eliminate fouling. If in doubt concerning the substitution of spark plugs, consult your Chevrolet or GMC dealer.

INSTALLATION

1. Lubricate the threads of the spark plugs with a drop of oil. Install the plugs and tighten them hand tight. Take care not to cross thread them.

2. Tighten the spark plugs with the socket. DO NOT apply the same amount of force you would use for a bolt; just snug them in. If a torque wrench is available, tighten to 11–15 ft. lbs.

3. Install the ignition wires on their respective plugs. Make sure the wires are firmly connected—you will be able to feel them click into place.

Spark Plug Wires

Every 15,000 miles, visually inspect the spark plug cables for burns, cuts or breaks in the insulation. Check the spark plug boots and the nipples on the distributor cap and coil. Replace any damaged wiring.

Every 30,000 miles or so, the resistance of the wires should be checked with an ohmmeter. Wires with excessive resistance will cause misfiring and may make the engine difficult to start in damp weather. Generally, the useful life of the cables is 30,000–45,000 miles.

To check spark plug wire resistance, remove the distributor cap, leaving the wires in place. Connect one lead of an ohmmeter to an electrode within the cap; connect the other lead to the corresponding spark plug terminal (remove it from the spark plug for this test). Replace any wire which shows a resistance over 30,000Ω. Generally speaking, resistance should not be over 25,000Ω.

HEI Plug Wire Resistance Chart

Wire Length	Minimum	Maximum
0–15 inches	3000 ohms	10,000 ohms
15–25 inches	4000 ohms	15,000 ohms
25–35 inches	6000 ohms	20,000 ohms
Over 35 inches	6000 ohms	25,000 ohms

It should be remembered that resistance is also a function of length; the longer the wire the greater the resistance. Thus, if the wires on your truck are longer than the factory originals, resistance will be higher, quite possibly outside these limits.

When installing a new set of spark plug wires, replace the wires one at a time so there will be no confusion. Start by replacing the longest cable first. Install the boot firmly over the spark plug. Route the wire exactly the same as the original. Insert the distributor end of the wire firmly into the distributor cap tower, then seat the boot over the tower. Repeat the process for each wire.

Firing order — 1.9L engine

FIRING ORDERS

NOTE: *To avoid confusion, replace spark plug wires one at a time.*

ELECTRONIC IGNITION

General Information

The High Energy Ignition (HEI) distributor is used on all gasoline engines. The ignition coil is either mounted to the top of the distributor cap or is externally mounted on the engine, using a secondary circuit high tension wire to connect the coil to the distributor cap. Interconnecting primary wiring is routed through the engine harness.

The HEI distributor is equipped to aid in spark timing changes, necessary for emissions, economy and performance. This system is called the Electronic Spark Timing Control (EST). HEI(EST) distributors use a magnetic pick-up assembly, located inside the distributor containing a permanent magnet, a pole piece

Firing order — 2.5L engine

Firing order — 2.0L engine

Firing order — 2.8L engine

Firing order — 4.3L engine

158. Distributor
159. Coil

Distributor and coil locations — 4.3L engine

with internal teeth and a pick-up coil. When the teeth of the rotating timer core and pole piece align, an induced voltage in the pick-up coil signals the electronic module to open the coil primary circuit. As the primary current decreases, a high voltage is induced in the secondary windings of the ignition coil, directing a spark through the rotor and high voltage leads to fire the spark plugs. The dwell period is automatically controlled by the electronic module and is increased with increasing engine rpm. The HEI system features a longer spark duration which is instrumental in firing lean and EGR (Exhaust Gas Recirculation) diluted fuel/air mixtures. The condenser (capacitor) located within the HEI distributor is provided for noise

(static) suppression purposes only and is not a regularly replaced ignition system component.

All spark timing changes in the HEI(EST) distributors are performed electronically by the Electronic Control Module (ECM), which monitors information from the various engine sensors, computes the desired spark timing and signals the distributor to change the timing accordingly. Vacuum advance and centrifugal advance is used only on distributors without EST.

The distributor on the 1.9L engine uses vacuum and centrifugal advance and does not use EST.

The distributor on the 2.5L engine contains a Hall Effect Switch. It is mounted above the pick-up coil in the distributor and takes the

Distributor and coil locations — 2.8L engines

158. Distributor
159. Coil
167. Electronic spark timing connector
168. To coil

Distributor and coil locations — 2.5L engines

Distributor and coil locations — 1.9L and 2.0L engines

place of the reference (R) terminal on the distributor module. The Hall Effect Switch provides a voltage signal to the ECM to tell it which cylinder will fire next.

The 2.8L and 4.3L engines are equipped with Electronic Spark Control (ESC). A knock sensor is mounted in the engine block. It is connected to the ESC module which is mounted on the cowl in the engine compartment. In response to engine knock, the sensor sends a signal to the ESC module. The module will then signal the ECM which will retard the spark timing in the distributor.

Electronic Spark Timing (EST) System

The High Energy Ignition (HEI) system controls fuel combustion by providing the spark to ignite the compressed air/fuel mixture in the combustion chamber at the correct time. To provide improved engine performance, fuel economy and control of the exhaust emissions, the ECM controls distributor spark advance (timing) using the Electronic Spark Timing (EST) system.

OPERATION

The HEI(EST) distributor uses a modified module. The module has seven terminals instead of the four used without EST. Two different terminal arrangements are used, depending upon engine application.

To properly control ignition/combustion timing, the ECM needs to know the following information:

- Crankshaft position
- Engine speed (rpm)
- Engine load (manifold pressure or vacuum)
- Atmospheric (barometric) pressure
- Engine temperature
- Transmission gear position (certain models)

The ECM uses information from the MAP and coolant sensors in addition to rpm to calculate spark advance as follows:

- Low MAP output voltage would require MORE spark advance.
- Cold engine would require MORE spark advance.
- High MAP output voltage would require LESS spark advance.
- Hot engine would require LESS spark advance.

Incorrect operation of the EST system can cause the following:

- Detonation—low MAP output or high resistance in the coolant sensor circuit.
- Poor performance—high MAP output or

low resistance in the coolant sensor circuit.

The EST system consists of the distributor module, ECM and its connecting wires. The distributor has 4 wires from the HEI module connected to a 4 terminal connector, which mates with a 4 wire connector from the ECM.

All Engines Except 2.5L

The distributor 4-terminal connector is labeled A, B, C, D. Circuit functions for these terminals (except the 2.5L Hall Effect Switch model) are as follows:

1. Reference ground—Terminal A—This wire is grounded in the distributor and makes sure the ground circuit has no voltage drop, which could affect performance. If this circuit is open, it could cause poor performance.

2. Bypass—Terminal B—At approximately 400 rpm, the ECM applies 5 volts to this circuit to switch the spark timing control from the HEI module to the ECM. An open or grounded bypass circuit will set a Code 42 and the engine will run at base timing, plus a small amount of advance built into the HEI module.

3. Distributor reference—Terminal C—This provides the ECM with rpm and crankshaft position information.

4. EST—Terminal D—This triggers the HEI module. The ECM does not know what the actual timing is, but it does know when it gets its reference signal. It then advances or retards the spark timing from that point. Therefore, if the base timing is set incorrectly, the entire spark curve will be incorrect.

2.5L Engine With Hall Effect Switch

Circuit functions for the 2.5L Hall Effect Switch distributor are as follows:

1. EST—Terminal A—This triggers the HEI module. The ECM does not know what the actual timing is, but it does know when it gets its reference signal. It then advances or retards the spark timing from that point. Therefore, if the base timing is set incorrectly, the entire spark curve will be incorrect.

2. Distributor reference—Terminal B—This provides the ECM with rpm and crankshaft position information.

3. Bypass—Terminal C—At approximately 400 rpm, the ECM applies 5 volts to this circuit to switch the spark timing control from the HEI module to the ECM. An open or grounded bypass circuit will set a Code 42 and the engine will run at base timing, plus a small amount of advance built into the HEI module.

4. Reference ground—Terminal D—This wire is grounded in the distributor and makes sure the ground circuit has no voltage drop, which could affect performance. If this circuit is open, it could cause poor performance.

Electronic Spark Control (ESC) System

The Electronic Spark Control (ESC) system is designed to retard spark timing up to 20° to reduce detonation in the engine. This allows the engine to use maximum spark advance to improve driveability and fuel economy. Varying octane levels in gasoline can cause detonation (spark knock) in any engine.

OPERATION

The ESC system has three components:
- ESC Module
- ESC Knock Sensor
- ECM

The knock sensor detects abnormal vibration in the engine. The sensor is mounted in the engine block near the cylinders. The ESC module receives the knock sensor information and sends a signal to the ECM. The ECM then adjusts the Electronic Spark Timing (EST) to reduce spark knocking.

The ESC module sends a voltage signal to the ECM when no spark knocking is detected by the ESC knock sensor, and the ECM provides normal spark advance. When the knock sensor detects spark knock, the module turns off the circuit to the ECM. The ECM then retards EST to reduce spark knock.

IGNITION TIMING ADJUSTMENT

The following procedure requires the use of a distributor wrench and a timing light. When using a timing light, be sure to consult the manufacturer's recommendations for installation and usage.

Gasoline Engine

- On 2.5L engines, ground the "A" and "B" terminals on the ALDL connector under the dash before adjusting the timing.
- On all other engines using the EST distributor, disconnect the timing connector wire, located below the heater case in the engine compartment or coming out of the wiring harness near the distributor, before adjusting the timing.

1. Timing specifications are listed on the Vehicle Emissions Control Information label, located on the radiator support. Use the timing specifications specific to your vehicle.

2. Using a timing light, connect it to the engine by performing the following procedures:

a. If using a non-inductive type, connect an adapter between the No. 1 spark plug and the spark plug wire; DO NOT puncture the

Timing marks

spark plug wire, for this will cause a voltage leak.

b. If using an inductive type, clamp it around the No. 1 spark plug wire.

c. If using a magnetic type, place the probe in the connector located near the damper pulley; this type must be used with special electronic timing equipment.

3. If equipped with Electric Spark Timing (EST), disconnect the timing connector wire; this allows the engine to operate in the by-pass timing mode.

4. Start the engine aim the timing light at the timing mark on the damper pulley; a line on the damper pulley will align the timing mark. If necessary (to adjust the timing), loosen the distributor hold down clamp and slowly turn the distributor slightly to align the marks. When the alignment is correct, tighten the hold down bolt.

5. Turn the engine OFF, remove the timing light and reconnect the timing connector wire (if disconnected).

DIESEL ENGINE INJECTION TIMING

NOTE: *This procedure requires the use of a Static Timing Gauge tool No. J-29763 or equivalent; DO NOT attempt any injection timing adjustments without this tool.*

1. Check that notched line on the injection pump flange is in alignment with notched line on the injection pump front bracket.

2. Bring the piston in No. 1 cylinder to top dear center on compression stroke by turning the crankshaft as necessary.

3. With the timing pulley housing cover re-

Injection pump and flange alignment

Removing the distributor screw — diesel engine

Number 1 piston at TDC

Aligning the timing marks — diesel engine

moved, check that the timing belt is properly tensioned and that timing marks are aligned.

4. Disconnect the injection pipe(s) from the injection pump, then remove the distributor head screw and washer. Using the Static Timing Gauge tool No. J-29763 or equivalent, install it into the distributor head screw hole and set the lift to approximately 0.04 in. (1mm) from the plunger.

5. Use a wrench to hold the delivery holder when loosening the sleeve nuts on the injection pump side.

6. Bring the piston in No. 1 cylinder to a point 45–60° before top dead center (TDC) by turning the crankshaft, then calibrate the dial indicator to zero.

7. Turn the crankshaft pulley slightly in both directions and check that gauge indication is stable.

8. Turn the crankshaft in the normal direction of rotation, then record the reading of the dial indicator when the timing mark (15°) on the crankshaft pulley is in alignment with the pointer; the reading should be 0.020 in. (0.5mm).

9. If the reading of dial indicator deviates from the specified range, hold the crankshaft in position 15° BTDC and loosen two nuts on injection pump flange.

10. Move the injection pump to a point where dial indicator gives reading of 0.020 in. (0.5mm), then tighten pump flange nuts.

Static timing gauge installed

No. 1 piston 45–60° BTDC

No. 1 piston 15° BTDC

VALVE LASH ADJUSTMENT

Valve adjustment determines how far the valves· enter the cylinder and how long they stay open and/or closed.

NOTE: *While all valve adjustments must be made as accurately as possible, it is better to have the valve adjustment slightly loose than slightly tight, as a burned valve may result from overly tight adjustments.*

1.9L and 2.2L Diesel

NOTE: *The valves are adjusted with the engine Cold.*

1. Remove the rocker arm cover.
2. Make sure that the rocker arm shaft nuts/bolts are torqued to 16 ft. lbs.
3. Using a wrench on the damper pulley bolt or a remote starter button, turn the crankshaft until the No. 1 piston is at TDC of the compression stroke.

NOTE: *You can tell when the piston is coming up on the compression stroke by removing the spark plug and placing your thumb over the hole, you will feel the air being forced out of the spark plug hole. Stop turning the crankshaft when the TDC timing mark on the crankshaft pulley is directly aligned with the timing mark pointer.*

4. With the No. 1 piston at TDC of the compression stroke, perform the following valve setting procedures:

    a. If working on the 1.9L engine, use a 0.006 in. (0.152mm) feeler gauge, to set intake valves of cylinders No. 1 & 2. Using a 0.010 in. (0.254mm) feeler gauge, set the exhaust valves of cylinders No. 1 & 3.
    b. If working on the 2.2L engine, use a 0.016 in. (0.40mm) feeler gauge, to set the intake valves of cylinders No. 1, 2 & 3, then set the exhaust valve of cylinder No. 1.

5. Rotate the engine one complete revolution, so that cylinder No. 4 is on the TDC of its compression stroke and the timing marks are aligned.
6. With cylinder No. 4 on the TDC of the compression stroke, perform the following valve setting procedures:

    a. If working on the 1.9L engine, use a 0.006 in. (0.152mm) feeler gauge, to set intake valves of cylinders No. 3 & 4. Using a 0.010 in. (0.254mm) feeler gauge, set the exhaust valves of cylinders No. 2 & 4.
    b. If working on the 2.2L engine, use a 0.016 in. (0.40mm) feeler gauge, to set the intake valve of cylinder No. 4, then the exhaust valves of cylinders No. 2, 3 & 4.

NOTE: *When adjusting the valve clearance, loosen the locknut with an open-end wrench, then turn the adjuster screw with a screwdriver and retighten the locknut. The proper thickness feeler gauge should pass between the camshaft and the rocker with a slight drag when the clearance is correct.*

Valve adjustment

Valve adjustment — 2.0L and 2.8L engine

2.0L and 2.8L

1. Remove the air cleaner and the rocker arm cover(s).

2. Rotate the crankshaft until the mark on the crankshaft pulley aligns with the **0** mark on the timing plate. Make sure that the No. 1 cylinder is positioned on the compression stroke.

NOTE: *You can tell when the piston is coming up on the compression stroke by removing the spark plug and placing your thumb over the hole, you will feel the air being forced out of the spark plug hole. Stop turning the crankshaft when the TDC timing mark on the crankshaft pulley is directly aligned with the timing mark pointer.*

3. With the engine in the No. 1 firing position, perform the following adjustments:

   a. If working on the 2.0L engine, adjust the intake valves of cylinders No. 1 & 2 and the exhaust valves of cylinders No. 1 & 3.

   b. If working on the 2.8L engine, adjust the intake valves of cylinders No. 1, 5 & 6 and the exhaust valves of cylinders No. 1, 2 & 3.

4. To adjust the valves, back-out the adjusting nut until lash can be felt at the push rod, then turn the nut until all of the lash is removed.

NOTE: *To determine is all of the lash is removed,, turn the push rod with your fingers until the movement is removed.*

5. When all of the lash has been removed, turn the adjusting an additional $1^1/2$ turns; this will center the lifter plunger.

6. Rotate the crankshaft one complete revolution and realign the timing marks; the engine is now positioned on the No. 4 firing position.

7. With the engine in the No. 4 firing position, perform the following procedures:

   a. If working on the 2.0L engine, adjust the intake valves of cylinders No. 3 & 4 and the exhaust valves of cylinders No. 2 & 4.

   b. If working on the 2.8L engine, adjust the intake valves of cylinders No. 2, 3 & 4

and the exhaust valves of cylinders No. 4, 5 & 6.

8. To compete the installation, reverse the removal procedures.

2.5L Engine

Valve lash is NOT adjustable on the 2.5L engine. Check that the rocker arm bolts are tightened to 22 ft. lbs. When valve lash falls out of specification (valve tap is heard), replace the rocker arm, pushrod and hydraulic lifter on the offending cylinder.

4.3L Engine

1. To prepare the engine for valve adjustment, rotate the crankshaft until the mark on the damper pulley aligns with the 0° mark on the timing plate and the No. 1 cylinder is on the compression stroke.

NOTE: *You can tell when the piston is coming up on the compression stroke by removing the spark plug and placing your thumb over the hole, you will feel the air being forced out of the spark plug hole. Stop turning the crankshaft when the TDC timing mark on the crankshaft pulley is directly aligned with the timing mark pointer.*

2. With the engine on the compression stroke, adjust the exhaust valves of cylinders No. 1, 5 & 6 and the intake valves of cylinders No. 1, 2 & 3 by performing the following procedures:

   a. Back out the adjusting nut until lash can be felt at the pushrod.

   b. While rotating the pushrod, turn the adjusting nut inward until all of the lash is removed.

   c. When the play has disappeared, turn the adjusting nut inward 1 additional turn.

3. Rotate the crankshaft one complete revolution and align the mark on the damper pulley with the 0° mark on the timing plate. With the engine on the compression stroke, adjust the exhaust valves of cylinders No. 2, 3 & 4 and the intake valves of cylinders No. 4, 5 & 6, by performing the following procedures:

   a. Back out the adjusting nut until lash can be felt at the pushrod.

   b. While rotating the pushrod, turn the adjusting nut inward until all of the lash is removed.

   c. When the play has disappeared, turn the adjusting nut inward $1^1/2$ additional turns.

4. To complete the installation, reverse the removal procedures. Start the engine, the check for oil leaks and engine operation.

VALVE ARRANGEMENT

1.9L
E-I-I-E-E-I-I-E (front-to-rear)
2.0L
E-I-I-E-E-I-I-E (front-to-rear)
2.2L
E-I-I-E-E-I-I-E (front-to-rear)
2.5L
I-E-I-E-E-I-E-I (front-to-rear)
2.8L
E-I-I-E-I-E (right bank—front-to-rear)
E-I-E-I-I-E (left bank—front-to-rear)
4.3L
E-I-I-E-I-E (right bank—front-to-rear)
E-I-E-I-I-E (left bank—front-to-rear)

IDLE SPEED AND MIXTURE ADJUSTMENTS

CARBURETED ENGINES

1.9L Engine

In order to adjust the idle mixture you must first remove the plug that covers the mixture screw.

1. Set the parking brake, block the drive wheels and place the transmission in Neutral.

2. Refer to the Carburetor, Removal and Installation procedures in Chapter 4, then remove the carburetor from the engine, place it on a work bench and turn it upside down.

3. Using a screwdriver and a hammer, carefully drive the idle mixture screw metal plug from the base of the carburetor.

4. Reinstall the carburetor onto the engine. Start the engine and adjust the idle speed.

5. Allow the engine to reach normal operat-ing temperatures, the choke must be Open and the A/C (if equipped) turned Off. Disconnect and plug the distributor vacuum line, the EGR vacuum line and the idle compensator vacuum lines.

6. Turn the mixture screw all the way in, then back it out $1^{1}/_{2}$ turns.

NOTE: *After adjustment, reconnect the vacuum lines.*

7. Adjust the throttle speed screw to 850 rpm (MT) or 950 rpm (AT).

8. Adjust the idle mixture screw to achieve the maximum speed.

9. Reset the throttle adjusting screw to 850 rpm (MT) or 950 rpm (AT).

10. Turn the idle mixture screw (clockwise) to until the engine speed is reduced to 800 rpm (MT) or 900 rpm (AT).

11. If equipped with A/C, perform the following procedures:

a. Turn the A/C to Max. Cold and the blower to High.

b. Open the throttle to $^{1}/_{3}$ and allow it to close; this allows the speed-up solenoid to reach full travel.

c. Adjust the speed-up controller adjusting screw to set the idle to 900 rpm.

2.0L and 2.8L Engines

NOTE: *The idle mixture adjustments are factory set and sealed; no adjustment attempt should be made, except by an authorized GM dealer.*

Adjusting the idle speed on the 2SE carburetor without air conditioning — 2.0L and 2.8L engines

Removing the mixture screw plug — 1.9L engine

Adjusting the idle speed — 1.9L engine

① PREPARE VEHICLE FOR ADJUSTMENTS - SEE EMISSION LABEL ON VEHICLE. NOTE: IGNITION TIMING SET PER LABEL

④ TURN SOLENOID SCREW TO ADJUST CURB IDLE SPEED TO SPECIFIED RPM (SOLENOID ENERGIZED)

② SOLENOID ENERGIZED - A/T IN DRIVE, M/T IN NEUTRAL

⑥ TURN IDLE SPEED SCREW TO SET BASIC IDLE SPEED TO SPECIFICATIONS. RECONNECT SOLENOID ELECTRICAL LEAD AFTER ADJUSTMENT

③ OPEN THROTTLE SLIGHTLY TO ALLOW SOLENOID PLUNGER TO FULLY EXTEND

⑤ DISCONNECT ELECTRICAL LEAD TO DE-ENERGIZE SOLENOID

Adjusting the idle speed on E2SE carburetors with air conditioning — 2.0L and 2.8L engines

WITHOUT A/C

1. Refer to the emission control label on the vehicle and prepare the engine for adjustments.

2. Remove the air cleaner, set the parking brake and block the drive wheels.

3. Connect a tachometer to the distributor connector.

4. Place the transmission in Drive (AT) or Neutral (MT); make sure that the solenoid is energized.

5. Open the throttle slightly to allow the solenoid plunger to extend. Adjust the curb idle speed to the specified rpm by turning the solenoid screw.

6. De-energize the solenoid by disconnecting the electrical lead.

7. Set the basic idle speed rpm by turning

① PREPARE VEHICLE FOR ADJUSTMENTS - SEE EMISSION LABEL ON VEHICLE. NOTE: IGNITION TIMING SET PER LABEL.

③ SOLENOID ENERGIZED - A/C COMPRESSOR LEAD DISCONNECTED AT A/C COMPRESSOR, A/C ON, A/T IN DRIVE, M/T IN NEUTRAL.

⑤ TURN SOLENOID SCREW TO ADJUST TO SPECIFIED RPM. (RECONNECT A/C COMPRESSOR LEAD AFTER ADJUSTMENT).

② TURN IDLE SPEED SCREW TO SET CURB IDLE SPEED TO SPECIFICATIONS - A/C OFF (SEE EMISSION LABEL)

④ OPEN THROTTLE SLIGHTLY TO ALLOW SOLENOID PLUNGER TO FULLY EXTEND.

ELECTRICAL CONNECTION

Adjusting the idle speed on E2SE carburetors without air conditioning — 2.0L and 2.8L engines the idle speed screw. After adjustment, reconnect the solenoid electrical lead.

8. Remove the tachometer and install the air cleaner.

WITH A/C

1. Refer to the emission label on the vehicle and prepare the engine for adjustments.

2. Remove the air cleaner, set the parking brake and block the drive wheels.

3. Connect a tachometer to the distributor connector.

4. Place the transmission in Drive (AT) or Neutral (MT); make sure that the solenoid is energized.

5. Turn the A/C Off and set the curb idle speed by turning the idle speed screw.

6. Disconnect the A/C lead from the A/C compressor; make sure the solenoid is energized. Open the throttle slightly to allow the solenoid plunger to extend.

7. Turn the solenoid screw to adjust to the specified rpm. After adjustment, reconnect the A/C compressor lead, remove the tachometer and install the air cleaner.

THROTTLE BODY ENGINES

2.5L EFI Engine

NOTE: *The following procedures require the use a tachometer, GM tool No. J-33047, BT-8207 or equivalent, GM Torx Bit No. 20, silicone sealant, a $\frac{5}{32}$ in. drill bit, a prick punch and a $\frac{1}{16}$ in. pin punch.*

The throttle stop screw, used in regulating the minimum idle speed, is adjusted at the factory and is not necessary to perform. This adjustment should be performed ONLY when the throttle body has been replaced.

NOTE: *The replacement of the complete throttle body assembly will have the minimum idle adjusted at the factory.*

Plug the idle passages of each throttle body as shown

IDLE STOP SCREW ASSEMBLY

IDLE STOP SCREW PLUG

Removing the idle stop screw plug

1. Remove the air cleaner and the gasket. Be sure to plug the THERMAC vacuum port (air cleaner vacuum line-to-throttle body) on the throttle body.

2. Remove the throttle valve cable from the throttle control bracket to provide access to the minimum air adjustment screw.

3. Using the manufacturer's instructions, connect a tachometer to the engine.

4. Remove the electrical connector from the Idle Air Control (IAC) valve, located on the throttle body.

5. To remove the throttle stop screw cover, perform the following procedures:

   a. Using a prick punch, mark the housing at the top over the center line of the throttle stop screw.

   b. Using a $\frac{5}{32}$ in. drill bit, drill (on an angle) a hole through the casting to the hardened cover.

   c. Using a $\frac{1}{16}$ in. pin punch, place it through the hole and drive out the cover to expose the throttle stop screw.

6. Place the transmission in Park (AT) or Neutral (MT), start the engine and allow the idle speed to stabilize.

7. Using the GM tool No. J-33047, BT-8207 or equivalent, install it into the idle air passage of the throttle body; be sure that the tool is fully seated in the opening and no air leaks exist.

8. Using the GM Torx Bit No. 20, turn the throttle stop screw until the engine speed is 475–525 rpm (AT in Park) or 750–800 rpm (MT in Neutral).

9. With the idle speed adjusted, stop the engine, remove the tool No. J-33047, BT-8207 or equivalent, from the throttle body.

10. Reconnect the Idle Air Control (IAC) electrical connector.

1. Screw
2. Throttle position sensor
3. Jumper wires
4. Electrical connector
5. Digital volt-ohm meter

Adjusting the throttle position sensor

11. Using silicone sealant or equivalent, cover the throttle stop screw.

12. Reinstall the gasket and the air cleaner assembly.

2.8L EFI Engine

1. Remove the idle stop screw plug by piercing it with an awl.

2. With the idle air control motor connected, ground the diagnostic connector.

3. Turn the ignition On and wait 30 seconds, DO NOT start the engine.

4. Disconnect the idle air control connector with the ignition On.

5. Remove the ground from the diagnostic connector and start the engine.

6. Adjust the idle stop screw to 700 rpm with the transmission in Neutral.

7. Turn the ignition Off and reconnect the idle air control motor connector.

8. Disconnect the electrical connector from the throttle position sensor (TPS), then install jumper wires between the TPS and the electrical connector.

9. Loosen the throttle position sensor screws.

10. With the ignition switch turned On, check the voltage between terminals **B** and **C**; they should be 0.420V and 0.450V. If necessary, rotate the TPS to obtain the correct voltage.

11. With the voltage correct, tighten the mounting screws.

12. Reconnect the electrical connector and the air cleaner.

NOTE: *After installing the electrical connector to the TPS, it is a good idea to recheck the TPS voltage.*

Fast Idle Adjustment

CARBURETOR ENGINES

2.0L and 2.8L Engines

NOTE: *Following the adjustment of the idle speed, the fast idle speed may be adjusted.*

1. Place the transmission in Park (AT) or Neutral (MT) and refer to the recommendation on the emission label.

2. Place the fast idle screw on the highest step of the fast idle cam.

3. Turn the fast idle screw to obtain the specified fast idle rpm.

① PREPARE VEHICLE FOR ADJUSTMENTS - SEE EMISSION LABLE ON VEHICLE. PLACE TRANSMISSION IN PARK/NEUTRAL .

② PLACE FAST IDLE SCREW ON HIGHEST STEP OF FAST IDLE CAM.

③ TURN FAST IDLE SCREW IN OR OUT TO OBTAIN SPECIFIED FAST IDLE R.P.M. - (SEE LABEL).

Fast idle adjustment procedure

Fast idle adjustment 1983 2.2L diesel engine

Idle speed adjustment points for the 1983 2.2L diesel engine

Diesel tachometer

Fast idle adjustment 1984–85 2.2L diesel engine

5. If the idle speed deviates from the specified range of 700–800 rpm, loosen the idle speed adjusting screw lock nut.

6. Turn the adjusting screw in or out until the idle speed is in the correct range. After tightening the lock nut, lock it in place.

DIESEL ENGINE FUEL SYSTEM

Slow Idle Speed Adjustment

1. Set parking brake and block drive wheels.

2. Place transmission in Neutral.

3. Start and warm up the engine. Engine coolant temperature above 176°F (80°C).

4. Connect a diesel tachometer according to the manufacturer's instructions.

Fast Idle Speed Adjustment

1. Start and warm up the engine. Engine coolant temperature above 176°F (80°).

2. Connect a diesel tachometer according to the manufacturer's instructions.

3. Disconnect the hoses from the vacuum switch valve, then connect a pipe (4mm dia.) in position between the hoses.

4. Loosen adjust nut and adjust engine idle speed by moving the nut. Fast idle should be 900–950 rpm.

5. Tighten the lock nut.

6. Remove engine tachometer.

ENGINE ELECTRICAL

Ignition Coil

The location of the ignition coil is as follows.

• 1.9L and 2.0L engines—the coil is attached to a bracket located on the inner fender at the right hand side of the engine compartment. These engines use a Non-EST distributor

• 2.5L engine—the coil is attached to the cylinder head at the right rear-side of the engine. This engine uses an EST distributor.

• 2.8L engine—the coil is attached to a valve cover bracket at the right rear-side of the engine. This engine uses an EST distributor.

• 4.3L engine—the coil is attached to a bracket attached to the intake manifold at the right rear of the engine. This engine uses an EST distributor.

TESTING

EST Distributor

NOTE: *Refer to the illustration "Testing the EST Ignition Coil" for this procedure.*

1. Disconnect the distributor lead and wiring from the coil.

2. Using the HIGH scale, connect an ohmmeter to the coil as shown in Step 1 of the illustration. The reading should be infinite. If not, replace the coil.

3. Using the LOW scale, connect the ohmmeter as shown in Step of the illustration.

4. The reading should be very low or zero. If not, replace the coil.

5. Using the HIGH scale, connect the ohmmeter as shown in Step 3 of the illustration.

6. The ohmmeter should **NOT** read infinite. If it does, replace the coil.

7. Reconnect the distributor lead and wiring to the coil.

Testing the EST ignition coil

Non-EST Distributor

NOTE: *Refer to the illustration "Testing the Non-EST Ignition Coil" for this procedure.*

1. Check the outer face of the ignition coil for cracking, rust or damage.

2. Check the resistance of the primary and secondary coils as shown in the illustration. If the resistance is not within specification, replace the coil.

• Primary coil resistance: 0.090–1.40 ohms

Ignition coil and distributor — 4.3L engine

Testing the Non-EST ignition coil

Ignition coil and distributor — 2.5L engine

Troubleshooting the Cooling System

Problem	Cause	Solution
High temperature gauge indication—overheating	• Coolant level low	• Replenish coolant
	• Fan belt loose	• Adjust fan belt tension
	• Radiator hose(s) collapsed	• Replace hose(s)
	• Radiator airflow blocked	• Remove restriction (bug screen, fog lamps, etc.)
	• Faulty radiator cap	• Replace radiator cap
	• Ignition timing incorrect	• Adjust ignition timing
	• Idle speed low	• Adjust idle speed
	• Air trapped in cooling system	• Purge air
	• Heavy traffic driving	• Operate at fast idle in neutral intermittently to cool engine
	• Incorrect cooling system component(s) installed	• Install proper component(s)
	• Faulty thermostat	• Replace thermostat
	• Water pump shaft broken or impeller loose	• Replace water pump
	• Radiator tubes clogged	• Flush radiator
	• Cooling system clogged	• Flush system
	• Casting flash in cooling passages	• Repair or replace as necessary. Flash may be visible by removing cooling system components or removing core plugs.
	• Brakes dragging	• Repair brakes
	• Excessive engine friction	• Repair engine
	• Antifreeze concentration over 68%	• Lower antifreeze concentration percentage
	• Missing air seals	• Replace air seals
	• Faulty gauge or sending unit	• Repair or replace faulty component
	• Loss of coolant flow caused by leakage or foaming	• Repair or replace leaking component, replace coolant
	• Viscous fan drive failed	• Replace unit
Low temperature indication—undercooling	• Thermostat stuck open	• Replace thermostat
	• Faulty gauge or sending unit	• Repair or replace faulty component
Coolant loss—boilover	• Overfilled cooling system	• Reduce coolant level to proper specification
	• Quick shutdown after hard (hot) run	• Allow engine to run at fast idle prior to shutdown
	• Air in system resulting in occasional "burping" of coolant	• Purge system
	• Insufficient antifreeze allowing coolant boiling point to be too low	• Add antifreeze to raise boiling point
	• Antifreeze deteriorated because of age or contamination	• Replace coolant
	• Leaks due to loose hose clamps, loose nuts, bolts, drain plugs, faulty hoses, or defective radiator	• Pressure test system to locate source of leak(s) then repair as necessary
	• Faulty head gasket	• Replace head gasket
	• Cracked head, manifold, or block	• Replace as necessary
	• Faulty radiator cap	• Replace cap
Coolant entry into crankcase or cylinder(s)	• Faulty head gasket	• Replace head gasket
	• Crack in head, manifold or block	• Replace as necessary
Coolant recovery system inoperative	• Coolant level low	• Replenish coolant to FULL mark
	• Leak in system	• Pressure test to isolate leak and repair as necessary
	• Pressure cap not tight or seal missing, or leaking	• Repair as necessary
	• Pressure cap defective	• Replace cap
	• Overflow tube clogged or leaking	• Repair as necessary
	• Recovery bottle vent restricted	• Remove restriction

Troubleshooting the Cooling System (cont.)

Problem	Cause	Solution
Noise	• Fan contacting shroud	• Reposition shroud and inspect engine mounts
	• Loose water pump impeller	• Replace pump
	• Glazed fan belt	• Apply silicone or replace belt
	• Loose fan belt	• Adjust fan belt tension
	• Rough surface on drive pulley	• Replace pulley
	• Water pump bearing worn	• Remove belt to isolate. Replace pump.
	• Belt alignment	• Check pulley alignment. Repair as necessary.
No coolant flow through heater core	• Restricted return inlet in water pump	• Remove restriction
	• Heater hose collapsed or restricted	• Remove restriction or replace hose
	• Restricted heater core	• Remove restriction or replace core
	• Restricted outlet in thermostat housing	• Remove flash or restriction
	• Intake manifold bypass hole in cylinder head restricted	• Remove restriction
	• Faulty heater control valve	• Replace valve
	• Intake manifold coolant passage restricted	• Remove restriction or replace intake manifold

NOTE: *Immediately after shutdown, the engine enters a condition known as heat soak. This is caused by the cooling system being inoperative while engine temperature is still high. If coolant temperature rises above boiling point, expansion and pressure may push some coolant out of the radiator overflow tube. If this does not occur frequently it is considered normal.*

• Secondary coil resistance: 7.3–11.1 kilo-ohms

• Insulation resistance: 10 megohms or more

3. When testing the insulation resistance, if the ohmmeter needle deflects even slightly, the ignition coil is poorly insulated and should be replaced.

REMOVAL AND INSTALLATION

1. Disconnect the negative battery terminal from the battery.

2. From the ignition coil, disconnect the primary electrical wiring connector and the coil-to-distributor high tension cable.

3. Remove the coil attaching bolts.

4. If necessary, replace the ignition coil.

Ignition coil and distributor — 1.9L and 2.0L engine

Troubleshooting the Serpentine Drive Belt

Problem	Cause	Solution
Tension sheeting fabric failure (woven fabric on outside circumference of belt has cracked or separated from body of belt)	• Grooved or backside idler pulley diameters are less than minimum recommended • Tension sheeting contacting (rubbing) stationary object • Excessive heat causing woven fabric to age • Tension sheeting splice has fractured	• Replace pulley(s) not conforming to specification • Correct rubbing condition • Replace belt • Replace belt
Noise (objectional squeal, squeak, or rumble is heard or felt while drive belt is in operation)	• Belt slippage • Bearing noise • Belt misalignment • Belt-to-pulley mismatch • Driven component inducing vibration • System resonant frequency inducing vibration	• Adjust belt • Locate and repair • Align belt/pulley(s) • Install correct belt • Locate defective driven component and repair • Vary belt tension within specifications. Replace belt.
Rib chunking (one or more ribs has separated from belt body)	• Foreign objects imbedded in pulley grooves • Installation damage • Drive loads in excess of design specifications • Insufficient internal belt adhesion	• Remove foreign objects from pulley grooves • Replace belt • Adjust belt tension • Replace belt
Rib or belt wear (belt ribs contact bottom of pulley grooves)	• Pulley(s) misaligned • Mismatch of belt and pulley groove widths • Abrasive environment • Rusted pulley(s) • Sharp or jagged pulley groove tips • Rubber deteriorated	• Align pulley(s) • Replace belt • Replace belt • Clean rust from pulley(s) • Replace pulley • Replace belt
Longitudinal belt cracking (cracks between two ribs)	• Belt has mistracked from pulley groove • Pulley groove tip has worn away rubber-to-tensile member	• Replace belt • Replace belt
Belt slips	• Belt slipping because of insufficient tension • Belt or pulley subjected to substance (belt dressing, oil, ethylene glycol) that has reduced friction • Driven component bearing failure • Belt glazed and hardened from heat and excessive slippage	• Adjust tension • Replace belt and clean pulleys • Replace faulty component bearing • Replace belt
"Groove jumping" (belt does not maintain correct position on pulley, or turns over and/or runs off pulleys)	• Insufficient belt tension • Pulley(s) not within design tolerance • Foreign object(s) in grooves • Excessive belt speed • Pulley misalignment • Belt-to-pulley profile mismatched • Belt cordline is distorted	• Adjust belt tension • Replace pulley(s) • Remove foreign objects from grooves • Avoid excessive engine acceleration • Align pulley(s) • Install correct belt • Replace belt
Belt broken (Note: identify and correct problem before replacement belt is installed)	• Excessive tension • Tensile members damaged during belt installation • Belt turnover • Severe pulley misalignment • Bracket, pulley, or bearing failure	• Replace belt and adjust tension to specification • Replace belt • Replace belt • Align pulley(s) • Replace defective component and belt

Troubleshooting the Serpentine Drive Belt (cont.)

Problem	Cause	Solution
Cord edge failure (tensile member exposed at edges of belt or separated from belt body)	• Excessive tension • Drive pulley misalignment • Belt contacting stationary object • Pulley irregularities • Improper pulley construction • Insufficient adhesion between tensile member and rubber matrix	• Adjust belt tension • Align pulley • Correct as necessary • Replace pulley • Replace pulley • Replace belt and adjust tension to specifications
Sporadic rib cracking (multiple cracks in belt ribs at random intervals)	• Ribbed pulley(s) diameter less than minimum specification • Backside bend flat pulley(s) diameter less than minimum • Excessive heat condition causing rubber to harden • Excessive belt thickness • Belt overcured • Excessive tension	• Replace pulley(s) • Replace pulley(s) • Correct heat condition as necessary • Replace belt • Replace belt • Adjust belt tension

158. Distributor
159. Coil

Ignition coil and distributor — 2.8L engine

Ignition Module

REMOVAL AND INSTALLATION

Non-EST Distributor

1. Remove the distributor from the engine and place it on a work bench.
2. Remove the distributor cap, the rotor, the packing ring and the cover.
3. Remove the electrical harness-to-distributor screw, then disconnect the electrical harness connectors from the ignition module.
4. Using two medium pry bars, pry the pole piece from the distributor shaft, then remove the roll pin.
5. Using a Phillips Head screwdriver, remove the ignition module-to-breaker plate screws and lift the module from the distributor; be sure to remove the spacers from the module.
6. If the module is suspected as being defective, take it to a module testing machine and have it tested.

Using two pry bars to remove the pole piece from the distributor shaft on the Non-EST distributor

7. To install, replace the ignition module, spacers and screws onto the breaker plate.

NOTE: *When replacing the module, ensure that the module-to-distributor surface is coated with silicone lubricant.*

8. Install the pole piece onto the distributor shaft, followed by the new roll pin.

NOTE: *If the breaker plate was loosened, use a 0.12–0.20 in. (3–5mm) feeler gauge to measure the air gap between the pole piece and the breaker plate stator.*

Exploded view of the ignition module and the breaker plate assembly

9. To complete the installation, reverse the removal procedures. Reinstall the distributor onto the engine.

EST Distributor

The ignition modules are located inside the distributor; they may be replaced without removing the distributor from the engine.

1. Disconnect the negative battery terminal.

2. Remove the distributor cap and the rotor.

3. If the flange, of the distributor shaft, is positioned above the module, place a socket on the crankshaft pulley bolt and rotate the crankshaft (turning the distributor shaft) to provide clearance to the ignition module.

4. Remove the ignition module-to-distributor screws, lift the module and disconnect the electrical connectors from it.

5. If the module is suspected as being defective, take it to a module testing machine and have it tested.

1. Cap assembly
2. Carbon point
3. Rotor head
4. Packing
5. Cover
6. Screw
7. Vacuum control assembly
8. Screw
9. Harness assembly
10. Pole piece
11. Roll pin
12. Screw
13. Breaker plate assembly
14. Screw
15. P/U coil module assembly
16. Spacer
17. Screw
18. Stator
19. Magnet set
20. Roll pin
21. Collar
22. Shaft assembly
23. Rotor shaft assembly
24. Packing
25. Screw
26. Governor weight
27. Governor spring

Exploded view of the Non-EST distributor

Using a non-magnetic feeler gauge, check the air gap between the pole piece and the breaker plate

153. "P" terminal
154. Module
155. Pickup coil assembly
156. Hall effect switch
157. Pickup coil leads

EST distributor used on the 2.5L 4-cylinder and all 6-cylinder engines

NOTE: *When replacing the module, ensure that the module-to-distributor surface is coated with silicone lubricant.*

6. To install, apply silicone lubricant to the module mounting area of the distributor and reverse the removal procedures. Install the rotor, the distributor cap and the negative battery terminal.

Distributor

REMOVAL

1. Disconnect the negative battery terminal from the battery.
2. Tag and disconnect the electrical connector(s) from the distributor.
3. Remove the distributor cap (DO NOT remove the ignition wires) from the distributor and move it aside.
4. Using a crayon or chalk, make locating marks (for installation purposes) on the rotor,

the ignition module, the distributor housing and the engine.
5. Loosen and remove the distributor clamp bolt and clamp, then lift the distributor from the engine.
NOTE: *Noting the relative position of the rotor and the module alignment marks, make a second mark on the rotor to align it with the one mark on the module.*

INSTALLATION

Undisturbed Engine

This condition exists if the engine has not been rotated with the distributor removed.
1. Install a new O-ring on the distributor housing.
2. Align the second mark on the rotor with the mark on the module, then install the distributor, taking care to align the mark on the housing with the one on the engine.
NOTE: *It may be necessary to lift the distributor and turn the rotor slightly to align the gears and the oil pump driveshaft.*
3. With the respective marks aligned, install the clamp and bolt finger tight.
4. Install and secure the distributor cap.
5. Connect the electrical connector(s) to the distributor.
6. Connect a timing light to the engine (following the manufacturer's instructions). Start the engine, then check and/or adjust the timing.
7. Turn the engine Off, tighten the distributor clamp bolt and remove the timing light.

Disturbed Engine

This condition exists when the engine has been rotated with the distributor removed.
1. Install a new O-ring on the distributor housing.
2. Rotate the crankshaft to position the No. 1 cylinder on the TDC of it's compression stroke. This may be determined by inserting a rag into the No. 1 spark plug hole and slowly turn the engine crankshaft. When the timing mark on the crankshaft pulley aligns with the 0° mark on the timing scale and the rag is blown out by the compression, the No. 1 piston is at top-dead-center (TDC).
3. Turn the rotor so that it will point to the No. 1 terminal of the distributor cap.
4. Install the distributor into the engine block. It may be necessary to turn the rotor, a little in either direction, in order to engage the gears.
5. Tap the starter a few times to ensure that the oil pump shaft is mated to the distributor shaft.
6. Bring the engine to No. 1 TDC again and

check to see that the rotor is indeed pointing toward the No. 1 terminal of the cap.

7. With the respective marks aligned, install the clamp and bolt finger tight.

8. Install and secure the distributor cap.

9. Connect the electrical connector(s) to the distributor.

NOTE: *If equipped with a vacuum line, reconnect it.*

10. Connect a timing light to the engine (following the manufacturer's instructions). Start the engine, then check and/or adjust the timing.

11. Turn the engine Off, tighten the distributor clamp bolt and remove the timing light.

Alternator

The alternator used in the charging system of 1982–86 S/10-S/15 trucks is the SI integral regulator alternator. The alternator will be one of the following types: 10-SI, 12-SI or 15-SI. Differences between the types are output current ratings, and drive end and slip ring end bearing stack up.

Starting in 1986, the CS-130 alternator was used in production. The CS-130 features a high ampere output per pound of weight. It has an integral regulator but DOES NOT use a diode

Schematic of the SI model alternator

57. Rotor
58. Stator
60. Rectifier bridge
64. Regulator
67. Double sealed ball bearing
68. Terminals
69. Internal fan

Sectional view of the CS model alternator

NO. 1 TERMINAL   NO. 2 TERMINAL

"BAT" TERMINAL

TEST HOLE

THRU-BOLT

CS-130 diagnostic test connections

trio. The stator, rectifier bridge, and rotor with slip rings and brushes are electrically similar to the SI model alternators.

The regulator voltage varies with temperature and limits system voltage by controlling rotor field current. It switches rotor field current on and off at a fixed frequency of about 400 cycles per second. By varying the on-off time, correct average field current for proper system voltage control is obtained. At high speeds, the on-time may be 10 percent and the off-time may be 90 percent. At low speeds, with high electrical loads, the on-off time may be 90 percent and 10 percent respectively.

NOTE: *The CS-130 alternator is not serviceable. If the alternator is found to be defective, replacement is the only alternative.*

ALTERNATOR PRECAUTIONS

To prevent damage to the on-board computer, alternator and regulator, the following precautionary measures must be taken when working with the electrical system.

• Never reverse the battery connections. Always check the battery polarity visually. This is to be done before any connections are made to be sure that all of the connections correspond to the battery ground polarity.

• Booster batteries for starting must be connected properly. Make sure that the positive cable of the booster battery is connected to the positive terminal of the battery that is getting the boost. This applies to both negative and ground cables.

• Make sure the ignition switch is OFF when connecting or disconnecting any electrical component, especially on trucks equipped with an on-board computer control system.

• Disconnect the battery cables before using a fast charger; the charger has a tendency to force current through the diodes in the opposite direction for which they were designed. This burns out the diodes.

• Never use a fast charger as a booster for starting the vehicle.

• Never disconnect the voltage regulator while the engine is running.

• Do not ground the alternator output terminal.

• Do not attempt to polarize an alternator.

NO. 2 TERMINAL (SENSING)

NO. 1 TERMINAL (FIELD)

"BAT" TERMINAL

DRIVE END FRAME

SLIP RING END FRAME

BEARING

REGULATOR

BRUSHES

SLIP RINGS

BEARING

SEAL

RECTIFIER BRIDGE

DIODE TRIO

ROTOR

STATOR ASSEMBLY

Sectional view of the SI model alternator

ALTERNATOR SPECIFICATIONS

Year	Engine	Alternator	Part No.	Model	Field Current	Output (amps)
1982	1.9L	—	1100140	10SI	4.0–5.0	37
	1.9L	—	1100146	15SI	4.0–5.0	63
	2.8L	—	1100201	10SI	4.0–5.0	37
	2.8L	—	1100202	15SI	4.0–5.0	66
1983–85	1.9L	K85	1105185	10SI	4.0–5.0	37
	1.9L	K81	1100207	12SI	4.0–5.0	63
	1.9L	K64	1100209	12SI	4.0–5.0	78
	2.0L	K85	1100204	10SI	4.0–5.0	37
	2.0L	K81	1100275	12SI	4.0–5.0	66
	2.0L	K64	1100276	12SI	4.0–5.0	78
	2.8L	K85	1100227	10SI	4.0–5.0	37
	2.8L	K81	1100249	12SI	4.0–5.0	66
	2.8L	K64	1100273	12SI	4.0–5.0	78
1986–87	2.5L	—	1105627	12SI	4.0–5.0	78
	2.8L	100	1105663	CS130	5.4–6.4	85
1988–91	2.5L	100	1101346	CS130	6.0–7.5	96
	2.8L	100	1101259	CS130	4.8–5.7	85
	4.3L	100	1101317	CS130	5.7–7.1	85
	4.3L	100	1101293	CS130	6.0–7.5	100

DIAGNOSIS

SI Alternator

A charge indicator lamp is used in most trucks to signal when there is a fault in the charging system. This lamp is located in the gauge package and is used in diagnosis. A voltmeter may be used instead of the charge indicator lamp in diagnosis. In this case, section "A" of the diagnosis chart should be omitted.

CS-130 Alternator

1. Check drive belt(s) for wear and tension. Check wiring for obvious damage.

2. Go to Step 5 for vehicles without a charge indicator lamp.

3. With the ignition switch ON and the engine stopped, the lamp should be ON. If not, detach the wiring harness at the generator and ground the "L" terminal lead.

4. If the lamp lights, replace the alternator. If the lamp does not light, locate the open circuit between the grounding lead and the ignition switch. Check the lamp, it may be open.

5. With the ignition switch ON, and the engine running at moderate speed, the lamp should be OFF. If not, detach the wiring harness at the alternator.

6. If the lamp goes out, replace the alternator. If the lamp stays ON, check for a grounded "L" terminal wire in the harness.

7. Determine if the battery is undercharged or overcharged.

• An undercharged battery is evidenced by slow cranking or a dark hydrometer.

• An overcharged battery is evidenced by excessive spewing of electrolyte from the vents.

8. Detach the wiring harness connector from the alternator.

9. With the ignition switch ON, and the engine OFF, connect a voltmeter from ground

Schematic of the CS model alternator

to the "L" terminal in the wiring harness, and to the "I" terminal, if used.

10. A zero reading indicates an open circuit between the terminal and the battery. Repair the circuit as necessary.

11. Connect the harness connector to the alternator and run the engine at moderate speed with accessories OFF.

12. Measure the voltage across the battery. If above 16 volts, replace the alternator.

13. Connect an ammeter at the alternator output terminal, turn ON all the accessories and load the battery with a carbon pile to obtain maximum amperage. Maintain voltage at 13 volts or above.

14. If the output is within 15 amps of the rated output of the alternator (stamped on the alternator case), the alternator is good. If the output is not within 15 amps, replace the alternator.

REMOVAL AND INSTALLATION

NOTE: *The following procedures require the use of GM Belt Tension Gauge No. BT-33-95-ACBN (regular V-belts) or BT-33-97M (poly V-belts). The belt should deflect about $^1/_4$ in. (6mm) over a 7–10 in. (178–254mm) span or $^1/_2$ in. (12.7mm) over a 13–16 in. (330–406mm) span at this point.*

1. Disconnect the negative battery terminal from the battery.

2. Remove other components as necessary to gain access to the alternator.

3. Label and disconnect the alternator's electrical connectors.

4. Remove the alternator brace bolt and the drive belt.

5. Support the alternator while removing the mounting bolts, then remove the alternator.

6. Installation is the reverse of removal.

7. If the vehicle is equipped with V-belts, adjust the belt tension. Serpentine drive belts are equipped with automatic tensioners; no adjustment is necessary.

8. Torque the top mounting bolt to 22 ft. lbs. and the lower mounting bolt to 24–35 ft. lbs.

9. Reconnect the negative battery terminal.

V-belt Adjustment Procedure

1. If the belt is Cold, operate the engine (at idle speed) for 15 minutes; the belt will seat itself in the pulleys allowing the belt fibers to relax or stretch. If the belt is hot, allow it to cool, until it is warm to the touch.

NOTE: *A used belt is one that has been rotated at least one complete revolution on the pulleys. This begins the belt seating process and it must never be tensioned to the new belt specifications.*

2. Loosen the component-to-mounting bracket bolts.

3. Place the GM Belt Tension Gauge [BT-33-95-ACBN (standard V-belts) or BT-33-97M (poly V-belts)] at the center of the belt between the longest span.

4. Applying belt tension pressure on the component, adjust the drive belt tension to the correct specifications.

5. While holding the correct tension on the component, tighten the component-to-mounting bracket bolt.

6. When the belt tension is correct, remove the tension gauge.

Battery

The battery is mounted in front, right-side of the engine compartment. It is a no maintenance type with side mounted terminals.

CURRENT DRAW TEST

1. Remove the negative battery cable.

2. Install a battery side terminal adapter to the negative battery terminal.

3. Connect the negative lead of a digital multimeter to the negative battery terminal.

4. Connect the positive lead of the digital multimeter to ground.

5. Set the multimeter on the DC, MA and 2000Ω scale. Take the reading with the engine and all accessories OFF.

6. Find the reserve capacity of the battery. This figure is usually noted on the top of the battery. If not, contact the battery manufacturer.

7. Divide the reserve capacity by 4. The current drain should not exceed this number. For example, if the battery has a reserve capacity of 100 minutes, the current draw should not exceed 25 milliamps.

8. If current draw is too high, check the system for causes such as shorted wires to a compartment lamp that does not shut off when it should.

REMOVAL AND INSTALLATION

1. Disconnect the negative battery terminal, then the positive battery terminal.

2. Remove the battery holddown retainer.

3. Remove the battery from the vehicle.

4. Inspect the battery, the cables and the battery carrier for damage.

5. To install, reverse the removal procedures. Torque the battery retainer to 11 ft. lbs., the top bar to 8 ft. lbs. (if equipped) and battery cable terminals to 10 ft. lbs.

Replacing the battery

Starter

The gasoline starter is located on the lower right-side (gasoline engines) or on the lower left-side (diesel engine). The diesel engine starter is a gear reduction type.

DIAGNOSIS

Before removing the starter for repair or replacement, check the condition of all circuit wiring for damage. Inspect all connection to the starter motor, solenoid, ignition switch, and battery, including all ground connections. Clean and tighten all connections as required.

Check all switches to determine their condition. Vehicles equipped with manual transmission have a neutral start switch attached to the clutch which closes when the clutch is depressed. Vehicles equipped with automatic transmissions have a manual interlock in the steering column which does not allow the ignition switch to turn to the start position unless the transmission is in the Park or Neutral position.

Check the battery to ensure that it is fully charged. Perform battery current draw test to determine battery condition.

Check the battery cables for excessive resistance as follows:

CAUTION: *To prevent possible injury from a moving vehicle or operating engine, engage*

Starter mounting on the 6-cylinder engines

the parking brakes, block the drive wheels, place the manual transmission in Neutral or the automatic transmission in Park, and disconnect the battery feed at the distributor before performing these tests.

• Check the voltage drop between the negative battery terminal and the vehicle frame by placing one lead of a voltmeter on the grounded battery post (not the cable clamp) and the other lead on the frame. Turn the ignition key to the START position and note the voltage drop.

• Check the voltage drop between the positive battery terminal (not the cable clamp) and the starter terminal stud. Turn the ignition key to the START position and note the voltage drop.

• Check the voltage drop between the starter housing and the frame. Turn the ignition key to the START position and note the voltage drop.

• If the voltage drop in any of the above is more than 1.0 volts, there is excessive resistance in the circuit. Clean and retest all cables not within specification. Replace as necessary.

REMOVAL AND INSTALLATION

1. Disconnect the negative battery terminal from the battery.
2. Raise and support the vehicle safely.
3. If equipped, remove any starter braces or shields that may be in the way.

Starter mounting on the 4-cylinder engines

4. Label and disconnect the electrical connectors from the starter solenoid. On the 4.3L engine, the electrical connections may be reached through the right wheel well.

NOTE: *It is helpful to have a floor jack handy to support the starter during removal and installation. The starter is heavier than it looks and can cause you injury if it falls.*

5. Remove the starter-to-engine bolts, nuts, washers and shims. Allow the starter to drop, then remove it from the engine.

NOTE: *Be sure to keep the shims in order so that they may be reinstalled in the same order.*

6. To install, reverse the removal procedures. Torque the starter-to-engine bolts to 30–33 ft. lbs. Connect the wires to the starter solenoid and connect the negative battery cable.

SOLENOID REPLACEMENT

Gasoline Engines

1. Remove the starter and place it on a workbench.
2. Remove the screw and the washer from the motor connector strap terminal.
3. Remove the two solenoid retaining screws.
4. Twist the solenoid housing clockwise to remove the flange key from the keyway in the housing and remove.
5. To install the solenoid, place the return spring on the plunger and place the solenoid body on the drive housing.
6. Turn solenoid counterclockwise to engage the flange key.
7. Install the two retaining screws, then install the screw and washer which secures the strap terminal.
8. Install the starter on the vehicle.

Starter mounting on the 2.2L diesel engine

Diesel Engine

1. Remove the starter from the vehicle.
2. Remove the two screws from the drive housing and separate the drive housing from the solenoid.
3. Remove the two pinion gears, then remove the overrunning clutch and retainer.
4. Remove the return spring from the solenoid.
5. Remove the steel ball from the overrunning clutch.
6. Installation is the reverse of removal.

ENGINE MECHANICAL

Six engines and three fuel systems are available to power your S-10/S-15 Truck, they are:
- 1982–85 Isuzu built 1.9L (118.9 cu. in.) 2-bbl.
- 1982–85 Chevy built 2.8L (173 cu. in.) 2-bbl.
- 1983–84 Chevy built 2.0L (121 cu. in.) 2-bbl.
- 1983–85 Isuzu built 2.2L (136.6 cu. in.) Diesel.

STARTER SPECIFICATIONS

Year	Engine	Part No.	Series	No Load Test @ 10V Amps	rpm
1982	2.8L	1109535	5MTPH3	45–70	7000–11900
1983	1.9L	94241705	—	—	—
	2.0L	1109561	5MTPH3	50–75	6000–11900
	2.8L	1109535	5MTPH3	45–70	7000–11900
1984–85	2.0L	1998431	5MTPH3	50–75	6000–11900
	2.8L	1998427	5MTPH3	50–75	6000–11900
1986–87	2.5L	1998532	5MT	50–75	6000–11900
	2.8L	1998524	5MT	50–75	6000–11900
1988–91	2.5L	10455018	5MT	50–70	6000–11900
	2.8L	10455016	SD200	50–75	6000–11900
	4.3L	9000735	PGMR②	50–90	2330–2660①
1991	4.3L	10455013	SD260	50–62	8500–10700

① Drive speed
② SD200

- 1985–91 Pontiac built 2.5L (151 cu. in.) TBI.
- 1986–91 Chevy built 2.8L (173 cu. in.) TBI.
- 1988–91 Chevy built 4.3L (262 cu. in.) TBI.

On the 1985, 2.5L EFI engine, the cylinder head and engine block are both constructed of cast iron. The valve guides are integral with the cylinder head and the rocker arms are retained by individual threaded shoulder bolts. Hydraulic roller lifters are incorporated to reduce the friction between the valve lifters and the camshaft lobes.

On the 1986–87, 2.5L TBI engine, a few changes appeared, such as: (1) the pistons were replaced with hypereutectic types (pistons embedded with silicone nodules in the walls to reduce the cylinder wall friction), (2) a reduced weight, high efficiency alternator and (3) a variable ratio A/C compressor.

The 2.8L engine, utilizes a 2-bbl (1982–85) or an TBI system (1986–87) and the use of swirl chamber heads (to increase power and fuel efficiency). The engine block and cylinder heads are constructed of cast iron. Other major features are: a wider oil pan flange, raised rails inside the cylinder heads (to improve oil return control), machined rocker cover seal surfaces, a trough along the rocker cover rails (to channel oil away from the gasket) and even distribution of the clamping loads, to make this engine one of the most leak-resistant on the road today.

In 1988, the 4.3L TBI engine was introduced. It features forged steel connecting rods and cast aluminum alloy pistons with full floating piston pins.

Engine Overhaul Tips

Most engine overhaul procedures are fairly standard. In addition to specific parts replacement procedures and complete specifications for your individual engine, this chapter also is a guide to acceptable rebuilding procedures. Examples of standard rebuilding practice are shown and should be used along with specific details concerning your particular engine.

Competent and accurate machine shop services will ensure maximum performance, reliability and engine life. Choose your machinist carefully. If the engine is not machined properly, engine failure will result within a short time period after installation.

On most instances it is more profitable for the home mechanic to remove, clean and inspect the component(s), buy the necessary parts and deliver these to a shop for actual machine work.

Troubleshooting Basic Fuel System Problems

Problem	Cause	Solution
Engine cranks, but won't start (or is hard to start) when cold	• Empty fuel tank • Incorrect starting procedure • Defective fuel pump • No fuel in carburetor • Clogged fuel filter • Engine flooded • Defective choke	• Check for fuel in tank • Follow correct procedure • Check pump output • Check for fuel in the carburetor • Replace fuel filter • Wait 15 minutes; try again • Check choke plate
Engine cranks, but is hard to start (or does not start) when hot— (presence of fuel is assumed)	• Defective choke	• Check choke plate
Rough idle or engine runs rough	• Dirt or moisture in fuel • Clogged air filter • Faulty fuel pump	• Replace fuel filter • Replace air filter • Check fuel pump output
Engine stalls or hesitates on acceleration	• Dirt or moisture in the fuel • Dirty carburetor • Defective fuel pump • Incorrect float level, defective accelerator pump	• Replace fuel filter • Clean the carburetor • Check fuel pump output • Check carburetor
Poor gas mileage	• Clogged air filter • Dirty carburetor • Defective choke, faulty carburetor adjustment	• Replace air filter • Clean carburetor • Check carburetor
Engine is flooded (won't start accompanied by smell of raw fuel)	• Improperly adjusted choke or carburetor	• Wait 15 minutes and try again, without pumping gas pedal • If it won't start, check carburetor

Troubleshooting Basic Turn Signal and Flasher Problems

Most problems in the turn signals or flasher system can be reduced to defective flashers or bulbs, which are easily replaced. Occasionally, problems in the turn signals are traced to the switch in the steering column, which will require professional service.

F = Front   R = Rear   • = Lights off   o = Lights on

Problem		Solution
Turn signals light, but do not flash		• Replace the flasher
No turn signals light on either side		• Check the fuse. Replace if defective. • Check the flasher by substitution • Check for open circuit, short circuit or poor ground
Both turn signals on one side don't work		• Check for bad bulbs • Check for bad ground in both housings
One turn signal light on one side doesn't work		• Check and/or replace bulb • Check for corrosion in socket. Clean contacts. • Check for poor ground at socket
Turn signal flashes too fast or too slow		• Check any bulb on the side flashing too fast. A heavy-duty bulb is probably installed in place of a regular bulb. • Check the bulb flashing too slow. A standard bulb was probably installed in place of a heavy-duty bulb. • Check for loose connections or corrosion at the bulb socket
Indicator lights don't work in either direction		• Check if the turn signals are working • Check the dash indicator lights • Check the flasher by substitution
One indicator light doesn't light		• On systems with 1 dash indicator: See if the lights work on the same side. Often the filaments have been reversed in systems combining stoplights with taillights and turn signals. Check the flasher by substitution • On systems with 2 indicators: Check the bulbs on the same side Check the indicator light bulb Check the flasher by substitution

Troubleshooting Basic Lighting Problems

Problem	Cause	Solution
Lights		
One or more lights don't work, but others do	• Defective bulb(s) • Blown fuse(s) • Dirty fuse clips or light sockets • Poor ground circuit	• Replace bulb(s) • Replace fuse(s) • Clean connections • Run ground wire from light socket housing to car frame
Lights burn out quickly	• Incorrect voltage regulator setting or defective regulator • Poor battery/alternator connections	• Replace voltage regulator • Check battery/alternator connections
Lights go dim	• Low/discharged battery • Alternator not charging • Corroded sockets or connections • Low voltage output	• Check battery • Check drive belt tension; repair or replace alternator • Clean bulb and socket contacts and connections • Replace voltage regulator
Lights flicker	• Loose connection • Poor ground • Circuit breaker operating (short circuit)	• Tighten all connections • Run ground wire from light housing to car frame • Check connections and look for bare wires
Lights "flare"—Some flare is normal on acceleration—if excessive, see "Lights Burn Out Quickly"	• High voltage setting	• Replace voltage regulator
Lights glare—approaching drivers are blinded	• Lights adjusted too high • Rear springs or shocks sagging • Rear tires soft	• Have headlights aimed • Check rear springs/shocks • Check/correct rear tire pressure
Turn Signals		
Turn signals don't work in either direction	• Blown fuse • Defective flasher • Loose connection	• Replace fuse • Replace flasher • Check/tighten all connections
Right (or left) turn signal only won't work	• Bulb burned out • Right (or left) indicator bulb burned out • Short circuit	• Replace bulb • Check/replace indicator bulb • Check/repair wiring
Flasher rate too slow or too fast	• Incorrect wattage bulb • Incorrect flasher	• Flasher bulb • Replace flasher (use a variable load flasher if you pull a trailer)
Indicator lights do not flash (burn steadily)	• Burned out bulb • Defective flasher	• Replace bulb • Replace flasher
Indicator lights do not light at all	• Burned out indicator bulb • Defective flasher	• Replace indicator bulb • Replace flasher

On the other hand, much of the rebuilding work (crankshaft, block, bearings, piston rods, and other components) is well within the scope of the home mechanic.

TOOLS

The tools required for an engine overhaul or parts replacement will depend on the depth of your involvement. With a few exceptions, they will be the tools found in a mechanic's tool kit (see Chapter 1). More in-depth work will require any or all of the following:
• A dial indicator (reading in thou-sandths) mounted on a universal base
• Micrometers and telescope gauges
• Jaw and screw-type pullers
• Scraper
• Valve spring compressor
• Ring groove cleaner
• Piston ring expander and compressor
• Ridge reamer
• Cylinder hone or glaze breaker
• Plastigage®
• Engine stand

Use of most of these tools is illustrated in this chapter. Many can be rented for a one-time use from a local parts jobber or tool supply house specializing in automotive work.

Occasionally, the use of special tools is called for. See the information on Special Tools and Safety Notice in the front of this book before substituting another tool.

INSPECTION TECHNIQUES

Procedures and specifications are given in this chapter for inspecting, cleaning and assessing the wear limits of most major components. Other procedures such as Magnaflux® and Zyglo® can be used to locate material flaws and stress cracks.

Magnaflux® is a magnetic process applicable only to ferrous materials. The Zyglo® process coats the material with a fluorescent dye penetrant and can be used on any material. Check for suspected surface cracks can be more readily made using spot check dye. The dye is sprayed onto the suspected area, wiped off and the area sprayed with a developer. Cracks will show up brightly.

OVERHAUL TIPS

Aluminum has become extremely popular for use in engines, due to its low weight. Observe the following precautions when handling aluminum parts:

• Never hot tank aluminum parts (the caustic hot tank solution will eat the aluminum.

• Remove all aluminum parts (identification tag, etc.) from engine parts prior to the tanking.

• Always coat threads lightly with engine oil or anti-seize compounds before installation, to prevent seizure.

• Never over-torque bolts or spark plugs especially in aluminum for you may strip the threads.

Stripped threads in any component can be repaired using any of several commercial repair kits (Heli-Coil®, Microdot®, Keenserts®, etc.).

When assembling the engine, any parts that will have frictional contact must be prelubed to provide lubrication at initial start-up. Any product specifically formulated for this purpose can be used, but engine oil is not recommended as a prelube.

When semi-permanent (locked, but removable) installation of bolts or nuts is desired, threads should be cleaned and coated with Loctite® or other similar, commercial non-hardening sealant.

REPAIRING DAMAGED THREADS

Several methods of repairing damaged threads are available. Heli-Coil® (shown here),

Keenserts® and Microdot® are among the most widely used. All involve basically the same principle—drilling out stripped threads, tapping the hole and installing a prewound insert—making welding, plugging and oversize fasteners unnecessary.

Two types of thread repair inserts are usually supplied—a standard type for most Inch Coarse, Inch Fine, Metric Course and Metric Fine thread sizes and a spark lug type to fit most spark plug port sizes. Consult the individual manufacturer's catalog to determine exact applications. Typical thread repair kits will contain a selection of prewound threaded inserts, a tap (corresponding to the outside diameter threads of the insert) and an installation tool. Spark plug inserts usually differ because they require a tap equipped with pilot threads and a combined reamer/tap section. Most manufacturers also supply blister-packed thread repair inserts separately in addition to a master kit containing a variety of taps and inserts plus installation tools.

Before effecting a repair to a threaded hole, remove any snapped, broken or damaged bolts or studs. Penetrating oil can be used to free frozen threads; the offending item can be removed with locking pliers or with a screw or

Using a specified drill bit to enlarge the damaged threads. Drill completely through the hole or to the bottom of a blind hole

Screw the threaded insert onto the installation tool until the tang engages the slot. Screw the insert into the tapped hole until it is $^1/_4$-$^1/_2$ turn below the top surface. After installation, break off the tang with a hammer and punch

Standard thread repair insert (left) and the spark plug repair insert (right)

With the supplied tapping bit, tap the hole to receive the thread insert. Keep the tap well oiled and back it out frequently to avoid clogging the threads

stud extractor. After the hole is clear, the thread can be repaired, as follows:

Checking Engine Compression

A noticeable lack of engine power, excessive oil consumption and/or poor fuel mileage measured over an extended period are all indicators of internal engine wear. Worn piston rings, scored or worn cylinder bores, blown head gaskets, sticking or burnt valves and worn valve seats are all possible culprits here. A check of each cylinder's compression will help you locate the problems.

As mentioned in the "Tools and Equipment" section of Chapter 1, a screw-in type compression gauge is more accurate that the type you simply hold against the spark plug hole. Although the screw in type gauge takes slightly longer to use, it is worth the accuracy you gain.

Gasoline Engines

1. Warm up the engine to normal operating temperature.
2. Remove all spark plugs.
3. Disconnect the high tension lead from the ignition coil.
4. Fully open the throttle, either by operating the carburetor throttle linkage by hand or by having an assistant hold the accelerator pedal to the floor.
5. Screw the compression gauge into the No. 1 spark plug hole until the fitting is snug.
   NOTE: *Be careful not to crossthread the plug hole. On aluminum cylinder heads use*

Using a thread insert to repair a damaged hole

extra care, as the threads in these heads are easily ruined.
6. Crank the engine through 4–5 compression strokes (complete revolutions) recording the highest reading on the compression gauge.
7. Repeat this procedure for each of the engine's cylinders. Compare the highest reading of each cylinder to the compression pressure specification in the Tune-Up Specifications chart in Chapter 2. The specs in this chart are maximum values.
   NOTE: *A cylinder's compression pressure is usually acceptable if it is not less than 80% of maximum. A more important measure is difference between each cylinder. The variance should be no more than 12–14 pounds.*
8. If a cylinder is unusually low, pour a tablespoon of clean engine oil (30W) into the cylinder through the spark plug hole and repeat the compression test. If the compression rises after adding the oil, it appears that the cylinder's piston rings or bore are damaged or worn.
9. If the pressure remains low, the valves may not be seating properly (a valve job is needed), or the head gasket may be blown near that cylinder.
10. If compression in any two adjacent cylinders is low and if the addition of oil doesn't help the compression, there is leakage past the head gasket. Oil and coolant water in the combustion chamber can result from this problem.

Screw-in type compression gauge

Diesel engines require a special compression gauge adaptor

There may be evidence of water droplets (sometimes seen as a milky white substance) on the engine dipstick when a head gasket has blown.

Diesel Engines

Checking the cylinder compression on diesel engines is basically the same procedures as on gasoline engines, except for the following:

1. A special compression gauge adaptor suitable for diesel engines (due to greater compression pressures) must be used.

2. Remove the injector tubes and the injectors from each cylinder.

NOTE: *Don't forget to remove the washer beneath each injector; otherwise, it may get lost when the engine is cranked.*

3. When fitting the compression gauge adaptor to the cylinder head, make sure the bleeder of the gauge (if equipped) is closed.

4. When reinstalling the injector assemblies, install new washers beneath each injector.

Engine

NOTE: *The following procedures require the use of an engine hoist with sufficient capacity to safely lift and support 500–1000 lbs.*

REMOVAL AND INSTALLATION

1. Remove the negative battery cable.

2. Matchmark the hood hinges for installation reference and remove the hood.

3. Drain the cooling system and remove the upper and lower radiator hoses. Disconnect the coolant overflow hose. Disconnect the heater hoses at the engine.

CAUTION: *When draining the coolant, keep in mind that cats and dogs are attracted by the ethylene glycol antifreeze, and are quite likely to drink any that is left in an uncovered container or in puddles on the ground. This will prove fatal in sufficient quantity. Always drain the coolant into a sealable container. Coolant should be reused unless it is contaminated or several years old.*

4. Remove the upper and lower fan shrouds. On automatic transmission equipped vehicles, disconnect and plug the transmission cooler lines.

5. Remove the air cleaner assembly and cover the carburetor/throttle body with a rag.

NOTE: *Refer to Chapter 5 for special procedures to release fuel system pressure.*

6. Label and disconnect all necessary hoses, vacuum lines and wires from the engine, transmission and transfer case (if equipped).

7. Disconnect the throttle cable, transmission TV cable and cruise control cable (if equipped).

8. Raise and support the vehicle safely. Disconnect the exhaust pipes at the manifold.

9. Remove the front driveshaft and skid plates on 4WD vehicles.

PISTON AND RING SPECIFICATIONS

(All measurements are given in inches. To convert inches to metric units, refer to the Metric Information section.)

Year	V.I.N. Code	Engine Type Disp. Liter (cu. in.)	Eng Mfg.	Piston-to-Bore Clearance	Ring Gap			Ring Side Clearance		
					Top Compression	Bottom Compression	Oil Control	Top Compression	Bottom Compression	Oil Control
1982–85	A	4-1.9 (118.9)	Isuzu	0.0018–0.0026	0.012–0.020	0.008–0.016	0.008–0.035	0.0059 max.	0.0059 max.	0.0059 max.
	B	6-2.8 (173)	Chev.	0.0017–0.0027	0.010–0.020	0.010–0.020	0.020–0.055	0.0012–0.0028	0.0016–0.0037	0.0078 max.
1983–84	Y	4-2.0 (121)	Chev.	0.0008–0.0018	0.010–0.020	0.010–0.020	0.020–0.055	0.0012–0.0027	0.0012–0.0038	0.0078 max.
1983–85	S	4-2.2 (136.6)	Isuzu	0.0062–0.0070	0.008–0.016	0.008–0.016	0.008–0.016	0.0018–0.0028	0.0012–0.0021	0.0008–0.0021
1985–91	E	4-2.5 (151)	Pontiac	0.0014–0.0022	0.010–0.020	0.010–0.020	0.020–0.060	0.002–0.003	0.001–0.003	0.0015–0.0055
1986–91	R	6-2.8 (173)	Chev.	0.0006–0.0017	0.010–0.020	0.010–0.020	0.020–0.055	0.0011–0.0027	0.0015–0.0037	0.0078 max.
1988–91	Z	6-4.3 (262)	Chev.	0.0007–0.0017	0.010–0.020	0.010–0.025	0.015–0.055	0.0012–0.0032	0.0012–0.0032	0.002–0.007

CRANKSHAFT AND CONNECTING ROD SPECIFICATIONS

(All measurements are given in inches)

Year	V.I.N. Code	Engine No. Cyl. Displacement Liter (cu. in.)	Eng. Mfg.	Crankshaft				Connecting Rod		
				Main Brg. Journal Dia.	Main Brg. Oil Clearance	Shaft End-Play	Thrust on No.	Journal Diameter	Oil Clearance	Side Clearance
1982–85	A	4-1.9 (118.9)	Isuzu	2.2050	0.0008–0.0025	0.0117 max.	3	1.9290	0.0007–0.0030	0.0137 max.
	B	6-2.8 (173)	Chev.	2.4940	0.0017–0.0030	0.0020–0.0067	3	1.9980	0.0014–0.0032	0.0063–0.0173
1983–84	Y	4-2.0 (121)	Chev.	①	②	0.0020–0.0071	3	1.9990	0.0010–0.0031	0.0034–0.0240
1983–85	S	4-2.2 (136.6)	Isuzu	2.3590	0.0011–0.0033	0.0018	3	2.0837	0.0016–0.0047	0.0024
1985–91	E	4-2.5 (151)	Pontiac	2.3000	0.0005–0.0022	0.0035–0.0085	5	2.000	0.0005–0.0026	0.0060–0.0220
1986–91	R	6-2.8 (173)	Chev.	③	0.0016–0.0032	0.0023–0.0082	3	1.9998–1.9983	0.0014–0.0037	0.0063–0.0173
1988–91	Z	6-4.3 (262)	Chev.	④	⑤	0.002–0.006	3	2.2487–2.2497	0.0013–0.0035	0.006–0.014

① Nos. 1, 2, 3, 4: 2.4940–2.4950
No. 5: 2.4930–2.4950
② Nos. 1, 2, 3, 4: 0.0006–0.0019
No. 5: 0.0014–0.0027

③ Nos. 1, 2, 4: 2.4937–2.4946
No. 3: 2.4934–2.4941
④ No. 1: 2.4484–2.4493
Nos. 2, 3: 2.4481–2.4490
No. 4: 2.4479–2.4488

⑤ No. 1: 0.0010–0.0015
Nos. 2, 3: 0.0010–0.0025
No. 4: 0.0025–0.0035

GENERAL ENGINE SPECIFICATIONS

Year	V.I.N. Code	Engine No. Cyl. Displ. Liter (Cu. In.)	Eng. Mfg.	Fuel Delivery system	Horsepower @ rpm	Torque @ rpm ft. lb.	Bore × Stroke	Compression Ratio	Oil Pressure 2000 rpm
1982–85	A	4-1.9 (118.9)	Isuzu	2-bbl	84 @ 4600	101 @ 3000	3.43 × 3.23	8.4:1	57
	B	6-2.8 (173)	Chev.	2-bbl	110 @ 4800	148 @ 2000	3.50 × 2.99	8.5:1	45
1983–84	Y	4-2.0 (121)	Chev.	2-bbl	83 @ 4600	108 @ 2400	3.50 × 3.15	9.3:1	45
1983–85	S	4-2.2 (136.6)	Isuzu	Diesel	58 @ 4300	93 @ 2200	3.46 × 3.62	21.0:1	55
1985–91	E	4-2.5 (151)	Pontiac	TBI	98 @ 4400	134 @ 2800	4.00 × 3.00	9.0:1	38
1986–91	R	6-2.8 (173)	Chev.	TBI	125 @ 4800	150 @ 2200	3.50 × 2.99	8.5:1	52
1988–91	Z	6-4.3 (262)	Chev.	TBI	160 @ 4000	230 @ 2800	4.00 × 3.48	9.3:1	18

① TBI—Throttle body injection

TORQUE SPECIFICATIONS

(All readings in ft. lbs.)

Year	V.I.N. Code	Engine No. Cyl. Displacement Liter (cu. in.)	Eng. Mfg.	Cylinder Head Bolts	Rod Bearing Bolts	Main Bearing Bolts	Crankshaft Bolt	Flywheel to Crankshaft Bolts	Manifold	
									Intake	Exhaust
1982–85	A	4-1.9 (118.9)	Isuzu	72	43	75	87	76	17	16
	B	6-2.8 (173)	Chev.	70	37	70	75	50	23	25
1983–84	Y	4-2.0 (121)	Chev.	70	37	70	75	50	23	25
1983–85	S	4-2.2 (136.6)	Isuzu	60	65	116–130	125–150	70	15	15
1985–91	E	4-2.5 (151)	Pontiac	90	32	70	160	55	①	①
1986–91	R	6-2.8 (173)	Chev.	70	39	70	70	52	23	25
1988–91	Z	6-4.3 (262)	Chev.	65	45	80	70	75	35	20 ②

① See text
② Except center (2) bolts 26 ft. lbs.

VALVE SPECIFICATIONS

Year	V.I.N. Code	Engine No. Cyl. Displacement Liter (cu. in.)	Eng. Mfg.	Seat Angle (deg.)	Face Angle (deg.)	Spring Test Pressure (lbs. @ in.)	Spring Installed Height (in.)	Stem-to-Guide Clearance (in.)		Stem Diameter (in.)	
								Intake	Exhaust	Intake	Exhaust
1982–85	A	4-1.9 (118.9)	Isuzu	45	45	①	NA	0.0009–0.0022	0.0015–0.0031	0.3102 min.	0.3091 min.
	B	6-2.8 (173)	Chev.	46	45	195 @ 1.180	1.5748	0.0010–0.0027	0.0010–0.0027	0.3410–0.3416	0.3410–0.3416
1983–84	Y	4-2.0 (121)	Chev.	46	45	182 @ 1.330	1.5984	0.0011–0.0026	0.0014–0.0031	0.3410–0.3416	0.3410–0.3416
1983–85	S	4-2.2 (136.6)	Isuzu	45	45	②	NA	0.0015–0.0027	0.0025–0.0037	0.3150–0.3100	0.3150–0.3090
1985–91	E	4-2.5 (151)	Pontiac	46	45	82 @ 1.660	1.690	0.0010–0.0027	0.0010–0.0027	0.343–0.342	0.342–0.343
1986–91	R	6-2.8 (173)	Chev.	46	45	195 @ 1.180	1.5748	0.0010–0.0027	0.0010–0.0027	0.3410–0.2416	0.3410–0.3416
1988–91	Z	6-4.3 (262)	Chev.	46	45	195 @ 1.250	1.7187	0.0010–0.0027	0.0010–0.0027	0.3410–0.2416	0.3410–0.3416

NA—Not available
① Outer: 35 @ 1.614
  Inner: 20 @ 1.516
② Outer: 145 @ 1.535
  Inner: 44 @ 1.457

CAMSHAFT SPECIFICATIONS
(All measurements in inches)

Year	V.I.N. Code	Engine	Eng. Mfg.	Journal Diameter					Bearing Clearance	Lobe Lift		Camshaft End Play
				1	2	3	4	5		Intake	Exhaust	
1982–85	A	4-1.9L (118.9)	Isuzu	1.3362–1.3370	1.3362–1.3370	1.3362–1.3370	1.3362–1.3370	1.3362–1.3370	0.0016–0.0035	NA	NA	0.0020–0.0059
	B	6-2.8L (173)	Chev.	1.8677–1.8696	1.8677–1.8696	1.8677–1.8696	1.8677–1.8696	—	0.0010–0.0039	0.231	0.262	NA
1983–84	Y	4-2.0L (121)	Chev.	1.8677–1.8696	1.8677–1.8696	1.8677–1.8696	1.8677–1.8696	1.8677–1.8696	0.0010–0.0039	0.262	0.262	NA
1983–85	S	4-2.2L (136.6)	Isuzu	1.8898–1.8741	1.8898–1.8741	1.8898–1.8741	—	—	0.0020–0.0097	NA	NA	0.0032–0.0079
1985–91	E	4-2.5L (151)	Pontiac	1.869	1.869	1.869	—	—	0.0007–0.0027	0.398	0.398	0.0015–0.0050
1986–91	R	6-2.8L (173)	Chev.	1.8677–1.8696	1.8677–1.8696	1.8677–1.8696	1.8677–1.8696	—	0.0010–0.0039	0.231	0.262	NA
1988–91	Z	6-4.3L (262)	Chev.	1.8682–1.8692	1.8682–1.8692	1.8682–1.8692	1.8682–1.8692	—	0.0010–0.0030	0.357	0.390	0.004–0.012

NA—Not available

10. Disconnect the strut rods at the bell housing.

11. Remove the body mounting bolts. Using a floor jack, raise and support the front of the body safely. Remove the top transmission-to-engine mounting bolts. Lower the body.

NOTE: *Vehicles equipped with automatic transmissions do not require transmission removal when removing the engine. Manual transmissions must be removed prior to removing the engine.*

13. Remove the rear driveshaft.

14. Support the transmission with a floor jack and remove the transmission crossmember.

15. For vehicles equipped with automatic transmissions:

• Remove the torque converter cover
• Remove the torque converter to flexplate attaching bolts
• Remove the transmission shift linkage
• If equipped with 4WD, remove the transfer case shift linkage
• Remove the remaining transmission-to-engine mounting bolts, and remove the transmission and transfer case (if equipped) as an assembly

16. For vehicles equipped with manual transmissions:

• Remove the clutch slave cylinder and set aside
• Remove the transmission shift linkage and shifter
• If equipped with 4WD, remove the trans-

fer case shift linkage and shifter
   • Remove the transmission-to-bell housing bolts and remove the transmission and
transfer case (if equipped) as an assembly
   • Leave the bell housing in place to protect
the clutch during engine removal
   17. Remove the accessory drive belts.
   18. Remove the fan.
   19. If equipped, remove the power steering
pump, A/C compressor and air pump with their
brackets and place aside in the engine compartment.
   NOTE: *DO NOT disconnect the fluid or refrigerant lines.*
   20. Check to see that nothing else is attached to the engine.
   21. Attach a suitable lifting device to the
engine and remove.
   22. Installation is the reverse of removal.
Torque engine mounting bolts to the following:
   • Engine mount-to-engine: 35 ft. lbs.
   • Engine mount-to-frame mount: 52 ft.
lbs.
   • Transmission   mount-to-transmission:
45 ft. lbs.
   • Transmission   mount-to-crossmember:
24 ft. lbs.

Rocker Arm Cover

REMOVAL AND INSTALLATION

1.9L Engine

   1. Remove the negative battery cable.
   2. Remove the air cleaner assembly.
   3. Remove the spark plug wires and the
evaporator pipe.
   4. Remove the rocker arm cover-to-engine
nuts/washers.
   5. Remove the rocker arm cover.
   6. Using a putty knife, clean the gasket
mounting surfaces.
   7. To install, use a new gasket and reverse
the removal procedures.

2.0L Engine

   1. Remove the negative battery cable.
   2. Remove the air cleaner assembly and the
distributor cap.
   3. Remove the fuel vapor canister harness
tubes from the rocker arm cover.
   4. Remove the accelerator cable and the
PCV valve.
   5. Remove the rocker arm cover-to-cylinder
head bolts and the cover.
   NOTE: *If the cover sticks, use a rubber
mallet to bump it or a prying tool to lift it
from the cylinder head.*
   6. Using a putty knife, clean the gasket
mounting surfaces.

   7. To install, place an $1/8$ in. bead of RTV
sealant around the sealing rail of the cover and
reverse the removal procedures. Torque the
rocker arm cover-to-cylinder head bolts to 8 ft.
lbs.

2.2L Diesel Engine

   1. Remove the negative battery cable.
   2. Remove the PCV valve from the rocker
arm cover and the PCV valve hose.
   3. Remove the air cleaner.
   4. Remove the rocker arm cover-to-cylinder
head bolts and the cover from the engine.
   5. Using a putty knife, clean the gasket
mounting surfaces.
   6. To install, use a new gasket and reverse
the removal procedures. Torque the rocker arm
cover-to-cylinder head bolts to 9–13 ft. lbs.

2.5L Engine

   NOTE: *A rocker arm cover removal tool (J
34144-A) is needed to perform this procedure
without damaging the sealing rail of the
rocker arm cover.*

   1. Remove the negative battery cable.
   2. Remove the air cleaner.
   3. Disconnect the Positive Crankcase Ventilation (PCV) valve hose, the ignition wires
from the rocker arm cover.
   4. Remove the Exhaust Gas Recirculation
(EGR) valve.
   5. Label and disconnect the vacuum hoses.
   6. Remove the rocker arm cover-to-cylinder

LEFT SIDE

RIGHT SIDE

Removing the fuel evaporation tubes — 2.0L engine

head bolts. Remove the cover using tool J 34144-A or equivalent.

7. Using a putty knife, clean the gasket mounting surfaces.

NOTE: *Be sure to use solvent to remove any oil or grease that may remain on the sealing surfaces.*

8. To install, place an $\frac{1}{8}$ in. bead of RTV sealant around the sealing rail of the cover (or use a new gasket) and reverse the removal procedures. Torque the valve cover-to-cylinder head bolts to 75 inch lbs.

2.8L Engine

LEFT-SIDE

1. Remove the negative battery cable.
2. Disconnect the air management hose, the vacuum hose(s), the electrical wires and the pipe bracket. Remove the spark plug wires and clips from the retaining stubs.
3. Disconnect the fuel line(s) from the carburetor or throttle body, if necessary.
4. Remove the rocker arm cover-to-cylinder head bolts/studs and the cover from the engine.

NOTE: *If the cover will not lift, use a rubber mallet to bump it loose from the cylinder head or use a small pry bar to lift the cover.*

5. Using a putty knife, clean the gasket mounting surfaces.
6. To install, place an $\frac{1}{8}$ in. bead of RTV sealant around the sealing rail of the cover (or use a new gasket) and reverse the removal procedures. Torque the rocker arm cover-to-cylinder head bolts/studs to 72 inch lbs.

Exploded view of the rocker arm cover — 2.0L engine

RIGHT-SIDE (1982–87)

1. Remove the negative battery cable.
2. Remove the air management and coil brackets.
3. Disconnect the air management hose, the vacuum hose(s), the electrical wires and the pipe bracket. Remove the spark plug wires and clips from the retaining stubs.
4. Disconnect the carburetor or throttle body controls and the brackets.
5. Remove the rocker arm cover-to-cylinder head bolts/studs and the cover from the engine.

A. Apply a continuous 5 mm ($\frac{3}{16}$-inch) diameter bead of RTV as shown.
5. Cylinder Head Bolt

Using tool J-34144-A to remove the rocker arm cover — 2.5L engine

NOTE: *If the cover will not lift, use a rubber mallet to bump it loose from the cylinder head or use a small pry bar to lift the cover.*

6. Using a putty knife, clean the gasket mounting surfaces.

7. To install, place an $1/8$ in. bead of RTV sealant around the sealing rail of the cover (or use a new gasket) and reverse the removal procedures. Torque the rocker arm cover-to-cylinder head bolts/studs to 72 inch lbs.

RIGHT-SIDE (1988–91)

1. Remove the negative battery cable.
2. Remove the ignition coil and bracket.
3. Remove spark plug wires, PCV valve and vacuum pipe.
4. Remove the throttle, cruise control and TVS cables and bracket at the throttle body.
5. Remove the alternator and lay it aside.
6. Remove the rocker arm cover-to-cylinder head bolts/studs and the cover from the engine.

NOTE: *If the cover will not lift, use a rubber mallet to bump it loose from the cylinder head or use a small pry bar to lift the cover.*

7. Using a putty knife, clean the gasket mounting surfaces.

8. To install, place an $1/8$ in. bead of RTV sealant around the sealing rail of the cover (or use a new gasket) and reverse the removal procedures. Torque the rocker arm cover-to-cylinder head bolts/studs to 72 inch lbs.

4.3L Engine

RIGHT SIDE

1. Remove the negative battery cable.
2. Remove the air cleaner, PCV valve and heater pipe.
3. Remove the emissions relays with their bracket and lay them aside.
4. Remove the wiring harness and lay it aside.
5. Remove the spark plug wires and move the dipstick tube aside.
6. Remove the rocker arm cover bolts and cover.

NOTE: *If the cover will not lift, use a rubber mallet to bump it loose from the cylinder head or use a small pry bar to lift the cover.*

7. Using a putty knife, clean the gasket mounting surfaces.

8. To install, place an $1/8$ in. bead of RTV sealant around the sealing rail of the cover (or use a new gasket) and reverse the removal procedures. Torque the rocker arm cover-to-cylinder head bolts/studs to 90 inch lbs.

LEFT SIDE

1. Remove the negative battery cable.
2. Remove the air cleaner, crankcase venti-

Rocker arm cover removal — 4.3L engine

lation pipe and heater pipe.

3. Remove the fuel pipes at the throttle body and move them aside.
4. Remove the generator rear bracket.
5. Remove the spark plug wires and the power brake vacuum line.
6. Remove the rocker arm cover bolts and cover.

NOTE: *If the cover will not lift, use a rubber mallet to bump it loose from the cylinder head or use a small pry bar to lift the cover.*

7. Using a putty knife, clean the gasket mounting surfaces.

8. To install, place an $1/8$ in. bead of RTV sealant around the sealing rail of the cover (or use a new gasket) and reverse the removal procedures. Torque the rocker arm cover-to-cylinder head bolts/studs to 90 inch lbs.

Rocker Arms and Push Rods

REMOVAL AND INSTALLATION

1.9L Engine

1. Remove the rocker arm cover.
2. Starting with the outer rocker arm shaft bracket, loosen the bracket nuts a little at a time (in sequence), then remove the nuts.
3. To disassemble the rocker arm shaft assembly, remove the spring from the rocker arm shaft, then the rocker arm brackets and arms.
4. Inspect the rocker arm shafts for runout. Runout should not exceed 0.0079 in.
5. Measure the rocker arm to shaft clearance. Clearance should not exceed 0.0078 in.
6. Check the face of the rocker arms for wear and/or damage, replace the rocker arms and/or shafts if not within specification.

7. Using engine oil, lubricate all of the moving parts.

8. Assemble the rocker arm shaft brackets and rocker arms to the shaft so that the cylinder number (on the upper face of the bracket) is pointed to the front of the engine.

9. Align the mark on the No. 1 rocker arm shaft bracket with the mark on the intake and exhaust valve side rocker arm shaft.

10. Check the amount of projection of the rocker arm shaft. The intake side should be longer when the holes in the shaft are aligned with the holes in the bracket.

11. Place the springs in position between the shaft bracket and rocker arm.

12. Check that the punch mark is turned upward, and install the shaft bracket assembly onto the head studs. Align the mark on the camshaft with the mark on the No. 1 rocker arm shaft bracket.

13. Tighten the bracket studs to 16 ft. lbs. and adjust the valves.

NOTE: *The valves are adjusted with the engine Cold.*

14. Using a wrench on the damper pulley bolt or a remote starter button, turn the engine's crankshaft until the No. 1 piston is at TDC of the compression stroke.

NOTE: *Crank the engine until the mark on the torsional damper lines up with the 0 in. mark on the timing tab. To determine if the No. 1 cylinder is on the compression stroke, place your fingers on the number one valve as the mark on the damper comes near the 0 in. mark on the timing tab. If the rocker arms are not moving, the engine is in the number one firing position. If the rocker arms are moving, the engine is in the number four firing position. Turn the engine over one revolution. Remove the distributor cap and ensure that the rotor is pointing to the No. 1 position on the cap.*

15. With the No. 1 piston at TDC of the compression stroke, use a 0.006 in. (0.152mm) feeler gauge, to set intake valves of cylinders No. 1 & 2. Using a 0.010 in. (0.254mm) feeler gauge, set the exhaust valves of cylinders No. 1 & 3. 16. Rotate the engine one complete revolution, so that cylinder No. 4 is on the TDC of its compression stroke and the timing marks are aligned.

17. With cylinder No. 4 on the TDC of the compression stroke, use a 0.006 in. (0.152mm) feeler gauge, to set intake valves of cylinders No. 3 & 18. Using a 0.010 in. (0.254mm) feeler gauge, set the exhaust valves of cylinders No. 2 & 4.

NOTE: *When adjusting the valve clearance, loosen the locknut with an open-end wrench, then turn the adjuster screw with a screw-driver and retighten the locknut. The proper thickness feeler gauge should pass between the camshaft and the rocker with a slight drag when the clearance is correct.*

2.0L Engine

1. Remove the rocker arm cover.

2. Remove the rocker arm nuts, the ball washers and the rocker arms off the studs, then lift out the push rods.

NOTE: *Always keep the rocker arm assemblies together and install them on the same stud.*

3. Coat the bearing surfaces of the rocker arms and the rocker arm ball washers with Molykote® or its equivalent.

4. Install the push rods making sure that they seat properly in the lifter.

5. Install the rocker arms, the ball washers and the nuts. Tighten the rocker arm nuts until all lash is eliminated.

6. Adjust the valves when the lifter is on the base circle of a camshaft lobe:

a. Crank the engine until the mark on the crankshaft pulley lines up with the 0° mark on the timing tab. Make sure that the engine is in the No. 1 firing position. Place your fingers on the No. 1 rocker arms as the mark on the crank pulley comes near the 0° mark.

NOTE: *If the valves are not moving, the engine is in the No. 1 firing position. If the valves move, the engine is in the No. 4 firing position; rotate the engine one complete revolution and it will be in the No. 1 position.*

b. When the engine is on the No. 1 firing position, adjust the following valves:

- Exhaust – 1, 3
- Intake – 1, 2

c. Back the adjusting nut out until lash can be felt at the push rod, then turn the nut until all lash is removed (this can be determined by rotating the push rod while turning the adjusting nut). When all lash has been

Rocker shaft removal/installation – 1.9L engine

removed, turn the nut in 1½ additional turns, this will center the lifter plunger.

d. Crank the engine one complete revolution until the timing tab (0° mark) and the crankshaft pulley mark are again in alignment. Now the engine is in the No. 4 firing position. Adjust the following valves:

- Exhaust – 2, 4
- Intake – 3, 4

7. Install the rocker arm cover, start the engine and check the timing and the idle speed.

2.2L Diesel Engine

1. Remove the rocker cover.
2. Remove the rocker arm bracket-to-cylinder head bolts in sequence, commencing with the outer ones.
3. Remove the rocker arm, the bracket and shaft assembly.
4. Remove the snapring, the rocker arms, the springs and the brackets.

NOTE: *Always keep the rocker arm assemblies together and install them on the same stud.*

5. Inspect the rocker arm shafts for runnout. Runnout should not exceed 0.0079 in..
6. Measure the rocker arm to shaft clearance. Clearance should not exceed 0.0078 in..
7. Check the face of the rocker arms for wear and/or damage, replace the rocker arms and/or shafts if not within specification.
8. Using engine oil, lubricate all of the moving parts.
9. To install, position the brackets with the "F" marks facing the front of the engine. Working from the center outward, torque the bracket-to-cylinder head bolts to 9–17 ft. lbs. Adjust the valves.

ROCKER ARM COVER

BALL

ROCKER ARM

PUSH ROD

PUSH ROD RETAINER

ROCKER ARM STUD

Rocker arm removal/installation — 2.0L engine

NOTE: *The valves are adjusted with the engine Cold.*

10. Using a wrench on the damper pulley bolt or a remote starter button, turn the crankshaft until the No. 1 piston is at TDC of the compression stroke.

NOTE: *Crank the engine until the mark on the torsional damper lines up with the 0 in. mark on the timing tab. To determine if the No. 1 cylinder is on the compression stroke, place your fingers on the number one valve as the mark on the damper comes near the 0 in. mark on the timing tab. If the rocker arms are not moving, the engine is in the number one firing position. If the rocker arms are moving, the engine is in the number four firing position. Turn the engine over one revolution. Remove the distributor cap and ensure that the rotor is pointing to the No. 1 position on the cap.*

11. With the No. 1 piston at TDC of the compression stroke, use a 0.016 in. (0.40mm) feeler gauge, to set the intake valves of cylinders No. 1, 2 & 3, then set the exhaust valve of cylinder No. 1. 12. Rotate the engine one complete revolution, so that cylinder No. 4 is on the TDC of its compression stroke and the timing marks are aligned.

13. With cylinder No. 4 on the TDC of the compression stroke, use a 0.016 in. (0.40mm) feeler gauge, to set the intake valve of cylinder No. 4, then the exhaust valves of cylinders No. 2, 3 & 4.

NOTE: *When adjusting the valve clearance, loosen the locknut with an open-end wrench, then turn the adjuster screw with a screwdriver and retighten the locknut. The proper thickness feeler gauge should pass between the camshaft and the rocker with a slight drag when the clearance is correct.*

2.5L Engine

1. Remove the rocker arm cover.
2. Using a socket wrench, remove the rocker arm bolts, the ball washer and the rocker arm.

ROCKER ARM

SNAP RING

ADJUSTING SCREW

SPRING

BRACKET

Rocker shaft assembly — 2.2L engine

10. Rocker arm bolt
11. Ball
12. Rocker arm
13. Pushrod
14. Pushrod guide

Rocker arm removal/installation — 2.5L engine

NOTE: *If only the pushrod is to be removed, back off the rocker arm bolt, swing the rocker arm aside and remove the pushrod. When removing more than one assembly, at the same time, be sure to keep them in order for reassembly purposes.*

3. Inspect the rocker arms and ball washers for scoring and/or other damage, replace them (if necessary).

NOTE: *If replacing worn components with new ones, be sure to coat the new parts with Molykote® before installation.*

4. To install, reverse the removal procedures. With the hydraulic lifter on the base circle of the camshaft, torque the rocker arm-to-cylinder head bolts to 22 ft. lbs.; DO NOT overtighten.

NOTE: *Valve lash is NOT adjustable on the 2.5L engine.*

2.8L Engine

1. Remove the rocker arm cover.
2. Remove the rocker arm nut, the rocker arm and the ball washer.

NOTE: *If only the push rod is to be removed, loosen the rocker arm nut, swing the rocker arm to the side and remove the pushrod.*

3. Inspect and replace components if worn or damaged.

4. Before installation, coat all of the working parts with Molykote®.

5. To adjust the valves, rotate the crankshaft until the mark on the crankshaft pulley aligns with the "0" mark on the timing plate. Make sure that the No. 1 cylinder is positioned on the compression stroke.

NOTE: *Crank the engine until the mark on the torsional damper lines up with the 0 in. mark on the timing tab. To determine if the*

No. 1 cylinder is on the compression stroke, place your fingers on the number one valve as the mark on the damper comes near the 0 in. mark on the timing tab. If the rocker arms are not moving, the engine is in the number one firing position. If the rocker arms are moving, the engine is in the number four firing position. Turn the engine over one revolution. Remove the distributor cap and ensure that the rotor is pointing to the No. 1 position on the cap.

6. Adjust the intake valves of cylinders No. 1, 5 & 6 and the exhaust valves of cylinders No. 1, 2 & 3.

7. To adjust the valves, back-out the adjusting nut until lash can be felt at the push rod, then turn the nut until all of the lash is removed.

NOTE: *To determine is all of the lash is removed, turn the push rod with your fingers until the movement is removed.*

8. When all of the lash has been removed, turn the adjusting an additional 1½ turns; this will center the lifter plunger.

9. Rotate the crankshaft one complete revolution and realign the timing marks; the engine is now positioned on the No. 4 firing position.

10. Adjust the intake valves of cylinders No. 2, 3 & 4 and the exhaust valves of cylinders No. 4, 5 & 6. 11. Install the rocker arm cover.

4.3L Engine

1. Remove the rocker arm cover.
2. Remove the rocker arm nut, the rocker arm and the ball washer.

NOTE: *If only the push rod is to be removed, loosen the rocker arm nut, swing the rocker arm to the side and remove the pushrod.*

3. Inspect and replace components if worn or damaged.

4. Before installation, coat all of the working parts with Molykote®.

5. To adjust the valves, rotate the crankshaft until the mark on the crankshaft pulley aligns with the "0" mark on the timing plate. Make sure that the No. 1 cylinder is positioned on the compression stroke.

NOTE: *Crank the engine until the mark on the torsional damper lines up with the 0 in. mark on the timing tab. To determine if the No. 1 cylinder is on the compression stroke, place your fingers on the number one valve as the mark on the damper comes near the 0 in. mark on the timing tab. If the rocker arms are not moving, the engine is in the number one firing position. If the rocker arms are moving, the engine is in the number four firing position. Turn the engine over one revolution. Remove the distributor cap and ensure that the rotor is pointing to the No. 1 position on the cap.*

6. Adjust the exhaust valves of cylinders No. 1, 5 & 6 and the intake valves of cylinders No. 1, 2 & 3.

7. To adjust the valves, back-out the adjusting nut until lash can be felt at the push rod, then turn the nut until all of the lash is removed.

NOTE: *To determine is all of the lash is removed, turn the push rod with your fingers until the movement is removed.*

8. When all of the lash has been removed, turn the adjusting an additional $1^1/_2$ turns; this will center the lifter plunger.

9. Rotate the crankshaft one complete revolution and realign the timing marks; the engine is now positioned on the No. 4 firing position.

10. Adjust the exhaust valves of cylinders No. 2, 3 & 4 and the intake valves of cylinders No. 4, 5 & 6. 11. Install the rocker arm cover.

Thermostat

DIAGNOSIS

Make an operational check of the thermostat by hanging the it on a hook in a hook in a pot of warm water. Insert a thermometer into the water and heat the water to the thermostat opening temperature (stamped on the top of the thermostat). With the temperature within 10° of the opening temperature, the thermostat should open. If not, replace the thermostat.

REMOVAL AND INSTALLATION

1.9L Engine

1. Drain the cooling system to a level below the thermostat.

CAUTION: *When draining the coolant, keep in mind that cats and dogs are attracted by the ethylene glycol antifreeze, and are quite likely to drink any that is left in an uncovered container or in puddles on the ground. This will prove fatal in sufficient quantity. Always drain the coolant into a sealable container. Coolant should be reused unless it is contaminated or several years old.*

2. Disconnect the PCV hose, the ECS hose, the AIR hose and the TCA hose.

3. Remove the air cleaner-to-carburetor bolts and loosen the clamp bolts, then lift the air cleaner and disconnect the TCA hose from the thermosenser (on the intake manifold). Remove the hoses from the air cleaner-to-carburetor slow actuator and the air cleaner-to-vacuum control (California), then remove the air cleaner assembly.

4. Remove the outlet pipe-to-inlet manifold bolts, the outlet pipe (with the radiator hose attached) and the thermostat from the engine.

5. Using a putty knife, clean the gasket mounting surfaces.

6. Installation is the reverse of removal. Use a new gasket and sealant. Torque the outlet pipe-to-intake manifold bolts to 21 ft. lbs.

7. Refill the cooling system with a 50% antifreeze solution. Start the engine and check for leaks.

2.0L Engine

The thermostat is connected to the water outlet and the thermostat housing, located at the top front-side of the engine.

1. Remove the negative battery cable.

2. Drain the cooling system to a level below the thermostat.

CAUTION: *When draining the coolant, keep in mind that cats and dogs are attracted by the ethylene glycol antifreeze, and are quite likely to drink any that is left in an uncovered container or in puddles on the ground. This will prove fatal in sufficient quantity. Always drain the coolant into a sealable container. Coolant should be reused unless it is contaminated or several years old.*

3. Remove the steel vacuum tubes.

4. Remove the water outlet-to-thermostat housing bolts, then lift the outlet from the thermostat housing and remove the thermostat.

5. Using a putty knife, clean the gasket mounting surfaces.

6. Place an $^1/_8$ in. bead of RTV sealant on the water outlet. Place the thermostat, with the power element down, in the housing and install water outlet while the RTV is still wet.

7. Torque the water outlet-to-thermostat housing bolts to 15–22 ft. lbs.

8. Refill the cooling system with a 50% antifreeze solution. Start the engine and check for leaks.

2.2L Diesel Engine

The thermostat is connected to the water outlet and the thermostat housing, located at the top front-side of the engine.

1. Remove the negative battery cable.

2. Drain the cooling system to a level below the thermostat.

CAUTION: *When draining the coolant, keep in mind that cats and dogs are attracted by the ethylene glycol antifreeze, and are quite likely to drink any that is left in an uncovered container or in puddles on the ground. This will prove fatal in sufficient quantity. Always drain the coolant into a sealable container. Coolant should be reused unless it is contaminated or several years old.*

WITH A/C

W/O A/C

Engine fan replacement — 2.2L diesel engine

20. Bolt
21. Water Outlet
22. Gasket
23. Thermostat
24. Inlet Manifold

Thermostat replacement — 4.3L engine

3. Disconnect the electrical wiring.

4. Remove the water outlet-to-thermostat housing bolts, then lift the outlet from the thermostat housing and remove the thermostat.

5. Using a putty knife, clean the gasket mounting surfaces.

6. Installation is the reverse of removal. Using a new gasket and sealant, install the water outlet while the sealant is wet. Torque the water outlet-to-thermostat housing bolts to 10–17 ft. lbs.

7. Refill the cooling system with a 50% antifreeze solution. Start the engine and check for leaks.

2.5L Engine

The thermostat is located inside the thermostat housing, which is attached to the front of the cylinder head.

1. Remove the negative battery cable.

THERMOSTAT

THERMOSTAT
HOUSING ADAPTER

Thermostat replacement — 2.0L engine

2. Drain the cooling system.

CAUTION: *When draining the coolant, keep in mind that cats and dogs are attracted by the ethylene glycol antifreeze, and are quite likely to drink any that is left in an uncovered container or in puddles on the ground. This will prove fatal in sufficient quantity. Always drain the coolant into a sealable container. Coolant should be reused unless it is contaminated or several years old.*

3. Remove the thermostat housing-to-engine bolts and the thermostat.

4. Using a putty knife, clean the gasket mounting surfaces.

5. Using RTV sealant or equivalent, place an $1/8$ in. bead of sealant in the groove of the water outlet.

6. Installation is the reverse of removal. Install the housing while the sealant is still wet.

7. Torque the thermostat housing-to-engine bolts to 21 ft. lbs.

8. Refill the cooling system, start the engine and check for leaks.

2.8L and 4.3L Engine

The thermostat is located between the water outlet and the intake manifold.

1. Remove the negative battery cable.

2. Drain the cooling system.

CAUTION: *When draining the coolant, keep in mind that cats and dogs are attracted by the ethylene glycol antifreeze, and are quite likely to drink any that is left in an uncovered container or in puddles on the ground. This will prove fatal in sufficient quantity.*

Always drain the coolant into a sealable container. Coolant should be reused unless it is contaminated or several years old.

3. Remove the thermostat housing-to-engine bolts and the thermostat.

4. Using a putty knife, clean the gasket mounting surfaces.

5. Using RTV sealant or equivalent, place an 1/8 in. bead of sealant in the groove of the water outlet.

6. Installation is the reverse of removal. Install the housing while the sealant is still wet.

7. Torque the thermostat housing-to-engine bolts to 21 ft. lbs.

8. Refill the cooling system, start the engine and check for leaks.

Intake Manifold

REMOVAL AND INSTALLATION

1.9L Engine

1. Remove the negative battery cable and the air cleaner assembly.

2. Drain the cooling system to a level below the intake manifold.

CAUTION: *When draining the coolant, keep in mind that cats and dogs are attracted by the ethylene glycol antifreeze, and are quite likely to drink any that is left in an uncovered container or in puddles on the ground. This will prove fatal in sufficient quantity. Always drain the coolant into a sealable container. Coolant should be reused unless it is contaminated or several years old.*

3. Disconnect the upper radiator hose, the vacuum hose and the heater hose (from the rear of the intake manifold).

4. Disconnect the accelerator control cable. Disconnect the automatic choke and the solenoid electrical connectors.

5. From the distributor, disconnect the vacuum advance hose and the thermo-unit wiring electrical connector.

6. Disconnect the PCV valve from the rocker arm cover, then remove the oil level gauge guide tube-to-intake manifold bolt.

7. Disconnect the EGR pipe from the EGR valve adapter, the EGR valve and the adapter. Remove the nut from under the EGR valve.

8. Disconnect the AIR vacuum hose from the 3-way connector.

9. Remove the intake manifold-to-cylinder head nuts and the intake manifold from the engine.

10. Using a putty knife, clean the gasket mounting surfaces.

11. Inspect the manifold for cracks or damage. Using a straight edge and a feeler gauge, check manifold distortion on the sealing surfaces. Have the manifold surface ground if distortion exceeds 0.0157 in.

12. Installation is the reverse of removal. Use a new gasket and sealant. tighten intake bolts to 17 ft. lbs.

2.0L Engine

1. Remove the negative battery cable.

2. Remove the air cleaner, distributor cap, distributor holddown nut and clamp.

60. Stud
61. Bolt
62. Bolt
63. Outlet
64. Gasket
65. Thermostat
66. Housing
67. Bolt
68. Gasket

72. Bolt
73. Gasket
74. Thermostat
75. Outlet

2.5 L ENGINE   2.8 L ENGINE

Thermostat replacement — 2.5L and 2.8L engine

3. Raise and support the vehicle safely. Remove the middle right hand bell housing to block bolt and remove the wiring harness.

4. Drain the cooling system.

CAUTION: *When draining the coolant, keep in mind that cats and dogs are attracted by the ethylene glycol antifreeze, and are quite likely to drink any that is left in an uncovered container or in puddles on the ground. This will prove fatal in sufficient quantity. Always drain the coolant into a sealable container. Coolant should be reused unless it is contaminated or several years old.*

5. Tag and disconnect the vacuum hose and the primary wires from the coil.

6. Remove the fuel pump-to-engine bolts and allow the pump to hang.

7. Lower the vehicle.

8. Disconnect the accelerator cable, the fuel inlet line, then the necessary vacuum hoses and wires. Remove the carburetor-to-intake manifold nuts, the carburetor and lift off the Early Fuel Evaporation (EFE) heater grid..

9. Disconnect the fuel vapor harness pipes from the cylinder head.

10. Disconnect the heater hose, bypass hose and any hoses and wires as necessary. Remove the intake manifold-to-cylinder head nuts/bolts, the intake manifold and the gasket.

11. Using a putty knife, clean the gasket mounting surfaces. Inspect the manifold for cracks, damage or distortion; if necessary, replace the intake manifold.

12. Installation is the reverse of removal. Using a new gasket and sealant, torque the intake manifold-to-cylinder head nuts/bolts to 25 ft. lbs.

13. Refill the cooling system. Adjust the drive belts. Check and/or adjust the engine timing and idle speed.

2.2L Diesel Engine

1. Remove the negative battery cable.
2. Remove the air cleaner.
3. Disconnect the heater pipe bracket, the PCV valve hose, the necessary wires and clips from the intake manifold.
4. Remove the intake manifold-to-cylinder head bolts and the intake manifold.

NOTE: *In order to replace the intake manifold gasket, it is necessary to remove the exhaust manifold.*

5. Using a putty knife, clean the gasket mounting surfaces.
6. Inspect the manifold for cracks, damage or distortion; if necessary, replace the intake manifold.
7. Using a new gasket, install the intake manifold onto the cylinder head. Torque the

Intake manifold removal/installation — 2.0L engine

intake manifold-to-cylinder head nuts/bolts to 10–17 ft. lbs. starting from the center and working outward.

8. The remainder of the installation procedure is the reverse of removal.

2.5L Engine

The intake manifold is located on the right-side of the cylinder head.

1. Remove the negative battery cable.
2. Drain the cooling system.

CAUTION: *When draining the coolant, keep in mind that cats and dogs are attracted by the ethylene glycol antifreeze, and are quite likely to drink any that is left in an uncovered container or in puddles on the ground. This will prove fatal in sufficient quantity. Always drain the coolant into a sealable container. Coolant should be reused unless it is contaminated or several years old.*

3. Remove the air cleaner assembly. Label and disconnect the wiring harnesses and connectors at the intake manifold.

4. Remove the accelerator, TVS, and cruise control cables and brackets.

5. Remove the EGR vacuum line.

6. Remove the emission sensor bracket at the manifold.

Intake manifold removal/installation — 2.2L engine

CAUTION: *Relieve the fuel system pressure before disconnecting any fuel line connection. Refer to Chapter 5 for the appropriate procedure.*

7. Remove the fuel lines, vacuum lines and wiring from the TBI unit.

8. Remove the water pump bypass hose at the intake manifold.

9. Remove the alternator rear bracket.

10. Remove the vacuum hoses and pipes from the intake manifold and the vacuum hold down at the thermostat and manifold.

11. Remove the coil wires.

12. Remove the intake manifold bolts and the manifold.

13. Using a putty knife, clean the gasket mounting surfaces.

14. Installation is the reverse of removal. Install a new gasket and torque the intake manifold-to-engine bolts to 25–37 ft. lbs. using the sequence in the illustration.

15. Refill the cooling system. Start the engine and check for leaks.

2.8L Engine

1. Drain the cooling system.

CAUTION: *When draining the coolant, keep in mind that cats and dogs are attracted by the ethylene glycol antifreeze, and are quite likely to drink any that is left in an uncovered container or in puddles on the ground. This will prove fatal in sufficient quantity. Always drain the coolant into a sealable container. Coolant should be reused unless it is contaminated or several years old.*

2. Remove the negative battery cable.

CAUTION: *Relieve the fuel system pressure before disconnecting any fuel line connection.*

Refer to Chapter 5 for the appropriate procedure.

3. Remove the air cleaner. Remove the electrical connectors, the vacuum hoses, the fuel lines and the accelerator cables from the carburetor or TBI unit.

4. If equipped with an AIR management system, remove the hose and the mounting bracket.

5. Label and disconnect the spark plug wires from the spark plugs and the electrical connectors from the ignition coil. Disconnect the coolant switch electrical connectors on the intake manifold.

6. Remove the distributor cap (with the wires connected). Mark the position of the rotor-to-distributor body and the distributor body-to-engine relationships, then remove the distributor from the engine.

NOTE: *DO NOT crank the engine with the distributor removed.*

7. Remove the EGR vacuum line and the evaporative emission hoses. Remove the pipe brackets from the rocker arm covers.

8. Remove the heater and upper radiator hoses from the intake manifold.

9. If equipped, remove the power brake vacuum hoses from the intake manifold.

10. Remove the rocker arm covers.

11. Remove the intake manifold-to-engine nuts and bolts, then the intake manifold from the engine.

11. Using a putty knife, clean the gasket mounting surfaces. Since the manifold is made from aluminum, be sure to inspect it for warpage and/or cracks; if necessary, replace it.

12. Installation is the reverse of removal. Use new intake manifold gaskets and a $\frac{3}{16}$ in.

A. Forward
B. 34 N·m (25 lb. ft.)
C. 50 N·m (37 lb. ft.)
D. 38 N·m (28 lb. ft.)
E. Apply sealant to bolt

Intake manifold removal/installation — 2.5L engine

INITIAL TIGHTENING SEQUENCE

FINAL TIGHTENING SEQUENCE

A. Front Of Engine

Intake manifold removal/installation with torque sequence — 2.8L engine

(5mm) bead of RTV sealant (applied to the front and rear of the engine block).

NOTE: *The gaskets are marked "Right-Side" and "Left-Side"; DO NOT interchange them. The gaskets will have to be cut slightly to fit past the center pushrods; DO NOT cut any more material than necessary. Hold the gaskets in place by extending the ridge bead of sealer ¹/₄ in. onto the gasket ends.*

13. Torque the intake manifold-to-cylinder head nuts and bolts (in sequence) to 23 ft. lbs.

14. Refill the cooling system with a 50% so-

Intake manifold torque sequence — 4.3L engine

lution of ethylene glycol anti-freeze.

15. Adjust the ignition timing, the idle speed (if possible) and check the coolant level after the engine has warmed up.

4.3L Engine

1. Remove the negative battery cable.
2. Drain the cooling system.

CAUTION: *When draining the coolant, keep in mind that cats and dogs are attracted by the ethylene glycol antifreeze, and are quite likely to drink any that is left in an uncovered container or in puddles on the ground. This will prove fatal in sufficient quantity. Always drain the coolant into a sealable con-*

VIEW A

VIEW B

C. Port Blocking Plate
D. RTV Sealant

Intake manifold removal/installation — 4.3L engine

tainer. Coolant should be reused unless it is contaminated or several years old.

3. Remove the air cleaner and heat stove tube.

4. Remove the two braces at the rear of the fan belt tensioner.

5. Remove the upper radiator hose.

6. Remove the emissions relays, wiring harness and ground cable.

CAUTION: *Relieve the fuel system pressure before disconnecting any fuel line connection. Refer to Chapter 5 for the appropriate procedure.*

7. Remove the power brake vacuum pipe, heater hose pipe and fuel lines to the TBI unit.

8. Remove the ignition coil, and electrical connectors at the sensors on the manifold.

9. Remove the distributor cap (with the wires connected). Mark the position of the rotor-to-distributor body and the distributor body-to-engine relationships, then remove the distributor from the engine.

NOTE: *DO NOT crank the engine with the distributor removed.*

10. Remove the EGR hose. Remove the throttle, TVS and cruise control cables.

11. Remove the intake manifold bolts, manifold and gaskets.

12. Using a putty knife, clean the gasket mounting surfaces. Since the manifold is made from aluminum, be sure to inspect it for warpage and/or cracks; if necessary, replace it.

13. Installation is the reverse of removal. Use new intake manifold gaskets and a $\frac{3}{16}$ in. (5mm) bead of RTV sealant (applied to the front and rear of the engine block).

14. Tighten the manifold bolts to 35 ft. lbs. using the sequence shown in the illustration.

Exhaust Manifold

REMOVAL AND INSTALLATION

1.9L Engine

1. Remove the negative battery cable, air cleaner assembly and hot air hose.

2. Raise and support the vehicle safely.

3. Disconnect the exhaust pipe and the EGR pipe from the exhaust manifold, then lower the vehicle.

4. If equipped with an A/C compressor or a P/S pump, remove the drive belt(s), the compressor/pump (move them aside) and the mounting brackets.

5. Remove the exhaust manifold shield and the heat stove (if equipped).

6. Remove the exhaust manifold-to-cylinder head nuts and the manifold from the engine.

7. Using a putty knife, clean the gasket

SHIELD

Exhaust manifold removal/installation — 2.0L engine

mounting surfaces. Inspect the exhaust manifold for distortion, cracks or damage; replace it, if necessary.

8. Installation is the reverse of removal. Use a new gasket and torque the exhaust manifold-to-cylinder head nuts to 16 ft. lbs., in sequence, starting with the center and working outwards.

2.0L Engine

1. Remove the negative battery cable and air cleaner assembly.

2. Raise and support the vehicle safely.

3. Disconnect the exhaust pipe from the exhaust manifold.

4. If equipped with an air injection reaction (AIR) system, remove the AIR hose, the AIR pipe bracket bolt and the dipstick tube bracket.

5. Remove the fuel vapor canister harness (steel) pipes.

6. Remove the exhaust manifold-to-cylinder head bolts and the manifold from the engine.

7. Using a putty knife, clean the gasket mounting surfaces. Inspect the exhaust manifold for distortion, cracks or damage; replace if necessary.

8. Installation is the reverse of removal. Using a new gasket, torque the exhaust manifold-to-cylinder head bolts to 26 ft. lbs., in sequence, starting with the center and working outwards.

2.2L Diesel Engine

1. Remove the negative battery cable.

2. Remove the air cleaner and the PCV valve.

3. Disconnect the exhaust pipe from the exhaust manifold at the flange.

4. Remove the exhaust manifold-to-cylinder head nuts and the exhaust manifold from the engine.

NOTE: *In order to replace the intake manifold gasket, it is necessary to remove the exhaust manifold.*

5. Using a putty knife, clean the gasket mounting surfaces.

6. Inspect the manifold for cracks, damage or distortion; if necessary, replace the intake manifold.

7. Using a new gasket, install the intake manifold onto the cylinder head. Torque the intake manifold-to-cylinder head nuts/bolts to 10–17 ft. lbs. starting from the center and working outward.

8. The remainder of the installation procedure is the reverse of removal.

2.5L Engine

The exhaust manifold is located on the left-side of the engine.

1. Remove the negative battery cable.

2. Remove the air cleaner and heat stove pipe.

3. Remove the A/C compressor (if equipped), drive belt, and the rear adjusting bracket (if used). Lay the compressor aside in the engine compartment.

4. Remove the dipstick tube and bracket.

5. Disconnect the exhaust pipe from the exhaust manifold.

6. Disconnect the electrical connector from the oxygen sensor.

7. Remove the exhaust manifold-to-engine bolts/washers and the manifold from the engine.

8. Using a putty knife, clean the gasket mounting surfaces.

9. Installation is the reverse of removal. Using a new gasket, torque the exhaust manifold-to-engine bolts to 36 ft. lbs. (center bolts) and 32 ft. lbs. (outer bolts).

2.8L Engine

LEFT-SIDE

1. Remove the negative battery cable.

2. Raise and support the vehicle safely.

3. Disconnect the exhaust pipe from the exhaust manifold.

4. Remove the rear exhaust manifold-to-cylinder head bolts, then lower the vehicle.

5. Disconnect the air management hoses and wiring.

6. If equipped, remove the P/S pump and bracket; DO NOT disconnect the power steering hoses.

7. Remove the front exhaust manifold-to-cylinder head bolts.

8. Using a putty knife, clean the gasket mounting surfaces. Inspect the exhaust manifold for distortion, cracks or damage; replace if necessary.

9. Installation is the reverse of removal. Using a new gasket, torque the exhaust manifold-to-cylinder head bolts to 25 ft. lbs., in a circular pattern, working from the center to the outer ends.

RIGHT-SIDE

1. Remove the negative battery cable.

2. Raise and support the vehicle safely.

3. Disconnect the exhaust pipe from the exhaust manifold.

4. Disconnect the air management hoses and wiring, then lower the vehicle.

5. Remove the exhaust manifold-to-cylinder head bolts.

"A" Group Bolts: (36 ft. lbs.)
"B" Group Bolts: (32 ft. lbs.)

Exhaust manifold removal/installation — 2.5L engine

6. Using a putty knife, clean the gasket mounting surfaces. Inspect the exhaust manifold for distortion, cracks or damage; replace if necessary.

7. Installation is the reverse of removal. Using a new gasket, torque the exhaust manifold-to-cylinder head bolts to 25 ft. lbs., in a circular pattern, working from the center to the outer ends.

A/C Compressor

REMOVAL AND INSTALLATION

4-Cyl Engines

1. Have the system discharged by a professional shop.

2. Remove the negative battery cable.

3. Disconnect the electrical connectors from the compressor.

4. At the rear of the compressor, remove the bracket from the exhaust manifold. If equipped, remove the power steering pump bracket.

Compressor replacement — 1.9L engine

1. Compressor
2. Compressor Mounting Bolts

Compressor replacement — 2.5L engine

Exhaust manifold removal/installation — 2.8L engine

5. Remove the compressor-to-front bracket bolts, the drive belt and the compressor from the vehicle.

6. Installation is the reverse of removal. Torque the compressor-to-front bracket bolts to 68 ft. lbs., the manifold-to-rear compressor bolt to 47 ft. lbs. and the engine brace-to-compressor nut to 37 ft. lbs.

7. Install the accessory drive belts and adjust the tension. Refer to Chapter 1 for the appropriate procedure.

8. Recharge the A/C system.

V6 Engine

1. Have the system discharged by a professional shop.

2. Remove the negative battery cable.

3. Disconnect the electrical connectors from the compressor.

4. Remove the intake manifold-to-compressor support bracket.

NOTE: *If the engine is equipped with a carburetor, disconnect the vacuum brake from the carburetor for access.*

5. Remove the drive belt idler bracket-to-intake manifold bolts, the drive belt and the bracket from the vehicle.

6. Remove the compressor-to-mounting bracket bolts and the compressor from the vehicle.

7. Installation is the reverse of removal. Torque the compressor-to-front bracket bolts to 68 ft. lbs. and the manifold-to-compressor bolt to 47 ft. lbs.

8. Install the accessory drive belts and adjust the tension. Refer to Chapter 1 for the appropriate procedure.

9. Recharge the A/C system.

Radiator

DIAGNOSIS

Test for restrictions in the radiator by warming the engine to operating temperature and

1. Compressor
2. Compressor Mounting Bolts

Compressor replacement — 2.8L engine

then turning the engine off. Feel the radiator, it should be hot along the left side and warm along the right side. The temperature should rise evenly from right to left. If cold spots are felt, have the radiator tested for clogged sections.

REMOVAL AND INSTALLATION

1. Remove the negative battery cable.
2. Drain the cooling system.
CAUTION: *When draining the coolant, keep in mind that cats and dogs are attracted by the ethylene glycol antifreeze, and are quite likely to drink any that is left in an uncovered container or in puddles on the ground. This will prove fatal in sufficient quantity. Always drain the coolant into a sealable container. Coolant should be reused unless it is contaminated or several years old.*
3. Remove the upper and lower radiator hoses, then remove the overflow hose.
4. If equipped with an A/T, disconnect and plug the oil cooler lines at the radiator.
5. If equipped with an engine oil cooler, dis-

1. Compressor
2. Bolt
105. Manifold

Compressor replacement — 4.3L engine

Radiator and shroud assembly

connect and plug the oil cooler lines at the radiator.
6. If equipped with A/C, remove the A/C hose retaining clip.
7. Remove the upper fan shroud, the radiator to chassis screws and the radiator.
8. Installation is the reverse of removal. Refill the cooling system with a 50% solution of anti-freeze. Start the engine, allow it to reach normal operating temperatures and check for leaks.

Engine Oil Cooler

REMOVAL AND INSTALLATION

1. Remove the negative battery cable.
2. Drain the cooling system.
CAUTION: *When draining the coolant, keep in mind that cats and dogs are attracted by the ethylene glycol antifreeze, and are quite likely to drink any that is left in an uncovered container or in puddles on the ground. This will prove fatal in sufficient quantity. Always drain the coolant into a sealable container. Coolant should be reused unless it is contaminated or several years old.*
3. Remove the oil filter.
4. Disconnect the coolant hoses from the oil cooler.
5. Remove oil cooler nut and the cooler from the vehicle.
6. Installation is the reverse of removal. Refill the cooling system with a 50% solution of anti-freeze. Start the engine, allow it to reach normal operating temperatures and check for leaks.

Air Conditioning Condenser

REMOVAL AND INSTALLATION

1. Have the system discharged by a professional shop.
2. Drain the cooling system.
3. Remove the upper and lower radiator hoses.

77. Fitting
78. Seal
79. Gasket
81. Power Steering Pump
84. Bolt
85. Clamp
86. Bracket
87. Radiator
89. Engine
91. Oil Filter
92. Oil Cooler Lines
93. Seals

VIEW A

Engine oil cooler — 4WD

4. Disconnect all coolant lines leading to the radiator.

5. Remove the radiator.

6. Remove the shields at both sides of the radiator support.

7. Remove the condenser retainers and lines. Remove the condenser.

8. Installation is the reverse of removal. Recharge the A/C system and fill the cooling system.

Clutch Fan

DIAGNOSIS

Start the engine and listen for fan noise. Fan noise is usually evident during the first few minutes after start-up and when the clutch is engaged for maximum cooling (during idle). If fan noise is excessive, the fan cannot be rotated by hand or there is a rough grating feel as the fan is turned, replace the clutch.

79. Gasket
80. Bracket
81. Power Steering Pump
84. Bolt
85. Clamp
86. Bracket
87. Radiator
89. Engine
91. Oil Filter
92. Oil Cooler Lines
93. Seals
94. Adapter

Engine oil cooler — 2WD

1. Belt
2. Fan
5. Bolt
6. Stud
7. Fan Clutch
8. Nut

Replacing the fan and fan clutch

2. Condenser
120. Insulator
121. Retainer
122. Bolt

Air conditioning condenser replacement

Check a loose fan assembly for wear and re-place as necessary. Under certain conditions, the fan may flex up to $1/4$ in.. This is not cause for replacement.

The fan clutch is not affected by small fluid leaks which may occur in the area around the bearing assembly. If leakage appears excessive, replace the fan clutch.

If the fan clutch free-wheels with no drag (re-volves more than five times when spun by hand), replace the clutch.

REMOVAL AND INSTALLATION

NOTE: *DO NOT use or repair a damaged fan assembly. An unbalanced fan assembly could fly apart and cause personal injury or property damage. Replace damaged assem-blies with new ones.*

1. Remove the upper radiator shroud.
2. Remove the fan attaching nuts and remove the fan and clutch assembly from the engine.
3. Remove clutch from the fan by removing the attaching nuts.
4. Installation is the reverse of removal. Tighten bolts to the following torque:
- 2.5L and 2.8L clutch-to-fan bolts: 9 ft. lbs.
- 4.3L clutch-to-fan bolts: 25 ft. lbs.
- All others clutch-to-fan bolts: 11–16 ft. lbs.
- Fan-to-pulley nuts: 27–40 ft. lbs.

Water Pump

DIAGNOSIS

Check the water pump operation by running the engine while squeezing the upper radiator hose. When the engine warms (thermostat opens) a pressure surge should be felt. Check for a plugged vent hole at the pump snout.

REMOVAL AND INSTALLATION

1.9L Engine

1. Remove the negative battery cable.
2. Raise and support the vehicle safely. Then, remove the lower fan shroud.
3. Drain the cooling system.
CAUTION: *When draining the coolant, keep in mind that cats and dogs are attracted by the ethylene glycol antifreeze, and are quite likely to drink any that is left in an uncov-ered container or in puddles on the ground. This will prove fatal in sufficient quantity. Always drain the coolant into a sealable con-tainer. Coolant should be reused unless it is contaminated or several years old.*

4. If not equipped with A/C, remove the fan-to-water pump nuts and fan from the vehicle.

5. If equipped with A/C, perform the following procedures:

a. Loosen the air pump and alternator adjusting bolts, pivot them toward the engine and remove the drive belt(s).

b. Remove the fan-to-water pump nuts and the fan (with the fan and air pump drive pulley) from the vehicle.

c. Remove the fan set plate/pulley-to-water pump bolts, then remove the set plate and the pulley.

6. Remove the coolant hoses at the water pump.

7. Remove the water pump-to-engine bolts and the water pump from the engine.

8. Using a putty knife, clean the gasket mounting surfaces.

9. Installation is the reverse of removal. Use a new gasket and sealant. tighten water pump bolts to 15–22 ft. lbs.

10. Refill the cooling system with a 50% solution of anti-freeze. Start the engine, allow it to reach normal operating temperatures and check for leaks.

2.0L Engine

1. Remove the negative battery cable.
2. Drain the cooling system.

CAUTION: *When draining the coolant, keep in mind that cats and dogs are attracted by the ethylene glycol antifreeze, and are quite likely to drink any that is left in an uncovered container or in puddles on the ground. This will prove fatal in sufficient quantity. Always drain the coolant into a sealable container. Coolant should be reused unless it is contaminated or several years old.*

3. Remove the upper fan shroud and all of the necessary drive belts.

4. Disconnect the radiator and heater hoses from the water pump.

5. Remove the water pump-to-engine bolts and the water pump from the vehicle.

6. Using a putty knife, clean the gasket mounting surfaces.

7. Installation is the reverse of removal.

Water pump replacement — 1.9L engine. 2.2L diesel engine similar

Water pump replacement — 2.0L engine

Use a new gasket and sealant. tighten water pump bolts to 15–22 ft. lbs.

8. Refill the cooling system with a 50% solution of anti-freeze. Start the engine, allow it to reach normal operating temperatures and check for leaks.

2.2L Diesel Engine

1. Remove the negative battery cable.
2. Disconnect the power steering reservoir. Remove the upper fan shroud.
3. Drain the cooling system.

CAUTION: *When draining the coolant, keep in mind that cats and dogs are attracted by the ethylene glycol antifreeze, and are quite likely to drink any that is left in an uncovered container or in puddles on the ground. This will prove fatal in sufficient quantity. Always drain the coolant into a sealable container. Coolant should be reused unless it is contaminated or several years old.*

4. Remove the drive belts, the fan and the A/C compressor (move it aside).

5. Disconnect the radiator pipe at the front cover.

6. Disconnect the radiator and heater hoses from the right-side of the water pump

7. Disconnect the PCV valve from the rocker cover. Remove the air cleaner and the heater pipe from the intake manifold.

8. Disconnect the heater hose from the left-side of the water pump, then the alternator brace.

9. Remove the water pump-to-engine bolts and the water pump from the engine.

10. Using a putty knife, clean the gasket mounting surfaces.

11. Installation is the reverse of removal. Using a new gasket install the water pump and tighten the water pump-to-engine bolts to 10–17 ft. lbs.

12. Refill the cooling system with a 50% solution of anti-freeze. Start the engine, allow it to reach normal operating temperatures and check for leaks.

2.5L Engine

1. Remove the negative battery cable.
2. Drain the cooling system.

CAUTION: *When draining the coolant, keep in mind that cats and dogs are attracted by the ethylene glycol antifreeze, and are quite likely to drink any that is left in an uncovered container or in puddles on the ground. This will prove fatal in sufficient quantity. Always drain the coolant into a sealable container. Coolant should be reused unless it is contaminated or several years old.*

3. Remove the accessory drive belt.
4. Remove the upper fan shroud. Remove the fan/clutch assembly-to-water pump bolts and the fan/clutch assembly from the water pump pulley.
5. Remove the drive belt pulley from the water pump.
6. Remove the clamps and the hoses from the water pump.
7. Remove the water pump-to-engine bolts and the water pump from the engine.
8. Using a putty knife, clean the gasket mounting surfaces.
9. Installation is the reverse of removal. Coat the bolt threads with sealant and using a new gasket, install the water pump and tighten the water pump-to-engine bolts to 22 ft. lbs.
10. Refill the cooling system with a 50% solution of anti-freeze. Start the engine, allow it to reach normal operating temperatures and check for leaks.

2.8L and 4.3L Engine

1. Remove the negative battery cable.
2. Drain the cooling system.

CAUTION: *When draining the coolant, keep in mind that cats and dogs are attracted by the ethylene glycol antifreeze, and are quite likely to drink any that is left in an uncovered container or in puddles on the ground. This will prove fatal in sufficient quantity.*

WATER PUMP

WATER INLET

Water pump replacement — 2.5L engine

Always drain the coolant into a sealable container. Coolant should be reused unless it is contaminated or several years old.

3. Remove the accessory drive belt.
4. Remove the upper fan shroud. Remove the fan/clutch assembly-to-water pump bolts and the fan/clutch assembly from the water pump pulley.
5. Remove the drive belt pulley from the water pump.
6. Remove the clamps and the hoses from the water pump.
7. Remove the water pump-to-engine bolts and the water pump from the engine.
8. Using a putty knife, clean the gasket mounting surfaces.
9. Installation is the reverse of removal. Coat the bolt threads with sealant. Place a $\frac{3}{32}$ in. (2mm) bead of sealer on the water pump mating surface and install the water pump. Tighten the water pump-to-engine bolts to 22 ft. lbs.
10. Refill the cooling system with a 50% solution of anti-freeze. Start the engine, allow it to reach normal operating temperatures and check for leaks.

41. Water Pump
42. Gasket
44. Bolt

Water pump replacement — 2.8L engine

2 mm DIAMETER BEAD OF
ANAEROBIC SEALANT
1052357
OR EQUIVALENT

Applying sealer to the V6 water pump

WATER PUMP

Water pump replacement — 4.3L engine

Cylinder Head

REMOVAL AND INSTALLATION

1.9L Engine

1. Remove the rocker arm cover.
2. Remove EGR pipe clamp bolt at the rear of the cylinder head.
3. Raise and support the vehicle safely.
4. Disconnect the exhaust pipe from the exhaust manifold, then lower the vehicle.
5. Drain the cooling system.

CAUTION: *When draining the coolant, keep in mind that cats and dogs are attracted by the ethylene glycol antifreeze, and are quite likely to drink any that is left in an uncovered container or in puddles on the ground. This will prove fatal in sufficient quantity. Always drain the coolant into a sealable container. Coolant should be reused unless it is contaminated or several years old.*

6. Disconnect the heater hoses from the intake manifold and the front of the cylinder head.
7. If equipped with an A/C compressor and/or a P/S pump, disconnect them and lay them aside.
8. Disconnect the accelerator linkage and the fuel line from the carburetor. Disconnect all necessary electrical connections, the spark plug wires and necessary vacuum lines.

9. Rotate the camshaft until the No. 4 cylinder is in the firing position. Remove the distributor cap and mark rotor-to-housing relationship, then remove the distributor.
10. Disconnect the fuel lines from the fuel pump and remove it.
11. Using two pry bars, depress the adjuster lock lever to lock the automatic adjuster shoe in its fully retracted position.
12. Remove timing sprocket-to-camshaft bolt, the sprocket and the fuel pump drive cam from the camshaft. Keep the sprocket on the chain damper and tensioner – DO NOT remove the sprocket from the chain.
13. Disconnect the AIR hose and check valve from the air manifold.
14. Remove the cylinder head-to-timing cover bolts.
15. Using the Extension Bar Wrench tool No. J-24239-01 or equivalent, remove cylinder head-to-engine bolts; remove the bolts in a progressional sequence, beginning with the outer bolts and working inward.
16. Remove the cylinder head, intake and exhaust manifold as an assembly.
17. Using a putty knife, clean the gasket mounting surfaces.

NOTE: *The gasket surfaces on both the head and block must be clean of any foreign matter*

Using two pry bars to lock the automatic adjuster into position — 1.9L engine

AUTO ADJUSTER
LOCK LEVER

FREE   LOCK

Locking the timing chain adjuster — 1.9L engine

Cylinder head bolt torque sequence — 2.0L engine

and free of nicks or heavy scratches. The cylinder bolt threads in the block and thread on the bolts must be cleaned (dirt will affect the bolt torque).

18. Installation is the reverse of removal. Place the new gasket over dowel pins with "TOP" side of gasket up.

NOTE: *Be sure to lubricate the cylinder head bolts with engine oil before installing them.*

19. Torque the cylinder head-to-engine bolts in several steps (in the proper sequence) to 61 ft. lbs. Then retighten to 72 ft. lbs.

20. Refill the cooling system. Start the engine, allow it to reach normal operating temperatures and check for leaks.

21. Check and/or adjust the engine timing and idle speed.

2.0L Engine

NOTE: *Let the vehicle sit overnight before attempting to remove the cylinder head. The engine must be cold.*

1. Remove the negative battery cable.
2. Drain the cooling system.

CAUTION: *When draining the coolant, keep in mind that cats and dogs are attracted by the ethylene glycol antifreeze, and are quite likely to drink any that is left in an uncovered container or in puddles on the ground. This will prove fatal in sufficient quantity. Always drain the coolant into a sealable container. Coolant should be reused unless it is contaminated or several years old.*

3. Remove the air cleaner. Raise and support the vehicle safely.
4. Remove the exhaust shield, then disconnect the exhaust pipe from the exhaust manifold. Lower the vehicle.
5. Disconnect the accelerator linkage, the necessary electrical wiring connectors and the vacuum lines.
6. Remove the fuel vapor canister harness (steel) pipes.
7. Remove the distributor cap, then mark the rotor-to-distributor housing and the distributor housing-to-engine.

8. Remove the rocker arm cover, the rocker arms and the push rods.
9. Remove the upper radiator hose, the heater hose, the upper fan shroud and the fan.
10. Remove the AIR management valve, the air pump and the upper AIR bracket.
11. Remove the fuel line from the fuel pump. Disconnect the wire from the rear of the cylinder head.
12. Remove the cylinder head-to-engine bolts and the cylinder head.
13. Using a putty knife, clean the gasket mounting surfaces.

NOTE: *The gasket surfaces on both the head and the block must be clean of any foreign matter and free of any nicks or heavy scratches. Cylinder bolt threads in the block and the bolt must be clean.*

14. Installation is the reverse of removal. Using a new head gasket, coat both sides of the gasket with sealing compound No. 10520026 and position the gasket on the locating pins.
15. Torque the cylinder head-to-engine bolts (in several steps) in sequence to 65–75 ft. lbs.
16. Refill the cooling system. Start the engine, allow it to reach normal operating temperatures and check for leaks.
17. Check and/or adjust the engine timing and idle speed.

2.2L Engine

NOTE: *The injection timing MUST BE reset after this procedure. See the Chapter 5 for details and special tools required.*

1. Remove the negative battery cable.
2. Drain the cooling system.

CAUTION: *When draining the coolant, keep in mind that cats and dogs are attracted by the ethylene glycol antifreeze, and are quite likely to drink any that is left in an uncovered container or in puddles on the ground. This will prove fatal in sufficient quantity. Always drain the coolant into a sealable container. Coolant should be reused unless it is contaminated or several years old.*

FRONT COVER FIXING SCREW

Cylinder head bolt torque sequence — 1.9L engine

3. Remove the rocker arm cover, the rocker arm shaft and the pushrods.

4. Remove the upper radiator hose and the heater hose from the cylinder head.

5. Disconnect the heater tube and remove the exhaust pipe from the exhaust manifold.

6. Remove the vacuum pump and the A/C compressor (if equipped, move it aside).

7. Disconnect the heater hose/bracket, the necessary electrical wiring connectors. Disconnect the PCV valve hose from the pipe and move it aside.

8. Disconnect the dipstick tube bracket and dipstick, the breather pipe and the oil jet pipe.

9. Disconnect the fuel injection lines and cover them with protective caps.

10. Remove the air conditioning bracket and disconnect the return hose.

11. Remove the cylinder head-to-engine bolts and the cylinder head from the vehicle.

12. Using a putty knife, clean the gasket mounting surfaces. Inspect the cylinder head for distortion, cracks and/or damage.

NOTE: *To install, the gasket surfaces on both the head and the block must be clean of any foreign matter and free of any nicks or heavy scratches. The cylinder bolt threads in the block and the bolt must be clean.*

13. Installation is the reverse of removal. Using a new head gasket with the "TOP" side facing upward, position the gasket on the locating pins, apply engine oil to the cylinder head bolt threads and torque the cylinder head-to-

CYLINDER HEAD BOLT
TIGHTENING SEQUENCE

Cylinder head bolt torque sequence — 2.2L engine

engine bolts (in sequence): First, to 40–47 ft. lbs. and then, to 54–61 ft. lbs. (new bolts) or 61–69 ft. lbs. (used bolts).

14. Refill the cooling system. Start the engine, allow it to reach normal operating temperatures and check for leaks.

15. Check and/or adjust the engine timing and idle speed.

2.5L Engine

NOTE: *Let the vehicle sit overnight before attempting to remove the cylinder head. The engine must be cold.*

CAUTION: *Relieve the pressure on the fuel system before disconnecting any fuel line connection. See Chapter 5 for the proper procedures.*

1. Remove the rocker arm cover.

2. Drain the cooling system.

CAUTION: *When draining the coolant, keep in mind that cats and dogs are attracted by the ethylene glycol antifreeze, and are quite likely to drink any that is left in an uncovered container or in puddles on the ground. This will prove fatal in sufficient quantity. Always drain the coolant into a sealable container. Coolant should be reused unless it is contaminated or several years old.*

3. Disconnect the accelerator, the cruise control and the TVS cables, if equipped.

4. Remove the water pump bypass and heater hoses from the intake manifold.

5. Remove the front and rear braces from the alternator, then move it aside.

6. Disconnect the A/C compressor brackets and move the compressor aside.

7. Remove the thermostat housing-to-cylinder head bolts and the housing from the engine.

8. Remove the ground cable and any necessary electrical connectors from the cylinder head. Disconnect the wires from the spark plugs and the oxygen sensor. Disconnect and remove the ignition coil from the intake manifold and the cylinder head.

9. Remove the vacuum lines and fuel hoses from the intake manifold and the TBI unit.

10. Disconnect the exhaust pipe from the exhaust manifold.

11. Remove the rocker arm nuts, the washers, the rocker arms and the pushrods from the cylinder head.

12. Remove the cylinder head-to-engine bolts and the cylinder head from the engine (with the manifolds attached). If necessary, remove the intake and the exhaust manifolds from the cylinder head.

13. Using a putty knife, clean the gasket mounting surfaces. Using a wire brush, clean

the carbon deposits from the combustion chambers.

14. Inspect the cylinder head and block for cracks, nicks, heavy scratches or other damage.

15. Installation is the reverse of removal. Using new gaskets and sealant (where necessary), torque the cylinder head bolts, in sequence, as follows:

- Torque all bolts gradually to 18 ft. lbs.
- Torque all bolts except the left front bolt (#9 in the sequence) to 26 ft. lbs. Torque number 9 to 18 ft. lbs.
- Torque all bolts an additional 1/4 turn (90°).

16. Refill the cooling system, start the engine and check for leaks.

2.8L Engine

CAUTION: *Relieve the pressure on the fuel system before disconnecting any fuel line connection. See Chapter 5 for the proper procedures.*

1. Remove the intake manifold.

2. Raise and support the vehicle safely.

3. Drain the cooling system.

CAUTION: *When draining the coolant, keep in mind that cats and dogs are attracted by the ethylene glycol antifreeze, and are quite likely to drink any that is left in an uncovered container or in puddles on the ground.*

This will prove fatal in sufficient quantity. Always drain the coolant into a sealable container. Coolant should be reused unless it is contaminated or several years old.

4. Disconnect the exhaust pipe from the exhaust manifold and remove the exhaust manifold-to-cylinder block bolts.

5. Lower the vehicle.

6. Remove the dipstick tube from the engine (left side only).

7. Remove the ground strap and the sensor connector from the cylinder head (left side only).

8. Remove the drive belt, alternator, and AIR pump with mounting bracket (right side only).

9. Loosen the rocker arm nuts, turn the rocker arms and remove the pushrods. Keep the pushrods in the same order as removed.

10. Remove the cylinder head bolts in stages and in the reverse order of the tightening sequence.

11. Remove the cylinder head; DO NOT pry on the head to loosen it.

12. Using a putty knife, clean the gasket mounting surfaces.

NOTE: *Coat the cylinder head bolts with sealer and torque to specifications in the sequence shown. Make sure the pushrods seat in the lifter seats and adjust the valves.*

MOUNTING SURFACES OF BLOCK ASM., HEAD ASM. AND BOTH SIDES OF GASKET MUST BE FREE OF OIL AND FOREIGN MATERIAL.

FRONT

LOCATING PINS

Cylinder head bolt torque sequence — 2.5L engine

13. Installation is the reverse of removal. Using a new gasket (position it on the dowel pins, with the words "This Side Up" facing upwards) and GM sealant No. 1052080 or equivalent, torque the cylinder head-to-engine bolts in sequence as follows:

- Torque all bolts to 40 ft. lbs.
- Torque all bolts an additional ¼ turn (90°).

14. Adjust the valves.

15. Refill the cooling system. Start the engine, allow it to reach normal operating temperatures and check for leaks.

16. Check and/or adjust the ignition timing and idle speed (if possible).

4.3L Engine

CAUTION: *Relieve the pressure on the fuel system before disconnecting any fuel line connection. See Chapter 5 for the proper procedures.*

1. Remove the negative battery cable.
2. Remove the rocker arm cover.
3. Drain the cooling system.

CAUTION: *When draining the coolant, keep in mind that cats and dogs are attracted by the ethylene glycol antifreeze, and are quite likely to drink any that is left in an uncovered container or in puddles on the ground. This will prove fatal in sufficient quantity. Always drain the coolant into a sealable container. Coolant should be reused unless it is contaminated or several years old.*

4. Remove the intake and exhaust manifolds.

5. Remove the following from the right cylinder head:

- Electrical connector at the sensor.
- Dipstick tube bracket.
- Air conditioning compressor (lay it aside).
- Air conditioning bracket and belt tensioner.

6. Remove the following from the left cylinder head:

- Alternator (lay it aside).
- Left side engine accessory bracket with power steering pump (lay it aside).

Cylinder head bolt torque sequence — 4.3L engine

Cylinder head bolt torque sequence — 2.8L engine

7. Remove the spark plug and wires.

8. Remove the rocker arms and pushrods.

9. Remove the cylinder head bolts by loosening them in sequence. Remove the cylinder head.

10. Using a putty knife, clean the gasket mounting surfaces.

NOTE: *If a steel head gasket is used, coat both sides with sealer. If a composition head gasket is used, DO NOT use sealer.*

11. Installation is the reverse of removal. Using a new gasket, position it on the dowel pins, with the words "This Side Up" facing upwards. Torque the cylinder head-to-engine bolts in sequence to 65 ft. lbs. Use three steps when torquing.

CLEANING AND INSPECTION

1. Remove the valve assemblies from the cylinder head. See the appropriate procedures in this Chapter.

2. Using a small wire power brush, clean the carbon from the combustion chambers and the valve ports.

3. Inspect the cylinder head for cracks in the exhaust ports, combustion chambers or external cracks to the water chamber.

4. Thoroughly clean the valve guides using a suitable wire bore brush.

NOTE: *Excessive valve stem-to-bore clearance will cause excessive oil consumption and may cause valve breakage. Insufficient clearance will result in noisy and sticky functioning of the valve and disturb engine smoothness.*

5. Measure the valve stem clearance as follows:

a. Clamp a dial indicator on the cylinder head.

b. Locate the indicator so that movement of the valve stem from side to side (horizontal to the head) will cause a direct movement of the indicator stem. The indicator stem

Remove the carbon from the cylinder head with a wire brush on an electric drill

Measuring cylinder head warpage

must contact the side of the valve stem just above the valve guide.

c. Prop the valve head about $\frac{1}{16}$ in. (1.6mm) off the valve seat.

d. Move the stem of the valve from side to side using light pressure to obtain a clearance reading. If the clearance exceeds specifications, it will be necessary to ream (for oversize valves) or knurl (raise the bore for original valves) the valve guides.

6. Inspect the rocker arm studs for wear or damage.

7. Install a dial micrometer into the valve guide and check the valve seat for concentricity.

Checking valve seat concentricity with a run-out gauge

RESURFACING

1. Using a straightedge, check the cylinder head for warpage.

2. If warpage exceeds 0.003 in. in a 6 in. span, or 0.006 in. over the total length, the cylinder head must be resurfaced. Resurfacing can be performed at most machine shops.

NOTE: *When resurfacing the cylinder head(s), the intake manifold mounting position is altered and must be corrected by machining a proportionate amount from the intake manifold flange.*

Valves and Valve Springs

REMOVAL AND INSTALLATION

Cylinder Head Removed

NOTE: *The following procedures requires the use of a Valve Spring Compressor tool.*

1. Remove the cylinder head.

2. Remove the rocker arm assemblies or rocker shaft assemblies.

3. Using a Valve Spring Compressor tool, compress the valve springs and remove the stem keys. Release the compressor tool and remove the rotators or spring caps, the oil shedders, the springs and damper assemblies, then remove the oil seals and the valve spring shims.

4. Remove the valve from the cylinder head and place them in a rack in their proper sequence so that they can be reassembled in their original positions. Discard any bent or damaged valves.

5. Installation is the reverse of removal. Always use new oil seals.

6. Adjust the valve lash (if necessary).

Cylinder Head Not Removed

This procedure requires the use of the following tools:

Measuring valve stem clearance with a dial indicator

• GM Air Adapter tool No. J-23590 or equivalent

• Valve Spring Compressor tool No. J-5892 or equivalent (2.0L, 2.5L, 2.8L and 4.3L engines)

• Valve Spring Compressor tool No. J-26513 or equivalent (1.9L engine)

• Valve Spring Compressor tool No. J-29760 or equivalent (2.2L engine)

1. Remove the spark plug (in the cylinder being worked on). Install the air adaptor tool and pressurize the cylinder.

NOTE: *The cylinder being worked on MUST BE at the TDC of its compression stroke.*

2. Using the appropriate valve spring compressor tool, compress the valve spring, then remove the valve keys and the retaining ring.

3. Release the compressor and remove the spring and valve stem seal. Keep the valves in order for installation.

4. Installation is the reverse of removal. Use new valve seals.

NOTE: *Keep all parts in order so that they may be assembled in their original locations.*

INSPECTION

Inspect the valve faces and seats (in the head) for pits, burned spots and other evidence of poor seating. Valves that are pitted must be

Valve Spring Compressor tool No. J-29760 — 2.2L engine

21. Valve keepers
22. Cap
23. Seal
24. Shield
25. Spring

Exploded view of the valve assembly

Valve Spring Compressor tool No. J-26513 — 1.9L engine

refaced to the proper angle (45°). Valves that are warped excessively must be replaced. When a valve head that is warped excessively is refaced, a knife edge will be ground on part or all of the valve head due to the amount of material that must be removed to completely reface the valve. Knife edges lead to breakage, burning or preignition due to heat localizing on the knife edge. If the edge of the valve head is less than $1/32$ in. after machining, replace the valve. All machine work should be performed by a reputable machine shop.

Check the valve stem for scoring and burned spots. If not noticeably scored or damaged, clean the valve stem with solvent to remove all gum and varnish. Clean the valve guides using solvent and an expanding wire-type valve guide cleaner. Use a dial indicator for measuring valve stem-to-guide clearance. Mount the dial indicator so that the stem of the indicator is at 90° to the valve stem and as close to the valve guide as possible. Move the valve off its seat, then measure the valve guide-to-stem clearance by rocking the stem back and forth to actuate the dial indicator. Measure the valve stem diameter using a micrometer and compare to specifications to determine whether the

Removing the valve springs with the head off the engine

Checking the valve spring pressure

Valve Spring Compressor tool No. J-5892 — 2.0L, 2.5L, 2.8L and 4.3L engines

Proper Tip Pattern	No Rotation Pattern	Partial Rotation Tip Pattern
Rotator Functioning Properly	Replace Rotator and check rotation	Replace Rotator and check rotation

Valve stem wear patterns on engines using rotator cups

stem or guide wear is responsible for the excess clearance.

Some of the engines covered in this guide are equipped with valve rotators which double as valve spring caps. In normal operation the rotators put a certain degree of wear on the tip of the valve stem; this wear appears as concentric rings on the stem tip. However, if the rotator is not working properly, the wear may appear as straight notches or "X" patterns across the valve stem tip. Whenever the valves are removed from the cylinder head, the tips should be inspected for improper pattern, which could indicate valve rotator problems. Valve stem tips will have to be ground flat if the rotator problems are severe.

Position the valve spring on a flat, clean surface next to a square. Measure the height of the spring and rotate it against the engine of the square to measure the distortion (out-of-roundness). If the spring height varies between the springs by more than $\frac{1}{16}$ in. (1.6mm), replace the spring. Using a valve spring tester, check

Valve inspection and head measurement

the spring pressure at the installed and compressed height.

VALVE REFACING

NOTE: *All valve grinding operations should be performed by a qualified machine shop; only the valve lapping operation is recommended to be performed by the home mechanic.*

Valve Lapping

When valve faces and seats have been refaced, or if they are determined to be in good condition, the valves MUST BE lapped to ensure efficient sealing when the valve closes against the seat.

1. Invert the cylinder head so that the com-

Checking the valve spring free length and squareness

bustion chambers are facing upward.

2. Lightly lubricate the valve stems with clean engine oil and coat the valve seats with valve lapping compound. Install the valves in the cylinder head as numbered.

3. Moisten and attach the suction cup of a valve lapping tool to a valve head.

4. Rotate the tool between your palms, changing position and lifting the tool often to prevent grooving. Lap the valve until a smooth polished seat is evident (you may have to add a bit more compound after some lapping is done).

5. Remove the valve and tool, then remove ALL traces of the grinding compound with a solvent-soaked rag or rinse the head with solvent.

Valve Seats

REMOVAL AND INSTALLATION

1.9L and 2.2L Engines

NOTE: *The following procedures requires the use of an arc welder, a wire brush, a slide hammer puller, dry ice and an arbor press.*

1. Weld pieces of welding rod to several points around the seat, then allow the head to cool for about 5 minutes.

2. Using a slide hammer puller, remove the valve seats attached to the welding rods.

3. Using a wire brush, clean the valve seat recess carefully.

4. Place the new valve seat in dry ice while heating the recess in the head with steam. Take about 5 minutes for this procedure. Perform the heating and cooling simultaneously.

5. Using protective gloves, insert the valve

VALVE SEAT INSERT

CYLINDER HEAD

WELDING BEAD

Valve seat removal

SUITABLE METAL PIECE

Valve seat installation using a bench press

Lapping the valves

seat into the cylinder head recess. The seat depth below the combustion chamber face should be 0.0031–0.0047 in. (0.08-0.12mm).

6. Cut the valve seat to the angle shown in the valve specifications chart. Valve seat contact width should be 0.0472–0.0630 in. (1.2-1.6mm).

7. Polish the seat using lapping compound and a suction type lapper.

8. Smear the seat and the face of a correctly ground and cleaned valve with a dye such as Prussian blue. Turn the valve against the seat several times, remove the valve and check that the dye shows and even contact.

NOTE: *The valve seats used on the 2.0L, 2.5L, 2.8L and 4.3 engines are an integral part of the cylinder head and are not replaceable; they should be refaced, cleaned and lapped, ONLY.*

Valve Guides

REMOVAL AND INSTALLATION

1.9L and 2.2L Engines

NOTE: *The following procedures requires the use of Valve Guide Removal and Installation tool No. J-26512 or equivalent.*

1. Insert the guide remover such as tool No. J-26512 or equivalent, into the guide from the combustion chamber side. Drive the guide upward and out. Remove the lower valve spring seat.

2. Apply clean engine oil to the outside of the new guide and position it on the head topside. Using opposite side of the tool No. J-26512 or equivalent, drive the guide in until it bottoms.

NOTE: *If the guides are replaced, the valves should be replaced also.*

3. The guide should protrude 0.4724 in. (12mm) above the head surface. Grind the end of the guide to achieve this height. Make certain that the guide has bottomed before grinding.

Valve guide installation

Valve guide removal

Cut-away view of a knurled valve guide

NOTE: *Valve guides on the 2.0L, 2.5L, 2.8L and 4.3L engines are not replaceable. The guides should be reamed to accommodate valves with oversized stems. Oversized stems are available in 0.089mm, 0.394mm and 0.775mm.*

KNURLING

Valve guides which are not excessively worn or distorted may, in some cases, be knurled. knurling is a process in which metal is displaced and raised, thereby reducing clearance. Knurling also provides excellent oil control.

This procedure should only be performed by a qualified machine shop.

Oil Pan

In most cases it will be necessary to remove the engine in order to gain access to the oil pan. It is a difficult and tedious task to remove the oil pan with the engine in the vehicle. The chances of contaminating the bearing surfaces or damaging other internal engine components is great. Also, working under the vehicle with the engine jacked up in the frame puts you at great risk for great personal injury.

REMOVAL AND INSTALLATION

1.9L Engine

1. Remove the engine.
2. Remove the bolts and nuts attaching the oil pan to the cylinder block and remove the oil pan.
3. Remove the oil level gage guide tube from the intake manifold and the oil pan.
4. Using a putty knife, clean the gasket

mounting surfaces. Make sure that the sealing surfaces on the pan, cylinder block and front cover are clean and free of oil.

5. Apply a thin coat of Permatex® number 2 or equivalent to the areas shown in the illustration.
6. Install the new oil pan gasket, aligning the holes, and then install the oil pan.
7. Install and tighten the bolts and nuts evenly to 4 ft. lbs.
8. Check the edge of the gasket to make certain the gasket is set in position correctly. If the projection of the gasket edge is beyond the oil pan flange is uneven, remove and reinstall.
9. Install the engine into the vehicle. Refill the crankcase with fresh oil. Start the engine, establish normal operating temperatures and check for leaks.

2.0L Engine

2-WHEEL DRIVE

1. Remove the negative battery cable.
2. Remove the engine from the vehicle.
3. Remove the oil pan.
4. Using a putty knife, clean the gasket mounting surfaces. Make sure that all sealing surfaces are clean and free of oil.
5. Apply a thin coat of RTV sealant to both ends of a new rear oil pan seal. Sealant must not extend beyond the tabs of the seal. Then install the seal firmly into the rear main bearing cap.
6. Apply a continuous 1/8 in. bead of RTV sealant on the oil pan side rails. This bead must be in line with the bolt holes and circled inboard at each hole location.

NOTE: *DO NOT apply sealant to the rear oil pan seal mating surface.*

7. Apply RTV sealant to the oil pan surface which fits to the engine front cover. Ensure the sealant meets both side rail beads.
8. Using care to avoid disturbing the RTV beads, install the oil pan onto the cylinder block. The sealant must be wet during oil pan

Oil pan sealer location — 1.9L engine

bolt torquing. 9. Torque attaching bolts to the following:

- Oil pan-to-cover: 6–9 ft. lbs.
- Oil pan-to-side rail: 4–9 ft. lbs.
- Oil pan-to-rear holes: 11–17 ft. lbs.

9. Install the engine into the vehicle. Refill the crankcase with fresh oil. Start the engine, establish normal operating temperatures and check for leaks.

4-WHEEL DRIVE

1. Remove the negative battery cable.
2. Remove the starter front brace bolt.
3. Remove the motor mount through bolts.
4. Raise and support the vehicle safely.
5. Remove the front splash shield, and the brake and fuel line clip retaining bolts.
6. Remove the crossmember bolts and cross-

Oil pan — 2.0L engine

member. Rotate the crossmember around the lines.

7. Drain the engine oil.
8. Remove the starter bolts and lay the starter aside.
9. Disconnect the steering damper at the frame.
10. Scribe the idler arm location and disconnect the idler arm and steering gear at the frame. Disconnect the front axle at the frame.
11. Disconnect the front driveshaft at the front differential and slide the differential forward.
12. Remove the oil pan bolts.
13. Raise the engine slightly and remove the pan.

NOTE: *Raising the engine too far could damage the EGR system.*

14. Remove the oil pan.
15. Using a putty knife, clean the gasket mounting surfaces. Make sure that all sealing surfaces are clean and free of oil.
16. Apply a thin coat of RTV sealant to both ends of a new rear oil pan seal. Sealant must not extend beyond the tabs of the seal. Then install the seal firmly into the rear main bearing cap.
17. Apply a continuous $1/8$ in. bead of RTV sealant on the oil pan side rails. This bead must be in line with the bolt holes and circled inboard at each hole location.

NOTE: *DO NOT apply sealant to the rear oil pan seal mating surface.*

18. Apply RTV sealant to the oil pan surface which fits to the engine front cover. Ensure the sealant meets both side rail beads.
19. Using care to avoid disturbing the RTV beads, install the oil pan onto the cylinder block. The sealant must be wet during oil pan bolt torquing.
20. Torque attaching bolts to the following:

- Oil pan-to-cover: 6–9 ft. lbs.
- Oil pan-to-side rail: 4–9 ft. lbs.
- Oil pan-to-rear holes: 11–17 ft. lbs.

21. Installation is the reverse of removal. Refill the crankcase with fresh oil. Start the engine, establish normal operating temperatures and check for leaks.

Oil pan gasket projection

2.2L Diesel Engine

1. Remove the negative battery cable.
2. Raise and support the vehicle safely.
3. Drain the engine oil.
4. Remove the oil pan bolts and remove the pan.
5. Using a putty knife, clean the gasket mounting surfaces. Make sure that all sealing surfaces are clean and free of oil.
6. Installation is the reverse of removal. Tighten bolts to 2–4 ft. lbs.
7. Refill the crankcase with fresh oil. Start the engine, establish normal operating temperatures and check for leaks.

2.5L Engine

2-WHEEL DRIVE

1. Remove the negative battery cable.
2. Remove the power steering reservoir at the fan shroud.
3. Remove the radiator fan shroud.
4. Raise and support the vehicle safely.
5. Drain the engine oil.
6. Remove the strut rods.
7. Remove the exhaust pipes at the manifolds.
8. Remove the catalytic converter and exhaust pipe.
9. Remove the flywheel cover.
10. Remove the starter and brace.
11. Remove the brake line at the crossmember. Remove the engine mount through bolts.
12. Remove the oil pan bolts and pan.
13. Using a putty knife, clean the gasket mounting surfaces. Make sure that all sealing surfaces are clean and free of oil.
14. Apply RTV sealant to the oil pan flange and block as shown in the illustration.
15. Using care to avoid disturbing the RTV beads, install the oil pan onto the cylinder block. The sealant must be wet during oil pan bolt torquing.
16. Tighten oil pan bolts to 90 inch lbs.
17. The remainder of the installation procedure is the reverse of removal. Refill the crankcase with fresh oil. Start the engine, establish normal operating temperatures and check for leaks.

4-WHEEL DRIVE

1. Remove the negative battery cable.
2. Remove the power steering reservoir at the fan shroud.
3. Remove the radiator fan shroud.
4. Remove the engine oil dipstick.
5. Raise and support the vehicle safely.
6. Drain the engine oil.
7. Remove the brake line at the crossmem-

Oil pan — 2.2L diesel engine

ber and remove the crossmember.
9. Remove the transmission cooler lines.
10. Remove the exhaust pipes at the manifolds.
11. Remove the catalytic converter hanger.
12. Remove the flywheel cover.
13. Remove the driveshaft splash shield.
14. Remove the idler arm assembly.
15. Remove the steering gear bolts. Pull the steering gear and linkage forward.
16. Remove the differential housing mounting bolts at the bracket on the right side and at the frame on the left side.
17. Remove the starter and brace.
18. Remove the engine mount through bolts.
19. Remove the oil pan bolts and pan.
21. Apply RTV sealant to the oil pan flange and block as shown in the illustration.
22. Using care to avoid disturbing the RTV beads, install the oil pan onto the cylinder block. The sealant must be wet during oil pan bolt torquing.
23. Tighten oil pan bolts to 90 inch lbs.
24. Installation is the reverse of removal. Refill the crankcase with fresh oil. Start the engine, establish normal operating temperatures and check for leaks.

2.8L and 4.3L Engine

2-WHEEL DRIVE

1. Remove the engine from the vehicle.
2. Remove the oil pan bolts and studs. Remove the oil pan.
3. Using a putty knife, clean the gasket mounting surfaces. Make sure that all sealing surfaces are clean and free of oil.
4. Apply RTV sealant to the rear oil pan rail where it contacts the rear bearing cap.
5. Using a new gasket, install the oil pan and tighten bolts as follows:
   • Two rear bolts: 18 ft. lbs.
   • All other bolts and nuts: 7 ft. lbs.
6. Install the engine into the vehicle. Refill the crankcase with fresh oil. Start the engine, establish normal operating temperatures and check for leaks.

4-WHEEL DRIVE

1. Remove the negative battery cable.
2. Remove the dipstick.
3. Raise and support the vehicle safely.
4. Remove the drive belt splash pan, the front axle shield and the transfer case shield.
5. Remove the brake line clips from the crossmember and the 2nd crossmember from the vehicle.
6. If equipped with an A/T, remove the hanger bolt and the exhaust pipe clamp from the catalytic converter, then disconnect the exhaust pipes from the exhaust manifolds and move the exhaust pipe rearward.
7. Remove the drive shaft-to-drive pinion nuts/bolts and the drive shaft from the vehicle.
8. Remove the flywheel cover-to-engine braces and the engine-to-chassis braces.
9. Remove the flywheel cover, the starter-to-engine bolts and the starter (lay it aside).
10. Remove the steering shock absorber from the frame bracket. Using a scribing tool, mark the position of the idler arm-to-chassis, then remove the steering gear-to-chassis bolts, the steering gear, the idler arm-to-chassis bolts and the idler arm from the vehicle.
11. Remove the front differential-to-bracket bolts from the sides of the chassis, then pull the steering gear and linkage forward.
12. Remove the motor mount through bolts.
13. Drain the engine oil.
14. Raise the engine slightly, then remove the oil pan-to-engine bolts and the oil pan from the engine.
15. Apply RTV sealant to the rear oil pan rail where it contacts the rear bearing cap.
16. Using a new gasket, install the oil pan and tighten bolts as follows:
- Two rear bolts: 18 ft. lbs.
- All other bolts and nuts: 7 ft. lbs.
17. Installation is the reverse of removal. Refill the crankcase with fresh oil. Start the engine, establish normal operating temperatures and check for leaks.

Oil Pump

REMOVAL AND INSTALLATION

Except 1.9L and 2.2L Diesel

NOTE: *The oil pump in the 1.9L engine is located in the front cover. See Front Cover Removal and Installation for oil pump service.*

1. Remove the oil pan.
2. Remove the oil pump attaching bolt and pickup tube bolt (if necessary).
3. Ensure that the pump pickup tube is tight in the pump body. If the tube should come loose, oil pressure will be lost and oil starvation will occur.
4. Install the replacement pump aligning the pump shaft with the distributor drive gear as necessary. Tighten oil pump bolts to the following:
- 2.0L Engine: 25–38 ft. lbs.
- 2.5L Engine: 31 ft. lbs.

A. 7.5 mm (5/16-Inch) Wide x
   2.5 mm (3/32-Inch) Thick
B. 4 mm (7/32-Inch) Wide x
   2.5 mm (3/32-Inch) Thick
C. 3 mm (1/8-Inch) Bead In
   Areas Shown
D. Front Of Engine
80. Block
81. Rear Main Bearing Cap
82. Oil Pan

Applying RTV sealant to the oil pan and block — 2.5L engine

1. PICK UP TUBE AND SCREEN.
2. PUMP COVER.
3. DRIVE GEAR AND SHAFT.
4. IDLER GEAR.
5. PUMP BODY.
6. PRESSURE REGULATOR SPRING.
7. PRESSURE REGULATOR VALVE.
8. RETAINING PIN.
9. GASKET.
10. ATTACHING BOLTS.

Oil pump components — 2.0L engine shown, others similar

Checking that the punch mark on the oil pump drive gear is turned to the rear side as viewed through the clearance between the front cover and the cylinder block — 1.9L engine

- 2.8L Engine: 30 ft. lbs.
- 4.3L Engine: 65 ft. lbs.

1.9L Engine

1. Remove the oil pan.
2. Remove the oil pickup tube from the oil pump.
3. Remove the distributor.
4. Remove the oil pump mounting bolt and remove the pump.
5. Install the pump as follows:

a. Align the oil pump drive gear punch mark with the oil filter side of cover; then align the center of dowel pin with alignment mark on the oil pump case.

b. Rotate the crankshaft until the No. 1 and No. 4 cylinders are at TDC of the compression stroke.

c. Install the pump by engaging the pinion gear with the oil pump drive gear on the crankshaft.

d. Check that the punch mark on the oil pump drive gear is turned to the rear side as viewed through clearance between front cover and cylinder block.

e. Check that the slit at the end of the oil pump shaft is parallel with front face of cylinder block and that it is offset forward.

6. With all parts correctly installed, the remainder of the installation procedure is the reverse the removal.

7. Check and/or adjust the engine timing. Inspect for leaks.

2.2L Diesel Engine

1. Remove the engine from the vehicle.
2. Disconnect the PCV hose at the crankcase.
3. Remove the dipstick tube.
4. Remove the oil pan.
5. Remove the crankcase bolts and using

Oil pump and pickup tube — 1.9L engine

Aligning the oil pump drive gear mark with the oil filter side of the cover and the center of the dowel pin with the mark on the oil pump case — 1.9L engine

Checking that the slit at the end of the oil pump shaft is parallel with the front face of the block — 1.9L engine

the slots provided, pry the crankcase from the engine.

6. Remove the oil pipe sleeve nut, the oil pump bolts and the oil pump.

7. Installation is the reverse of removal.

Timing (Front) Cover and Seal

On most vehicles it is possible to replace the timing cover front seal without removing the timing cover. Simply remove the torsional damper or crankshaft hub assembly and pry the seal from the cover.

REMOVAL AND INSTALLATION

1.9L Engine

1. Remove the cylinder head.
2. Remove the oil pan.
3. Remove the oil pickup tube from the oil pump.
4. Remove the crankshaft hub and pulley.
5. Remove the AIR pump drive belt.
6. If equipped with air conditioning, remove the compressor and mounting brackets and lay aside. DO NOT remove the refrigerant lines.
7. Remove the distributor.
8. Remove the front cover attaching bolts and remove the front cover.
9. Check the front cover inner and outer faces for cracking or damage. Replace as necessary.
10. Install a new gasket onto the engine.
11. Align the oil pump drive gear punch mark with the oil filter side of cover; then align the center of dowel pin with alignment mark on the oil pump case.
12. Rotate the crankshaft until the No. 1 and No. 4 cylinders are at TDC of the compression stroke.
13. Install the front cover by engaging the pinion gear with the oil pump drive gear on the crankshaft.
14. Check that the punch mark on the oil pump drive gear is turned to the rear side as viewed through clearance between front cover and cylinder block.
15. Check that the slit at the end of the oil pump shaft is parallel with front face of cylinder block and that it is offset forward.
16. With all parts correctly installed, the remainder of the installation procedure is the reverse the removal.
17. Check and/or adjust the engine timing. Inspect for leaks.

2.0L Engine

NOTE: *The following procedure requires the use of the Centering tool No. J-23042 or equivalent.*

Oil pump — 2.2L diesel engine

1. Remove the negative battery cable.
2. Drain the cooling system.

CAUTION: *When draining the coolant, keep in mind that cats and dogs are attracted by the ethylene glycol antifreeze, and are quite likely to drink any that is left in an uncovered container or in puddles on the ground. This will prove fatal in sufficient quantity. Always drain the coolant into a sealable container. Coolant should be reused unless it is contaminated or several years old.*

3. Remove the upper fan shroud.
4. Loosen the accessory drive belt adjusters and remove the drive belts from the crankshaft pulley.
5. Remove the cooling fan-to-water pump bolts and the pulley.
6. Remove the radiator hose and the heater hose from the water pump. Remove the water pump-to-engine bolts and the water pump from the engine.
7. Remove the crankshaft pulley-to-hub bolt and the pulley from the crankshaft.
8. Using the puller tool No. J-24420 or equivalent, pull the hub assembly from the crankshaft.
9. Remove the front cover-to-engine bolts and the cover from the engine.
10. Using a putty knife, clean the gasket mounting surfaces. Using solvent, clean the oil and grease from the gasket mounting surfaces.
12. Apply a 2–3mm bead of RTV sealant to the front cover, oil pan and water pump sealing surfaces.

NOTE: *When applying RTV sealant to the front cover, be sure to keep it out of the bolt holes. The sealant must be wet to the touch when the bolts are torqued down.*

13. Installation is the reverse of removal. Torque the hub-to-crankshaft bolt to 66–88 ft. lbs. and the damper pulley-to-hub bolts to 29–44 ft. lbs.
14. Adjust the drive belts.

Crankshaft pulley alignment — 2.2L diesel

2.2L Diesel Engine

1. Remove the negative battery cable.
2. Remove the power steering reservoir.
3. Remove the upper fan shroud and fan.
4. Loosen the drive belts and remove the fan drive pulley.
5. Remove the upper cover attaching bolts and cover.
6. Remove the alternator belt.
7. Align the crankshaft pulley and remove the attaching bolts. Remove the pulley.
8. Remove the lower cover attaching bolts and cover.
9. Installation is the reverse of removal.

2.5L and 2.8L Engine

NOTE: *The following procedure requires the use of the GM Seal Installer/Centering tool No. J-34995 or equivalent.*

1. Remove the negative battery cable.
2. Remove the accessory drive belts.
3. Remove the power steering reservoir from the fan shroud. Remove the fan shroud.
4. Remove the alternator and brackets (lay them aside).
5. Remove the crankshaft pulley bolt, crankshaft pulley and hub (torsional damper).

NOTE: *The outer ring (weight) of the torsional damper is bonded to the hub with rubber. The damper must be removed with a puller which acts on the inner hub only. Pulling on the outer portion of the damper will break the rubber bond or destroy the tuning of the unit.*

6. Drain the cooling system. Remove the lower radiator hose at the water pump.

CAUTION: *When draining the coolant, keep in mind that cats and dogs are attracted by the ethylene glycol antifreeze, and are quite likely to drink any that is left in an uncovered container or in puddles on the ground.*

Pulley and hub assembly — 2.0L engine

50. Bolts
51. Crankshaft pulley
52. Bolt
53. Washer
54. Hub
55. Bolts
56. Front crankshaft seal
57. Timing gear cover

Crankshaft pulley and timing cover assembly — 2.5L engine

This will prove fatal in sufficient quantity. Always drain the coolant into a sealable container. Coolant should be reused unless it is contaminated or several years old.

7. Remove the timing cover bolts and cover.

8. If the front seal is to be replaced, it can be pryed out of the cover with a suitable tool.

9. Using the GM Seal Installer/Centering Tool J-34995 or equivalent, install the replacement cover seal.

10. Clean all sealing surfaces and apply a 3/8 in. bead of RTV sealant to the oil pan and timing gear cover sealing surfaces.

11. Use the GM Seal Installer/Centering Tool J-34995 or equivalent align the front cover. Install the cover while the RTV sealant is still wet.

12. Installation is the reverse of removal.

13. Tighten front cover bolts as follows:
- 2.5L Engine: 8 ft. lbs.
- 2.8L Engine: 18 ft. lbs.

4.3L Engine

1. Remove the torsional damper center bolts and remove the damper with suitable puller.

NOTE: *The outer ring (weight) of the torsional damper is bonded to the hub with rubber. The damper must be removed with a puller which acts on the inner hub only. Pulling on the outer portion of the damper will break the rubber bond or destroy the tuning of the unit.*

2. Drain the cooling system.

CAUTION: *When draining the coolant, keep in mind that cats and dogs are attracted by the ethylene glycol antifreeze, and are quite likely to drink any that is left in an uncovered container or in puddles on the ground. This will prove fatal in sufficient quantity. Always drain the coolant into a sealable container. Coolant should be reused unless it is contaminated or several years old.*

3. Remove the water pump.

4. Remove the oil pan.

5. Remove the upper radiator hose, air conditioner compressor (lay it aside) and right side engine accessory bracket.

6. Remove the front cover bolts and front cover.

7. If the front cover seal is to be replaced, it may be pried front the front cover with a pry bar. Use tool J-35468 to install the seal.

8. Clean all sealing surfaces and install a new gasket to the front cover. Use sealant to hold it in place.

9. Install the front cover and tighten the bolts to 10 ft. lbs.

10. Installation is the reverse of removal.

Timing Chain and Gears

REMOVAL AND INSTALLATION

1.9L Engine

NOTE: *The following procedure requires the use of the Wheel Puller tool No. J-25031 or equivalent, and Timing Sprocket Installation tool No. J-26587 or equivalent.*

1. Remove the timing (front) cover.

2. Lock the shoe on the automatic adjuster in fully retracted position by depressing the adjuster lock lever.

3. Remove timing chain from crankshaft sprocket.

NOTE: *To remove the timing chain, it may be necessary to remove the camshaft sprocket. Before removing the timing chain, be sure to align the timing marks.*

4. Check the timing sprockets for wear or damage. If crankshaft sprocket must be replaced, remove the sprocket and the pinion gear from crankshaft using the Puller tool No. J-25031 or equivalent.

5. Check timing chain for wear or damage; replace as necessary. Measure distance (L) with chain stretched with a pull of approximately 22 lbs. (98N). Standard (L) valve is 15 in. (381mm); replace chain of (L) is greater than 15.16 in. (385mm).

6. Remove the automatic chain adjuster-to-engine bolt and the adjuster.

7. To check the operation of the automatic chain adjuster, push the shoe inwards, if it becomes locked, the adjuster is working properly. The adjuster assembly must be replaced if rack teeth are found to be worn excessively.

8. To remove the chain tensioner, remove the "E" clip and the tensioner. Check the tensioner for wear or damage; if necessary, replace it.

9. Inspect the tensioner pin for wear or

Timing chain guide and tensioner — 1.9L engine

damage. If replacement is necessary, remove the pin from the cylinder block using a pair of locking pliers. Lubricate the NEW pin tensioner with clean engine oil. Start the pin into block, then place the tensioner over the appropriate pin. Position the E-clip onto the pin, then (using a hammer) tap it into the block until clip just clears tensioner. Check the tensioner and adjuster for freedom of rotation on the pins.

10. Inspect the guide for wear or damage and plugged lower oil jet. If replacement or cleaning is necessary, remove the guide bolts, the guide and the oil jet. Install a new guide and upper attaching bolt. Install the lower oil jet and bolt, so that the oil port is pointed toward crankshaft.

11. Install the timing sprocket and the pinion gear (groove-side toward the front cover). Align the key groove with crankshaft key, then drive it into position using Installing tool No. J-26587 or equivalent.

12. Turn the crankshaft so that key is turned toward the cylinder head-side (No. 1 and No. 4 pistons at TDC).

13. Install the timing chain, align the timing chain mark plate with the mark on the crankshaft timing sprocket. The side of the chain with the mark plate is on the front-side and the side of chain with the most links between mark plates is on the chain guide-side. Keep the timing chain engaged with the camshaft timing sprocket until the camshaft timing sprocket is installed on the camshaft.

14. Install the camshaft timing sprocket so that it's marked-side faces forward and it's triangular mark aligns with the chain mark plate.

15. Install the automatic chain adjuster.

16. Release the lock by depressing the shoe on adjuster by hand, and check to make certain the chain is properly tensioned when the lock is released.

17. Install from cover assembly as outlined previously.

2.0L Engine

NOTE: *The following procedure requires the use of the Spring compressor tool No. J-33875 or equivalent, the Gear Puller tool No. J-22888-20 or equivalent.*

1. Remove the timing cover.

2. Rotate the crankshaft to position the No. 4 piston on TDC of the compression stroke; the marks on the camshaft and crankshaft sprockets should be in alignment.

3. Loosen the timing chain tensioner nut (as far as possible) without actually removing it.

4. Remove the camshaft sprocket-to-camshaft bolts and the sprocket; remove the timing

Timing chain alignment — 1.9L engine

chain with the sprocket. If the sprocket does not slide from the camshaft easily, a light blow with a soft mallet at the lower edge of the sprocket will dislodge it.

5. Using the Gear Puller tool No. J-22888-20 or equivalent, remove the crankshaft sprocket.

6. Using a putty knife, clean the gasket mounting surfaces. Inspect the timing chain and the sprocket teeth for wear and/or damage; replace the parts, if necessary.

7. Install the crankshaft sprocket onto the crankshaft, position the timing chain over the camshaft sprocket and then around the crankshaft sprocket. Make sure that the marks on the two sprockets are aligned. Lubricate the thrust surface with Molykote® or equivalent.

8. Align the dowel in the camshaft with the dowel hole in the sprocket and then install the sprocket onto the camshaft. Torque the camshaft sprocket-to-camshaft bolts to 27–33 ft. lbs.

9. Lubricate the timing chain with clean engine oil. Using the Spring Compressor tool

Timing chain alignment — 2.0L engine

No. J-33875 or equivalent, position the tangs under the sliding block and pull the tool to compress the spring. Tighten the chain tensioner.

10. To complete the installation, reverse the removal procedures.

2.8L and 4.3L Engine

NOTE: *The following procedure requires the use of the Crankshaft Sprocket Removal tool No. J-5825 or equivalent, and the Crankshaft Sprocket Installation tool No. J-5590 or equivalent.*

1. Remove the timing cover.

2. Rotate the crankshaft until the No. 4 cylinder is on the TDC of it's compression stroke and the camshaft sprocket mark (No. 4 cylinder) aligns with the mark on the crankshaft sprocket (facing each other) and in line with the shaft centers.

3. Remove the camshaft sprocket-to-camshaft bolts and the camshaft sprocket (with timing chain). If camshaft is difficult to remove, use a plastic mallet to bump the sprocket from the camshaft.

NOTE: *The camshaft sprocket (located by a dowel) is lightly pressed onto the camshaft and will come off readily. The chain comes off with the camshaft sprocket.*

4. Using the Crankshaft Sprocket Removal tool No. J-5825 or equivalent, remove the timing sprocket from the crankshaft.

5. Inspect the timing chain and the timing sprockets for wear or damage, replace the damaged parts (if necessary).

6. Using a putty knife, clean the gasket mounting surfaces. Using solvent, clean the oil and grease from the gasket mounting surfaces.

7. Using the Crankshaft Sprocket Installation tool No. J-5590 or equivalent, and a hammer, without disturbing the position of the engine, drive the crankshaft sprocket onto the crankshaft.

8. Position the timing chain over the camshaft sprocket. Arrange the camshaft sprocket

in such a way that the timing marks will align between the shaft centers and the camshaft locating dowel will enter the dowel hole in the cam sprocket.

9. Place the cam sprocket, with its chain mounted over it, in position on the front of the camshaft and torque the camshaft sprocket-to-camshaft bolts to 17 ft. lbs.

10. With the timing chain installed, turn the crankshaft two complete revolutions, then check to make certain that the timing marks are in correct alignment between the shaft centers.

11. Install the timing cover.

Timing Belt

REMOVAL AND INSTALLATION

2.2L Diesel Engine

NOTE: *The following procedure requires the use of the Belt Tension Gauge tool No. J-29771 or equivalent.*

1. Remove the negative battery cable.

2. Align the mark on the crankshaft pulley with the timing pointer and remove the crankshaft pulley. Remove the front covers.

3. Remove the bolts attaching the injection pump timing pulley flange. Remove the tension spring.

NOTE: *When removing tension spring, avoid using excess force, or distortion of spring will result.*

4. Remove the timing belt tension pulley-to-engine fixing nut, then the tension pulley and tension center.

5. Remove the timing belt. Avoid twisting or kinking the belt and keep it free from water, oil, dust and other foreign matter.

NOTE: *No attempt should be made to readjust belt tension. If the belt has been loosened*

Removing the crankshaft sprocket — 2.8L engine

1 CYLINDER AT T.D.C.

4 CYLINDER AT T.D.C.

Timing chain alignment — 2.8L engine

Installing the timing belt — 2.2L diesel

Torquing the tension pulley — 2.2L diesel

J—29771

Using tool No. J-29771 to check the belt tension — 2.2L diesel

through service of the timing system, it should be replaced with a new one.

6. Check that the setting marks on the crank pulley, injection pump timing pulley, and camshaft pulley are in alignment, then install the timing belt in sequence of crankshaft timing pulley, camshaft timing pulley and injection pump timing pulley.

7. Make an adjustment, so that slackness of the belt is taken up by the tension pulley. When installing the timing belt, care should be taken so as not to damage the belt.

8. Install the tension center and tension pulley, making certain the end of the tension center is in proper contact with two pins on the timing pulley housing.

9. Hand-tighten the nut, so that tension pulley can slide freely.

10. Install the tension spring correctly and semi-tighten the tension pulley fixing nut.

11. Turn the crankshaft 2 turns in normal direction of rotation to permit seating of the belt. Further rotate the crankshaft 90° beyond TDC to settle the injection pump. Never at-

tempt to turn the crankshaft in reverse direction.

NOTE: *If the engine is turned past the timing marks, keep rotating the engine in the normal direction of rotation until the marks align properly.*

12. Loosen the tension pulley fixing nut completely, allowing the pulley to take up looseness of the belt. Then, tighten the nut to 78–95 ft. lbs.

13. Install the flange on the injection pump pulley. The hole in the outer circumference of the flange should be aligned with the timing mark "triangle" on the injection pump pulley.

14. Turn the crankshaft 2 (clockwise) turns to position the No. 1 cylinder on to TDC of it's compression stroke, then check that the "triangle" mark on the timing pulley is in alignment with the hole in the flange.

15. The belt tension should be checked at a point between the injection pump pulley and crankshaft pulley using tool No. J-29771 or equivalent, to 33–55 lbs. as read on the scale.

Aligning the timing marks — 2.2L diesel

Aligning the tension pulley to make proper contact with the two housing pins — 2.2L diesel

TDC

Bringing the No. 1 cylinder to TDC — 2.2L diesel

16. Adjust valve clearances and reverse the removal procedures.

17. Check the injection timing.

Timing Gear

REMOVAL AND INSTALLATION

2.5L Engine

The 2.5L engine uses a direct drive timing assembly. The sprocket on the crankshaft drives the camshaft sprocket by direct action. The timing gear (camshaft sprocket) is pressed onto the camshaft and requires the use of an arbor press to remove.

NOTE: *The following procedure requires the use of an arbor press, a press plate, the GM Gear Removal tool No. J-971 or equivalent, the GM Gear Installation tool No. J-21474-13, J-21795-1 or equivalent.*

1. Remove the camshaft.

2. Using an arbor press, a press plate and the GM Gear Removal tool No. J-971 or equivalent, press the timing gear from the camshaft.

NOTE: *When pressing the timing gear from the camshaft, be certain that the position of the press plate does not contact the woodruff key.*

3. To assemble, position the press plate to support the camshaft at the back of the front journal. Place the gear spacer ring and the thrust plate over the end of the camshaft, then install the woodruff key. Press the timing gear onto the camshaft, until it bottoms against the gear spacer ring.

NOTE: *The end clearance of the thrust plate should be 0.0015–0.005 in. (0.038–0.127mm). If less than 0.0015 in. (0.038mm), replace the spacer ring; if more than 0.005 in. (0.127mm), replace the thrust plate.*

4. To complete the installation, align the marks on the timing gears and install the camshaft.

Camshaft Sprocket—OHC Engine

REMOVAL AND INSTALLATION

1.9L Engine

1. Remove timing cover.

2. Rotate camshaft until No. 4 cylinder is on the TDC of it's compression stroke.

3. Remove the distributor cap. Using a marking tool, mark the rotor-to-housing and the housing-to-engine positions, then remove the distributor from the engine.

4. Disconnect the fuel lines and remove the fuel pump from the engine.

5. Using a screwdriver or equivalent, de-

Removing the timing gear from the crankshaft — 2.5L engine

Removing the camshaft thrust plate-to-engine screws — 2.5L engine

press the automatic shoe adjuster lock lever into the fully retracted position. After locking the automatic adjuster, check that the chain is in free state.

6. Remove the timing sprocket-to-camshaft bolt, the sprocket and the fuel pump drive cam from the camshaft. Keep the timing sprocket on the chain damper and the tensioner without removing the chain from the sprocket.

7. Check that the mark on the No. 1 rocker arm shaft bracket is in alignment with the mark on the camshaft and that the crankshaft pulley groove is aligned with the TDC mark (0°) on the front cover.

8. Assemble the timing sprocket to the camshaft by aligning it with the pin on the camshaft; use care not to remove the chain from the sprocket.

9. Install the fuel pump drive cam, the sprocket retaining bolt and washer. Remove

Timing mark alignment — 2.5L engine

Separating the timing gear from the camshaft — 2.5L engine

the half-moon seal in from end of head; then install torque wrench and torque bolt to 58 ft. lbs; replace the half-moon seal in cylinder head.

10. Using the alignment marks, install the distributor.

11. Using a medium pry bar, depressing the adjuster shoe to release the lock, check the timing chain tension.

12. Check valve timing, the rotor and mark on distributor housing should be in alignment when the No. 4 cylinder on TDC. The timing mark on damper pulley should align with TDC mark (0° mark) on front cover.

13. Installation is the reverse of removal.

Valve Lifter

REMOVAL AND INSTALLATION

2.0L Engine

1. Remove the rocker arm covers.

2. Loosen the rocker arms and remove the pushrods and guide plates.

3. Using Valve Lifter Removal tool J-29834, or equivalent, remove the valve lifters.

NOTE: *Keep all components in order. If reusing components, install them into their original positions.*

4. For proper rotation during engine operation, the lifter bottom must be convex. Check the lifter bottom for proper shape using a straight edge. If the lifter bottom is not convex, replace the lifter. Chances are if lifters are in need of replacement, so is the camshaft.

5. Using the valve lifter tool, install the lifters into the block.

6. Installation is the reverse of removal. Adjust the valve lash.

2.2L Diesel

NOTE: *The diesel engine uses solid type lifters.*

1. Remove the rocker arm cover and side cover.

Using a feeler gauge to check thrust plate clearance — 2.5L engine

2. Remove the rocker arm shaft assembly.

3. Remove the pushrods.

4. Remove the hydraulic lifters using an appropriate lifter removal tool.

5. Installation is the reverse of removal.

6. Adjust the valve lash.

2.5L Engine

1. Remove the rocker arm and pushrod covers.

NOTE: *Keep all components in order. If reusing components, install them into their original positions. If a new hydraulic lifter is being installed, all sealer coating inside the lifter must be removed.*

2. Remove the pushrods.

3. Remove the lifter studs and retainers.

4. Remove the lifter guides and lifters.

5. Inspect the lifter and lifter bore for wear and scuffing. Examine the roller for freedom of movement and/or flat spots on the roller surface.

6. Installation is the reverse of removal.

2.8L Engine

Some engines have both standard size and 0.25mm (0.010 in.) oversize valve lifters. The cylinder block will be marked with a white

Valve lifter removal/installation tool

1.	Lifter Body	6.	Push Rod Seat
2.	Push Rod Seat		Retainer
3.	Metering Valve	7.	Plunger
4.	Check Ball	8.	Check Ball Spring
5.	Check Ball Retainer	9.	Plunger Spring

Valve lifter components

Removing the side cover — 2.2L diesel

paint mark and 0.25mm O.S. stamp where the oversize lifters are used. If lifters replacement is necessary, use new lifters with a narrow flat along the lower ³/₄ of the body length. This provides additional oil to the cam lobe and lifter surfaces.

NOTE: *This procedure requires the use of a Hydraulic Lifter Remover tool J-9290-1.*

1. Remove the rocker arm covers.
2. Remove the intake manifold.
3. Remove the rocker arm nuts and balls.
4. Remove the rocker arms and pushrods.

NOTE: *Keep all components in order. If reusing components, install them into their original positions.*

5. Using the Hydraulic Lifter Remover tool, remove the lifters.
6. For proper rotation during engine operation, the lifter bottom must be convex. Check the lifter bottom for proper shape using a straight edge. If the lifter bottom is not convex, replace the lifter. Chances are if lifters are in need of replacement, so is the camshaft.

Hydraulic lifters and components — 2.5L engine

7. Lubricate and install the lifters.
8. Installation is the reverse of removal.
9. Adjust the valve lash.

4.3L Engine

1. Remove the rocker arm cover.
2. Remove the intake manifold.

NOTE: *Keep all components in order. If reusing components, install them into their original positions.*

3. Remove the rocker arms and pushrods.
4. Remove the hydraulic lifter retainer bolts, retainers and restrictors.
5. Inspect the lifter and lifter bore for wear and scuffing. Examine the roller for freedom of movement and/or flat spots on the roller surface.
6. Installation is the reverse of removal.
7. Adjust the valve lash.

Camshaft and Bearings

REMOVAL AND INSTALLATION

1.9L Engine

1. Remove timing cover.
2. Rotate camshaft until No. 4 cylinder is on the TDC of it's compression stroke.
3. Remove the distributor cap. Using a marking tool, mark the rotor-to-housing and the housing-to-engine positions, then remove the distributor from the engine.

Oversize lifter marking — 2.8L engine

4. Disconnect the fuel lines and remove the fuel pump from the engine.

5. Using a screwdriver or equivalent, depress the automatic shoe adjuster lock lever into the fully retracted position. After locking the automatic adjuster, check that the chain is in free state.

6. Remove the timing sprocket-to-camshaft bolt, the sprocket and the fuel pump drive cam from the camshaft. Keep the timing sprocket on the chain damper and the tensioner without removing the chain from the sprocket.

7. Remove rocker arm, the shaft and the bracket assembly, the remove the camshaft assembly.

8. Using set of "V" blocks and a dial indicator, inspect the camshaft for damage and/or wear; replace it, if necessary.

9. Using a generous amount of clean engine oil, lubricate the camshaft and journals.

10. Install the camshaft, the rocker arm, the shaft and the bracket assembly.

11. Check that the mark on the No. 1 rocker arm shaft bracket is in alignment with the mark on the camshaft and that the crankshaft pulley groove is aligned with the TDC mark (0°) on the front cover.

12. Assemble the timing sprocket to the camshaft by aligning it with the pin on the camshaft; use care not to remove the chain from the sprocket.

13. Install the fuel pump drive cam, the sprocket retaining bolt and washer. Remove the half-moon seal in from end of head; then install torque wrench and torque bolt to 58 ft. lbs; replace the half-moon seal in cylinder head.

14. Using the alignment marks, install the distributor.

15. Using a medium pry bar, depressing the adjuster shoe to release the lock, check the timing chain tension.

16. Check valve timing, the rotor and mark on distributor housing should be in alignment when the No. 4 cylinder on TDC. The timing mark on damper pulley should align with TDC mark (0° mark) on front cover.

17. To complete the installation, reverse the removal procedures. Adjust the drive belts. Refill the cooling system.

2.0L Engine

NOTE: *The following procedure requires the use of the Camshaft Bearing Removal/Installation tool No. J-6098 or equivalent.*

1. Remove the timing chain and the rocker arm assemblies.

2. Drain the cooling system.

CAUTION: *When draining the coolant, keep in mind that cats and dogs are attracted by the ethylene glycol antifreeze, and are quite*

Locking the timing chain adapter — 1.9L engine

likely to drink any that is left in an uncovered container or in puddles on the ground. This will prove fatal in sufficient quantity. Always drain the coolant into a sealable container. Coolant should be reused unless it is contaminated or several years old.

3. Remove the radiator hoses, the radiator-to-engine bolts and the radiator.

4. Remove the distributor cap, mark the rotor-to-housing and the housing-to-engine positions, then remove the distributor.

5. Raise and support the vehicle safely.

6. Disconnect the fuel lines and remove the fuel pump.

7. Lower the vehicle.

8. Remove the rocker arm studs and the push rod guides.

9. Remove the valve lifters.

NOTE: *When removing the pushrods and the valve lifters, keep them in order.*

10. Carefully pull the camshaft from the front of the block, being sure that the camshaft lobes do not contact the bearings.

11. If removal of camshaft bearings is necessary, use the following procedure:

　a. Using Camshaft Bearing Removal/Installation tool J-6098, install the tool with the shoulder toward the bearing. Ensure that enough threads are engaged.

　b. Using two wrenches, hold the puller

Depressing the adjuster lock lever — 1.9L engine

screw while turning the nut. When the bearing has been released from the bore, remove the tool.

c. Assemble the tool on the driver to remove the front and rear bearings.

d. Install the rear and intermediate bearings with the oil hole between the 2 and 3 o'clock position. Install the front bearing with the holes at 11 o'clock and 2 o'clock.

e. Install a fresh camshaft bearing rear cover using sealant.

12. Lubricate the camshaft journals with clean engine oil and install the camshaft into the block being extremely careful not to contact the bearings with the cam lobes.

NOTE: *If installing a new camshaft, be sure to coat the lobes with GM Part No. 1051396 or equivalent.*

13. Install the camshaft sprocket and timing chain. Align the timing chain and sprockets and tighten the camshaft sprocket bolt.

14. Installation is the reverse of removal.

15. Adjust the valve lash. Adjust the drive belts. Refill the cooling system.

2.2L Diesel Engine

NOTE: *The following procedure requires the use of the Camshaft Bearing Removal/ Installation tool No. J-29764 or equivalent.*

1. Remove the engine from the vehicle and mount it on a workstand.

2. Disconnect the PCV hoses from the rocker arm cover.

3. Remove the rocker arm cover, the rocker arm shaft and the push rods.

4. Remove the upper timing housing cover. Turn the crankshaft to align the timing marks, then install a holding bolt into the injection pump gear.

5. Remove the crankshaft damper pulley and the lower timing housing cover.

6. Remove the injection pump timing gear flange, the timing belt tension spring and the pulley, then remove the timing belt.

7. Remove the camshaft sprocket, the hub and the camshaft oil seal retainer.

8. Remove the oil pump and the valve lifters.

9. Remove the camshaft from the front of the engine, using care not to damage the camshaft bearings.

10. Inspect the inner bearing faces for damage. Using an inside micrometer, measure the inside diameter of the camshaft bearings; if bearing clearance is greater than 0.0047 in. (0.12mm), replace the bearing(s).

11. Using Camshaft Bearing Removal/Installation tool No. J-29764 or equivalent, remove the camshaft bearings.

12. Using the same tool, install the replacement bearings into the engine block; be sure to align the oil ports in the bearings with those in the cylinder body.

13. Installation is the reverse of removal.

2.5L Engine

1. Remove the rocker arm cover, pushrods and valve lifters from the engine.

NOTE: *When removing the pushrods and the valve lifters, be sure to keep them in order for reassembly purposes.*

2. Drain the cooling system.

CAUTION: *When draining the coolant, keep in mind that cats and dogs are attracted by the ethylene glycol antifreeze, and are quite likely to drink any that is left in an uncovered container or in puddles on the ground. This will prove fatal in sufficient quantity. Always drain the coolant into a sealable container. Coolant should be reused unless it is contaminated or several years old.*

3. Remove the power steering reservoir from the fan shroud, then the upper fan shroud, the radiator. Remove the grille, the headlight bezel and the bumper filler panel.

4. Remove the accessory drive belts, the cooling fan and the water pump pulley.

5. If equipped with A/C, disconnect the condenser baffles and the condenser, then raise the condenser and set it aside without disconnecting the refrigerant lines.

6. Remove the crankshaft drive belt pulley

Timing mark alignment — 2.0L engine

Timing chain and camshaft assembly — 2.0L engine

Camshaft bearing removal — OHV engines only

and the damper hub. Remove the timing gear cover-to-engine bolts and the cover.

7. Label and disconnect the distributor electrical connectors, then the holddown bolt and the distributor from the engine. Remove the oil pump driveshaft.

8. Label and disconnect the vacuum lines from the intake manifold and the thermostat housing, then remove the Exhaust Gas Recirculation (EGR) valve from the intake manifold.

9. Remove the camshaft thrust plate-to-engine bolts. While supporting the camshaft (to prevent damaging the bearing or lobe surfaces), remove it from the front of the engine.

10. Inspect the camshaft for scratches, pitting and/or wear on the bearing and lobe surfaces. Check the timing gear teeth for damage.

11. Replace the camshaft bearings as follows:

a. Using a Camshaft Bearing Removal/Installation tool, install the tool with the shoulder toward the bearing. Ensure that enough threads are engaged.

b. Using two wrenches, hold the puller screw while turning the nut. When the bearing has been released from the bore, remove the tool.

c. Assemble the tool on the driver to remove the front and rear bearings.

d. Install the bearings at the correct clocking to ensure the oil holes in the block and bearings align.

e. Install a fresh camshaft bearing rear cover using sealant.

12. Lubricate the camshaft with engine oil and install.

13. Torque the camshaft thrust plate-to-engine bolts to 90 inch lbs.

14. Installation is the reverse of removal. Refill the cooling system, start the engine, allow it to reach operating temperatures and check for leaks.

2.8L and 4.3L Engines

1. Remove the negative battery cable.
2. Drain the cooling system.

CAUTION: *When draining the coolant, keep in mind that cats and dogs are attracted by*

the ethylene glycol antifreeze, and are quite likely to drink any that is left in an uncovered container or in puddles on the ground. This will prove fatal in sufficient quantity. Always drain the coolant into a sealable container. Coolant should be reused unless it is contaminated or several years old.

3. Remove the upper fan shroud and radiator.

4. Remove the intake manifold and rocker arm covers.

5. Remove the rocker arms, pushrods and lifters.

6. Remove the drive belt(s), fan and water pump.

7. Remove the torsional damper and the front (timing) cover.

8. Align the timing marks on the crankshaft and camshaft sprockets.

9. Remove the camshaft sprocket and timing chain.

10. Remove the thrust plate screws and remove the camshaft front the front of the engine. Take care not to damage the camshaft bearings when removing the camshaft.

11. If removal of camshaft bearings is necessary, use the following procedure:

a. Using a Camshaft Bearing Removal/Installation tool, install the tool with the shoulder toward the bearing. Ensure that enough threads are engaged.

b. Using two wrenches, hold the puller screw while turning the nut. When the bearing has been released from the bore, remove the tool.

c. Assemble the tool on the driver to remove the front and rear bearings.

d. Install the bearings so that the oil holes in the block and the bearing align.

e. Install a fresh camshaft bearing rear cover using sealant.

12. Lubricate the camshaft journals with clean engine oil and install the camshaft into the

2.2L diesel camshaft oil hole alignment — others similar

Camshaft lobe measurement

block being extremely careful not to contact the bearings with the cam lobes.

13. Install the camshaft thrust plate and tighten the bolts to 105 inch lbs. Install the timing chain and camshaft sprocket. Align the timing marks an tighten the sprocket bolt to 21 ft. lbs.

14. Installation is the reverse of removal.

INSPECTION

Using solvent, degrease the camshaft and clean out all of the oil holes. Visually inspect the cam lobes and bearing journals for excessive wear. If a lobe is questionable, check all of the lobes as indicated. If a journal or lobe is worn, the camshaft MUST BE reground or replaced.

NOTE: *If a journal is worn, there is a good chance that the bearings are worn and need replacement.*

If the lobes and journals appear intact, place the front and rear journals in V-blocks and rest a dial indicator on the center journal. Rotate the camshaft to check the straightness. If deviation exceeds 0.001 in. (0.0254mm), replace the camshaft.

Check the camshaft lobes with a micrometer, by measuring the lobes from the nose to the base and again at 90° (see illustration). The lobe lift is determined by subtracting the second measurement from the first. If all of the exhaust and intake lobes are not identical, the camshaft must be reground or replace.

Pistons and Connecting Rods

REMOVAL

1. Remove the engine from the vehicle.

2. Remove the intake manifold and the cylinder head(s).

3. Remove the oil pan and the oil pump assembly.

4. Stamp the cylinder number on the machined surfaces of the bolt bosses on the connecting rod and cap for identification when reinstalling. If the pistons are to be removed from the connecting rod, mark the cylinder number on the piston with a silver pencil or quick

Checking the camshaft for straightness

drying paint for proper cylinder identification and cap to rod location.

NOTE: *The cylinders on a 4-cylinder engine are numbered 1-2-3-4 (front-to-rear); on the V6 (2.8L and 4.3L) engine, are numbered 1-3-5 (front-to-rear) on the right-side and 2-4-6 (front-to-rear) on the left-side.*

5. Examine the cylinder bore above the ring travel. If a ridge exists, remove it with a ridge reamer before attempting to remove the piston and rod assembly.

6. Remove the connecting rod bearing cap and bearing.

7. Install a $^3/_8$ in. rubber guide hose over the rod bolt threads; this will prevent damage to the bearing journal and rod bolt threads.

8. Remove the rod and piston assembly through the top of the cylinder bore; remove

A. Align Marks as Shown

Timing mark alignment — 4.3L engine

the other rod and piston assemblies in the same manner.

9. Clean and inspect the engine block, the crankshaft, the pistons and the connecting rods.

CLEANING AND INSPECTION

Using a piston ring expanding tool, remove the piston rings from the pistons; any other method (screwdriver blades, pliers, etc.) usually results in the rings being bent, scratched or distorted and/or the piston itself being damaged.

Pistons

Clean the varnish from the piston skirts and pins with a cleaning solvent. DO NOT WIRE BRUSH ANY PART OF THE PISTON. Clean the ring grooves with a groove cleaner and make sure that the oil ring holes and slots are clean.

Inspect the piston for cracked ring lands, scuffed or damaged skirts, eroded areas at the top of the piston. Replace the pistons that are damaged or show signs of excessive wear.

Inspect the grooves for nicks of burrs that might cause the rings to hang up.

Measure the piston skirt (across the center

Match the connecting rods to their caps with a scribe mark

Match the connecting rods to their cylinders with a number stamp

RIDGE CAUSED BY CYLINDER WEAR

CYLINDER WALL

TOP OF PISTON

The ridge at the top of the cylinder wall must be removed prior to removing the piston

line of the piston pin) and check the piston clearance. If installing replacement pistons, follow the manufacturers recommendations on where to measure the piston.

Connecting Rods

Wash the connecting rods in cleaning solvent and dry with compressed air. Check for twisted or bent rods and inspect for nicks or cracks. Replace the connecting rods that are damaged.

Cylinder Bores

Using a telescoping gauge or an inside micrometer, measure the diameter of the cylinder bore, perpendicular (90°) to the piston pin, at $1-2\frac{1}{2}$ in. below the surface of the cylinder block. The difference between the two measurements is the piston clearance.

If the clearance is within specifications or slightly below (after the cylinders have been bored or honed), finish honing is all that is nec-

USE A SHORT PIECE OF 3/8" HOSE AS A GUIDE

Install a short piece of rubber hose over the connecting rod bolts to protect the crankshaft journals during removal/installation

Carefully tap the piston and rod assembly out of the cylinder with a wooden hammer handle

Cylinder bore measuring points

Measuring the piston diameter

Cylinder bore cross-hatch pattern after honing

essary, If the clearance is excessive, try to obtain a slightly larger piston to bring the clearance within specifications. If this is not possible obtain the first oversize piston and hone the cylinder or (if necessary) bore the cylinder to size. Generally, if the cylinder bore is tapered more than 0.005 in. (0.127mm) or is out-of-round more than 0.003 in. (0.0762mm), it is advisable to rebore for the smallest possible oversize piston and rings. After measuring, mark the pistons with a felt-tip pen for reference and for assembly.

NOTE: *Boring of the cylinder block should be performed by a reputable machine shop with the proper equipment. In some cases, clean-up honing can be done with the cylinder block in the vehicle, but most excessive honing and all cylinder boring MUST BE*

done with the block stripped and removed from the vehicle.

PISTON PIN REPLACEMENT

All Engines — Except 2.2L Diesel

NOTE: *The following procedure requires the use of the GM Fixture/Support Assembly tool No. J-24086-20 or equivalent, the GM Piston Pin Removal tool No. J-24086-8 or equivalent, and the GM Piston Pin Installation tool No. J-24086-9 or equivalent.*

Use care at all times when handling and servicing the connecting rods and pistons. To prevent possible damage to these units, DO NOT clamp the rod or piston in a vise since they may become distorted. DO NOT allow the pistons to

Measuring the cylinder bore with a dial gauge

Clean the piston ring grooves using a ring groove cleaner

Removing the piston pin from the piston assembly

strike one another, against hard objects or bench surfaces, since distortion of the piston contour or nicks in the soft aluminum material may result.

1. Using an arbor press, the GM Fixture/Support Assembly tool No. J-24086-20 or equivalent, and the GM Piston Pin Removal tool No. J-24086-8 or equivalent, place the piston assembly in the fixture/support tool and press the pin from the piston assembly.

NOTE: *The piston and the piston pin are a matched set which are not serviced separately.*

2. Using solvent, wash the varnish and oil from the parts, then inspect the parts for scuffing or wear.

3. Using a micrometer, measure the diameter of the piston pin. Using a inside micrometer or a dial bore gauge, measure the diameter of the piston bore.

NOTE: *If the piston pin-to-piston clearance is in excess of 0.001 in. (0.0254mm), replace the piston and piston pin assembly.*

4. Before installation, lubricate the piston pin and the piston bore with engine oil.

5. To install the piston pin into the piston assembly, use an arbor press, the GM Fixture/Support Assembly tool No. J-24086-20 or equivalent, and the GM Piston Pin Installation tool No. J-24086-9 or equivalent, then press the piston pin into the piston/connecting rod assembly.

NOTE: *When installing the piston pin into the piston/connecting rod assembly and the installation tool bottoms onto the support assembly, DO NOT exceed 5000 lbs. of pressure for structural damage may occur to the tool.*

6. After installing the piston pin, make sure that the piston has freedom of movement with the piston pin. The piston/connecting rod assembly is ready for installation into the engine block.

2.2L Diesel Engine

1. Using a pair of snapring pliers, remove the piston pin snapring from the piston.

2. Slide the piston pin from the connecting rod and piston assembly.

NOTE: *When separating the piston from the connecting rod, be sure to mark them for reassembly purposes.*

3. Clean and inspect the piston and the connecting rod bearing surfaces for damage and/or wear; if necessary, replace the damaged part.

4. Lubricate the piston pin and bearing surfaces with clean engine oil.

5. Installation is the reverse of removal.

PISTON RING REPLACEMENT AND SIDE CLEARANCE MEASUREMENT

Check the pistons to see that the ring grooves and oil return holes have been properly

Installing the piston pin into the piston assembly

Replacing the piston pin snapring — 2.2L diesel engine

cleaned. Slide a piston ring into its groove and check the side clearance with a feeler gauge. Make sure the feeler gauge is inserted between the ring and its lower land (lower edge of the groove), because any wear that occurs forms a step at the inner portion of the lower land. If the piston grooves have been worn to the extent that relatively high steps exist on the lower land, the piston should be replaced, because these will interfere with the operation of the new rings and ring clearances will be excessive. Piston rings are not furnished in oversize widths to compensate for ring groove wear.

Install the rings on the piston, bottom ring first, using a piston ring expander. There is a high risk of breaking or distorting the rings and/or scratching the piston, if the rings are installed by hand or other means.

Position the rings on the piston as illustrated; spacing of the various piston ring gaps is crucial to the proper oil retention and cylinder wear. When installing the new rings, refer to the installation diagram furnished with the new parts.

CHECKING RING END GAP

The piston ring end gap should be checked while the rings are removed from the pistons. Incorrect end gap indicates that the wrong size rings are being used; **ring breakage could result.**

1. Compress the new piston ring into a cylinder (one at a time).
2. Squirt some clean oil into the cylinder so that the ring and the top 2 in. (51mm) of the cylinder wall are coated.
3. Using an inverted piston, push the ring approximately 1 in. (25.4mm) below the top of the cylinder.
4. Using a feeler gauge, measure the ring gap and compare it to the Ring Gap chart in this chapter. Carefully remove the ring from the cylinder.

CONNECTING ROD BEARING REPLACEMENT

Replacement bearings are available in standard size and undersize (for reground crankshafts). Connecting rod-to-crankshaft bearing clearance is checked using Plastigage® at either the top or the bottom of each crank journal. The Plastigage® has a range of 0.001–0.003 in. (0.0254–0.0762mm).

1. Remove the rod cap with the bearing shell. Completely clean the bearing shell and the crank journal, blow any oil from the oil hole in the crankshaft; place the Plastigage® lengthwise along the bottom center of the lower bearing shell, then install the cap with the shell and torque the bolt or nuts to specification. DO NOT turn the crankshaft with the Plastigage® on the bearing.
2. Remove the bearing cap with the shell. The flattened Plastigage® will be found sticking to either the bearing shell or the crank journal. DO NOT remove it yet.
3. Use the scale printed on the Plastigage® envelope to measure the flattened material at its widest point. The number within the scale which most closely corresponds to the width of the Plastigage® indicates the bearing clearance in thousandths of an inch.
4. Check the specifications chart in this chapter for the desired clearance. It is advisable to install a new bearing if the clearance exceeds 0.003 in. (0.0762mm); however, if the bearing is in good condition and is not being checked because of bearing noise, bearing replacement is not necessary.
5. If you are installing new bearings, try a

Removing the piston rings with a piston ring expander

Checking piston ring side clearance

Checking piston ring end gap with a feeler gauge

Measuring Plastigage® to determine main bearing clearance

standard size, then each undersize in order until one is found that is within the specified limits when checked for clearance with Plastigage®; each undersize shell has its size stamped on it.

6. When the proper size shell is found, clean off the Plastigage®, oil the bearing thoroughly, reinstall the cap with its shell and torque the rod bolt nuts to specifications.

NOTE: *With the proper bearing selected and the nuts torqued, it should be possible to move the connecting rod back and forth freely on the crank journal as allowed by the specified connecting rod end clearance. If the rod cannot be moved, either the rod bearing is too far undersize or the rod is misaligned.*

INSTALLATION

NOTE: *The following procedure requires the use of the Ring Compressor tool No. J-8037 or equivalent, and the ring installation tool.*

Position the rings on the piston; **spacing of the various piston ring gaps is crucial to proper oil retention and even cylinder wear.** When installing new rings, refer to the installation diagram furnished with the new parts.

Install the connecting rod to the piston, making sure that the piston installation notches and marks (if any) on the connecting rod are in proper relation to one another.

1. Make sure that the connecting rod big-end bearings (including the end cap) are of the correct size and properly installed.

2. Fit rubber hoses over the connecting rod bolts to protect the crankshaft journals, as in the Piston Removal procedure. Lubricate the connecting rod bearings with clean engine oil.

3. Using the Ring Compressor tool No. J-8037 or equivalent, compress the rings around the piston head. Insert the piston assembly into the cylinder, so that the notch (on top of the piston) faces the front of the engine.

4. From beneath the engine, coat each crank journal with clean oil. Using a hammer handle, drive the connecting rod/piston assembly into the cylinder bore. Align the connecting rod (with bearing shell) onto the crankshaft journal.

5. Remove the rubber hoses from the studs. Install the bearing cap (with bearing shell) onto the connecting rod and the cap nuts. Torque the connecting rod cap nuts to the following:

- 1.9L engine: 43 ft. lbs.
- 2.0L engine: 36 ft. lbs.
- 2.2L diesel: 62 ft. lbs.
- 2.5L engine: 32 ft. lbs.
- 2.8L engine: 39 ft. lbs.
- 4.3L engine: 45 ft. lbs.

NOTE: *When more than one connecting rod/piston assembly are being installed, the connecting rod cap nuts should only be tightened enough to keep each rod in position until the all have been installed. This will ease the installation of the remaining piston assemblies.*

6. Check the clearance between the sides of the connecting rods and the crankshaft using a feeler gauge. Spread the rods slightly with a small pry bar to insert the feeler gauge. If the

Undersize mark are stamped on the bearing shells. The tang fits in the notch on the connecting rod and cap

Piston ring positioning — 1.9L engine

"A" OIL RING SPACER GAP
(Tang in Hole or Slot within Arc)
"B" OIL RING RAIL GAPS
"C" 2ND COMPRESSION RING GAP
"D" TOP COMPRESSION RING GAP

Piston ring positioning — 2.0L and 2.5L engine

"A" OIL RING SPACER GAP
(Tang in Hole or Slot within Arc)

"B" OIL RING RAIL GAPS

"C" 2ND COMPRESSION RING GAP

"D" TOP COMPRESSION RING GAP

Piston ring positioning — 2.8L engine

Piston ring positioning — 2.2L engine

A. Oil Ring Rail Gaps
B. 2nd Compression Ring Gap
C. Notch In Piston
D. Oil Ring Spacer Gap
   (Tang In Hole Or Slot With Arc)
E. Top Compression Ring Gap

Piston ring positioning — 4.3L engine

Installing the piston rings

Install the piston ring compressor, then tap the piston into the cylinder bore with a wooden hammer handle

Check the connecting rod side clearance with a feeler gauge. Use a small pry bar to carefully spread the rods to specified clearance

Install the pistons with the notch facing the front of the engine

clearance is below the minimum tolerance, the rod may be machined to provide adequate clearance. If the clearance is excessive, substitute an unworn rod and recheck. If clearance is still outside specifications, the crankshaft must be welded and reground or replaced.

7. To complete the installation, reverse the removal procedures. Refill the cooling system. Refill the engine crankcase. Start the engine, allow it to reach normal operating temperatures and check for leaks.

Freeze Plugs

REMOVAL AND INSTALLATION

1. Remove the negative battery cable.
2. Drain the cooling system.

CAUTION: *When draining the coolant, keep in mind that cats and dogs are attracted by the ethylene glycol antifreeze, and are quite likely to drink any that is left in an uncovered container or in puddles on the ground. This will prove fatal in sufficient quantity. Always drain the coolant into a sealable container. Coolant should be reused unless it is contaminated or several years old.*

3. If equipped, remove the engine coolant drain plugs (located at the bottom of the block near the oil pan rail) and drain the coolant from the block. If the engine is not equipped with coolant drain plugs, drill a small hole in the leaking freeze plug and allow the coolant to drain.

4. Remove any components that restrict access to the freeze plug.

5. Using a chisel, tap the bottom edge of the freeze plug to cock it in the bore. Remove the plug using pliers. An alternate method is to

drill an $1/8$ in. hole in the plug and remove it using a dent puller.

6. Clean the freeze plug hole and using an appropriate driver tool or socket, install the freeze plug into the hole. Coat the freeze plug with sealer before installation.

7. Fill the engine with coolant, install the negative battery cable, start the engine and check for leaks.

Block Heater

REMOVAL AND INSTALLATION

1. Remove the negative battery cable.
2. Drain the cooling system.

CAUTION: *When draining the coolant, keep in mind that cats and dogs are attracted by the ethylene glycol antifreeze, and are quite likely to drink any that is left in an uncovered container or in puddles on the ground. This will prove fatal in sufficient quantity. Always drain the coolant into a sealable container. Coolant should be reused unless it is contaminated or several years old.*

3. If equipped, remove the engine coolant drain plugs (located at the bottom of the block near the oil pan rail) and drain the coolant from the block. If the engine is not equipped with coolant drain plugs, be ready to catch the coolant

that will drain from the block when the block heater is removed.

4. Disconnect the block heater electrical connector.

5. Loosen the block heater retaining screw and remove the block heater from the engine.

6. Coat the block heater O-ring with engine oil and clean the block heater hole of rust.

7. Install the block heater and tighten the retaining screw.

8. Fill the engine with coolant, install the negative battery cable, start the engine and check for leaks.

Rear Main Oil Seal

Replacing a rear main seal is a formidable task. Before replacing the seal, care should be taken in determining the exact source of the leak.

REPLACEMENT

1.9L Engine

NOTE: *The following procedure requires the use of the Seal Installer tool No. J-22928-A or equivalent*

Rear main seal — 1.9L engine

OIL SEAL RETAINER   SEAL   REAR PLATE

J-22345

Rear main seal installation — 1.9L engine

1. Remove the negative battery cable.

2. Raise and support the vehicle safely.

3. Remove the starter motor and lay it aside. DO NOT allow the starter to hang by the wires.

4. Remove driveshaft.

5. Support the rear of the engine and remove the transmission.

6. If equipped with a manual transmission, remove the clutch assembly.

7. Remove the flywheel-to-crankshaft bolts and the flywheel.

8. Remove the rear main seal retainer from the engine.

9. Using a medium pry bar, remove the rear main oil seal from the retainer and discard it.

10. Lubricate the seal lips and fill the space between the seal and the crankshaft with grease.

11. Using the Seal Installer tool No. J-22928-A or equivalent, drive the new rear main oil seal into the housing.

12. Installation is the reverse of removal.

2.0L and 2.8L Engine

To determine the type of oil seal on 2.0L engines, it will be necessary to look for an identification mark (oval) stamped on the right rear side of the engine where it connects to the transmission. If the oval appears, the engine uses an 11mm second design (one-piece) seal. If the oval does not appear the engine uses a 5mm first design seal. The first design seals may come in either a one or two piece configuration.

On 2.8L engines, the year of the vehicle (engine) determines the seal used as follows:

• 1982–85 engines use a 5mm first design rear main seal.

• 1986–91 engines use an 11mm second design rear main seal.

5MM TWO PIECE

1. Remove the oil pan and pump.

2. Remove the rear main bearing cap.

3. Remove the upper and lower seal. Clean the seal channel of any oil.

NOTE: *To install the replacement seal, you may need to loosen numbers 2, 3, and 4 rear main bearing caps.*

4. Apply a very thin coat of gasket sealant to the outside diameter of the upper seal. Install the seal with the lip inward, turning the crankshaft to ease installation.

5. Install the lower seal in the rear main bearing cap after applying sealant to the outside diameter.

6. Check the bearing clearance of the rear main bearing with Plastigage®. Repair as necessary if out of specification.

7. Lightly oil the rear main bearing after re-

moving the Plastigage®. Apply a 1mm bead of RTV to the rear main bearing cap between the rear main seal end and the oil pan rear seal groove. DO NOT allow sealant to come in contact with the rear main seal or the drain slot.

8. Lightly oil the rear main seal and install the rear main bearing cap. Torque the cap bolts to 70 ft. lbs.

9. Installation is the reverse of removal.

5MM ONE PIECE

1. Remove the engine.
2. Remove the oil pan and pump.
3. Remove the front (timing) cover and lock the chain tensioner with the pin.
4. Rotate the crankshaft until the timing marks on the cam and crank sprockets line up.
5. Remove the camshaft bolt, cam sprocket and timing chain.
6. Rotate the crankshaft to a horizontal position and remove the rod bearing nuts, caps and bearings.

NOTE: *The rod bearings and caps must be replaced in order. DO NOT mix them up.*

7. Remove the main bearing bolts, caps and bearings. Remove the crankshaft.
8. Remove the old rear main seal and clean the sealant from the crankshaft and block.
9. Apply a light coat of sealant to the outside diameter of the replacement seal.
10. Place a Seal Tool assembly on the rear area of the crankshaft. Position the seal tool so that the arrow points toward the engine. Place the crankshaft in the engine with the tool in this position. Remove and discard the tool.
11. Seal the rear main bearing split line (use sealant No. 1052756) and replace the rear main bearing and cap.
12. Replace the other bearings and caps. Tighten bolts to 63–75 ft. lbs.
13. Replace the rod bearings and caps. Tighten bolts to 34–50 ft. lbs.
14. Install the oil pump and tighten the bolt to 26–35 ft. lbs.
15. Align the crank sprocket timing mark

COATED AREA INDICATED
WITH #1052357 SEALER
OR EQUIVALENT.

SEALER

DRAIN
SLOT

Applying sealant to the rear main bearing — 2.0L and 2.8L engine with 5mm two-piece seal

OVAL MARKING
IN THIS LOCATION
INDICATES "THICK
REAR MAIN SEAL"

FRT

Seal identification mark — 2.0L engine

and install the cam sprocket and timing chain. Tighten bolt to 66–85 ft. lbs.

16. Installation is the reverse of removal.

11MM ONE PIECE

NOTE: *The following procedure requires the use of the Seal Installation tool No. J-34686 or equivalent.*

1. Support the rear of the engine and remove the transmission.
2. Remove the flywheel and verify the rear main seal is leaking.
3. Remove the seal by inserting a pry bar through the dust lip and prying the seal out.
4. Check the seal bore for nicks or damage. Repair as necessary.
5. Install the new seal using a Seal Installer tool No. J-34686.
6. Install the seal over the mandrill and bottom the dust lip (back of seal) squarely against the collar of the tool.
7. Align the dowel pin of the tool with the dowel pin hole in the crankshaft and attach the tool to the crankshaft by hand.
8. Turn the handle of the tool until the collar is tight against the case. This will ensure the seal is completely seated.
9. Turn the handle of the tool out until it stops. Check the seal making sure it is seated squarely in the bore.
10. Installation is the reverse of removal.

2.2L Diesel Engine

NOTE: *The following procedure requires the use of the Seal Installation tool No. J-22928 or equivalent.*

1. Raise and support the vehicle safely.
2. Remove the transmission. If equipped with a manual transmission, remove the clutch assembly.
3. Remove the flywheel-to-crankshaft bolts and the flywheel.
4. Using a medium pry bar, pry the rear main seal from the rear of the engine.

5. Using clean engine oil, lubricate the lips of the new seal.

6. Using the Seal Installation tool No. J-22928 or equivalent, drive the new seal into the rear of the engine until it seats.

7. Installation is the reverse of removal.

2.5L and 4.3L Engine

NOTE: *The following procedure requires the use of the Seal Installation tool (2.5L – No. J-34924 or 4.3L No. J-35621) or equivalent.*

1. Support the rear of the engine and remove the transmission.

2. Remove the flywheel and verify the rear main seal is leaking.

3. Remove the seal by inserting a pry bar through the dust lip and prying the seal out.

4. Check the seal bore for nicks or damage. Repair as necessary.

CAUTION RETAINER SPRING SIDE OF SEAL MUST FACE TOWARD FRONT OF CYLINDER & CASE.

Installing the 5mm one-piece rear main seal — 2.0L and 2.8L engine

A. Alignment hole in crankshaft
B. Dust lip
C. Dowel pin
D. Collar
E. Mandrel
F. Screws
85. Crankshaft rear oil seal

Installing the 11mm one-piece rear main seal

Rear main seal installation — 2.2L diesel

5. Install the new seal using a Seal Installer tool.

6. Install the seal over the mandrel and bottom the dust lip (back of seal) squarely against the collar of the tool.

7. Align the dowel pin of the tool with the dowel pin hole in the crankshaft and attach the tool to the crankshaft by hand.

8. Turn the handle of the tool until the collar is tight against the case. This will ensure the seal is completely seated.

9. Turn the handle of the tool out until it stops. Check the seal making sure it is seated squarely in the bore.

10. Installation is the reverse of removal.

Crankshaft and Main Bearings

REMOVAL AND INSTALLATION

1. Remove the engine from the vehicle.

2. Remove the flywheel and mount the engine onto a workstand.

3. Disconnect the spark plug wires from the plugs, then remove the spark plugs.

4. Remove the drive belt pulley from the damper pulley/hub, the damper pulley/hub-to-crankshaft bolt, the damper pulley/hub from the crankshaft and the timing cover from the engine.

NOTE: *After removing the damper pulley/hub from the crankshaft, be sure to remove the woodruff key from the crankshaft. When removing the damper pulley/hub from the crankshaft, the oil seal should be replaced.*

5. Rotate the crankshaft, until the timing marks on the timing gears or sprockets align with each other, then remove the timing gear or sprocket from the crankshaft.

NOTE: *After removing the timing gear or sprocket from the crankshaft, be sure to remove the woodruff key from the crankshaft.*

6. Drain the engine oil.

7. Remove the oil pump as necessary.

8. Inspect the connecting rods and bearing caps for identification marks (numbers); if there are none, mark them for reassembly purposes.

9. Remove the connecting rod nuts and caps, then store them in the order of removal. Place short pieces of rubber hose on the con-

necting rod studs to prevent damaging the crankshaft bearing surfaces.

10. Check the main bearing caps for identification marks (if not identified, mark them). Remove the main bearing caps and store them in order, for reassembly purposes; the caps must be reinstalled in their original position.

11. Remove the crankshaft, the main bearing inserts and the rear main oil seal.

NOTE: *On engines equipped with an 11mm one-piece rear main seal, it will be necessary to remove the seal first before removing the crankshaft.*

12. Using solvent, clean all of the parts and inspect for damage.

13. To install, use new bearing shell inserts and check the bearing clearances.

NOTE: *If necessary, deliver the crankshaft to an automotive machine shop, have the crankshaft journals ground and new bearing shells matched.*

14. Lubricate all of the parts and oil seals with clean engine oil.

15. Using a feeler gauge and a medium pry bar, move the crankshaft forward-and-rearward. Check the crankshaft endplay by inserting a feeler gauge between the crankshaft and the thrust bearing shell. An alternate method is to use a dial indicator at the crankshaft snout. Install the indicator, move the crankshaft rearward, zero the indicator and then move the crankshaft forward. the dial indicator will read the endplay. Thrust bearing location is as follows:

- 1.9L engine: No. 3
- 2.0L engine: No. 4
- 2.2L engine: No. 3
- 2.5L engine: No. 5
- 2.8L engine: No. 3
- 4.3L engine: No. 4

16. Tighten main bearing caps (in three steps) to the following:

- 1.9L engine: 75 ft. lbs.
- 2.0L engine: 70 ft. lbs.
- 2.2L engine: 116–130 ft. lbs.
- 2.5L engine: 70 ft. lbs.
- 2.8L engine: 70 ft. lbs.
- 4.3L engine: 80 ft. lbs.

17. Install connecting rod caps and torque rod bolts to the following:

- 1.9L engine: 43 ft. lbs.
- 2.0L engine: 37 ft. lbs.
- 2.2L engine: 65 ft. lbs.
- 2.5L engine: 32 ft. lbs.
- 2.8L engine: 39 ft. lbs.
- 4.3L engine: 45 ft. lbs.

18. Check connecting rod side clearance by inserting a feeler gauge between the side of the rod and the crankshaft. If not within specification, repair as necessary.

FRONT OF ENGINE

1. Rubber hose
2. #4 rod
3. #3 rod
4. Oil pan bolt
5. Note overlap of adjacent rods
6. Rubber bands

Support the connecting rods with rubber bands and install rubber rod bolt caps to protect the crankshaft during removal/installation

19. The remainder of the installation procedure is the reverse of removal.

20. Fill the cooling system (with the saved coolant) and the crankcase (with new oil). Start the engine, allow it to reach normal operating temperatures and check for leaks.

CLEANING AND INSPECTION

NOTE: *The following procedure requires the use of Plastigage® or a micrometer set consisting of inside and outside micrometers, and a dial indicator.*

1. Remove the bearing cap and wipe the oil from the crankshaft journal and outer/inner surfaces of the bearing shell.

2. To check the crankshaft/rod bearing clearances using a micrometer, perform the following procedures:

a. Set the crankshaft in the block with the bearings inserted. Using a dial indicator

OIL GROOVE

Thrust bearing location

Aligning the thrust bearings and torquing the main caps

Checking crankshaft runout

set on the center bearing journal, check the crankshaft runout. Repair or replace the crankshaft if out of specification.

b. Using an outside micrometer, measure the bearing journals for diameter and out-of-round conditions; if necessary, regrind the bearing journals.

c. Install the bearings and caps and torque the nuts/bolts to specifications. Using an inside micrometer, check the bearing bores in the engine block. If out of specification, regrind the bearing bores to the next largest oversize.

d. The difference between the two readings is the bearing clearance. If out of specification, inspect for the cause and repair as necessary.

3. To inspect the main bearing surfaces, using the Plastigage® method, perform the following procedures:

a. Using a piece of Plastigage® material, position it in the center of the bearing surface(s).

b. Install the bearing caps and torque the cap nuts/bolts to specifications.

NOTE: *When the Plastigage® material is installed on the bearing surfaces, DO NOT rotate the crankshaft.*

c. Remove the bearing caps and determine the bearing clearance by comparing the width of the flattened Plastigage® material at its widest point with the graduations on the gauging material container.

Checking crankshaft endplay with a feeler gauge

Checking main bearing journal diameter

Measuring connecting rod side clearance

Position Plastigage® on the bearing surface. The surface must be clean and dry

Checking main bearing bore diameter with bearings installed

NOTE: *The number within the graduation on the envelope indicates the clearance in millimeters or thousandths of an inch. If the clearance is greater than allowed. Replace bearings with the next largest oversize. Recheck the clearance after replacing the shells.*

Flywheel

The flywheel and the ring gear are machined from one piece of metal and cannot be separated.

REMOVAL AND INSTALLATION

NOTE: *The following procedure requires the use of the Clutch Disc Aligner tool No. J-33169 (2.5L & 2.8L), J-33034 (all others) or equivalent.*

1. Refer to the "Manual Transmission, Removal and Installation" procedures in Chapter 6 and remove the transmission from the bell housing.

2. Remove the slave cylinder-to-bell housing bolts and move the slave cylinder aside; DO NOT disconnect the hydraulic line from the cylinder.

3. Remove the bell housing-to-engine bolts and the bell housing from the engine. When removing the bell housing, slide the clutch fork from the ball stud.

NOTE: *The clutch fork ball stud is threaded into the bell housing and can easily be replaced, if necessary.*

4. Position the clutch disc aligner tool in the pilot bushing (to support the clutch disc).

5. Inspect the flywheel/pressure plate assembly for match marks (a stamped or a painted **X** mark); if no mark exists, mark the flywheel and the pressure plate.

6. Loosen the clutch-to-flywheel bolts, evenly (one turn at a time), until the spring tension is relieved, then remove the retaining bolts, the pressure plate and the clutch assembly.

7. Remove the flywheel-to-crankshaft bolts and the flywheel from the engine.

8. Clean the clutch disc (use a stiff brush), the pressure plate and the flywheel of all dirt, oil and grease. Inspect the flywheel, the pressure plate and the clutch disc for scoring, cracks, heat checking and/or other defects.

NOTE: *When the flywheel is removed, it is a good idea to replace the rear main oil seal, the pilot bushing and/or the clutch plate (if necessary).*

9. To install, align flywheel with the crankshaft, then torque the flywheel-to-crankshaft bolts to the following:
   • 1.9L engine: 76 ft. lbs.
   • 2.0L engine: 50 ft. lbs.
   • 2.2L diesel: 70 ft. lbs.
   • 2.5L engine: 55 ft. lbs.
   • 2.8L engine: 52 ft. lbs.
   • 4.3L engine: 75 ft. lbs.

10. Position the clutch disc aligner tool in the pilot bushing (to support the clutch disc), then assemble the clutch disc (the damper springs facing the transmission), the pressure plate and the retaining bolts onto the flywheel.

NOTE: *When installing the pressure plate onto the flywheel, be sure to align the **X** marks.*

11. Tighten the pressure plate-to-flywheel bolts gradually and evenly (to prevent clutch plate distortion), then remove the alignment tool.

12. Installation is the reverse of removal.

13. Lubricate the pilot bushing and the clutch release lever.

EXHAUST SYSTEM

Two types of pipe connections are used on the exhaust system, they are: the ball joint (to allow angular movement for alignment purposes) and the slip joint. Gaskets are used only with the ball joint type connections.

2.8 L ENGINE

1.9 LITER ENGINE

VIEW A

TIGHTEN TO
32 N•m (23 FT LBS)

SEAL

TIGHTEN TO
20 N•m (15 FT LBS)

TIGHTEN TO
34 N•m (25 FT LBS)

VIEW B

MOUNT

TIGHTEN TO
10 N•m (85 IN. LBS)

TIGHTEN TO
47 N•m (35 FT LBS)

TIGHTEN TO
34 N•m (25 FT LBS)

VIEW C

TIGHTEN TO
10 N•m (85 IN. LBS)

TIGHTEN TO
34 N•m (25 FT LBS)

TIGHTEN TO
15 N•m (10 FT LBS)

TIGHTEN TO
17 N•m (12 FT LBS)

VIEW D

VIEW E

Exhaust system components — typical

The system is supported by free hanging rubber mountings which permit some movement of the exhaust system but do not allow the transfer of noise and vibration into the passenger compartment. Any noise vibrations or rattles in the exhaust system are usually caused by misalignment of the parts.

CAUTION: *Before performing any operation on the exhaust system, be sure to allow it to cool.*

Front Pipe

REMOVAL AND INSTALLATION

NOTE: *The following procedure requires the use of GM Sealing Compound No. 1051249 or equivalent, at the slip joint connection.*

1. Raise and support the vehicle safely.
2. Remove the front pipe(s)-to-manifold(s) nuts and separate (pry, if necessary) the front pipe (ball joint) from the exhaust manifold(s).
3. At the catalytic converter, loosen the

front pipe-to-converter clamp nuts, then slide the clamp away from the converter and separate the front pipe from the converter.

NOTE: *Use a twisting motion to separate the front pipe-to-converter slip joint connection. If the front pipe cannot be removed from the catalytic converter, use a hammer (to loosen the connection) or wedge tool to separate the connection.*

4. Inspect the pipe for holes, damage or deterioration; if necessary, replace the front pipe.

5. Installation is the reverse of removal.

6. Lubricate the front pipe-to-manifold(s) studs/nuts and the front pipe-to-converter clamp threads. Torque the front pipe-to-exhaust manifold bolts to 15 ft. lbs. and the front pipe-to-converter clamp nuts to 35 ft. lbs.

7. Start the engine and check for exhaust leaks.

Catalytic Converter

The catalytic converter is an emission control device added to the exhaust system to reduce the emission of hydrocarbon and carbon monoxide pollutants.

NOTE: *The following procedure requires the use of GM Sealing Compound No. 1051249 or equivalent, at the slip joint connection.*

REMOVAL AND INSTALLATION

1. Raise and support the vehicle safely.

2. Remove the catalytic converter-to-muffler bolts and separate the muffler from the converter.

NOTE: *The connection between the converter and the muffler is a ball joint type, which can be easily separated.*

3. Remove the catalytic converter-to-front pipe clamp nuts and move the clamp forward.

4. Remove the converter-to-mounting bracket bolts, then twist the converter to separate it from the front pipe.

5. Inspect the condition of the catalytic converter for physical damage, replace it, if necessary.

NOTE: *When installing the catalytic converter, be sure that it is installed with adequate clearance from the floor pan, to prevent overheating of the vehicle floor.*

6. Align the components and reverse the removal procedures.

7. Torque the converter-to-mounting bracket bolts to 25 ft. lbs., the converter-to-front pipe clamp nuts to 35 ft. lbs. and the converter-to-muffler bolts to 23 ft. lbs. Be careful not to damage the pipe sealing surfaces when tightening the retaining clamps.

8. Start the engine and check for exhaust leaks.

Muffler

REMOVAL AND INSTALLATION

1. Remove the catalytic converter-to-muffler flange bolts and separate the items.

2. Remove the intermediate and rear tail pipe-to-bracket clamp nuts/bolts.

3. Remove the muffler bracket-to-chassis bolts and lower the muffler from the vehicle.

4. Coat the slip joints with GM Sealing Compound No. 1051249 or equivalent, and loosely install the components onto the vehicle.

5. After aligning the components, tighten the connecting bolts and clamps. Torque the muffler bracket-to-chassis bolts 12 ft. lbs., the rear tail pipe-to-bracket clamp nuts/bolts to 25 ft. lbs., the intermediate pipe-to-chassis bracket bolt to 85 inch lbs. and the muffler-to-converter bolts to 23 ft. lbs.

NOTE: *When torquing the exhaust system connectors, be careful not to tighten the pipe clamps too tight.*

6. Start the engine and check for exhaust leaks.

TROUBLESHOOTING

Engine Speed Oscillates at Idle

When the engine idle speed will not remain constant, replace or repair the following items or systems, as necessary:

• A faulty fuel pump.
• A leaky Exhaust Gas Recirculation (EGR) valve.
• A blown head gasket.
• A worn camshaft.
• Worn timing gears, chain or sprockets.
• Leaking intake manifold-to-engine gasket.
• A blocked Positive Crankcase Ventilation (PCV) valve.
• Overheating of the cooling system.

Low Power Output of Engine

When the engine power output is below normal, replace or repair the following items or systems, as necessary:

• Overheating of the cooling system.
• Leaks in the vacuum system.
• Leaking of the fuel pump or hoses.
• Unadjusted valve timing.
• A blown head gasket.
• A slipping clutch disc or unadjusted pedal.

- Excessive piston-to-bore clearance.
- Worn piston rings.
- A worn camshaft.
- Sticking valve(s) or weak valve spring(s).
- A poorly operating diverter valve.
- A faulty pressure regulator valve (Auto. Trans.).
- Low fluid level (Auto. Trans.).

Poor High Speed Operation

When the engine cannot maintain high speed operations, replace or repair the following items or systems, as necessary:
- A faulty fuel pump producing low fuel volume.
- A restriction in the intake manifold.
- A worn distributor shaft.
- Unadjusted valve timing.
- Leaking valves or worn valve springs.

Poor Acceleration

When the engine experiences poor acceleration characteristics, replace or repair the following items or systems, as necessary:
- Incorrect ignition timing.
- Poorly seated valves.
- Improperly adjusted accelerator pump stroke (carburetor equipped).
- Worn accelerator pump diaphragm or piston (carburetor equipped).

Backfire—Intake Manifold

When the engine backfires through the intake manifold, replace or repair the following items or systems, as necessary:
- Incorrect ignition timing.
- Incorrect operation of the choke (carburetor equipped).
- Choke setting (initial clearance) too large (carburetor equipped).
- Defective Exhaust Gas Recirculation (EGR) valve.
- A very lean air/fuel mixture (carburetor equipped).

Backfire—Exhaust Manifold

When the engine backfires through the exhaust manifold, replace or repair the following items or systems, as necessary:
- Leaks in the vacuum hose system.
- Leaks in the exhaust system.
- Faulty choke adjustments or operation (carburetor equipped).
- Faulty vacuum diverter valve.

Engine Detonation (Dieseling)

When the engine operates beyond the controlled limits, replace or repair the following items or systems, as necessary:

- Faulty ignition electrical system components.
- The ignition timing may be too far advanced.
- Inoperative Exhaust Gas Recirculation (EGR) valve.
- Inoperative Positive Crankcase Ventilation (PCV) valve.
- Faulty or loose spark plugs.
- Clogged fuel delivery system.
- Sticking, leaking or broken valves.
- Excessive deposits in the combustion chambers.
- Leaks in the vacuum system.

Excessive Oil Leakage

When large amounts of oil are noticed under the engine after each operation, replace or repair the following items or systems, as necessary:
- Damaged or broken oil filter gasket.
- Leaking oil pressure sending switch.
- Worn rear main oil seal gasket.
- Worn front main oil seal gasket.
- Damaged or broken fuel pump gasket (mechanical pump).
- Damaged or loose valve cover gasket.
- Damaged oil pan gasket or bent oil pan.
- Improperly seated oil pan drain plug.
- Broken timing chain cover gasket.
- Blocked camshaft bearing drain hole.

Heavy Oil Consumption

When the engine is burning large amounts of oil, replace or repair the following items or systems, as necessary:
- The engine oil level may be to high.
- The engine oil may be to thin.
- Wrong size of piston rings.
- Clogged piston ring grooves or oil return slots.
- Insufficient tension of the piston rings.
- Piston rings may be sticking in the grooves.
- Excessively worn piston ring grooves.
- Reversed (up-side-down) compression rings.
- Non-staggered piston ring gaps.
- Improper Positive Crankcase Ventilation (PCV) valve operation.
- Damaged valve O-ring seals.
- Restricted oil drain back holes.
- Worn valve stem or guides.
- Damaged valve stem oil deflectors.
- Too long intake gasket dowels.
- Mismatched rail and expander of the oil ring.
- Excessive clearance of the main and connecting rods.

• Scored or worn cylinder walls.

Negative Oil Pressure

When the engine presents no oil pressure, replace or repair the following items or systems, as necessary:
• Low oil level in the crankcase.
• Broken oil pressure gauge or sender.
• Blocked oil pump passages.
• Blocked oil pickup screen or tube.
• Malfunctioning oil pump.
• Sticking oil pressure relief valve.
• Leakage of the internal oil passages.
• Worn (loose) camshaft bearings.

Low Oil Pressure

When the engine presents low oil pressure, replace or repair the following items or systems, as necessary:
• Low oil level in the crankcase.
• Blocked oil pickup screen or tube.
• Malfunctioning or excessive clearance of the oil pump.
• Sticking oil pressure relief valve.
• Very thin engine oil.
• Worn main, rod or camshaft bearings.

High Oil Pressure

When the engine presents high oil pressure, replace or repair the following items or systems, as necessary:
• Sticking (closed) oil pressure relief valve.
• Wrong grade of oil.
• Faulty oil pressure gauge or sender.

Knocking Main Bearings

When the main bearings are constantly making noise, replace or repair the following items or systems, as necessary:
• Oval shaped crankshaft journals.
• Loose torque converter or flywheel mounting bolts.
• Loose damper pulley hub.
• Excessive clearance of the main bearings.
• Excessive belt tension.
• Low oil supply to the main bearings.
• Extreme crankshaft end play.

Knocking Connecting Rods

When the connecting rod bearings are constantly making noise, replace or repair the following items or systems, as necessary:
• Misaligned connecting rod or cap.
• Missing bearing shell or excessive bearing clearance.
• Incorrectly torqued connecting rod bolts.

• Connecting rod journal of the crankshaft is out-of-round.

Knocking Pistons and Rings

When the pistons and/rings are constantly making noise, replace or repair the following items or systems, as necessary:
• Misaligned connecting rods.
• Out-of-round or tapered cylinder bore.
• Loose or tight ring side clearance.
• Build-up of carbon on the piston(s).
• Piston-to-cylinder bore clearance is excessive.
• Broken piston rings.
• Loose or seized piston pin(s).

Knocking Valve Train

When the valve train is constantly making noise, replace or repair the following items or systems, as necessary:
• Retighten any loose rocker arms.
• Remove any dirt or chips in the valve lifters.
• Excessive valve stem-to-guide clearance.
• Remove restrictions from valve lifter oil holes.
• Incorrect valve lifter may be installed in the engine.
• Valve lock(s) may be missing.
• Valve lifter check ball may be faulty.
• Valve lifter leak down may be excessive.
• Rocker arm nut may be reversed (installed up-side-down).
• Camshaft lobes may be excessively worn.
• Bent or worn pushrods.
• Excessively worn bridged pivots or rocker arms.
• Cocked or broken valve springs.
• Bent valve(s).
• Worn valve lifter face(s).
• Damaged lifter plunger or pushrod seat.

Knocking Valves

When the valves are constantly noisy, replace or repair the following items or systems, as necessary:
• Unadjusted valve lash.
• Valve springs may be broken.
• Pushrods may be bent.
• Camshaft lobes may be excessively worn.
• Dirty or worn valve lifters.
• Valve guides may be worn.
• Valve seat or face runout may be excessive.
• Loose rocker arm studs.

Emission Controls

4

EMISSION CONTROLS

Crankcase Ventilation System

OPERATION

The Positive Crankcase Ventilation (PCV) system is used on all vehicles to evacuate the crankcase vapors. Outside vehicle air is routed through the air cleaner to the crankcase where it mixes with blow-by gases and is passed through the PCV valve. The air is then routed into the intake manifold to be burned in the combustion process. The PCV valve meters the air flow rate, which varies under engine operation, depending on manifold vacuum. In order to maintain idle quality, the PCV valve limits the air flow when intake manifold vacuum is high. If abnormal operating conditions occur, the system will allow excessive blow-by gases to back flow through the crankcase vent tube into the air cleaner. These blow-by gases will then be burned by normal combustion.

On the 1.9L engine, the blow by gases are forced back into the intake manifold through a closed loop system which consists of a baffle plate and an orifice mounted in the intake manifold.

A plugged PCV valve or hose may cause rough idle, stalling or slow idle speed, oil leaks, oil in the air cleaner or sludge in the engine. A leaking PCV valve or hose could cause rough idle, stalling or high idle speed.

Positive crankcase ventilation (PCV) system diagram

Inspect the PCV system hose(s) and connections at each tune-up and replace any deteriorated hoses. Check the PCV valve at every tune-up and replace it at 30,000 mile intervals.

TESTING

1. Remove the PCV valve from the rocker arm cover.

2. Operate the engine at idle speed.

3. Place your thumb over the end of the valve to check for vacuum. If no vacuum exists, check the valve, the hoses or the manifold port for a plugged condition.

4. Remove the valve from the hose(s), then shake it and listen for a rattling of the check needle (inside the valve); the rattle means the valve is working. If no rattle is heard, replace the valve.

REMOVAL AND INSTALLATION

1. Pull the PCV valve from the rocker arm cover grommet.

2. Remove the hose(s) from the PCV valve.

PCV system — 2.8L engine

3. Shake the valve to make sure that it is not plugged.

4. Installation is the reverse of removal. Always install a new PCV valve.

Evaporative Emission Control System (EECS)

OPERATION

The Evaporative Emission Control System (EECS) is designed to prevent fuel tank vapors

← BLOW-BY GAS

--- FRESH AIR

⇐ BLOW-BY GAS & FRESH AIR

PCV system — 1.9L engine

1	TUBE ASSEMBLY
2	PCV VALVE
3	GROMMET
4	BOLT—TIGHTEN TO 25 N·m (18 LBS. FT.)
5	CONNECTOR
6	HOSE

PCV system — 2.5L engine

1	PCV	4	GROMMET
2	TBI UNIT PORT "C"	5	TUBE ASSEMBLY
3	HOSE	6	AIR CLEANER EXTENSION

PCV valve — 4.3L engine

from being emitted into the atmosphere. Gasoline vapors are absorbed and stored by a fuel vapor charcoal canister. The charcoal canister absorbs the gasoline vapors and stores them

1. TBI
2. Canister purge port
3. Vacuum signal
4. Purge valve
5. Vapor storage canister
6. Purge air
7. Fuel tank
8. Fuel
9. Vapor
10. Pressure-vacuum relief gas cap
11. Vent restricter
12. Fuel tank vent
13. Purge line

EEC system — 2.5L and 4.3L engines

until certain engine conditions are met, then the vapors are purged and burned in the combustion process.

The charcoal canister purge cycle is controlled either by a thermostatic vacuum switch or by a timed vacuum source. The thermostatic vacuum switch is installed in the coolant passage and prevents canister purge when engine operating temperature is below 115°F (46°C). The timed vacuum source uses a manifold vacuum-controlled diaphragm to control canister purge. When the engine is running, full manifold vacuum is applied to the top tube of the purge valve which lifts the valve diaphragm and opens the valve.

A vent, located in the fuel tank, allows fuel vapors to flow to the charcoal canister. A tank pressure control valve, used on high altitude applications, prevents canister purge when the engine is not running. The fuel tank cap does not normally vent to the atmosphere but is designed to provide both vacuum and pressure relief.

Poor engine idle, stalling and poor driveability can be caused by a damaged canister or split, damaged or improperly connected hoses.

Evidence of fuel loss or fuel vapor odor can be caused by a liquid fuel leak; a cracked or damaged vapor canister; disconnected, misrouted, kinked or damaged vapor pipe or canister hoses; a damaged air cleaner or improperly seated air cleaner gasket.

1. Port "B" ported vacuum
2. Port "F" bowl vent
3. Fuel bowl vent solenoid
4. Fuel vapor connector
5. Fuel vapor purge solenoid
6. Tank pressure control valve
7. Vent/purge hose
8. Canister
9. Tank vapor vent pipe
10. Ported vacuum line

EEC system — 2.8L engines

TESTING

Charcoal Canister

This fuel vapor canister is used to absorb and store fuel vapors from the fuel tank. Engines employing the timed vacuum source purge system use a canister purge valve which is integral to the vapor canister. The valve consists of a housing and tube molded into the canister cover, valve assembly, diaphragm and valve spring. The diaphragm cover has a built-in control vacuum signal tube.

NOTE: *The 2.2L diesel engine is not equipped with a charcoal canister.*

1. Remove the lower tube of the canister (purge valve) and install a short length of tube, then try to blow through it (little or no air should pass).

2. Using a vacuum source, apply 15 in.Hg to the upper tube of the canister (purge valve). The diaphragm should hold the vacuum for at least 20 seconds, if not replace the canister.

3. While holding the vacuum on the upper tube, blow through the lower tube (air should now pass); if not, replace the canister.

Thermostatic Vacuum Switch (TVS)

NOTE: *The number stamped on the base of the switch (valve) is the calibration temperature.*

1. With engine temperature below 100°F (38°C), apply vacuum to the manifold side of the switch. The switch should hold vacuum.

2. As the engine temperature increases above 122°F (50°C), vacuum should drop off.

3. Replace the switch if it fails either test.

NOTE: *A leakage of up to 2 in.Hg/2 min. is allowable and does not mean that the valve is defective.*

REMOVAL AND INSTALLATION

Charcoal Canister

1. Label and disconnect the hoses from the canister.

2. Loosen the retaining bolt and remove the canister from the vehicle.

NOTE: *If necessary to replace the canister filter, simply pull the filter from the bottom of the charcoal filter and install a new one.*

3. Installation is the reverse of removal.

Thermostatic Vacuum Switch (TVS)

The TVS is located near the engine coolant outlet housing.

1. Drain the cooling system to a level below the TVS.

CAUTION: *When draining the coolant, keep in mind that cats and dogs are attracted by the ethylene glycol antifreeze, and are quite likely to drink any that is left in an uncovered container or in puddles on the ground. This will prove fatal in sufficient quantity. Always drain the coolant into a sealable container. Coolant should be reused unless it is contaminated or several years old.*

1. EGR valve
2. TVS

Location of the Thermostatic Vacuum Switch on the 2.8L engine — others similar

2. Disconnect the vacuum hoses from the TVS.

3. Using a wrench, remove the TVS from the engine.

4. Inspect and test the TVS; if defective, replace it.

5. Apply a soft setting sealant to the TVS threads. Install the TVS and torque to 120 inch lbs.

6. Reconnect the vacuum hoses. Refill the cooling system.

NOTE: *DO NOT apply sealant to the sensor end of the TVS.*

Exhaust Gas Recirculation (EGR) System

OPERATION

The EGR system is used to reduce oxides of nitrogen (NOx) emission levels caused by high combustion chamber temperatures. This is accomplished by the use of an EGR valve which opens, under specific engine operating conditions, to admit a small amount of exhaust gas into the intake manifold, below the throttle plate. The exhaust gas mixes with the incoming air charge and displaces a portion of the oxygen in the air/fuel mixture entering the combustion chamber. The exhaust gas does not support combustion of the air/fuel mixture but it takes up volume, the net effect of which is to lower the temperature of the combustion process.

The EGR valve is a mounted on the intake manifold and has an opening into the exhaust manifold. The EGR valve is opened by manifold vacuum to permit exhaust gas to flow into the intake manifold. If too much exhaust gas enters, combustion will not occur. Because of this, very little exhaust gas is allowed to pass through the valve. The EGR system will be activated once the engine reaches normal operating temperature and the EGR valve will open when engine operating conditions are above idle speed and, in some applications, below Wide Open Throttle (WOT). The EGR system is deactivated on vehicles equipped with a Transmission Converter Clutch (TCC) when the TCC is engaged. There are 2 basic types of systems as described below.

Ported EGR Valve

This valve is controlled by a flexible diaphragm. It is spring-loaded in order to hold the valve closed. When ported vacuum is applied to the top side of the diaphragm, spring pressure is overcome and the valve in the exhaust gas port is opened. This allows the exhaust gas to be pulled into the intake manifold and enter the cylinders with the air/fuel mixture. Port EGR valves have no identification stamped below the part number.

Negative Backpressure EGR Valve

The negative backpressure EGR valve is similar to the positive backpressure EGR valve, except that the bleed valve spring is moved from above the diaphragm to below and the valve is normally closed. The negative backpressure valve varies the amount of exhaust gas flow into the intake manifold depending on manifold vacuum and variations in exhaust backpressure. The diaphragm on the valve has an internal air bleed hole which is held closed by a small spring when there is no exhaust backpressure. Engine vacuum opens the EGR valve against the pressure of a spring. When manifold vacuum combines with negative exhaust backpressure, the vacuum bleed hole opens and the EGR valve closes. This valve will open if vacuum is applied with the engine not running. Negative backpressure EGR valves will have a "N" stamped on the top side of the valve below the part number and after the date built.

ELECTRONIC EGR CONTROL

On certain vehicle applications, EGR flow is regulated by an ECM-controlled Electronic Vacuum Regulator Valve (EVRV). The EGR valve is controlled by a vacuum solenoid that uses pulse width modulation. This means that the ECM turns the solenoid on and off many times a second and varies the amount of ON time (pulse width) which in turn varies the amount of EGR.

INCORRECT EGR OPERATION

Too much EGR flow at idle, cruise or during cold operation may result in the engine stalling after cold start, the engine stalling at idle after deceleration, vehicle surge during cruise and

TO CARBURETOR VIA THERMAL VACUUM SWITCH

SPRING

DIAPHRAGM CHAMBER

SEAL

DIAPHRAGM

VALVE CHAMBER

VALVE OPEN

SHAFT

TO INTAKE MANIFOLD

EXHAUST GAS INLET PORT

METERING VALVE

Cross section of a typical EGR valve

EGR system — 1.9L engine

EGR system — 2.0L engine

1. EGR valve
2. Exhaust gas
4. Intake flow
6. Vacuum port
7. Throttle valve
8. Vacuum chamber
9. Valve return spring
10. Thermal vacuum switch
11. Coolant
12. Diaphragm

EGR system — 2.8L carbureted engine

EGR valve — 2.8L engine

1	EGR VALVE
2	VACUUM HARNESS
3	EGR SOLENOID
4	MANIFOLD VACUUM

EGR system — 2.8L TBI engine

rough idle. If the EGR valve is always open, the vehicle may not idle. Too little or no EGR flow allows combustion temperatures to get too high which could result in spark knock (detonation), engine overheating and/or emission test failure.

TESTING (Except TBI Engines)

EGR Valve

1. Check hose routing (Refer to Vehicle Emission Control Information Label).

2. Check the EGR valve signal tube orifice for obstructions.

3. Connect a vacuum gauge between EGR valve and carburetor, then check the vacuum; the engine must be at operating temperature of 195°F (90°C). With the engine running at approximately 3000 rpm there should be at least 5 in.Hg.

4. Check the EGR solenoid for correct operation.

5. To check the valve, perform the following procedures:

   a. Depress the valve diaphragm.

   b. With the diaphragm still depressed

1	EGR VALVE	4	MANIFOLD VACUUM (PORT – J)
2	VACUUM HARNESS	5	BOLT – TIGHTEN TO 2 N·m (18 lb.in.)
3	EGR SOLENOID	6	HARNESS CONNECTOR

EGR system – 4.3L engine

hold finger over source tube and release the diaphragm.

   c. Check the diaphragm and seat for movement. The valve is good if it takes over 20 seconds for the diaphragm to move to the seated position (valve closed).

   d. Replace the EGR valve if it takes less than 20 seconds to move to the seated position.

EGR VALVE CLEANING

NOTE: *DO NOT wash valve assembly in solvents or degreaser — permanent damage to valve diaphragm may result. Also, sand blasting of the valve is recommended since this can affect the operation of the valve.*

1. Remove the EGR valve-to-intake manifold bolts and the valve, discard the gasket.

2. With a wire brush, remove the exhaust deposits from the mounting surface and around the valve.

3. Depress the valve diaphragm and look at the valve seating area through the valve outlet for cleanliness. If the valve and/or seat are not completely clean, repeat Step 2.

4. Look for exhaust deposits in the valve

1	EGR VALVE	4	PORTED MANIFOLD VACUUM (PORT F)
2	VACUUM HARNESS	5	BOLT TIGHTEN TO 4 N·m (35 LBS. IN.)
3	EGR SOLENOID		

EGR system – 2.5L engine

TESTING (TBI Engines)

EGR SYSTEM CHECK
2.5L

ASSUMES NO CODE 24 OR 32 IS STORED

- CHECK VACUUM SOURCE TO EGR SOLENOID (IF NOT OK, REPAIR).
- IGNITION "OFF".
- DISCONNECT EGR SOLENOID VACUUM HARNESS.
- INSTALL HAND HELD VACUUM PUMP ON MANIFOLD SIDE OF SOLENOID.
- APPLY VACUUM. DOES SOLENOID HOLD VACUUM?

YES
- IGNITION "ON", ENGINE STOPPED.
- DOES VACUUM DROP?

NO
FAULTY SOLENOID

NO
- GROUND DIAGNOSTIC TEST TERMINAL. DOES VACUUM DROP?

YES
CKT 435 SHORTED TO GROUND OR FAULTY ECM. SEE "DIAGNOSTIC AIDS" ON FACING PAGE.

YES
- REMOVE GROUND FROM DIAGNOSTIC TEST TERMINAL.
- IGNITION "OFF".
- CONNECT A VACUUM PUMP TO EGR SIDE OF VACUUM HARNESS.
- USING A MIRROR, OBSERVE EGR DIAPHRAGM WHILE APPLYING VACUUM
- DIAPHRAGM SHOULD MOVE FREELY AND HOLD VACUUM FOR AT LEAST 20 SECONDS.

NO
DISCONNECT SOLENOID ELECTRICAL CONNECTOR. PROBE CKT 439 WITH A TEST LIGHT TO GROUND.

LIGHT "ON"
CONNECT TEST LIGHT BETWEEN HARNESS CONNECTOR TERMINALS.

LIGHT "OFF"
OPEN CKT 439

OK

NOT OK
CHECK FOR RESTRICTION IN VACUUM LINE TO VALVE OR IN VALVE VACUUM PORT ORIFACE. IF OK, REPLACE EGR VALVE.

LIGHT "ON"
FAULTY SOLENOID

LIGHT "OFF"
OPEN CKT 435, SHORT TO VOLTAGE OR FAULTY ECM.

- APPLY VACUUM TO EGR VALVE.
- START ENGINE AND IMMEDIATELY OBSERVE VACUUM AND VALVE POSITION.
- VALVE IS GOOD IF VALVE MOVES TO SEATED POSITION (VALVE CLOSED) AND VACUUM DROPPED WHILE STARTING ENGINE.

OK
A/T CHECK P/N SWITCH

NOT OK
- REMOVE EGR VALVE AND CHECK PASSAGES FOR BEING PLUGGED.
- IF NOT PLUGGED REPLACE EGR VALVE.

OK
NO TROUBLE FOUND

NOT OK
REPAIR AS NECESSARY

CONFIRM "CLOSED LOOP" OPERATION AND NO "SERVICE ENGINE SOON" LIGHT.

EGR SYSTEM CHECK
2.8L & 4.3L

ASSUMES NO CODE 24 OR 32 IS STORED

- DISCONNECT EGR SOLENOID VACUUM HOSE (MANIFOLD SIDE)
- CHECK VACUUM SOURCE TO SOLENOID (IF NOT OK , REPAIR).
- INSTALL A HAND HELD VACUUM PUMP WITH GAGE ON MANIFOLD SIDE OF EGR SOLENOID .
- IGNITION "ON" ENGINE STOPPED .
- DIAGNOSTIC TERMINAL NOT GROUNDED .
- APPLY VACUUM .
- OSBSERVE EGR VALVE .
- VALVE SHOULD NOT MOVE . DOES IT?

NO

- GROUND DIAGNOSTIC TERMINAL .
- REPEAT TEST . DOES VALVE MOVE?

YES

- START AND IDLE ENGINE .
- LIFT UP ON EGR VALVE AND OBSERVE IDLE .

NO

- INSTALL A VACUUM GAGE IN VACUUM LINE AT VALVE.
- REPEAT TEST.
- DOES GAGE INDICATE VACUUM.

YES

CHECK EGR VALVE VACUUM PORT ORIFACE FOR BEING PLUGGED. IF NOT PLUGGED. REPLACE EGR VALVE.

NO

SEE CODE 32 CHART TO DIAGNOSE SOLENOID.

YES

- DISCONNECT EGR SOLENOID ELECTRICAL CONNECTOR .
- REPEAT TEST . DOES VALVE MOVE?

YES

REPLACE SOLENOID

NO

CHECK CKT 435 FOR SHORT TO GROUND . IF NOT SHORTED IT IS A FAULTY ECM. SEE "DIAGNOSTIC AIDS."

outlet. Remove the deposit build-up with a small scraper.

5. Clean the mounting surfaces of the intake manifold and the valve assembly, then using a new gasket install the valve assembly to the intake manifold. Torque the bolts to 25 ft. lbs.

6. Connect the vacuum hoses.

REMOVAL AND INSTALLATION

EGR Valve

1. Remove the air cleaner.
2. Detach the vacuum hose from the EGR valve.
3. On the 2.8L engine, disconnect the temperature switch from the EGR valve.
4. Remove the EGR valve-to-intake manifold bolts and the valve from the manifold.
5. Using a new gasket, install the EGR valve and torque the EGR valve-to-manifold bolts to 15 ft. lbs.

EGR Solenoid (2.8L TBI Engine)

1. Disconnect the negative battery cable from the battery.
2. Remove the air cleaner.
3. Disconnect the electrical connector and the vacuum hoses from the solenoid.
4. Remove the mounting nut and the solenoid.
5. Installation is the reverse of removal. Torque the solenoid mounting nut to 17 ft. lbs.

Back Pressure Transducer

1. Remove the back pressure transducer from the clamp bracket.
2. Remove the hoses from the transducer.
3. Inspect and/or replace the transducer.
4. Installation is the reverse of removal.

Thermostatic Air Cleaner (THERMAC)

OPERATION

Fresh air supplied to the air cleaner comes either from the snorkel, which supplies the engine with outside air, or a tube underneath the snorkel, which is connected to a heat stove surrounding the exhaust manifold. The purpose of the heat stove is to supply the engine with warm air during cold running to reduce choke-on time and bring the engine to normal operating temperature as quickly as possible.

An actuator motor in the snorkel operates the door which regulates the source of incoming air. The snorkel door is controlled either by a temperature sensor actuator or a vacuum diaphragm motor. The temperature sensor actuator is controlled by means of a self-contained, wax pellet assembly mounted in the air cleaner. When the engine is cold, the wax material sealed in the actuator is in a solid state, causing the damper to close off the cold air inlet. All air supplied to the engine is routed through the heat stove. As the incoming air warms the wax material, it changes to a liquid state and expands forcing out the piston to reposition the damper, allowing a hot/cold air mix or all cold air to enter the engine.

The vacuum diaphragm operated system uses a vacuum operated motor, mounted to the snorkel, to operate the damper door and a thermostatic bi-metal switch inside the air cleaner. When the engine is cold, the bi-metal switch is cold allowing vacuum to be supplied to the motor. As that the engine warms up, the bi-metal switch opens and bleeds off the vacuum. A spring inside the vacuum motor overcomes the vacuum and opens the damper door to the cold air inlet. Some applications use a delay valve on the hose connecting the vacuum motor to the temperature sensor. When vacuum in this hose drops for any reason, the check valve will bleed off the vacuum to the vacuum motor slowly.

On certain vehicles, the snorkel is connected to a tube, which is routed to the front of the vehicle in order to take in cooler air from outside the engine compartment.

Incorrect Thermostatic Air Cleaner (THERMAC) operation can result in warm up hesitation, lack of power or sluggishness on a hot engine. Inspect the system for any of the following:

1. Disconnected heat stove tube.
2. Vacuum diaphragm motor or temperature sensor actuator inoperative.
3. No damper door operation.
4. Absence of manifold vacuum source.
5. Air cleaner not seated properly.

TESTING

Vacuum Motor

1. With the engine Off, disconnect the hose from the vacuum diaphragm motor.
2. Using a vacuum source, apply 7 in.Hg to the vacuum motor; the door should close and block off the outside air, completely.
3. Bend the vacuum hose (to trap the vacuum in the motor) and make sure that the door stays closed; if not, replace the vacuum motor.

NOTE: *Before replacing the vacuum motor (if defective), be sure to check the motor linkage, for binding.*

4. If the vacuum motor is OK and the problem still exists, check the temperature sensor.

Temperature Sensor

1. Remove the air cleaner cover and place a thermometer near the temperature sensor; the temperature MUST BE below 86°F (30°C). When the temperature is OK, replace the air cleaner.
2. Start the engine and allow it to idle. Watch the vacuum motor door, it should close immediately (if the engine is cool enough).
3. When the vacuum motor door starts to open, remove the air cleaner cover and read the thermometer, it should be about 131°F (55°C).
4. If the door does not respond correctly, replace the temperature sensor.

REMOVAL AND INSTALLATION

Vacuum Motor

1. Remove the air cleaner.
2. Disconnect the vacuum hose from the motor.
3. Using a 1/8 in. drill bit, drill out the spot

THERMAC vacuum door operation

THERMAC AIR CLEANER ASSEMBLY

TEMPERATURE SENSOR

VACUUM DIAPHRAGM MOTOR

LINKAGE

SNORKEL

DAMPER DOOR

HOT AIR DUCT

AIR BLEED VALVE

VACUUM HOSE TO INTAKE MANIFOLD TEE

Thermostatic Air Cleaner (THERMAC) Assembly

welds, then enlarge as necessary to remove the retaining strap.

4. Remove the retaining strap.

5. Lift up the motor and cock it to one side to unhook the motor linkage at the control damper assembly.

6. Install the new vacuum motor as follows:

a. Using a $7/64$ in. drill bit, drill a hole in the snorkel tube at the center of the vacuum motor retaining strap.

b. Insert the vacuum motor linkage into the control damper assembly.

c. Use the motor retaining strap and a sheet metal screw to secure the retaining strap and motor to the snorkel tube.

NOTE: *Make sure the screw does not interfere with the operation of the damper assembly; shorten the screw, if necessary.*

Temperature Sensor

1. Remove the air cleaner.

2. Disconnect the hoses from the sensor.

3. Pry up the tabs on the sensor retaining clip and remove the clip and sensor from the air cleaner.

4. Installation is the reverse of removal.

Air Injection Reactor (AIR)

OPERATION

The AIR system uses an air pump, air check valve(s), a mixture control (deceleration) valve, an air switching (diverter) valve, an air manifold (with air injector nozzles).

The air pump transmits filtered air received from the air cleaner assembly, through the air switching valve and the check valve, into an air manifold assembly which is mounted on the cylinder head. As the hot exhaust gas comes out from the combustion chamber, it meets with a blast of air from the air injection nozzle located in the exhaust port to burn some of the hydrocarbon and carbon monoxide emissions.

Upon receiving a high vacuum signal from the intake manifold, the mixture control valve introduces ambient air through the air filter into the intake manifold to dilute the momentarily rich fuel mixture that occurs on initial throttle closing. This eliminates backfire.

On California and TBI models, the Electronic Control Module (ECM) operates the electric air control valve which directs the air flow to the engine exhaust manifold ports or the air cleaner. When the engine is cold or in wideopen throttle, the ECM energizes the solenoid to direct the air flow into the exhaust manifold check valves. When the engine warms, operating at high speeds or deceleration, the ECM deenergizes the electric air control valve, changing the air flow from the exhaust manifold to the air cleaner. The diversion of the air flow to the air cleaner acts as a silencer.

A check valve(s) prevents back flow of the exhaust gases into the air pump, if there is an exhaust backfire or pump drive belt failure.

TESTING

Air Injection Pump

Accelerate the engine to approximately 1500 rpm and observe the air flow from hose(s). If the air flow increases as the engine is accelerated, the pump is operating satisfactorily. If the air flow does not increase or is not present, proceed as follows:

1. Check for proper drive belt tension. The Air Management System is not completely noiseless. Under normal conditions, noise rises in pitch as the engine speed increases. To determine if excessive noise is the present, operate the engine with the pump drive belt removed. If excessive noise does not exist with the belt removed, proceed as follows:

2. Check for a seized Air Injection Pump. DO NOT oil the air pump.

3. Check the hoses, the pipes and all connections for leaks and proper routing.

4. Check the air control valve.

5. Check air injection pump for proper mounting and bolt torque.

6. Repair irregularities in these components, as necessary.

7. If no irregularities exist and the air injection pump noise is still excessive, replace the pump.

Check Valves

1. The check valve should be inspected whenever the hose is disconnected from the check valve or whenever check valve failure is suspected (A pump that had become inoperative and had shown indications of having exhaust gases in the pump would indicate check valve failure).

2. Blow through the check valve (toward the cylinder head) then attempt to suck back

1. Electrical air control (EAC) valve
2. Decel timing assembly
3. Manifold vacuum signal tube
4. Electrical terminal
5. EAC solenoid
6. Decel Timing chamber
7. Air to air cleaner
8. Air from air pump
9. Air to exhaust ports or manifold
10. Pressure relief assembly

Electric air control valve — TBI engines

through check valve. The flow should only be in one direction (toward the exhaust manifold). Replace the valve which does not function correctly.

Air Hoses and Injection Pipes

1. Inspect all hoses for deterioration or holes.

2. Inspect all air injection pipes for cracks of holes.

3. Check all hose and pipe connections.

4. Check pipe and hose routing; interference may cause wear.

5. If a leak is suspected on the pressure side of the system or any hose has been disconnected on the pressure side, the connection should be checked for leaks with a soapy water solution.

6. If a hose, manifold and/or pipe assembly replacement is required, note the routing, then replace the item as required.

7. When installing the new item, be sure to connect the hoses correctly.

Air Switching (Diverter) Valve (ASV)

The diverter valve directs air to the exhaust ports unless there is a sudden rise in manifold vacuum due to deceleration. In such a case air is diverted to the intake manifold.

If the diverter valve is functioning properly, the secondary air will continue to blow out from the valve for a few seconds when the accelerator pedal is pressed to the floor and released quickly. If the secondary air continues to blow out for more than 5 seconds, replace the air switching valve.

fig. 414/415 must run together, as 1 piece, if possible.

Mixture Control (Deceleration) Valve

1. Install a tachometer to the engine and allow the engine to establish normal operating temperatures.

2. Remove the air cleaner and plug the air cleaner vacuum hose(s).

3. Operate the engine at idle speed, then remove the deceleration valve-to-intake manifold (diaphragm) hose.

4. Reconnect the hose and listen for a noticeable air flow (hiss) through the air cleaner-to-deceleration valve hose; there should also be a noticeable drop in idle speed.

5. If the air flow does not continue for at least one second or the engine speed does not drop, check the hoses (of the deceleration valve) for restrictions or leaks.

6. If no restrictions are found, replace the deceleration valve.

ASSUMES MANIFOLD VACUUM SIGNAL AT VALVE WITH
ENGINE IDLING, AND VOLTAGE ON PIN A WITH IGNITION ON.

AIR MANAGEMENT CHECK
(ELECTRONIC AIR CONTROL VALVE)

- IGNITION OFF. DIAGNOSTIC TERMINAL NOT GROUNDED.
- TRANSMISSION IN PARK OR NEUTRAL.
- PARKING BRAKE ENGAGED.
- COOLANT AT NORMAL OPERATING TEMPERATURE (ABOVE 15°.
- DISCONNECT HOSE TO AIR CLEANER. START ENGINE.
- LET VEHICLE IDLE. AIR SHOULD GO TO EXHAUST PORTS.
- RUN AT PART THROTTLE TO WARM UP O2 SENSOR, UNTIL ENGINE GOES CLOSED LOOP. (USE SCAN TOOL TO VERIFY CLOSED LOOP)
- AFTER VEHICLE HAS BEEN IN CLOSED LOOP STATUS FOR AT LEAST 10 SECONDS, MAINTAIN A PART THROTTLE (APPROX. 1500 RPM CONDITION FOR AT LEAST 10 SEC.
- DOES AIR GO TO CLEANER

NO

- CONNECT HOSE TO AIR CLEANER.
- DIAGNOSTIC TERMINAL NOT GROUNDED.
- IGNITION "ON" AND ENGINE STOPPED.
- DISCONNECT CONNECTOR FROM VALVE SOLENOID AND CONNECT A TEST LIGHT BETWEEN HARNESS CONNECTOR TERMINALS. IS THE TEST LIGHT "ON"?

YES

- AIR MANAGEMENT SYSTEM IS OPERATING PROPERLY.

NO

- GROUND DIAGNOSTIC TERMINAL.
- IS THE TEST LIGHT "ON"?

YES

- CHECK FOR GROUNDED WIRE FROM SOLENOID TO ECM.
- IF NOT GROUNDED, REPLACE ECM.

NO

- CONNECT TEST LIGHT BETWEEN HARNESS TERMINAL "A" TO GROUND.
- IS THE TEST LIGHT "ON"?

YES

- IT IS A FAULTY VALVE SOLENOID CONNECTOR OR SOLENOID. REPLACE EAC VALVE.

NO

- CHECK FOR OPEN FUSE OR OPEN IN WIRE TO IGNITION

YES

- CHECK FOR AN OPEN IN WIRE FROM SOLENOID TO ECM.
- IF OK, CHECK RESISTANCE OF SOLENOID WINDINGS.
- IF UNDER 20 OHMS, REPLACE EAC VALVE AND PERFORM ECM QDR CHECK IN SECTION "3".
- IF OVER 20 OHMS, REPLACE ECM ONLY.

Check for at least 34 kPa (10'') of vacuum at valve with engine idling.

①
- "Test" terminal ungrounded.
- Run engine at part throttle (under 2000 RPM).
- Air should go to exhaust ports until system goes closed loop, then divert to air cleaner.

Not OK

OK

No trouble found

②
- Test term. ungrounded.
- Ignition "ON," engine stopped.
- Remove connector from divert valve and connect a test light between connector terminals.

Light Off

Light On

- Check for grounded wire from sol. to ECM.
- If not grounded, replace ECM.

③
- Ground "Test" Terminal
- Note Check Engine Light.

Light Off

Light On

It is faulty divert valve connections or valve.

- Connect test light across connector terms.
- Note test light.

Light Off

Light On

- Check for blown fuse or open in pink wire to ignition.

- Check for an open in wire from sol. to ECM.
- If OK, check resistance of solenoid winding.
- If under 20 ohms, replace solenoid and ECM.
- If over 20 ohms, replace ECM only.

ECM

B — Ignition

Divert Valve

Air injection reactor system — 1.9L engine

REMOVAL AND INSTALLATION

Air Injection Pump

NOTE: *The air pump is non-serviceable, it must be replaced as an assembly, if defective.*

1. Compress the drive belt to keep the pump pulley from turning, then loosen the pump pulley bolts.

2. Loosen the pump-to-mounting brackets, release the tension on the drive belt and remove the drive belt.

3. Unscrew the mounting bolts and then remove the pump pulley.

4. If necessary, use a pair of needle nose pliers to pull the fan filter from the hub.

5. Remove the hoses, the vacuum lines, the electrical connectors (if equipped) and the air control or diverter valve.

6. Unscrew the pump mounting bolts and then remove the pump.

7. Installation is the reverse of removal. Torque the pump pulley bolts to 90 inch lbs. and the pump-to-bracket nuts/bolts to 25 ft. lbs. Adjust the drive belt tension after installation.

Air Pump Drive Belt Adjustment and Replacement

NOTE: *Vehicles using a serpentine accessory drive belt are equipped with an automatic tensioner, no adjustment is necessary.*

1. Inspect the drive belt for wear, cracks or deterioration.

2. Loosen the pump adjustment and the pivot bolts.

3. Replace the drive belt, if necessary.

4. Move the air pump until the drive belt is at proper tension, then retighten bolts.

5. Check the drive belt tension using a belt tension gauge.

Air Pump Pulley Replacement

1. Hold the pump pulley from turning by compressing the drive belt, then loosen the pump pulley bolts.

2. Loosen the pump through bolt and the adjusting bolt.

3. Remove the drive belt, the pump pulley and the pulley spacer.

4. Install the pump pulley and spacer with the retaining bolts hand tight.

5. Install the drive belt and adjust to proper tension.

TIGHTEN TO
25 N•m (18 FT. LBS)

AIR CONTROL
VALVE

CHECK VALVE

AIR PUMP

Air injection reactor system — 2.8L carbureted engine

FRT

FRT

VIEW A

FRT

A

1	AIR PUMP	6	AIR INJECTION PIPE — TIGHTEN NUTS TO 28 N·m (20 FT. LBS.)
2	SILENCER	7	BOLT — TIGHTEN TO 15 N·m (11 FT. LBS.)
3	EAC VALVE	8	GASKET
4	HOSE	9	SHIELD
5	CHECK VALVE — TIGHTEN TO 85 N·m (26 FT. LBS.)	10	PORT VACUUM HARNESS

Air injection reactor system — 2.8L TBI engine

Air injection reactor system — 2.0L engine

6. Hold the pump pulley from turning by compressing the drive belt, then torque the pump pulley bolts to 24 ft. lbs.

7. Recheck drive belt tension and adjust it, if necessary.

Air Pump Filter Fan Replacement

Before starting this operation, note the following:

• DO NOT allow any filter fragments to enter the air pump intake hole.

• DO NOT remove the filter fan by inserting a screwdriver between pump and filter fan. Air damage to the sealing lip pump will result.

• DO NOT remove the metal drive hub from the filter fan.

• It is seldom possible to remove the filter fan without destroying it.

1. Remove the drive belt, the pump pulley and spacer.

2. Insert needle nose pliers and pull the filter fan from hub.

3. Position a new filter fan onto the pump hub.

4. Position the spacer and the pump pulley against the centrifugal filter fan.

5. Install the pump pulley bolts and torque them equally to 80 inch lbs. This will compress the centrifugal filter fan into the pump hole. DO NOT drive the filter fan on with a hammer.

NOTE: *A slight amount of interference with the housing bore is normal. After a new filter fan has been installed, it may squeal upon initial operation or until O.D. sealing lip has worn in. This may require a short period of pump operation at various engine speeds.*

6. To complete the installation, replace the pump drive belt. Adjust the belt tension if necessary.

Check Valve(s)

1. Remove the clamp(s) and disconnect the hose from the valve(s).

2. Unscrew the valve(s) from the air injection pipe(s).

3. To test the valve(s), air should pass only in one direction only.

4. Installation is the reverse of removal.

Air Control Valve

1. Disconnect the negative battery cable.

2. Disconnect the air inlet and outlet hoses from the valve.

3. Disconnect the electrical connector (if equipped) and the vacuum hoses at the valve. Remove the electric air control or the diverter valve.

4. Installation is the reverse of removal. For California models, check the system operation.

NOTE: *The air switching (diverter) valve is replaced in the same manner as the air control valve.*

Mixture Control (Deceleration) Valve

1. Remove the vacuum hoses from the valve.

2. Remove the deceleration valve-to-engine bracket screws.

3. Remove the deceleration valve.

4. Installation is the reverse of removal. Torque the deceleration valve-to-engine bracket screws to 30 inch lbs.

Vacuum Switching Valve (VSV)

1. Disconnect the electrical wiring connector.

2. Remove the hoses from the valve.

3. Remove the vacuum switching valve.

4. Installation is the reverse of removal.

Electronic Spark Timing (EST) System

All HEI distributors used in S/10-S/15 vehicles are equipped to aid in spark timing changes, necessary for emissions control, economy and performance. The system used is called the Electronic Spark Timing Control (EST).

Electronic Spark Control (ESC) System

OPERATION

Varying octane levels of gasoline can cause detonation (spark knock) in an engine. Spark knock is a condition caused by temperatures inside the cylinder rising so high as to ignite the air/fuel mixture prior to the spark plug firing.

This early ignition causes a down force on the piston as it is rising in the cylinder toward TDC. In light cases, the only damage to the engine may be broken spark plug insulators. In extreme cases, pistons may become severely damaged (holes blown through the top of the piston) requiring the engine to be rebuilt.

The ESC system has been added to the engine to remedy spark knock by retarding the spark timing by as much as 20°; this allows the engine to maximize the spark advance to improve the fuel economy and driveability.

A sensor is mounted on the left side of the block (near the cylinders) to detect the knock and send the information to the Electronic Spark Control (ESC) module. The ESC module sends a signal to the Electronic Control Module (ECM) which adjusts the Electronic Spark Timing (EST) to reduce the spark knock. If no signal is received from the ESC sensor, the ECM provides normal spark advance.

NOTE: *Loss of spark knock sensor signal (through a bad ESC sensor, ESC module or a poor ground) will cause the engine to operate sluggishly and cause a Code 43 to be set.*

TESTING

1. With the engine operating at 1,500 rpm, the transmission in Neutral or Park, tap on the engine block in the area of the knock sensor, the engine rpm should drop.

NOTE: *If the speed does not drop, the timing is not retarding or it is retarded all of the time.*

2. Disconnect the ESC module connector (the engine rpm should drop); after 4 seconds, the "CHECK ENGINE" light should turn ON and the Code 43 will be stored.

3. Using a digital voltmeter (set on the low AC scale), check the knock sensor voltage; low or no voltage will indicate an open circuit at terminal **E** or a bad sensor.

4. Check the CHECK ENGINE light and the Code 43 in the ESC system. If no light turns ON, the ECM is not retarding the engine spark for there may be voltage on the **C** terminal or the ECM may be faulty, replace the ECM.

5. Disconnect the electrical connector from the knock sensor; if the rpm increases with the sensor disconnected, the sensor is bad and should be replaced.

REMOVAL AND INSTALLATION

Knock Sensor

The knock sensor is mounted on the right side of the engine in front of the starter.

1. Disconnect the negative battery terminal from the battery.

2. Disconnect the electrical harness connector from the knock sensor.

3. Remove the knock sensor from the engine block.

4. Apply teflon tape to the threads. Installation is the reverse of removal.

ESC Module

The ESC module is located at the top-rear of the engine.

1. Disconnect the electrical harness connector from the ESC module.

2. Remove the mounting screws and the ESC module from the vehicle.

3. Installation is the reverse of removal.

Transmission Converter Clutch (TCC) System

All vehicles equipped with an automatic transmission use the TCC system. The ECM controls the converter by means of a solenoid mounted in the outdrive housing of the trans-

1. ESC knock sensor

Typical knock sensor

Electronic spark control (ESC) system schematic

mission. When the vehicle speed reaches a certain level, the ECM energizes the solenoid and allows the torque converter to mechanically couple the transmission to the engine. When the operating conditions indicate that the transmission should operate as a normal fluid coupled transmission, the ECM will de-energize the solenoid. Depressing the brake pedal will also return the transmission to normal automatic operation.

The ECM monitors the following sensors to control the transmission converter clutch operation.

• Throttle Position Sensor (TPS) — Acceleration and deceleration conditions are used to the clutch.

• Coolant Temperature Sensor — The

engine MUST BE warmed before the clutch can be applied.

• Pulse Switch — During a 4-to-3 downshift condition, the clutch switch is opened momentarily.

• Brake Switch — Depressing the brake pedal will de-energize the clutch system.

Early Fuel Evaporation System Carbureted Engines

OPERATION

The early fuel evaporation system provides a rapid heat source to the engine induction system. The heat generated provides quick fuel evaporation and more uniform fuel distribution during cold starts. The system also reduces

1. ESC module
2. Electrical connector

Electronic spark control (ESC) module

1. TCC solenoid
2. Check ball
3. Check ball seat

Transmission converter clutch (TCC) solenoid

TORQUE CONVERTER CLUTCH (TCC)
(ELECTRICAL DIAGNOSIS)
4.3L ENGINE

TORQUE CONVERTER CLUTCH (TCC)
(ELECTRICAL DIAGNOSIS)
2.5L ENGINE

USE A "SCAN" TOOL TO CHECK THE FOLLOWING AND
CORRECT IF NECESSARY:
- COOLANT TEMPERATURE
- TPS
- VSS
- CODES - IF 24 IS PRESENT, SEE CODE CHART 24. ALSO,
  PERFORM MECHANICAL CHECKS, SUCH AS LINKAGE,
  OIL LEVEL, ETC., BEFORE USING THIS CHART.

- ENGINE AT NORMAL OPERATING TEMPERATURE AND "CLOSED LOOP".
- CONNECT TEST LIGHT FROM TCC TEST POINT, ALDL TERM "F" AND GROUND.
- NOTE LIGHT.

LIGHT "ON"

TEST LIGHT SHOULD GO OUT AS
BRAKE PEDAL IS DEPRESSED.

OK

- IGNITION ON. ENGINE STOPPED.
- INSTEAD OF GROUND. CONNECT
  TEST LIGHT TO 12 VOLTS AND
  PROBE ALDL TERMINAL "F".
- GROUND DIAGNOSTIC TERMINAL
- NOTE TEST LIGHT.

LIGHT "ON"

CHECK FOR OPEN CKT 422
FROM ALDL TO ECM.

CKT 422 OK. FAULTY ECM
CONNECTION OR ECM. SEE
"DIAGNOSTIC AIDS" ON
FACING PAGE.

LIGHT "OFF"

CHECK FOR:
- LOW COOLANT LEVEL.
- FAULTY OR INCORRECT
  THERMOSTAT.
- VSS CODE 24 CHART.
IF OK, NO ELECTRICAL TROUBLE
FOUND. IF TCC DOES NOT
WORK, SEE APPROPRIATE
SERIES SERVICE MANUAL FOR
TCC SERVICE.

NOT OK

FAULTY BRAKE SWITCH
OR ADJUSTMENT.

LIGHT "OFF"

③ • CHECK FOR BLOWN FUSE. IF OK,
  DISCONNECT CONNECTOR AT
  TRANSMISSION AND CONNECT TEST LIGHT
  FROM HARNESS CONNECTOR "A" TO "D"
  WITH IGNITION "ON", ENGINE STOPPED.

LIGHT "OFF"

- CONNECT A TEST
  LIGHT FROM
  TERM "A" TO
  GROUND.

LIGHT "ON"

CHECK FOR SHORT TO
GROUND IN CKT 422. IF
NOT GROUNDED.
REPLACE ECM. SEE
"DIAGNOSTIC AIDS".

LIGHT "OFF"

REPAIR OPEN
IN TCC BRAKE
SWITCH
CIRCUIT OR
ADJ. SWITCH.

LIGHT "ON"

FAULTY:
- TRANSMISSION TCC
  CONNECTION
- TCC SOLENOID.

LIGHT "ON"

- GROUND TCC TEST POINT
  AND AGAIN CONNECT
  TEST LIGHT BETWEEN
  HARNESS CONNECTOR
  TERMS "A" AND"D".

LIGHT "OFF"

REPAIR OPEN IN
WIRE FROM
TRANSMISSION TO
ALDL TEST POINT,
TERM "F".

TRANSMISSION CONVERTER CLUTCH (TCC) CHECK

ELECTRICAL DIAGNOSIS

Mechanical checks, such as linkage, oil level, etc., should be performed prior to using this chart.

①
- Connect test light from T.C.C. test point in Term. "F" in ALCL connector to ground.
- Four wheel drive vehicle should be in Two-wheel drive.
- With drive wheels off floor, key "ON", engine not running.
- Note light.

Light on
- Test light should go out as brake pedal is momentarily depressed.

②

OK
- Increase speed to 50-55 mph and note light.

Not OK
- It is faulty brake switch or adj.

Light "on"
- Lightly depress parking brake and open throttle to maintain 50-55 mph for 5 seconds and note light.

Light "off"
- TCC Electrical System OK

③

Light "on"
- Check volt. from ECM term. "2" to ground with digital V.M. with ign. on, eng. stopped, throttle wide open.

Light off
- Check TPS adjustment.
- If OK, no trouble found.

Over 1 volt

Under 1 volt
- Check for gn'd. in wire to ECM term. "2".
- If not grounded, replace ECM.

- Check TPS adj. Check for low coolant level and higher than normal resistance in coolant sensor circuit.
- If OK, see ECM Replacement Check

Light off

④
- Check for blown fuse. If OK, disconnect connector at trans. and connect test light from harness connector "A" to "D" terminal.
- With ignition on, engine stopped, note test light.

Light off
- Connect test light from term. "A" to ground.
- Note light.

Light on
- Check for ground in wire to ECM term. "P".
- If not grounded, see ECM.

Light on

⑤
- Connect test light between harness connector term's. again. Ground trans. test point & note light.

Light off
- Repair open in TCC brake switch circuit or adj. switch.

Light off
- Repair open in wire from trans. to test point or faulty 4WD relay.

Light on
- It is faulty conn. at trans. or trans. sol. circuit.

the length of carburetor choking time, thus reducing exhaust emissions.

The system consists of a ceramic heater grid (located between the carburetor and the intake manifold) and a temperature switch (non-ECM models) or a relay (ECM models) which activates the heater during cold operation. The relay, located under the right fender, is operated by the ECM.

As the coolant temperature increases, the temperature switch (non-ECM models) or the relay (ECM models) turns Off the current to the ceramic heater, allowing the engine to operate normally.

NOTE: *Operational checks should be made at normal maintenance intervals.*

TESTING

REMOVAL AND INSTALLATION

EFE Heater

1. Remove the air cleaner.
2. Disconnect all electrical, vacuum and fuel connections from carburetor.
3. Disconnect the EFE Heater electrical connector.
4. Remove the carburetor-to-intake manifold nuts/bolts and the carburetor.
5. Remove the EFE Heater isolator assembly.
6. To install, reverse the removal procedures.
7. Start the engine and check for leaks.

12 VOLT
IGNITION

TO IGN COIL

HEATER SWITCH

PNK

PNK

CLOSED ON
COLD ENGINE

BLK

HEATER
GRID

**ELECTRIC EFE
NON-ECM CONTROLLED**

① • Ign. on, engine cold.
   • Back probe both terminals of heater switch
     connecter with test light connected to gnd.

| Two lights | One light | No light |

Replace heater switch.

Repair circuit to ign. switch.

② • Probe pink wire
     at heater connector
     (near carburetor base)
     with test light connected
     to ground.

| Light | No light |

③ Disconnect heater
   harness and connect
   test light across
   harness terminals.

Repair wire
at connector
between heater
switch and heater
connector.

| Light | No light |

④ Check resistance
   of heater.

Repair open
ground wire.

| Under 3 ohms | Over 3 ohms |

⑤ • Reconnect circuit.
   • Probe pink wire (at
     EFE grid conn.)
     with test light to gnd.
   • Engine running at
     normal operating
     temp.

Replace
heater.

| No light | Light |

No trouble
found.

Replace heater
switch.

EFE RELAY
(N.O. CONTACTS)

EFE
RELAY
CONNECTOR

A B C E

EFE
HEATER

DASH
CONN.

F

ECM FUSE
10 AMP

IGNITION

IGNITION

ECM

6

EFE RELAY
CONNECTOR

A B C D E

ECM CONNECTOR
(BACK VIEW)

DASH CONNECTOR
(FRONT VIEW)

J

A F H

**EARLY FUEL EVAPORATION (EFE) CHECK
(ELECTRICALLY HEATED)**

An intermittent coolant sensor connection could cause the relay to click

(1)
- Ignition "ON", engine not running
- Disconnect connector at heater.
- Connect test light between harness connector terminals.
- Ground "Test" terminal.

Light "On"

- Remove ground from "Test" terminal.

Light "Off"

(2)
- Ground term. "B" at relay.

Light "Off"

- Check resistance of heater.

Light "On"

- Remove EFE relay conn.
- Connect test light from relay conn. term. "B" to battery.

Light "On"

- Check for open in wire to ECM term. "6". If not open,
- See ECM Replacement Check, Chart, C-1.

Light "Off"

- Jumper relay terminals "A-E".

Under 3 ohms

Over 3 ohms

Light "ON"

Light "OFF"

Light "Off"

Light "On"

- No trouble found.

- Replace heater.

- Replace relay.

- Connect test light from relay terminal "A" to ground.

- Jumper relay term. C-E.

- Check for grounded wire from relay term. "B" to ECM term. "6". If not grounded,
- See ECM Replacement Check, Chart C-1

Light "Off"

Light "On"

- Repair open in circuit to relay term. "C".

- Replace relay.

RELAY

HEATER

A B C E

IGNITION

6

ECM

IGNITION

Light "On" one terminal

Light "Off"

- Repair open in wire from relay to heater connector or ground wire.

- Repair open from relay term. "A" to ignition.

Early fuel evaporation (EFE) grid — 2.0L engine

Early fuel evaporation (EFE) relay — 2.8L engine

Temperature Switch — Non-ECM Models

The temperature switch is located on the rear (2.0L) of the intake manifold coolant outlet housing or behind the engine coolant housing (2.8L).

1. Disconnect the electrical connector from the temperature switch.

2. Place a catch pan under the radiator, open the drain cock and drain the coolant to a level below the intake manifold coolant housing.

CAUTION: *When draining the coolant, keep in mind that cats and dogs are attracted by the ethylene glycol antifreeze, and are quite likely to drink any that is left in an uncov-*

ered container or in puddles on the ground. This will prove fatal in sufficient quantity. Always drain the coolant into a sealable container. Coolant should be reused unless it is contaminated or several years old.

NOTE: *If replacing the temperature switch, refer to the calibration number stamped on the base.*

3. Apply soft setting sealant to the male threads of the temperature switch Installation is the reverse of removal.

4. Torque the temperature switch-to-intake manifold coolant housing to 10 ft. lbs. Refill the cooling system. Start the engine, run the engine to normal operating temperatures and check the operation.

NOTE: *When applying sealant to the temperature switch, be sure not to coat the sensor end with sealant.*

Relay — ECM Models

1. Disconnect negative battery terminal from the battery.

2. Disconnect electrical connector from the relay.

3. Remove relay-to-bracket bolts and the relay.

4. Installation is the reverse of removal.

Early fuel evaporation (EFE) grid — 2.8L engine

Early fuel evaporation (EFE) temperature switch 2.8L engine

Oxygen sensor and connector

Closed Loop Emission Control System

NOTE: *When troubleshooting the system, always check the electrical and vacuum connectors which may cause the problem before testing or replacing a component.*

VACUUM CONTROLLER REPLACEMENT

1. Disconnect the electrical connector.
2. Disconnect the vacuum hoses from the vacuum regulator and solenoid.
3. Remove the vacuum controller.
4. Installation is the reverse of removal.

IDLE AND WIDE OPEN THROTTLE (WOT) VACUUM SWITCH REPLACEMENT

1. Disconnect the electrical harness connector.
2. Disconnect the vacuum hoses from the sensors.
3. Remove the idle and the WOT vacuum switch.
4. Installation is the reverse of removal.

Closed loop emission system — 1.9L engine

1. Carburetor
2. Top view of canister
3. Fuel tank
4. Canister
5. TVS
6. PVC
7. Carburetor bowl vent line
8. Fuel tank vapor line
9. Ported vacuum line
10. Fuel vapor purge line
11. Canister purge valve
12. Control vacuum tube (ported vac)
13. Purge tube (PCV)
14. Canister vent
15. Vapor vent valve
16. Vapor from carburetor tube
17. Control vacuum tube (manifold vac)
18. Sealed fuel tank cap
19. Fuel tank vapor line restriction

Emissions control system schematic — 2.0L and 2.8L carbureted engines

Vacuum hose routing — 1.9L engine (except California)

1	TBI UNIT	3	FUEL TANK	5	VAPOR PIPE
2	VAPOR CANISTER			6	FUEL CAP
		4	VAPOR RESTRICTION	7	CANISTER HOSE

Emissions control system schematic — 2.5L and 4.3L TBI engine

VACUUM HOSE ROUTING DIAGRAM · CALIFORNIA ·

* ON AIR CLEANER
=== FOR AUTO. TRANS. (ADDITIONAL)

AIR CLEANER
INTAKE MANIFOLD
CARBURETOR
CARBURETOR MAIN ACTUATOR
CARBURETOR SLOW ACTUATOR
MIXTURE CONTROL
THERMAL VACUUM SWITCH
VACUUM CONTROL VALVE
(BROWN)
VACUUM SWITCH (WOT)
(BLACK)
IGNITION COIL
VACUUM SWITCH (IDLE)
DISTRIBUTOR
TO LOCK-UP CONVERTOR

GAS FILTER
* PIPE PCV

* IDLE COMPENSATOR
* THERMO SENSOR
* VACUUM MOTOR
BACK PRESSURE TRANSDUCER
AIR SWITCHING VALVE
EGR VALVE (UNDER INTAKE MANIFOLD)
TO FUEL TANK
TO ATMOSPHERE
CANISTER
AIR CLN
PCV
CARB. BOWL
FUEL TANK

RADIATOR

Vacuum hose routing — 1.9L engine (California)

1	TBI UNIT	3	FUEL TANK	6	FUEL CAP
2	VAPOR CANISTER	4	VAPOR RESTRICTION	7	CANISTER HOSE
		5	VAPOR PIPE	8	THERMOSTATIC VACUUM SWITCH

Emissions control system schematic — 2.8L TBI engine

Fuel System

5

CARBURETED FUEL SYSTEM

Fuel Pump

All carbureted engines use a mechanical fuel pump, driven off the camshaft and located on the engine block.

REMOVAL AND INSTALLATION

1.9L and 2.0L Engines

The fuel pump is located near the front right side of the engine.

1. Disconnect the negative battery terminal from the battery.
2. Remove the distributor.
3. Disconnect the fuel hoses from the fuel pump.
4. Remove the engine lifting hook.
5. Remove the fuel pump-to-engine bolts and the fuel pump, then discard the gasket.

NOTE: *Before installing the fuel pump, rotate the crankshaft so that the cam lobe is on the down stroke.*

6. Use a new gasket and RTV sealant. Installation is the reverse of removal. Torque the fuel pump-to-engine bolts to 15 ft. lbs. Check and/or adjust the timing.

2.8L Engine

The fuel pump is located near the front left side of the engine.

1. Disconnect the negative battery terminal from the battery.
2. Disconnect the fuel hoses the from pump.
3. Remove the fuel pump-to-engine bolts and the fuel pump from the engine, then discard the gasket.

NOTE: *Before installing the fuel pump, rotate the crankshaft so that the cam lobe is on the down stroke.*

Mechanical fuel pump and hoses — 1.9L and 2.0L engines

Mechanical fuel pump — 2.8L engine

4. To install, use a new gasket, RTV sealant and reverse the removal procedures. Torque the fuel pump-to-engine bolts to 15 ft. lbs.

TESTING

To determine if the pump is in good condition, tests for both volume and pressure should be performed. The tests are made with the pump installed, and the engine at normal operating temperature and idle speed. Never replace a fuel pump without first performing these simple tests.

Be sure that the fuel filter has been changed at the specified interval. If in doubt, install a new filter first.

Pressure Test

1. Disconnect the fuel line from the carburetor and connect a fuel pump pressure gauge.

2. Start the engine and check the pressure with the engine at idle. If the pump has a vapor return hose, squeeze it off so that an accurate reading can be obtained. Pressure should not be below 4.5 psi.

3. If the pressure is incorrect, replace the pump. It if is OK, perform the volume test.

Volume Test

1. Disconnect the fuel line from the carburetor.

2. Place the fuel line into a graduated container.

3. Run the engine at idle until one pint of gasoline has been pumped. One pint should be delivered in 30 seconds or less. There is normally enough fuel in the carburetor float bowl to perform this test, but refill it if necessary.

4. If the delivery rate is below the minimum, check the lines for restrictions or leaks. If none are found, replace the pump.

DCH340 Carburetor

ADJUSTMENTS

NOTE: *Idle Speed and Mixture Adjustment procedures are located in Chapter 2.*

Float Level

The fuel level is normal if it is seen to be within the mark on the float bowl window. If not, Remove the top of the carburetor and bend the float seat to regulate the level.

Primary Throttle Valve

When the choke plate is completely closed, the primary throttle valve should be opened by the fast idle screw to an angle of 16° (M/T) or 18° (A/T). To check this adjustment, perform the following procedures:

1. Close the choke plate completely, then measure between the throttle plate and the air horn wall; the clearance should be 0.050–0.059 in. (1.3–1.5mm), M/T or 0.059–0.069 in. (1.50–1.75mm), A/T.

NOTE: *The measurement should be made at the center point of the choke plate.*

2. If necessary, adjust the opening by turning the fast idle screw.

Throttle Linkage

1. Turn the primary throttle valve plate until the adjustment plate is in contact with the kickdown lever. This is a primary throttle plate opening of about 47°.

2. Measure the clearance between the

Adjusting the float level — 1.9L engine

Adjusting the primary throttle valve — 1.9L engine

center point of the primary throttle plate and the air horn wall; the clearance should be 0.24–0.30 in. (6.0–7.6mm), if not, bend the kickdown lever tab.

Kickdown Lever

1. Turn the primary throttle lever until the plate is completely closed. Back off the throttle adjustment screw, if necessary.

2. Loosen the locknut on the kickdown lever screw and turn the screw until it just contacts the return plate, then tighten the locknut.

REMOVAL AND INSTALLATION

1.9L Engine

1. Remove the PCV valve from the rocker arm cover.

2. Disconnect the ECS hose from the air cleaner.

3. Disconnect the AIR hose from the pump.

4. On California models, disconnect the air hose from the slow carburetor.

5. Unbolt the air cleaner, lift it slightly, disconnect the hoses and remove the unit.

6. Disconnect the rubber piping from the TVS switch.

Adjusting the throttle linkage — 1.9L engine

7. Disconnect the vacuum advance hose (if equipped) from the distributor.

8. If equipped with an A/T, disconnect the vacuum hose from the converter housing.

9. On California models, disconnect the vacuum hoses from the slow and main actuator.

10. Disconnect the carburetor solenoid lead wire, the accelerator control cable and the cruise control cable.

11. On automatic transmission models, disconnect the control cable.

12. Disconnect the fuel line(s) from the carburetor.

13. Disconnect the ECS hose from the carburetor.

14. Remove the carburetor-to-intake manifold bolts and the carburetor; discard the mounting gasket.

15. To install, reverse the removal procedures. Make sure all of the linkage is properly adjusted and operates smoothly. Check that there are no leaks.

2SE and E2SE Carburetor

ADJUSTMENTS

Float Level

1. With the engine Cold, remove the top of the carburetor.

2. While holding a finger lightly but firmly, on the float retainer, press down lightly on the float tab to seat the needle valve.

3. Measure the distance between the float bowl gasket surface and the point on the float farthest from the needle valve.

4. If the measurement is not correct, remove the float and bend the tab.

Pump

1. With the throttle plate in the Closed position and the fast idle screw off the steps of the fast idle cam, measure the distance from the air horn casting to the top of the pump stem.

2. To adjust, remove the retaining screw, the washer and the pump lever. Bend the end

Adjusting the kickdown lever — 1.9L engine

of the lever to correct the stem height. DO NOT twist the lever or bend it sideways.

3. Install the lever, washer and screw, then check the adjustment. When correct, open and close the throttle a few times to check the linkage movement and alignment.

Fast Idle

1. Set the ignition timing and curb idle speed, then disconnect and plug the hoses as directed on the emission control decal.

2. Position the fast idle screw on the highest step of the fast idle cam.

3. Start the engine and adjust the engine speed to specification with the fast idle screw.

Choke Coil Lever

NOTE: *The following procedure requires the use of the Choke Valve Angle Gauge tool No. J–26701 or BT–7704 or equivalent.*

1. Remove the three retaining screws, the choke cover and coil. On models with a riveted choke cover, drill out the three rivets, then remove the cover and the choke coil.

NOTE: *A choke stat cover retainer kit is required for reassembly.*

2. Place the fast idle screw on the high step of the fast idle cam.

3. Close the choke plate by pushing in on the intermediate choke lever.

4. Insert a drill or plug gauge, of the specified size, into the hole in the choke housing. The choke lever in the housing should be up against the side of the gauge.

5. If the lever does not just touch the gauge, bend the intermediate choke rod to adjust.

Fast Idle Cam (Choke Rod)

NOTE: *The following procedure requires the use of the Choke Valve Angle Gauge tool No. J–26701 or BT–7704 or equivalent.*

① HOLD RETAINER
FIRMLY IN PLACE

(INSET)

③ GAUGE AT LARGE TOE OF
FLOAT AT POINT FURTHES'
AWAY FROM FLOAT HINGE
PIN (SEE INSET)

④ REMOVE FLOAT AND
BEND FLOAT ARM UP
OR DOWN TO ADJUST

② PUSH FLOAT DOWN
LIGHTLY AGAINST NEEDLE

⑤ VISUALLY CHECK FLOAT
ALIGNMENT AFTER
ADJUSTING

Adjusting the float level — 2.0L and 2.8L engines

① REMOVE RIVETS AND CHOKE
COVER AND COIL ASSEMBLY
FOLLOWING INSTRUCTIONS
IN CHOKE STAT COVER
RETAINER KIT (SEE NOTE).

NOTE: DO NOT REMOVE
RIVETS AND RETAINERS
HOLDING CHOKE COVER AND
COIL ASSEMBLY IN PLACE
UNLESS NECESSARY TO
CHECK THE CHOKE COIL
LEVER ADJUSTMENT. IF RIVETS
AND COVER ARE REMOVED, A
CHOKE STAT COVER RETAINER
KIT IS REQUIRED FOR REASSEMBLY.

.085" (2.18mm)

④ INSERT SPECIFIED
PLUG GAUGE INTO
HOLE PROVIDED

⑤ EDGE OF LEVER SHOULD
JUST CONTACT SIDE OF
PLUG GAUGE AS SHOWN

⑥ BEND INTERMEDIATE CHOKE
ROD AT THIS POINT TO ADJUST

② PLACE FAST IDLE
SCREW ON HIGH STEP
OF FAST IDLE CAM

③ PUSH ON INTER-
MEDIATE CHOKE
LEVER UNTIL
CHOKE VALVE
IS CLOSED

Adjusting the choke coil lever — 2.0L and 2.8L engines

① DEGREE SCALE
② POINTER
③ CHOKE VALVE CLOSED
④ LEVELING BUBBLE (CENTERED)
⑤ SPECIFIED ANGLE (SEE SPECS.)
MAGNET
⑧ BEND ROD TO ADJUST
⑦ HOLD CHOKE VALVE TOWARD CLOSED POSITION BY LIGHTLY PUSHING ON INTER-MEDIATE CHOKE LEVER.
FIGURE 1
⑥ PLACE FAST IDLE SCREW ON SECOND STEP OF CAM AGAINST RISE OF HIGH STEP
FAST IDLE CAM
⑨ REMOVE GAUGE

Adjusting the choke rod — 2.0L and 2.8L engines

1. First, adjust the choke coil lever and fast idle speed.

2. Rotate the degree scale until it is zeroed.

3. Close the choke and install the degree scale onto the choke plate. Center the leveling bubble.

4. Rotate the scale so that the specified degree is opposite the scale pointer.

5. Place the fast idle screw on the second step of the cam (against the high step). Close the choke by pushing in the intermediate lever.

6. Push on the vacuum break lever, to Open the choke, until the lever is against the rear tang on the choke lever.

7. Bend the fast idle cam rod at the U to adjust the angle to specifications.

Air Valve Rod

NOTE: *The following procedure requires the use of the Choke Valve Angle Gauge tool No. J–26701 or BT–7704 or equivalent.*

1. Align the 0° mark with the pointer on an angle gauge.

2. Close the air valve and place a magnet on top of it.

3. Rotate the bubble until it is centered.

4. Rotate the degree scale until the specified degree mark is aligned with the pointer.

5. Seat the vacuum diaphragm using an external vacuum source.

6. On four cylinder models plug the end cover. Unplug after adjustment.

7. Apply a light pressure to the air valve

shaft in the direction to open the air valve until all the slack is removed between the air link and plunger slot.

8. Bend the air valve link until the bubble is centered.

Primary Side Vacuum Break

NOTE: *The following procedure requires the use of the Choke Valve Angle Gauge tool No. J–26701 or BT–7704 or equivalent.*

1. Rotate the degree scale on the measuring gauge until the 0° is opposite the pointer.

NOTE: *Prior to adjustment, remove the vacuum break from the carburetor. Place the bracket in a vise and using the proper safety precautions, grind off the adjustment screw cap then reinstall the vacuum break.*

2. Seat the choke vacuum diaphragm by applying an external vacuum source of over 5 in.Hg to the vacuum break.

NOTE: *If the air valve rod is restricting the vacuum diaphragm from seating, it may be necessary to bend the air valve rod slightly to gain clearance. Make the air valve rod adjustment after the vacuum break adjustment.*

3. Read the angle gauge while lightly pushing on the intermediate choke lever so that the choke valve is toward the Closed position.

4. Using an $1/8$ in. (3mm) hex wrench, turn the screw in the rear cover until the bubble is centered. Apply a silicone sealant over the screw head to seal the setting.

Adjusting the air valve rod — 2.0L and 2.8L engines

⑤ SPECIFIED ANGLE (SEE SPECS.)

⑦ ROTATE AIR VALVE IN THE DIRECTION OF OPEN AIR VALVE BY APPLYING A LIGHT PRESSURE TO THE AIR VALVE SHAFT.

① DEGREE SCALE

④ LEVELING BUBBLE (CENTERED)

② AIR VALVE CLOSED

MAGNET

③ POINTER

FIGURE 1

⑥ SEAT VACUUM DIAPHRAGM USING OUTSIDE VACUUM SOURCE

⑧ TO ADJUST, BEND AIR VALVE ROD UNTIL BUBBLE IS CENTERED.

Adjusting the primary vacuum break — 2.0L and 2.8L engines

① DEGREE SCALE

④ LEVELING BUBBLE (CENTERED)

MAGNET

② POINTER

③ CHOKE VALVE CLOSED (FAST IDLE SCREW MUST BE ON HIGH STEP OF FAST IDLE CAM).

⑦ DURING READING OF ANGLE GAUGE, HOLD CHOKE VALVE TOWARD CLOSED POSITION BY LIGHTLY PUSHING ON INTERMEDIATE CHOKE LEVER.

⑤ SPECIFIED ANGLE (SEE SPECS.)

⑥ SEAT DIAPHRAGM USING VACUUM SOURCE (OVER 5" Hg VACUUM AND AIR VALVE ROD NOT RESTRICTING).

⑧ TO ADJUST, USING 1/8" HEX WRENCH, TURN SCREW IN REAR COVER UNTIL BUBBLE IS CENTERED.

Electric Choke

This procedure is only for those carburetors with choke covers retained by screws. Riveted choke covers are preset and nonadjustable.

1. Loosen the three retaining screws.
2. Place the fast idle screw on the high step of the cam.
3. Rotate the choke cover to align the cover mark with the specified housing mark.

Secondary Vacuum Break

NOTE: *The following procedure requires the use of the Choke Valve Angle Gauge tool No. J–26701, BT–7704 or equivalent.*

1. Rotate the degree scale on the measuring gauge until the 0° is opposite the pointer.

NOTE: *Prior to adjustment, remove the vacuum break from the carburetor. Place the bracket in the vise and using the proper safety precautions, grind off the adjustment screw cap then reinstall the vacuum break. Plug the end cover using an accelerator pump plunger cup or equivalent. Remove the cup after the adjustment.*

2. Seat the choke vacuum diaphragm by applying an external vacuum source of over 5 in.Hg to the vacuum break.

NOTE: *If the air valve rod is restricting the vacuum diaphragm from seating it may be necessary to bend the air valve rod slightly to gain clearance. Make an air valve rod adjustment after the vacuum break adjustment.*

3. Read the angle gauge while lightly pushing on the intermediate choke lever so that the choke valve is toward the Closed position.

4. Using an 1/8 in. (3mm) hex wrench, turn the screw in the rear cover until the bubble is centered. Apply silicone sealant over the screw head to seal the setting.

Choke Unloader

1. Follow Steps 1-4 of the Fast Idle Cam Adjustment.

2. If removed, install the choke cover and the coil, then align the housing marks with the cover marks, as specified.

3. Hold the primary throttle valve Wide Open.

4. If the engine is Warm, push inward on the intermediate choke lever to close the choke valve.

5. Bend the unloader tang until the bubble is centered.

Secondary Lockout

1. Place the choke in the Wide Open position by pushing outward on the intermediate choke lever.

2. Open the throttle valve until the end of the secondary actuating lever is opposite the toe of the lockout lever.

3. Gauge the clearance between the lockout lever and secondary lever, as specified.

4. To adjust, bend the lockout lever where it contacts the fast idle cam.

REMOVAL AND INSTALLATION

2.0L Engine

1. Remove the air cleaner and the gasket.
2. Disconnect the fuel pipe and all of the vacuum lines.
3. Label and disconnect all of the electrical connections.
4. Disconnect the downshift cable.
5. If equipped with cruise control, disconnect the linkage.
6. Remove the carburetor-to-intake manifold bolts and the carburetor, then discard the mounting gasket.

NOTE: *Before installing the carburetor, fill the float bowl with gasoline to reduce the battery strain and the possibility of backfiring when the engine is started again.*

7. Inspect the EFE heater for damage. Using a putty knife, clean the gasket mounting surfaces. Be sure that the throttle body and EFE mating surfaces are clean.

8. To install, use a new gasket and the carburetor; tighten the nuts alternately.

Adjusting the secondary vacuum break — 2.0L and 2.8L engines

Adjusting the choke unloader — 2.0L and 2.8L engines

⑤ SPECIFIED ANGLE (SEE SPECS.)

④ LEVELING BUBBLE (CENTERED)

① DEGREE SCALE

② POINTER

MAGNET

③ CHOKE VALVE CLOSED

FIGURE 1

⑦ DURING READING OF ANGLE GAUGE, LIGHTLY PUSH CLOCKWISE ON INTERMEDIATE CHOKE LEVER (IN DIRECTION OF CLOSED CHOKE VALVE) AND HOLD IN POSITION WITH RUBBER BAND.

⑧ BEND TANG TO ADJUST UNTIL BUBBLE IS CENTERED.

⑥ HOLD PRIMARY THROTTLE VALVE WIDE OPEN

FIGURE 2

① HOLD CHOKE VALVE WIDE OPEN BY PUSHING COUNTERCLOCKWISE ON INTERMEDIATE CHOKE LEVER.

④ IF NECESSARY TO ADJUST, BEND LOCKOUT LEVER TANG CONTACTING FAST IDLE CAM.

③ GAUGE CLEARANCE - DIMENSION SHOULD BE AS SPECIFIED.

② OPEN THROTTLE LEVER UNTIL END OF SECONDARY ACTUATING LEVER IS OPPOSITE TOE OF LOCKOUT LEVER.

Adjusting the secondary lockout — 1.9L engine

9. To complete the installation, reverse the removal procedures.

2.8L Engine

1. Remove the air cleaner.
2. Disconnect the fuel and vacuum lines from the carburetor.
3. Disconnect all of the electrical connectors from the carburetor.

4. Disconnect the linkage from carburetor.
5. Remove the carburetor-to-intake manifold nuts or bolts and the carburetor from the vehicle; discard the gasket.
6. Using a putty knife, clean the gasket mounting surfaces.
7. To install, use a new gasket and reverse the removal procedures. Check that the linkage works smoothly and is properly adjusted. Make sure there are no leaks.

CHILTON'S
FUEL ECONOMY & TUNE-UP TIPS

Tune-up • Spark Plug Diagnosis • Emission Controls

Fuel System • Cooling System • Tires and Wheels

General Maintenance

CHILTON'S FUEL ECONOMY & TUNE-UP TIPS

Fuel economy is important to everyone, no matter what kind of vehicle you drive. The maintenance-minded motorist can save both money and fuel using these tips and the periodic maintenance and tune-up procedures in this Repair and Tune-Up Guide.

There are more than 130,000,000 cars and trucks registered for private use in the United States. Each travels an average of 10-12,000 miles per year, and, and in total they consume close to 70 billion gallons of fuel each year. This represents nearly ⅔ of the oil imported by the United States each year. The Federal government's goal is to reduce consumption 10% by 1985. A variety of methods are either already in use or under serious consideration, and they all affect you driving and the cars you will drive. In addition to "down-sizing", the auto industry is using or investigating the use of electronic fuel delivery, electronic engine controls and alternative engines for use in smaller and lighter vehicles, among other alternatives to meet the federally mandated Corporate Average Fuel Economy (CAFE) of 27.5 mpg by 1985. The government, for its part, is considering rationing, mandatory driving curtailments and tax increases on motor vehicle fuel in an effort to reduce consumption. The government's goal of a 10% reduction could be realized — and further government regulation avoided — if every private vehicle could use just 1 less gallon of fuel per week.

How Much Can You Save?

Tests have proven that almost anyone can make at least a 10% reduction in fuel consumption through regular maintenance and tune-ups. When a major manufacturer of spark plugs sur-

---

TUNE-UP

1. Check the cylinder compression to be sure the engine will really benefit from a tune-up and that it is capable of producing good fuel economy. A tune-up will be wasted on an engine in poor mechanical condition.

2. Replace spark plugs regularly. New spark plugs alone can increase fuel economy 3%.

3. Be sure the spark plugs are the correct type (heat range) for your vehicle. See the Tune-Up Specifications.

Heat range refers to the spark plug's ability to conduct heat away from the firing end. It must conduct the heat away in an even pattern to avoid becoming a source of pre-ignition, yet it must also operate hot enough to burn off conductive deposits that could cause misfiring.

The heat range is usually indicated by a number on the spark plug, part of the manufacturer's designation for each individual spark plug. The numbers in bold-face indicate the heat range in each manufacturer's identification system.

Manufacturer	Typical Designation
AC	R **45** TS
Bosch (old)	WA **145** T30
Bosch (new)	HR **8** Y
Champion	RBL **15** Y
Fram/Autolite	**415**
Mopar	P-**62** PR
Motorcraft	BRF-**42**
NGK	BP **5** ES-15
Nippondenso	W **16** EP
Prestolite	14GR **5** 2A

Periodically, check the spark plugs to be sure they are firing efficiently. They are excellent indicators of the internal condition of your engine.

On AC, Bosch (new), Champion, Fram/Autolite, Mopar, Motorcraft and Prestolite, a higher number indicates a hotter plug. On Bosch (old), NGK and Nippondenso, a higher number indicates a colder plug.

4. Make sure the spark plugs are properly gapped. See the Tune-Up Specifications in this book.

5. Be sure the spark plugs are firing efficiently. The illustrations on the next 2 pages show you how to "read" the firing end of the spark plug.

6. Check the ignition timing and set it to specifications. Tests show that almost all cars have incorrect ignition timing by more than 2°.

veyed over 6,000 cars nationwide, they found that a tune-up, on cars that needed one, increased fuel economy over 11%. Replacing worn plugs alone, accounted for a 3% increase. The same test also revealed that 8 out of every 10 vehicles will have some maintenance deficiency that will directly affect fuel economy, emissions or performance. Most of this mileage-robbing neglect could be prevented with regular maintenance.

Modern engines require that all of the functioning systems operate properly for maximum efficiency. A malfunction anywhere wastes fuel. You can keep your vehicle running as efficiently and economically as possible, by being aware of your vehicle's operating and performance characteristics. If your vehicle suddenly develops performance or fuel economy problems it could be due to one or more of the following:

PROBLEM	POSSIBLE CAUSE
Engine Idles Rough	Ignition timing, idle mixture, vacuum leak or something amiss in the emission control system.
Hesitates on Acceleration	Dirty carburetor or fuel filter, improper accelerator pump setting, ignition timing or fouled spark plugs.
Starts Hard or Fails to Start	Worn spark plugs, improperly set automatic choke, ice (or water) in fuel system.
Stalls Frequently	Automatic choke improperly adjusted and possible dirty air filter or fuel filter.
Performs Sluggishly	Worn spark plugs, dirty fuel or air filter, ignition timing or automatic choke out of adjustment.

Check spark plug wires on conventional point type ignition for cracks by bending them in a loop around your finger.

Be sure that spark plug wires leading to adjacent cylinders do not run too close together. (Photo courtesy Champion Spark Plug Co.)

7. If your vehicle does not have electronic ignition, check the points, rotor and cap as specified.

8. Check the spark plug wires (used with conventional point-type ignitions) for cracks and burned or broken insulation by bending them in a loop around your finger. Cracked wires decrease fuel efficiency by failing to deliver full voltage to the spark plugs. One misfiring spark plug can cost you as much as 2 mpg.

9. Check the routing of the plug wires. Misfiring can be the result of spark plug leads to adjacent cylinders running parallel to each other and too close together. One wire tends to pick up voltage from the other causing it to fire "out of time".

10. Check all electrical and ignition circuits for voltage drop and resistance.

11. Check the distributor mechanical and/or vacuum advance mechanisms for proper functioning. The vacuum advance can be checked by twisting the distributor plate in the opposite direction of rotation. It should spring back when released.

12. Check and adjust the valve clearance on engines with mechanical lifters. The clearance should be slightly loose rather than too tight.

SPARK PLUG DIAGNOSIS

Normal

APPEARANCE: This plug is typical of one operating normally. The insulator nose varies from a light tan to grayish color with slight electrode wear. The presence of slight deposits is normal on used plugs and will have no adverse effect on engine performance. The spark plug heat range is correct for the engine and the engine is running normally.

CAUSE: Properly running engine.

RECOMMENDATION: Before reinstalling this plug, the electrodes should be cleaned and filed square. Set the gap to specifications. If the plug has been in service for more than 10-12,000 miles, the entire set should probably be replaced with a fresh set of the same heat range.

Oil Deposits

APPEARANCE: The firing end of the plug is covered with a wet, oily coating.

CAUSE: The problem is poor oil control. On high mileage engines, oil is leaking past the rings or valve guides into the combustion chamber. A common cause is also a plugged PCV valve, and a ruptured fuel pump diaphragm can also cause this condition. Oil fouled plugs such as these are often found in new or recently overhauled engines, before normal oil control is achieved, and can be cleaned and reinstalled.

RECOMMENDATION: A hotter spark plug may temporarily relieve the problem, but the engine is probably in need of work.

Incorrect Heat Range

APPEARANCE: The effects of high temperature on a spark plug are indicated by clean white, often blistered insulator. This can also be accompanied by excessive wear of the electrode, and the absence of deposits.

CAUSE: Check for the correct spark plug heat range. A plug which is too hot for the engine can result in overheating. A car operated mostly at high speeds can require a colder plug. Also check ignition timing, cooling system level, fuel mixture and leaking intake manifold.

RECOMMENDATION: If all ignition and engine adjustments are known to be correct, and no other malfunction exists, install spark plugs one heat range colder.

Carbon Deposits

APPEARANCE: Carbon fouling is easily identified by the presence of dry, soft, black, sooty deposits.

CAUSE: Changing the heat range can often lead to carbon fouling, as can prolonged slow, stop-and-start driving. If the heat range is correct, carbon fouling can be attributed to a rich fuel mixture, sticking choke, clogged air cleaner, worn breaker points, retarded timing or low compression. If only one or two plugs are carbon fouled, check for corroded or cracked wires on the affected plugs. Also look for cracks in the distributor cap between the towers of affected cylinders.

RECOMMENDATION: After the problem is corrected, these plugs can be cleaned and reinstalled if not worn severely.

Photos Courtesy Fram Corporation

MMT Fouled

APPEARANCE: Spark plugs fouled by MMT (Methycyclopentadienyl Maganese Tricarbonyl) have reddish, rusty appearance on the insulator and side electrode.

CAUSE: MMT is an anti-knock additive in gasoline used to replace lead. During the combustion process, the MMT leaves a reddish deposit on the insulator and side electrode.

RECOMMENDATION: No engine malfunction is indicated and the deposits will not affect plug performance any more than lead deposits (see Ash Deposits). MMT fouled plugs can be cleaned, regapped and reinstalled.

High Speed Glazing

APPEARANCE: Glazing appears as shiny coating on the plug, either yellow or tan in color.

CAUSE: During hard, fast acceleration, plug temperatures rise suddenly. Deposits from normal combustion have no chance to fluff-off; instead, they melt on the insulator forming an electrically conductive coating which causes misfiring.

RECOMMENDATION: Glazed plugs are not easily cleaned. They should be replaced with a fresh set of plugs of the correct heat range. If the condition recurs, using plugs with a heat range one step colder may cure the problem.

Ash (Lead) Deposits

APPEARANCE: Ash deposits are characterized by light brown or white colored deposits crusted on the side or center electrodes. In some cases it may give the plug a rusty appearance.

CAUSE: Ash deposits are normally derived from oil or fuel additives burned during normal combustion. Normally they are harmless, though excessive amounts can cause misfiring. If deposits are excessive in short mileage, the valve guides may be worn.

RECOMMENDATION: Ash-fouled plugs can be cleaned, gapped and reinstalled.

Detonation

APPEARANCE: Detonation is usually characterized by a broken plug insulator.

CAUSE: A portion of the fuel charge will begin to burn spontaneously, from the increased heat following ignition. The explosion that results applies extreme pressure to engine components, frequently damaging spark plugs and pistons.

Detonation can result by over-advanced ignition timing, inferior gasoline (low octane) lean air/fuel mixture, poor carburetion, engine lugging or an increase in compression ratio due to combustion chamber deposits or engine modification.

RECOMMENDATION: Replace the plugs after correcting the problem.

Photos Courtesy Champion Spark Plug Co.

EMISSION CONTROLS

13. Be aware of the general condition of the emission control system. It contributes to reduced pollution and should be serviced regularly to maintain efficient engine operation.

14. Check all vacuum lines for dried, cracked or brittle conditions. Something as simple as a leaking vacuum hose can cause poor performance and loss of economy.

15. Avoid tampering with the emission control system. Attempting to improve fuel econ-

FUEL SYSTEM

Check the air filter with a light behind it. If you can see light through the filter it can be reused.

Extremely clogged filters should be discarded and replaced with a new one.

18. Replace the air filter regularly. A dirty air filter richens the air/fuel mixture and can increase fuel consumption as much as 10%. Tests show that ⅓ of all vehicles have air filters in need of replacement.

19. Replace the fuel filter at least as often as recommended.

20. Set the idle speed and carburetor mixture to specifications.

21. Check the automatic choke. A sticking or malfunctioning choke wastes gas.

22. During the summer months, adjust the automatic choke for a leaner mixture which will produce faster engine warm-ups.

COOLING SYSTEM

29. Be sure all accessory drive belts are in good condition. Check for cracks or wear.

30. Adjust all accessory drive belts to proper tension.

31. Check all hoses for swollen areas, worn spots, or loose clamps.

32. Check coolant level in the radiator or expansion tank.

33. Be sure the thermostat is operating properly. A stuck thermostat delays engine warm-up and a cold engine uses nearly twice as much fuel as a warm engine.

34. Drain and replace the engine coolant at least as often as recommended. Rust and scale

TIRES & WHEELS

38. Check the tire pressure often with a pencil type gauge. Tests by a major tire manufacturer show that 90% of all vehicles have at least 1 tire improperly inflated. Better mileage can be achieved by over-inflating tires, but never exceed the maximum inflation pressure on the side of the tire.

39. If possible, install radial tires. Radial tires deliver as much as ½ mpg more than bias belted tires.

40. Avoid installing super-wide tires. They only create extra rolling resistance and decrease fuel mileage. Stick to the manufacturer's recommendations.

41. Have the wheels properly balanced.

omy by tampering with emission controls is more likely to worsen fuel economy than improve it. Emission control changes on modern engines are not readily reversible.

16. Clean (or replace) the EGR valve and lines as recommended.

17. Be sure that all vacuum lines and hoses are reconnected properly after working under the hood. An unconnected or misrouted vacuum line can wreak havoc with engine performance.

23. Check for fuel leaks at the carburetor, fuel pump, fuel lines and fuel tank. Be sure all lines and connections are tight.

24. Periodically check the tightness of the carburetor and intake manifold attaching nuts and bolts. These are a common place for vacuum leaks to occur.

25. Clean the carburetor periodically and lubricate the linkage.

26. The condition of the tailpipe can be an excellent indicator of proper engine combustion. After a long drive at highway speeds, the inside of the tailpipe should be a light grey in color. Black or soot on the insides indicates an overly rich mixture.

27. Check the fuel pump pressure. The fuel pump may be supplying more fuel than the engine needs.

28. Use the proper grade of gasoline for your engine. Don't try to compensate for knocking or "pinging" by advancing the ignition timing. This practice will only increase plug temperature and the chances of detonation or pre-ignition with relatively little performance gain.

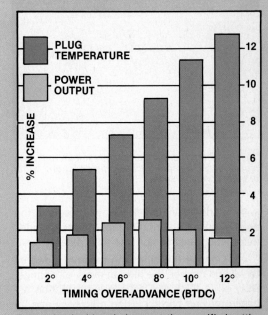

Increasing ignition timing past the specified setting results in a drastic increase in spark plug temperature with increased chance of detonation or preignition. Performance increase is considerably less. (Photo courtesy Champion Spark Plug Co.)

that form in the engine should be flushed out to allow the engine to operate at peak efficiency.

35. Clean the radiator of debris that can decrease cooling efficiency.

36. Install a flex-type or electric cooling fan, if you don't have a clutch type fan. Flex fans use curved plastic blades to push more air at low speeds when more cooling is needed; at high speeds the blades flatten out for less resistance. Electric fans only run when the engine temperature reaches a predetermined level.

37. Check the radiator cap for a worn or cracked gasket. If the cap does not seal properly, the cooling system will not function properly.

42. Be sure the front end is correctly aligned. A misaligned front end actually has wheels going in differed directions. The increased drag can reduce fuel economy by .3 mpg.

43. Correctly adjust the wheel bearings. Wheel bearings that are adjusted too tight increase rolling resistance.

Check tire pressures regularly with a reliable pocket type gauge. Be sure to check the pressure on a cold tire.

GENERAL MAINTENANCE

Check the fluid levels (particularly engine oil) on a regular basis. Be sure to check the oil for grit, water or other contamination.

A vacuum gauge is another excellent indicator of internal engine condition and can also be installed in the dash as a mileage indicator.

44. Periodically check the fluid levels in the engine, power steering pump, master cylinder, automatic transmission and drive axle.

45. Change the oil at the recommended interval and change the filter at every oil change. Dirty oil is thick and causes extra friction between moving parts, cutting efficiency and increasing wear. A worn engine requires more frequent tune-ups and gets progressively worse fuel economy. In general, use the lightest viscosity oil for the driving conditions you will encounter.

46. Use the recommended viscosity fluids in the transmission and axle.

47. Be sure the battery is fully charged for fast starts. A slow starting engine wastes fuel.

48. Be sure battery terminals are clean and tight.

49. Check the battery electrolyte level and add distilled water if necessary.

50. Check the exhaust system for crushed pipes, blockages and leaks.

51. Adjust the brakes. Dragging brakes or brakes that are not releasing create increased drag on the engine.

52. Install a vacuum gauge or miles-per-gallon gauge. These gauges visually indicate engine vacuum in the intake manifold. High vacuum = good mileage and low vacuum = poorer mileage. The gauge can also be an excellent indicator of internal engine conditions.

53. Be sure the clutch is properly adjusted. A slipping clutch wastes fuel.

54. Check and periodically lubricate the heat control valve in the exhaust manifold. A sticking or inoperative valve prevents engine warm-up and wastes gas.

55. Keep accurate records to check fuel economy over a period of time. A sudden drop in fuel economy may signal a need for tune-up or other maintenance.

CARBURETOR SPECIFICATIONS

Type DCH340 4-1.9L Engine

Primary Throttle Plate Gap (in.)	Primary Main Jet Number	Secondary Main Jet Number	Primary Slow Jet Number	Secondary Slow Jet Number	Power Jet Number	Primary Main Air Bleed Number	Secondary Main Air Bleed Number	Slow Air Bleed Number
.050–.059 (MT)	114 Fed.	170	50 Fed.	100	50	120 Fed.	70 Fed.	150 Fed.
.059–.069 (AT)	85 Cal.		54 Cal.			110 Cal.	90 Cal.	130 Cal.

Type E2SE 6-2.8L (Code B) (California)

Carb. Number	Float Level (in.)	Fast Idle Cam. (deg.)	Primary Vacuum Break (deg.)	Air Valve Rod (deg.)	Secondary Vacuum Break (deg.)	Choke Unloader (deg.)
17082356	13/32	22	25	1	30	30
17082357	13/32	22	25	1	32	30
17082358	13/32	22	25	1	30	30
17082359	13/32	22	25	1	32	30
17072683	9/32	28	25	1	35	45
17074812	9/32	28	25	1	35	45
17084356	9/32	22	25	1	30	30
17084357	9/32	22	25	1	30	30
17084358	9/32	22	25	1	30	30
17084359	9/32	22	25	1	30	30
17084368	1/8	22	25	1	30	30
17084370	1/8	22	25	1	30	30
17084430	11/32	15	26	1	38	42
17084431	11/32	15	26	1	38	42
17084434	11/32	15	26	1	38	42
17084435	11/32	15	26	1	38	42
17084452	5/32	28	25	1	35	45
17084453	5/32	28	25	1	35	45
17084455	5/32	28	25	1	35	45
17084456	5/32	28	25	1	35	45
17084458	5/32	28	25	1	35	45
17084532	5/32	28	25	1	35	45
17084534	5/32	28	25	1	35	45
17084535	5/32	28	25	1	35	45
17084537	5/32	28	25	1	35	45
17084538	5/32	28	25	1	35	45
17084540	5/32	28	25	1	35	45
17084542	1/8	28	25	1	35	45
17084632	9/32	28	25	1	35	45
17084633	9/32	28	25	1	35	45
17084635	9/32	28	25	1	35	45
17084636	9/32	28	25	1	35	45

GASOLINE FUEL INJECTION SYSTEM

Fuel Pressure Relief

Prior to servicing any component of the fuel injection system, the fuel pressure must relieved. If fuel pressure is not relieved, serious injury could result.

2.5L TBI ENGINE

1. From the fuse block, located in the passenger compartment, remove the fuse labeled, Fuel Pump.

2. Start the engine.

NOTE: *The engine wil start and run for a short period of time, until the remaining fuel is used up.*

3. Engage the starter, a few more times, to relieve any remaining pressure.

4. Turn the ignition switch Off and install the Fuel Pump fuse into the fuse block.

Type 2SE 6-2.8L (Code B) (excluding California)

Carb. Number	Float Level (in.)	Fast Idle Cam. (deg.)	Primary Vacuum Break (deg.)	Air Valve Rod (deg.)	Secondary Vacuum Break (deg.)	Choke Unloader (deg.)
17082348	7/16	22	26	1	32	40
17082349	7/16	22	28	1	32	40
17082350	7/16	22	26	1	32	40
17082351	7/16	22	28	1	32	40
17082353	7/16	22	28	1	35	30
17082355	7/16	22	28	1	35	30
17083348	7/16	22	30	1	32	40
17083349	7/16	22	30	1	32	40
17083350	7/16	22	30	1	32	40
17083351	7/16	22	30	1	32	40
17083352	7/16	22	30	1	35	40
17083353	7/16	22	30	1	35	40
17083354	7/16	22	30	1	35	40
17083355	7/16	22	30	1	35	40
17083360	7/16	22	30	1	32	40
17083361	7/16	22	28	1	32	40
17083362	7/16	22	30	1	32	40
17083363	7/16	22	28	1	32	40
17083364	7/16	22	30	1	35	40
17083365	7/16	22	30	1	35	40
17083366	7/16	22	30	1	35	40
17083367	7/16	22	30	1	35	40
17083390	13/32	28	30	1	35	38
17083391	13/32	28	30	1	35	38
17083392	13/32	28	30	1	35	38
17083393	13/32	28	30	1	35	38
17083394	13/32	28	30	1	35	38
17083395	13/32	28	30	1	35	38
17083396	13/32	28	30	1	35	38
17083397	13/32	28	30	1	35	38
17084410	11/32	15	23	1	38	42
17084412	11/32	15	23	1	38	42
17084425	11/32	15	26	1	36	40
17084427	11/32	15	26	1	36	40
17084560	11/32	15	24	1	34	38
17084562	11/32	15	24	1	34	38
17084569	11/32	15	24	1	34	38

2.8L and 4.3L TBI ENGINE

Allow the engine to set for 5–10 minutes; this will allow the orifice (in the fuel system) to bleed off the pressure.

Electric Fuel Pump

The electric fuel pump is attached to the fuel sending unit, located in the fuel tank.

REMOVAL AND INSTALLATION

NOTE: *The following procedure requires the use of the GM Fuel Gauge Sending Unit Retaining Cam tool No. J–24187 or equivalent, a brass drift and a hammer.*

1. Relieve the system fuel pressure.
2. Disconnect the negative battery terminal from the battery.

NOTE: *Be sure to keep a Class B (dry chemical) fire extinguisher nearby.*

CAUTION: *Due to the possibility of fire or explosion, never drain or store gasoline in an open container.*

3. Using a hand pump or a siphon hose, drain the gasoline into an approved container.
4. Raise and support the vehicle on jackstands.
5. Support the fuel tank and remove the fuel tank-to-vehicle straps.

Splash Cup Liquid
Vapor Separator

Return Tube

Fuel Tube

Rubber Coupler and
Sound Isolator

Fuel Level Sender

Electric Fuel Pump

Filter Strainer

TBI fuel pump and fuel gauge sender assembly

6. Lower the tank slightly, then remove the sender unit wires, the hoses and the ground strap.

7. Remove the fuel tank from the vehicle.

8. Using the GM Fuel Gauge Sending Unit Retaining Cam tool No. J–24187 (or equivalent) or a brass drift and a hammer, remove the cam locking ring (fuel sending unit) counterclockwise, then lift the sending unit from the fuel tank.

9. Remove the fuel pump from the fuel sending unit, by performing the following procedures:

a. Pull the fuel pump up into the mounting tube, while pulling outward (away) from the bottom support.

NOTE: *When removing the fuel pump from the sending unit, be careful not to damage the rubber insulator and the strainer.*

b. When the pump assembly is clear of the bottom support, pull it out of the rubber connector.

10. Inspect the fuel pump hose and bottom sound insulator for signs of deterioration, then replace it, if necessary.

11. Push the fuel pump onto the sending tube.

12. Using a new sending unit-to-fuel tank O-ring, install the sending unit into the fuel tank.

NOTE: *When installing the sending unit, be careful not to fold or twist the fuel strainer, for it will restrict the fuel flow.*

13. Using the GM Fuel Gauge Sending Unit Retaining Cam tool No. J–24187 (or equivalent) or a brass drift and a hammer, turn the sending unit-to-fuel tank locking ring clockwise.

14. To install the fuel tank, align the insulator strips and reverse the removal procedures. Torque the inner fuel tank strap-to-vehicle

bolts to 26 ft. lbs. and the outer fuel tank strap-to-vehicle nuts/bolts to 26 ft. lbs.

TESTING AND ADJUSTMENTS

Flow Test

1. Remove the fuel pump-to-throttle body line from the throttle body.

2. Place the fuel line in a clean container.

3. Turn the ignition switch On; approximately $1/2$ pint of the fuel should be delivered in 15 seconds.

4. If the fuel flow is below minimum, inspect the fuel system for restrictions; if no restrictions are found, replace the fuel pump.

Pressure Test

NOTE: *The following procedure requires the use of a GM Fuel Pressure Gauge tool No. J–29658–A or equivalent.*

1. If equipped with an EFI equipped engine, refer to the Fuel Pressure Relief procedures in this Chapter and relieve the fuel pressure.

2. Remove the air cleaner, then disconnect and plug the THERMAC vacuum port on the throttle body unit.

3. Place a rag (to catch excess fuel) under the fuel line-to-throttle body connection. Disconnect the fuel line from the throttle body.

NOTE: *When disconnecting the fuel line, use a back-up wrench to hold the fuel nut on the throttle body.*

4. Using a GM Fuel Pressure Gauge tool No. J–29658–A or equivalent, install it into the fuel line.

5. Start the engine and observe the fuel pressure, it should be 9–13 psi.

NOTE: *If the fuel pressure does not meet specifications, inspect the fuel system for restrictions or replace the fuel pump.*

6. Turn the engine Off, relieve the fuel pressure and remove the GM Fuel Pressure Gauge tool No. J–29658–A or equivalent.

7. Install a new fuel line-to-throttle body O-ring and reverse the removal procedures. Unplug from the THERMAC vacuum port. Start the engine and check for fuel leaks.

Fuel Pump Relay

The fuel pump relay is mounted on the left front fender in the engine compartment. Check for loose electrical connections; no other service is possible, except replacement.

REMOVAL AND INSTALLATION

1. Disconnect the negative battery terminal from the battery.

2. Disconnect the relay/electrical connector assembly from the bracket.

A. Front
B. Left front inner fender
21. Bracket
22. Fuel pump relay

Fuel pump relay location

3. Pull the fuel pump relay from the electrical connector.

4. If necessary, use a new fuel pump and reverse the removal procedures.

Throttle Body

The Model 220 throttle body assembly is used on the 2.8L and 4.3L engines. It consists of three major casting assemblies:

• Fuel pressure cover with pressure regulator.

• Fuel metering body with fuel injectors.

• Throttle body with an Idle Speed Control (IAC) Valve and a Throttle Position Sensor (TPS).

The Model 300 throttle body assembly is used on early 2.5L engines. It consists of three major casting assemblies:

• Fuel pressure cover with pressure regulator.

• Fuel metering body with fuel injectors.

• Throttle body with an Idle Speed Control (IAC) Valve and a Throttle Position Sensor (TPS).

The Model 700 throttle body assembly is used on later 2.5L engines. It consists of two major casting assemblies:

• Fuel metering assembly with pressure regulator and fuel injector.

• Throttle body with an Idle Speed Control (IAC) Valve and a Throttle Position Sensor (TPS).

The Throttle Position Sensor (TPS) is a variable resistor used to convert the degree of throttle plate opening to an electrical signal to the ECM. The ECM uses this signal as a reference point of throttle valve position. In addition, an Idle Air Control (IAC) assembly, mounted in the throttle body is used to control idle speeds. A cone-shaped valve in the IAC assembly is lo-

cated in an air passage in the throttle body that leads from the point beneath the air cleaner to below the throttle valve. The ECM monitors idle speeds and, depending on engine load, moves the IAC cone in the air passage to increase or decrease air bypassing the throttle valve to the intake manifold for control of idle speeds.

The operation of all throttle bodies is basically the same. Each is constantly monitored by the ECM to produce a 14.7:1 air/fuel ratio, which is vital to the catalytic converter operation.

REMOVAL AND INSTALLATION

1. Relieve the system fuel pressure.

2. Remove the air cleaner. Disconnect the negative battery cable from the battery.

3. Disconnect the electrical connectors from the idle air control valve, the throttle position sensor and the fuel injector(s).

4. Remove the throttle return spring(s), the cruise control (if equipped) and the throttle linkage.

5. Label and disconnect the vacuum hoses from the throttle body.

1. Gasket
5. Fuel inlet O ring
6. Fuel outlet O ring
10. Flange gasket
20. Fuel meter assembly
22. Fuel meter screws
25. Fuel meter to throttle body gasket
35. Injector retainer screw
36. Injector retainer
40. Fuel injector
42. Upper injector O-ring
43. Lower injector O ring
60. Pressure regulator cover
61. Pressure regulator screw
65. Spring seat
66. Pressure regulator spring
70. Pressure regulator diaphragm
90. Fuel inlet nut
91. Fuel nut seal
96. Fuel outlet nut
200. Throttle body assembly
205. Idle stop screw plug
207. Idle stop screw and washer
208. Idle stop screw spring
230. Throttle position sensor
232. TPS attaching screw
250. Idle air control valve
251. IAC valve screw
255. IAC O-ring
270. Tube module
272. Tube module attaching screw
275. Tube module gasket

Exploded view of the model 700 TBI unit — late 2.5L engines

1. Screw & washer assembly
2. Screw & washer assembly
3. Fuel meter cover assembly
4. Gasket—fuel meter cover
5. Gasket—fuel meter outlet
6. Dust seal—pressure regulator
7. Pressure regulator
11. Filter—fuel injector nozzle
12. Lower "O" ring
13. Upper "O" ring
14. Back-up washer—fuel injector
20. Screw & washer assembly
21. Fuel meter body assembly
22. Gasket—fuel meter body
23. Gasket—air filter
30. Fuel return line "O" ring
31. Nut—fuel return

32. Gasket—fuel return nut
37. Fuel inlet line "O" ring
38. Nut—fuel inlet
39. Gasket—fuel inlet nut
50. Screw—TPS lever attaching
51. Lever—TPS
52. Screw & washer assembly
55. Retainer—TPS attaching screw
58. Sensor—throttle position
60. Plug—idle stop screw
61. Screw—throttle stop
62. Spring—throttle stop screw
65. Throttle body assembly
70. Gasket—flange mounting
75. Idle air control assembly
76. Gasket—IAC to throttle body

Exploded view of the model 300 TBI unit — early 2.5L engines

1. Screw assembly—fuel meter cover attaching—long
2. Screw assembly—fuel meter cover attaching—short
3. Fuel meter cover assembly
4. Gasket—fuel meter cover
5. Gasket—fuel meter outlet
6. Seal—pressure regulator
7. Pressure regulator
10. Injector—fuel
11. Filter—fuel injector inlet
12. O-ring—fuel injector—lower
13. O-ring—fuel injector—upper
14. Washer—fuel injector
20. Screw assembly—fuel meter body—throttle body attaching
21. Fuel meter body assembly
22. Gasket—throttle body to fuel meter body
23. Gasket—air filter
30. O-ring—fuel return line
31. Nut—fuel outlet
37. O-ring—fuel inlet line
38. Nut—fuel inlet
40. Gasket—fuel outlet nut
41. Gasket—fuel inlet nut

50. Screw—TPS lever attaching
51. Lever—TPS
52. Screw assembly—TPS attaching
55. Retainer—TPS attachingscrew
58. Sensor—throttle position (TPS)
60. Plug—idle stop screw
61. Screw assembly—idle stop
62. Spring—idle stop screw
65. Throttle body assembly
70. Gasket—flange
75. Valve assembly—idle air control (IAC)
76. Gasket—idle air control valve assembly

Exploded view of the model 220 TBI unit — 2.8L and 4.3L engines

1. TBI unit
2. Bolts and nut—tighten to 18 N·m (13 ft. lbs.)
3. Stud—tighten to 5 N·m (45 in. lbs.)
4. Gasket

Removing the model 300 TBI unit — early 2.5L engine

1. TBI unit
2. Nut-tighten to 25 N·m (18 ft. lbs.)
3. Gasket
4. Engine inlet manifold

Removing the model 220 TBI unit — 2.8L and 4.3L engine

6. Place a rag (to catch the excess fuel) under the fuel line-to-throttle body connection, then disconnect the fuel line from the throttle body.

7. Remove the attaching hardware, the

1	STUD - TIGHTEN TO 17 N·m (12 FT. LBS.)
2	TBI UNIT
3	GASKET
4	ENGINE INTAKE MANIFOLD

Removing the model 700 TBI unit — late 2.5L engine

throttle body-to-intake manifold bolts, the throttle body and the gasket.

NOTE: *Be sure to place a cloth in the intake manifold to prevent dirt from entering the engine.*

8. Using a putty knife (if necessary), clean the gasket mounting surfaces.

9. To install, use a new gasket and reverse the removal procedures. Torque the throttle body-to-intake manifold nuts/bolts to 13 ft. lbs. Depress the accelerator pedal to the floor and release it, to see if the pedal returns freely. Turn the ignition switch On and check for fuel leaks.

INJECTOR REPLACEMENT

CAUTION: *When removing the injector(s), be careful not to damage the electrical connector pins (on top of the injector), the injector fuel filter and the nozzle. The fuel injector is serviced as a complete assembly ONLY, it is an electrical component and should not be immersed in any kind of cleaner.*

1. Remove the air cleaner. Disconnect the negative battery terminal from the battery.

2. Relieve the system fuel pressure.

3. At the injector connector, squeeze the two tabs together and pull it straight up.

4. Remove the fuel meter cover and leave the cover gasket in place.

5. Using a small pry bar or tool No. J–26868, carefully lift the injector until it is free from the fuel meter body.

6. Remove the small O-ring form the nozzle

1. Fuel meter cover gasket
2. Removing fuel injector

Fuel injector removal — model 220

1. Fuel injector
2. Filter
3. Small "O" ring
4. Large "O" ring
5. Steel back-up washer

Fuel injector removal — model 300

1. Fuel meter body
2. Fuel injector
A. Suitable prybar
B. Fulcrum

Fuel injector removal — model 700

end of the injector. Carefully rotate the injector's fuel filter back-and-forth to remove it from the base of the injector.

7. Discard the fuel meter cover gasket.

8. Remove the large O-ring and back-up washer from the top of the counterbore of the fuel meter body injector cavity.

9. To install, lubricate the O-rings with automatic transmission fluid and push it into the

fuel injector cavity. To complete the installation, reverse the removal procedures. Start the engine and check for fuel leaks.

IDLE AIR CONTROL (IAC) VALVE RE-PLACEMENT

NOTE: *The following procedure requires the use of the GM Removal tool No. J–33031 or equivalent.*

1. Remove the air cleaner. Disconnect the negative battery terminal from the battery.

2. Disconnect the electrical connector from the idle air control valve.

3. Using a $1^{1}/4$ in. (32mm) wrench or the GM Removal tool No. J–33031, remove the idle air control valve.

CAUTION: *Before installing a new idle air control valve, measure the distance that the valve extends (from the motor housing to the end of the cone); the distance should be no greater than $1^{1}/8$ in. (28mm). If it extends to far, damage will occur to the valve when it is installed.*

4. To install, use a new gasket and reverse the removal procedures. Start the engine and allow it to reach normal operating temperatures.

NOTE: *The ECM will reset the idle speed when the vehicle is driven at 30 mph.*

THROTTLE POSITION SENSOR (TPS)

1. Remove the air cleaner.

2. Disconnect the electrical connector from the throttle position sensor (TPS).

1. Idle air control valve
A. Less than 28mm ($1^{1}/8$ in.)
B. Type I (with collar)
C. Type II (without collar)
D. Gasket (part of IAC valve service kit)

Idle air control valve

1. Throttle position sensor
2. Screw & washer
3. TPS pick up lever
4. Screw
5. Lever
6. Throttle body assembly

Throttle position sensor — 2.5L engine

1. Screw assembly
2. Retainer
3. Throttle position sensor
4. Screw
5. Lever
6. Throttle body assembly

Throttle position sensor — 2.8L and 4.3L engines

3. Remove the TPS mounting screws, the lockwashers and the retainers.

4. Remove the TPS sensor.

5. To install, make sure that the throttle valve is in the closed position, then install the TPS sensor.

NOTE: *Make sure the the TPS pickup lever is located ABOVE the tang on the throttle actuator lever.*

6. To complete the installation, lubricate the mounting screws with Loctite® (thread locking compound) No. 262 or equivalent, then reverse the removal procedures.

ADJUSTMENTS

Idle Speed and Mixture Adjustment

2.5L TBI ENGINE

NOTE: *The following procedures require the use a tachometer, GM tool No. J–33047, BT–8207 or equivalent, GM Torx Bit No. 20, silicone sealant, a $\frac{5}{32}$ in. (4mm) drill bit, a prick punch and a $\frac{1}{16}$ in. (1.5mm) pin punch.*

The throttle stop screw, used in regulating the minimum idle speed, is adjusted at the factory and is not necessary to perform. This adjustment should be performed ONLY when the throttle body has been replaced.

NOTE: *The replacement of the complete throttle body assembly will have the minimum idle adjusted at the factory.*

1. Remove the air cleaner and the gasket. Be sure to plug the THERMAC vacuum port (air cleaner vacuum line-to-throttle body) on the throttle body.

2. Remove the throttle valve cable from the throttle control bracket to provide access to the minimum air adjustment screw.

3. Using the manufacturer's instructions, connect a tachometer to the engine.

4. Remove the electrical connector from the Idle Air Control (IAC) valve, located on the throttle body.

5. If necessary to remove the throttle stop screw cover, perform the following procedures:

a. Using a prick punch, mark the housing at the top over the center line of the throttle stop screw.

b. Using a $\frac{5}{32}$ in. (4mm) drill bit, drill (on an angle) a hole through the casting to the hardened cover.

c. Using a $\frac{1}{16}$ in. (1.5mm) pin punch, place it through the hole and drive out the cover to expose the throttle stop screw.

6. Place the transmission in Park (A/T) or Neutral (M/T), start the engine and allow the idle speed to stabilize.

7. Using the GM tool No. J-33047, BT-8207 or equivalent, install it into the idle air passage of the throttle body; be sure that the

1. Idle air passage plug (J33047/BT 8207-A)
2. Idle air passage

Plug the idle passages of each throttle body as illustrated

tool is fully seated in the opening and no air leaks exist.

8. Using the GM Torx Bit No. 20, turn the throttle stop screw until the engine speed is 475–525 rpm (A/T in Park or Neutral) or 750–800 rpm (M/T in Neutral).

9. With the idle speed adjusted, stop the engine, remove the tool No. J–33047, BT–8207 or equivalent, from the throttle body.

10. Reconnect the Idle Air Control (IAC) electrical connector.

11. Using silicone sealant or equivalent, cover the throttle stop screw.

12. Reinstall the gasket and the air cleaner assembly.

2.8L TBI ENGINE

NOTE: *The following procedure requires the use of a tachometer, a prick punch, a $5/32$ in. (4mm) drill bit, a $1/16$ in. (1.5mm) pin punch, a grounding wire and silicone sealant.*

1. Remove the air cleaner and the gasket.

2. If necessary to remove the throttle stop screw cover, perform the following procedures:

a. Using a prick punch, mark the housing at the top over the center line of the throttle stop screw.

b. Using a $5/32$ in. (4mm) drill bit, drill (on an angle) a hole through the casting to the hardened cover.

c. Using a $1/16$ in. (1.5mm) pin punch, place it through the hole and drive out the cover to expose the throttle stop screw.

NOTE: *The following adjustment should be performed ONLY when the throttle body assembly has been replaced; the engine should be at normal operating temperatures before making this adjustment.*

3. With the Idle Air Control (IAC) connected, ground the diagnostic terminal of the Assembly Line Communications Link (ALCL) connector.

NOTE: *The Assembly Line Communications Link (ALCL) connector is located in the engine compartment on the left side firewall.*

4. Turn the ignition switch On but DO NOT start the engine. Wait 30 seconds, this will allow the IAC valve pintle to extend and seat in the throttle body.

5. With the ignition switch turned On, disconnect the Idle Air Control (IAC) valve electrical connector.

6. Remove the ground from the Diagnostic Terminal ALCL connector and start the engine.

7. Adjust the idle stop screw to obtain 700 rpm (M/T) or 400–450 rpm (A/T in Drive).

8. Turn the ignition switch Off and reconnect the IAC valve electrical connector.

9. Using silicone sealant or equivalent, cover the throttle stop screw.

10. Reinstall the gasket and the air cleaner assembly.

Throttle Position Sensor (TPS)

The throttle position sensor is non-adjustable. However, a test should be performed when throttle body parts have been replaced or AFTER the minimum idle speed has been adjusted.

NOTE: *The following procedure requires the use of the Digital Voltmeter tool No. J–29125–A or equivalent.*

1. Using the Digital Voltmeter tool No. J–29125–A or equivalent, set it on the 0–5.0V scale, then connect the probes to the center terminal **B** and the outside terminal **C**.

NOTE: *To attach probes to the TPS electrical connector, disconnect the TPS electrical connector, install thin wires into the sockets and reconnect the connector.*

2. Turn the ignition On (engine stopped).

3. On the Model 220 and 700 throttle body units, output voltage should be 1.25V. If the voltage is more that 1.25V, replace the TPS.

4. On the Model 300 throttle body unit, the output voltage should be 0.420–0.450V; if not, rotate the TPS to obtain the correct voltage.

5. Remove the voltmeter and the jumper wires.

DIESEL ENGINE FUEL SYSTEM –

2.2L ENGINE

CAUTION: *The following procedures should not be attempted unless all tools necessary to adjust the injection pump timing are available.*

Fuel Injectors

The primary function of the nozzles is to distribute the fuel in the combustion chamber, which effects the combustion efficiency and engine performance.

REMOVAL AND INSTALLATION

1. Disconnect the negative battery terminal from the battery.

2. From the fuel injector nozzle(s), disconnect the fuel return line(s).

3. From the fuel injector nozzle(s), disconnect the fuel injection line(s).

4. Remove the fuel injector nozzle(s) from the engine.

5. Inspect and test the fuel injector nozzle(s).

6. To install, reverse the removal procedures.

TESTING

NOTE: *The following procedure requires the use of a reliable pressure tester and Calibrating Oil No. SAE J9670 or equivalent (70°F).*

CAUTION: *DO NOT use diesel fuel; it is unstable with the respect to corrosion inhibition and may cause skin problems.*

Opening Pressure

1. Using a reliable pressure tester, connect the test line to a fuel nozzle and tighten the fittings.

CAUTION: *Exercise extreme care, when using the pressure tester, not to damage the gauge with excessive pressure during the test procedure. When testing the nozzle(s), be sure not to position your hands or arms near the nozzle tip. The atomized high pressure fuel spray has enough penetrating power to puncture the flesh and destroy tissue and may also cause blood poisoning. The nozzle tip should always be enclosed in a transparent receptacle, to contain the spray.*

2. Close the gauge valve and operate the handle several times, then check for proper nozzle spray pattern.

3. Open the gauge valve and operate the handle slowly to determine the injector opening pressure. Observe the gauge reading just before the oil is sprayed from the tip; a buzzing noise will occur when the spray is injected. The minimum opening pressure is 1493 psi.

Spray Pattern

1. Close the pressure gauge.

2. Operate the handle slowly, one stroke every 2 seconds, and observe the spray pattern.

3. The spray should be uniform and injected at the correct angle of the nozzle being tested.

Leakage

1. Operate the handle to increase the fuel pressure to 284 psi.

2. Observe the nozzle tip, it should remain dry without an accumulation of fuel at the spray holes; a slight wetting is permitted after 10 seconds, if no droplets are formed.

Injection Pump

REMOVAL

1. Raise the hood.

2. Disconnect the negative battery terminal from the battery. Remove the battery.

3. Remove the undercover.

4. Place a drain pan under the radiator, open the drain cock and on the cylinder block, then drain the cooling system.

CAUTION: *When draining the coolant, keep in mind that cats and dogs are attracted by the ethylene glycol antifreeze, and are quite likely to drink any that is left in an uncovered container or in puddles on the ground. This will prove fatal in sufficient quantity. Always drain the coolant into a sealable container. Coolant should be reused unless it is contaminated or several years old.*

5. Disconnect the upper water hose from the engine side.

6. Loosen the compressor drive belt by

CORRECT   INCORRECT   INCORRECT   INCORRECT

RESTRICTIONS IN ORIFICE   DRIPPING

Description of the fuel nozzle spray pattern — 2.2L diesel engine moving the power steering oil pump or idler, if equipped.

7. Remove the cooling fan and the fan shroud.

8. Disconnect the lower water hose from the engine side.

9. Remove the air conditioner compressor, if equipped.

10. Remove the fan belt, the crankshaft pulley and the timing pulley housing covers.

11. Remove the tension spring and the fixing bolt, then remove the tension center and pulley.

12. Remove the timing belt, the engine control cable and the wiring harness of the fuel cut solenoid.

13. Remove the fuel hoses and the injection pipes. Using a wrench to hold the delivery holder, loosen the sleeve nuts on the injection pump side.

14. Install a 6mm bolt (with pitch of 1.25) into threaded hole in the timing pulley housing through the hole in pulley to prevent turning of the pulley.

15. Remove the bolt fixing the injection pump timing pulley, then remove the pulley using pulley puller.

16. Remove injection pump flange fixing nuts and rear bracket bolts, then remove the injection pump.

INSTALLATION

1. Install the injection pump by aligning the notched line on the flange with the line on the front bracket.

2. Install the injection pump timing pulley by aligning it with the key groove, then torque the bolts to 42–52 ft. lbs.

3. Position the piston of the No. 1 cylinder to TDC of the compression stoke and align marks on the timing pulleys.

4. Refer to the "Timing Belt, Installation" procedures in Chapter 3, then install and adjust the timing belt.

5. Check the injection timing.

6. To complete the installation, reverse the removal procedures.

Diesel Injection Pump Timing

CHECK AND ADJUSTMENT

NOTE: *The following procedure requires the use of the Static Timing Gauge tool No. J–29763 or equivalent.*

1. Check that notched line on the injection pump flange is in alignment with notched line on the injection pump front bracket.

2. Position the No. 1 piston on TDC of the compression stroke by turning crankshaft as necessary.

Injection pump and flange alignment

Correct timing mark alignment at TDC

Loosen the tension pulley

Removing the tension pulley

NOTE: *Make sure No. 1 cylinder is on the compression stroke; it is possible to align the timing marks incorrectly.*

3. Remove the upper fan shroud, if not already done.

4. With the upper cover removed, check that the timing belt is properly tensioned and that the timing marks are properly aligned. If the marks are not aligned properly, the timing belt will have to be removed and readjusted.

5. With the injection lines removed, remove the distributor head screws and washer from the injection pump.

6. Install the Static Timing Gauge tool No. J–29763 or equivalent, and set the lift to approximately 0.04 in. (1mm) from the plunger.

7. Position the piston, of the No. 1 cylinder, to a point 45–60° BTDC by turning the crankshaft, then calibrate the dial indicator to 0°. Turn the crankshaft pulley slightly in both directions and check that the gauge indication is stable.

8. Turn the crankshaft in the normal direction of rotation and record the reading of the dial indicator when the timing mark (15°) on the crankshaft pulley is in alignment with the TDC pointer. The dial indicator should read 0.020 in. (0.5mm).

9. If the reading of the dial indicator is not as described, hold the crankshaft in position (15°) before TDC and loosen two nuts on the injection pump flange. Move the injection pump to a point where the dial indicator gives reading of 0.020 in. (0.5mm), then tighten pump flange nuts.

10. Recheck the dial indicator reading and readjust the injection pump as necessary. Remove the dial indicator from the pump.

11. Install the distributor screw and washer into injection pump, then tighten.

12. Install the injection lines; DO NOT overtighten the connections.

13. To complete the installation, reverse the removal procedures. Adjust the idle speed and the fast idle speed as described in Chapter 2.

No. 1 piston at TDC

Location of the distributor head screw (arrow) that must be removed to install the dial gauge

Before adjusting the injection timing, bring the No. 1 piston to 45-60° BTDC and then zero the dial gauge

Injection timing dual gauge installed in injection pump

Location of the injection pump flange and bracket bolts

Check for leaks in the fuel system and correct, if necessary.

FUEL TANK

REMOVAL AND INSTALLATION

1. Drain the tank.
2. Raise and support the truck on jackstands.
3. Disconnect the wiring and ground strap at the tank.

4. Disconnect the filler neck hose and vent hose from the tank.
5. Disconnect the fuel feed line and vapor line at the tank.
6. Place a floor jack under the tank to take up its weight.
7. Remove the fuel tank support bolts and lower the tank.
8. To install, reverse the removal procedures.

Fuel tank assembly

Fuel pump and fuel sender unit assembly

HEATING AND
AIR CONDITIONING

Blower Motor

REMOVAL AND INSTALLATION

1. Disconnect the negative battery terminal from the battery.

2. Disconnect the electrical connectors from the blower motor.

NOTE: *On some earlier models equipped with A/C, it may be necessary to remove the A/C vacuum tank and move it aside.*

3. Remove the blower motor-to-case screws, then lift the blower motor from the case.

4. To install, reverse the removal procedures. Torque the blower motor-to-case screws to 18 ft. lbs.

Heater Core

The heater core is removable from under the right side of the instrument panel.

REMOVAL AND INSTALLATION

1. Disconnect the negative battery terminal from the battery.

2. Position a drain pan under the radiator,

DASH & TOE PANEL

STUD
(HEATER & DEFROSTER ASM)

SEAL

Heater case and blower motor

14. Screw
151. Seal
152. Bracket
153. Bracket
154. Core
155. Strap
156. Screw
157. Bracket
158. Case (rear)
159. Baffle
160. Valve (temperature)
161. Clip
162. Case (front)

Exploded view of the heater core assembly

4. Accumulator
108. Inlet line (accumulator)
130. Plate
131. Washer
132. Fan
133. Nut
134. Gasket
135. Wire
136. Screw
137. Seal
138. Tube
139. Screw
140. Case
141. Seal
142. Orifice
143. Core
144. Screw
145. Resistor
146. Case
147. Nut
148. Screw
149. Clamp
150. Clamp
151. Seal
152. Relay
153. Gasket
154. Switch
155. Motor
156. Screw
157. Inlet (evaporator)

Exploded view of the A/C evaporator

open the drain cock and drain the cooling system to a level below the heater core.

CAUTION: *When draining the coolant, keep in mind that cats and dogs are attracted by the ethylene glycol antifreeze, and are quite likely to drink any that is left in an uncovered container or in puddles on the ground. This will prove fatal in sufficient quantity. Always drain the coolant into a sealable container. Coolant should be reused unless it is contaminated or several years old.*

3. Disconnect the heater-to-engine coolant hoses from the core tubes on the fire wall, in the engine compartment.

NOTE: *Plug the heater core tubes to avoid spilling coolant in the passenger compartment during removal.*

4. Remove the heater core cover-to-cowl screws and the cover from the vehicle.

5. Remove the brackets from each end of the heater core.

6. Lift out the heater core.

7. To install, reverse the removal procedures. Torque the rear cover-to-case screws to 27 inch lbs. Refill the cooling system, the start the engine, allow the engine to reach normal operating temperatures, then check for leaks.

Control Head

REMOVAL AND INSTALLATION

1. Disconnect the negative battery terminal from the battery.

2. Remove the instrument panel trim bezel(s).

3. Remove the control head-to-instrument panel screws and pull the control head from the instrument panel.

4. Disconnect the vacuum hoses, the electrical connectors and the control cables from the control head.

5. Remove the control head assembly from the vehicle.

6. To install, reverse the removal procedures.

Evaporator Core

REMOVAL AND INSTALLATION

1. Have the system discharged by a professional shop.

2. Disconnect the negative battery terminal from the battery.

3. Disconnect the electrical connectors from the resistor and the blower motor.

4. Remove the inlet line from the A/C evaporator.

5. Remove the blower motor-to-case nuts/screws and the blower motor assembly from the vehicle.

6. Remove the accumulator inlet line from the evaporator and the accumulator.

7. Remove the blower motor case-to-evaporator case screws and separate the cases, then remove the evaporator core.

8. To install, reverse the removal procedures. Recharge the A/C system.

Expansion Tube

REMOVAL AND INSTALLATION

NOTE: *An orifice tube removal and installation tool (J–26549–D) is required to perform this procedure.*

1. Refer to Chapter 1 and evacuate the refrigerant from the A/C system.

2. Disconnect the refrigerant inlet line at the accumulator.

3. Remove the orifice from the refrigerant line using tool J–26549–D.

4. Install the new orifice into the inlet line with the shorter screen end toward the expansion tube.

5. Install the refrigerant line onto the accumulator and tighten to 18 ft. lbs.

6. Recharge the A/C system and check for leaks.

Accumulator

The accumulator assembly has a service replacement kit which includes two seals for the inlet and outlet connections. The dessicant is not serviced separately, it is part of the sealed accumulator assembly. Replace the accumulator only when:

• A physical perforation produces a leak.

170. Control assembly
171. Screws
172. Instrument panel
173. Nuts

Heater and A/C control head

• The orifice screen experiences continued or repeated plugging.

• An evaporator fail because of internal and external corrosion.

REMOVAL AND INSTALLATION

1. Remove the negative battery cable.

2. Refer to Chapter 1 and evacuate the refrigerant from the A/C system.

3. Disconnect the electrical connector from the dual pressure switch.

4. Remove the inlet line at the accumulator. Remove the evaporator outlet line at the accumulator and cap or plug both lines.

5. Remove the accumulator attaching screw and clamp. Remove the accumulator.

6. Drain excess refrigerant into a clean container. Measure to determine how much oil needs to be added to the system.

7. Install the accumulator attaching clamp and screw.

8. Add 2 oz. of clean refrigerant oil plus an amount equal to the oil drained from the system. Use clean 525 viscosity refrigerant oil on the seals.

9. Install the inlet and outlet lines and tighten to 18 ft. lbs.

10. Install the electrical connector. Install the negative battery cable.

11. Evacuate, charge and leak test the system.

RADIO

Receiver

REMOVAL AND INSTALLATION

1. Disconnect the negative battery terminal from the battery.

2. Remove the ash tray and any necessary wires.

3. Remove the instrument panel center bezel and the support clip nuts.

4. Remove the radio bracket-to-instrument panel bracket screws and pull the radio forward.

5. Disconnect the antenna, the clock connector, the speaker connectors and any electrical wires, then remove the radio.

WARNING: *DO NOT let the antenna cable touch the clock connector. It is very important when changing speakers or performing any radio work to avoid pinching the wires. A short circuit-to-ground from any wire will cause damage to the output circuit in the radio.*

Using the GM Windsheild Wiper Blade/Arm Removal tool No. J-8966 to remove the wiper arms

6. Installation is the reverse of removal.

NOTE: *In order to prevent damage to the receiver, always connect the speaker wire to the receiver before applying power to it.*

WINDSHIELD WIPERS

The windshield wiper units are of the 2-speed, non-depressed park type, a washer pump mounted under the washer bottle and turn signal type wiper/washer switch. A single wiper motor operates both wiper blades. Rotating the switch to either **LO** or **HI** speed position completes the circuit and the wiper motor runs at that speed.

The pulse/demand wash functions are controlled by a plug-in printed circuit board enclosed in the wiper housing cover.

Blade and Arm

REMOVAL AND INSTALLATION

NOTE: *The following procedure requires the use of GM Windshield Wiper Blade/Arm Removal tool No. J–8966 or equivalent.*

If the wiper assembly has a press type release tab at the center, simply depress the tab and remove the blade. If the blade has no release tab, use a screwdriver to depress the spring at the center; this will release the assembly. To install the assembly, position the blade over the pin (at the tip of the arm) and press until the spring retainer engages the groove in the pin.

To remove the element, either depress the release button or squeeze the spring type retainer clip (at the outer end) together and slide the blade element out. To install, slide the new element in until it latches.

1. Insert the tool under the wiper arm and lever the arm off the shaft.

2. Disconnect the washer hose from the arm (if equipped), then remove the arm.

3. To install, operate the wiper motor (momentarily) to position the pivot shafts into the Park position and reverse the removal procedures. The proper Park position for the arms is with the blades approximately 2 in. (51mm) on the driver's side, or 2³⁄₄ in. (70mm) on the passenger's side, above the lower windshield molding.

Wiper Motor

REMOVAL AND INSTALLATION

1. Disconnect the negative battery terminal from the battery.

2. Using the GM Windshield Wiper Blade/Arm Removal tool No. J-8966 or equivalent, remove the wiper arms.

3. Remove the cowl, vent and grille.

4. Loosen but DO NOT remove the nuts which hold the drive link to the motor crank arm.

5. Detach the drive link from the crank arm.

6. Disconnect the wiring from the wiper motor.

7. Remove the wiper motor-to-cowl screws. Turn the motor upward, then move it outward and remove it from the vehicle.

8. To install, reverse the removal procedures. Torque the wiper motor-to-cowl screws to 50–75 inch lbs.

Wiper Linkage

REMOVAL AND INSTALLATION

1. Disconnect the negative battery terminal from the battery.

2. Using the GM Windshield Wiper Blade/Arm Removal tool No. J-8966 or equivalent, remove the wiper arms.

3. Remove the cowl vent and the grille.

4. Remove the wiper linkage-to-motor clamp.

5. Remove the wiper linkage-to-cowl panel screws.

6. To install, reverse the removal procedures. Torque the wiper linkage-to-panel screws to 50–80 inch lbs.

INSTRUMENTS AND SWITCHES

Instrument Cluster

REMOVAL AND INSTALLATION

1. Disconnect the negative battery terminal from the battery.

2. Remove the lamp switch trim plate-to-instrument panel screws and the trim plate, then disconnect the electrical connector from the lamp switch.

3. Remove the air conditioning/heater control assembly-to-instrument panel screws and

1. Arm, windshield wiper
2. Blade
   insert
3. Nozzle
4. Spacer, nozzle
5. Nut, type R stamped (M16)
6. Transmission, left hand
   transmission, right hand
7. Lever
8. Module
9. Lens, pulse switch
10. Knob, pulse switch
11. Nut, pulse module retaining
12. Reservoir
13. Bolt, (M6 × 1 × 25)
14. Hose, (5/32" ID)
15. Strap
16. Connector
17. Motor assembly
18. Bolt (M5 × .8 × 28)
19. Screw, (M6.3 × 1.69 × 20)
20. Pump

Windshield wiper motor

1. Instrument panel
10. Nut
11. Instrument cluster
12. Instrument cluster housing
13. Screw
14. Filler panel

Exploded view of the instrument panel

the assembly, the disconnect the electrical connector from the lamp switch.

4. Remove the filler panel (under the steering column) to instrument panel screws and the filler panel.

5. Remove the instrument cluster-to-instrument panel nuts, the instrument cluster, the nuts and the instrument cluster.

6. Disconnect the speedometer drive cable from the instrument cluster.

7. Disconnect the cluster electrical connectors and remove the instrument cluster.

8. To install, reverse the removal procedures.

Windshield Wiper Switch

The windshield wiper switch is located on the end of the combination switch, attached to the steering column. Refer to the Combination Switch Removal and Installation procedures in Chapter 8 for servicing procedures.

Headlight Switch

The headlight switch, a push button switch to turn the lights On and Off, is located on the left side of the instrument panel. A rheostat dial, located just above the headlight/parking light switch, is used to control the illumination of the instrument panel.

A dimmer switch (part of the combination switch), to control the HI and LO beam operation, is located on the steering column; the lights are changed by pulling the combination switch lever toward the driver.

REMOVAL AND INSTALLATION

1. Disconnect the negative battery terminal from the battery.

2. From under the headlight switch assembly, remove the switch assembly-to-instrument panel screws.

3. Pull the switch trim plate from the instrument panel.

4. Disconnect the electrical wiring connectors from the rear of the headlight switch assembly.

5. Remove the headlight switch from the trim plate assembly; if necessary, replace the switch.

6. To install, reverse the removal procedures.

Back-Up Light Switch

REMOVAL AND INSTALLATION

Automatic Transmission

1. Disconnect the negative battery terminal from the battery.

2. From the steering column, disconnect the electrical harness connector from the back-up light switch.

3. Using a small pry bar, expand the back-up switch-to-steering column retainers and remove the switch from the steering column.

4. To install, reverse the removal procedures. Place the gear shift lever in the reverse position and check that the back-up lights turn On.

Manual Transmission

To replace the back-up light switch, refer to the Back-Up Light Switch, Removal and Installation procedures in Chapter 7.

Speedometer Cable

REMOVAL AND INSTALLATION

1. Refer to the Instrument Cluster Removal and Installation procedures in this Chapter and remove the instrument cluster.

2. From the rear of the instrument cluster, remove the speedometer cable-to-head fitting.

3. If replacing ONLY the speedometer cable core, perform the following procedures:

a. Disconnect the speedometer casing from the speedometer head.

b. Pull the speedometer cable core from the speedometer casing.

c. Using a graphite-based lubricant, lubricate a new speedometer cable and install the cable into the casing.

4. If replacing the speedometer cable assembly, perform the following procedures:

a. Disconnect the speedometer casing from the speedometer head.

b. Disconnect the speedometer casing from the transmission.

c. Remove the various speedometer cable/casing retaining clips.

d. Remove the speedometer cable/casing assembly from the vehicle.

5. To install the speedometer cable, reverse the removal procedures.

1. Screws
2. Bezel
3. Headlamp
4. Spring
5. Adjuster

Exploded view of the headlight assembly

LIGHTING

Headlights

REMOVAL AND INSTALLATION

1. Disconnect the negative battery terminal from the battery.

2. Remove the headlight-to-fender bezel and the retaining spring.

3. Rotate the headlight to the right and remove it from the adjusters.

4. Disconnect the electrical harness connector from the rear of the headlight and remove the headlight from the vehicle.

5. To install, reverse the removal procedures.

Signal and Marker Lights

REMOVAL AND INSTALLATION

Front Turn Signal/Marker Lights

1. Disconnect the negative battery terminals from the battery.

2. Remove the headlight bezel-to-fender screws and the bezel; allow the bezel to hang by the turn signal/marker light wires.

3. At the rear of the headlight bezel, turn

49. Screw
50. Instrument panel switch trim plate
51. Instrument panel harness

Headlight switch assembly

6. Nut
7. Front marker lamp

Turn signal/marker light assembly

the turn signal/marker bulb socket ¼ turn and remove it from the headlight bezel.

4. Remove the bulb from the turn signal/marker bulb socket; if necessary, replace the bulb.

5. To install, use a new bulb (if necessary) and reverse the removal procedures. Check the turn signal/marker light operations.

Parking Lights

1. Disconnect the negative battery terminal from the battery.

2. At the rear of the front bumper, turn the bulb socket ¼ turn and remove the socket from the parking brake housing.

3. Remove the bulb from the socket; if necessary, replace the bulb.

4. To install, reverse the removal procedures. Check the parking light operations.

Rear Turn Signal, Brake and Parking Lights

1. Disconnect the negative battery terminal from the battery.

2. Remove the rear turn signal/brake/park-

ing lamp-to-vehicle screws and the lamp housing from the vehicle.

3. Turn the bulb socket ¼ turn and remove the socket from the lamp housing.

4. Remove the bulb from the bulb socket; if necessary, replace the bulb.

5. To install, reverse the removal procedures. Check the turn signal/brake/parking light operations.

Cargo Light

REMOVAL AND INSTALLATION

1. Disconnect the negative battery terminal from the battery.

2. Remove the lens-to-housing screws and the lens.

3. Remove the bulb from the cargo light housing; if necessary, replace the bulb.

4. To install, reverse the removal procedures.

TRAILER WIRING

Wiring the truck for towing is fairly easy. There are a number of good wiring kits available and these should be used, rather than

Parking light assembly

10. Screw
11. Rear lamp

Rear turn signal/brake/parking light assembly

18. Lamp assembly
19. Screw
20. Lens
21. Bulb
22. Screw
23. Insulator
24. Wire assembly

Exploded view of the cargo light assembly

trying to design your own. All trailers will need brake lights and turn signals as well as tail lights and side marker lights. Most states require extra marker lights for overly wide trailers. Also, most states have recently required back-up lights for trailers, and most trailer manufacturers have been building trailers with back-up lights for several years.

Additionally, some Class I, most Class II and just about all Class III trailers will have electric brakes.

Add to this number an accessories wire, to operate trailer internal equipment or to charge the trailer's battery, and you can have as many as seven wires in the harness.

Determine the equipment on your trailer and buy the wiring kit necessary. The kit will contain all the wires needed, plus a plug adapter set which included the female plug, mounted on the bumper or hitch, and the male plug, wired into, or plugged into the trailer harness.

When installing the kit, follow the manufacturer's instructions. The color coding of the wires is standard throughout the industry.

One point to note: some domestic vehicles, and most imported vehicles, have separate turn signals. On most domestic vehicles, the brake

lights and rear turn signals operate with the same bulb. For those vehicles with separate turn signals, you can purchase an isolation unit so that the brake lights won't blink whenever the turn signals are operated, or you can go to your local electronics supply house and buy four diodes to wire in series with the brake and turn signal bulbs. Diodes will isolate the brake and turn signals. The choice is yours. The isolation units are simple and quick to install, but far more expensive than the diodes. The diodes, however, require more work to install properly, since they require the cutting of each bulb's wire and soldering in place of the diode.

One, final point, the best kits are those with a spring loaded cover on the vehicle mounted socket. This cover prevent dirt and moisture from corroding the terminals. Never let the vehicle socket hang loosely; always mount it securely to the bumper or hitch.

CIRCUIT PROTECTION

Fuses

The fuses are of the miniaturized (compact) size and are located on a fuse block, they provide increased circuit protection and reliability. Access to the fuse block is gained through a swing-down unit at the far left side of the dash panel. Each fuse receptacle is marked as to the circuit it protects and the correct amperage of the fuse.

REPLACEMENT

1. Pull the fuse from the fuse block.
2. Inspect the fuse element (through the clear plastic body) to the blade terminal for defects.
NOTE: *When replacing the fuse, DO NOT use one of a higher amperage.*
3. To install, reverse the removal procedures.

1	Circuit breaker
A	Fuse—choke
B	Fuse—heater or air condition
C	Fuse—radio
D	Fuse—stop, hazard lamps
E	Power accessory
F	Fuse—windshield wiper
G	Receptacle—power door locks
H	Fuse—horn
J	Receptacle—clock, courtesy lamp, dome lamp, I/P compt lamp & hdlp wrng buzzer
K	Fuse—tail & ctsy lamps
L	Receptacle—headlamp on warning
M	Fuse—instrument panel lamps
N	Fuse—turn & back up lamps
P	Receptacle—cruise control & auto trans
R	Fuse—ignition & gauges
S	Connector—seat belt warning buzzer & timer

Fuse box

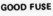

GOOD FUSE   BLOWN FUSE

Remove and inspect the fuse to determine if the element is broken or burned. If so, determine the reason why the fuse blew and replace the fuse with one of the same rating

1. Horn relay
2. Seat belt–ignition key–headlight buzzer
3. Choke relay (vacant w/EFI)
4. Hazard flasher
5. Signal flasher

Convenience center and components

Convenience Center

The Convenience Center is a swing-down unit located on the underside of the instrument panel, near the steering column. The swing-down feature provides central location and easy access to buzzers, relays and flasher units. All units are serviced by plug-in replacement.

Fusible Links

In addition to fuses, the wiring harness incorporates fusible links (in the battery feed circuits) to protect the wiring. Fusible links are 4 in. (102mm) sections of copper wire, 4 gauges smaller than the circuit(s) they are protecting, designed to melt under electrical overload. There are four different gauge sizes used. The fusible links are color coded so that they may be installed in their original positions.

REPLACEMENT

1. Disconnect the negative battery terminal from the battery.
2. Locate the burned out link.
3. Strip away the melted insulation and cut the burned link ends from the wire.
4. Strip the wire back ½ in. (13mm) to allow soldering of the new link.
5. Using a new fusible link 4 gauges smaller than the protected circuit — approx. 10 in. (254mm) long — solder it into the circuit.

New fusible links are spliced into the wire

NOTE: *Whenever splicing a new wire, always bond the splice with rosin core solder, then cover with electrical tape. Using acid core solder may cause corrosion.*

6. Tape and seal all splices with silicone to weatherproof repairs.
7. After taping the wire, tape the electrical harness leaving an exposed 5 in. (127mm) loop of wire.
8. Reconnect the battery.

Circuit Breakers

A circuit breaker is an electrical switch which breaks the circuit in case of an overload. The circuit breaker is located on the lower center of the fuse block. The circuit breaker will remain open until the short or overload condition in the circuit is corrected.

RESETTING

Locate the circuit breaker on the fuse block, then push the circuit breaker in until it locks. If the circuit breaker kicks itself Off again, locate and correct the problem in the electrical circuit.

MANUAL TRANSMISSION

Identification

Manual transmissions are officially identified by using the following descriptions:

    a. The number of forward gears.

    b. The measured distance between the center lines of the mainshaft and the countergear.

The 4-speed (77.5mm) transmission is a fully synchronized unit with blocker ring synchronizers and a sliding mesh reverse gear. It is contained in an aluminum alloy case with an integral clutch housing, a center support and an extension housing, which houses some of the gears, bearings and shafts. The shift lever is mounted on top of the extension housing. This transmission is used with the 2.8L 6 cylinder and the 1.9L 4 cylinder engines. The easiest way to identify the 77.5mm transmission is

BRAKE & CLUTCH PEDAL BRACKET ASM

CLUTCH PEDAL ASM

On some models the clutch safety start switch is adjustable

that the gear box and bell housing are one casting.

The 4-speed (77mm) and 5-speed (77mm) model transmissions are fully synchronized units with blocker ring synchronizers and a sliding mesh reverse gear. They have the more familiar aluminum gear box type of transmission case that houses the various gears, bearings and shafts. The floor-mounted gearshift lever assembly is located on top of the extension housing. The ML2 model is used with the 2.5L 4 cylinder engine; the ML3 model is used with the V6 engine. The easiest way to identify 77mm transmissions is that the gear box can be removed from the bell housing.

Adjustments

CLUTCH SWITCH

A clutch switch is located under the instrument panel and attached to the top of the clutch pedal. Its function is to prevent starter operation unless the clutch pedal is depressed. On some vehicles, the switch must be adjusted for reliable starter operation.

1. Remove the lower steering column-to-instrument panel cover.

2. Disconnect the electrical connector from the clutch switch.

3. Be sure to leave any carpets and floor mats in place when making the adjustment.

4. At the clutch switch, move the slider (A) rearward (towards the clutch switch) on the clutch switch shaft (B).

5. Push the clutch pedal to the floor. A clicking noise will be heard as the switch adjusts itself.

6. Release the clutch pedal; the adjustment is complete.

7. Reconnect the switch and test it.

38. Adapter
39. Skid plate
46. Catalytic converter hanger
47. Transmission mount
49. Bolt
50. Support
51. Nut
52. Bolt
53. Catalytic converter

Catalytic converter hanger assembly under transmission

Shift Lever

REMOVAL AND INSTALLATION

1. With the transmission in Neutral, loosen the lock nut under the shift knob and unscrew the knob from the lever.

2. Unscrew and remove the shifter boot.

3. On 1984–91 models, there is another lock nut which can be loosened to remove upper portion of the lever.

4. Remove the bolts to remove the shift lever from the housing assembly.

5. When reassembling, lightly lubricate the shifter with molybdenum disulphide grease and use a new gasket or silicone sealer. Torque the bolts to 10 ft. lbs. (13 Nm).

Back-Up Light Switch

REMOVAL AND INSTALLATION

1. Disconnect the negative battery terminal from the battery.

2. At the left-rear of the transmission, the back-up light switch is threaded into the transmission case. The speed sensor is held in with a separate bracket. Disconnect the electrical connector from the back-up light switch.

3. Remove the back-up light switch from the transmission.

4. To install, reverse the removal procedures. Place the gear shift lever in the reverse position and check the back-up lights work.

Transmission

REMOVAL AND INSTALLATION

2-Wheel Drive

1. Disconnect the negative battery terminal from the battery.

2. If the bell housing is being removed with the transmission (77.5mm 4-speed) remove the starter. The 77mm 4- and 5-speed can be removed without removing the bell housing.

3. Shift the transmission into Neutral. Remove the shift lever boot-to-console screws and slide the boot up the shift lever.

4. Remove the shift lever.

5. Raise and safely support the truck on jackstands. Remove the drain plug and drain the oil. Dispose of old oil properly at a reclamation center, such as a gas station or parts retailer.

6. Disconnect the speedometer cable and/or the electrical wiring connectors from the transmission.

7. Remove the driveshaft(s). Refer to the Driveline section if necessary.

8. Disconnect the exhaust pipe-to-exhaust manifold nuts and separate the exhaust pipe from the manifold.

9. On the 1982–83 models, disconnect the clutch cable from the clutch lever. On the 1984–91 models, remove the clutch slave cylinder from the clutch release lever. It can be secured out of the way without disconnecting the hydraulic line.

10. Position a floor jack under the transmission and support the transmission. Secure the jack to the transmission so it won't slip

11. Remove the transmission-to-crossmember mount bolts.

12. Remove the catalytic converter-to-chassis hanger bolts.

13. Remove the crossmember-to-chassis bolts and the crossmember from the vehicle.

14. If the bell housing is being removed, remove the clutch cover from the front of the housing.

15. Unbolt the bell housing from the engine, or the transmission from the bell housing and carefully roll the floor jack straight back away from the engine. Carefully lower it from the vehicle.

To install

16. Lightly coat the input shaft spline with high temperature or molybdenum grease. Don't use too much or the clutch disc will be ruined.

17. If the clutch was removed, make sure it is properly aligned or it will be impossible to install the transmission.

18. Put the transmission into high gear.

19. With the transmission properly placed behind the engine, turn the output shaft slowly to engage the splines of the input shaft into the clutch while pushing the transmission forward into place. Don't force it, the transmission will easily fall into place when everything is properly aligned.

20. On 4 cylinder engines with the 77.5mm transmission, torque the bell housing-to-engine bolts to 25 ft. lbs. On all others, torque all the bolts to 55 ft. lbs.

21. Install the cross member and torque the bolts to 25 ft. lbs.

22. Install the support braces and catalyst hanger and torque the nuts and bolts to 35 ft. lbs.

23. Install the clutch inspection cover and starter.

24. On 1984–91 models, install the slave cylinder and if necessary, attach the hydraulic line and bleed the system.

25. On earlier models, attach the clutch cable and push the pedal to test its operation.

26. Install the shift lever and boot.

27. Reassemble the exhaust system.

28. Install the driveshaft and refill the transmission with the proper oil.

20. Connect the wiring for the back-up lights and speed sensor, or the speedometer cable.

30. Lower the vehicle to the ground and reconnect the battery.

4-Wheel Drive

1. Shift the transfer case into **4H**.

2. Disconnect the negative battery cable.

3. Raise and support the vehicle safely. Remove the skid plate.

4. Drain the lubricant from the transfer case.

5. Mark the transfer case front output shaft yoke and driveshaft for assembly reference. Disconnect the front driveshaft from the transfer case.

6. Mark the rear axle yoke and driveshaft for assembly reference. Remove the rear driveshaft.

7. Disconnect the speedometer cable and vacuum harness at the transfer case. Remove the shift lever from the transfer case.

8. Remove the catalytic converter hanger bolts at the converter.

D. Gage Pin
E. Lock Bolt
1. Upper Boot
3. Lower Boot
5. Switch
9. Bracket
10. Washer
11. Bolt
16. Rod
18. Bolt
21. Lever
31. Detent
36. Console

Transfer case shift linkage

1. Fluid reservoir
2. Clutch master cylinder
3. Boot
4. Push rod

5. Shipping strap
6. Boot
7. Clutch slave cylinder

Hydraulic clutch system

9. Raise the transmission and transfer case and remove the transmission mount attaching bolts. Remove the mount and catalytic converter hanger and lower the transmission and transfer case.

10. If the bell housing is being removed, remove the clutch cover from the front of the housing.

11. Unbolt the bell housing from the engine, or the transmission from the bell housing and carefully roll the floor jack straight back away from the engine. Carefully lower it from the vehicle.

To install

12. Lightly coat the input shaft spline with high temperature or molybdenum grease. Don't use too much or the clutch disc will be ruined.

13. If the clutch was removed, make sure it is properly aligned or it will be impossible to install the transmission.

14. Put the transmission into high gear.

15. With the transmission properly placed behind the engine, turn the output shaft slowly to engage the splines of the input shaft into the clutch while pushing the transmission forward into place. Don't force it, the transmission will easily fall into place when everything is properly aligned.

16. On 4 cylinder engines with the 77.5mm transmission, torque the bell housing-to-engine bolts to 25 ft. lbs. On all others, torque all the bolts to 55 ft. lbs.

17. Install the cross member and torque the bolts to 25 ft. lbs.

18. Install the support braces and catalyst hanger and torque the nuts and bolts to 35 ft. lbs.

19. Install the clutch inspection cover and starter.

20. On 1984–91 models, install the slave cylinder and if necessary, attach the hydraulic line and bleed the system.

21. On earlier models, attach the clutch cable and push the pedal to test its operation.

22. Install the transmission shift lever and transfer case shift linkage.

23. Reassemble the exhaust system.

24. Install the driveshafts. Note the alignment marks and make sure the

shafts are installed the same way.

25. Refill the transmission and transfer case with the proper fluids.

26. Connect the wiring for the back-up lights and speed sensor, or the speedometer cable. Connect the transfer case vacuum lines.

27. Lower the vehicle to the ground and reconnect the battery.

CLUTCH

The 1984–91 trucks use a hydraulic clutch system which consists of a master and a slave cylinder. When pressure is applied to the clutch pedal (pedal depressed), the push rod contacts the plunger and pushes it up the bore of the master cylinder. In the first $\frac{1}{32}$ in. (0.8mm) of movement, the center valve seal closes the port to the fluid reservoir tank and as the plunger continues to move up the bore of the cylinder, the fluid is forced through the outlet line to the slave cylinder mounted on the clutch housing. As fluid is pushed down the pipe from the master cylinder, this in turn forces the piston in the slave cylinder outward. A push rod is connected to the slave cylinder and rides in the pocket of the clutch fork. As the slave cylinder piston moves rearward the push rod forces the clutch fork and the release bearing to disengage the pressure plate from the clutch disc. On the return stroke (pedal released), the plunger moves back as a result of the return pressure of the clutch. Fluid returns to the master cylinder and the final movement of the plunger lifts the valve seal off the seat, allowing an unrestricted flow of fluid between the system and the reservoir.

A piston return spring in the slave cylinder preloads the clutch linkage and assures contact of the release bearing with the clutch release fingers at all times. As the driven disc wears, the diaphragm spring fingers move rearward forcing the release bearing, fork and push rod to move. This movement forces the slave cylinder piston forward in its bore, displacing hydraulic fluid up into the master cylinder reservoir, thereby providing the self-adjusting feature of the hydraulic clutch linkage system.

Before attempting to repair the clutch, transmission, hydraulic system or related linkages for any reason other than an obvious failure, the problem and probable cause should be identified. A large percentage of clutch and manual transmission problems are manifested by shifting difficulties such as high shift effort, gear clash and grinding or transmission blockout. When any of these problems occur, a careful analysis of these difficulties should be made, then the basic checks and adjustments performed before removing the clutch or transmission for repairs. Run the engine at a normal idle with the transmission in Neutral (clutch engaged). Disengage the clutch, wait about 10 seconds and shift the transmission into Reverse (no grinding noise should be heard). A grinding noise indicates incorrect clutch travel, lost motion, clutch misalignment or internal problems such as failed dampers, facings, cushion springs, diaphragm spring fingers, pressure plate drive straps, pivot rings or etc.

Adjustment

Since the hydraulic system provides automatic clutch adjustment, no adjustment of the clutch linkage or pedal height is required.

CLUTCH CABLE — 1982-83

1. Lift up on the pedal to allow the self adjuster to adjust the cable length.

2. Depress the pedal several times to set the pawl into mesh with the detent teeth.

3. Check the linkage for lost motion caused by loose or worn swivels, mounting brackets or a damaged cable.

Clutch Disc and Pressure Plate

REMOVAL AND INSTALLATION

CAUTION: *The clutch plate contains asbestos, which has been determined to be a cancer causing agent. Never clean the clutch surfaces with compressed air! Avoid inhaling any dust from any clutch surface! When cleaning clutch surfaces, use a commercially available brake cleaning fluid.*

1. Refer to the "Transmission, Removal and Installation" procedures in this Chapter and remove the transmission.

NOTE: *If equipped with a clutch cable (1982–83), disconnect the cable from the clutch lever and move it aside. If equipped with a hydraulic clutch system (1984–87), disconnect the slave cylinder from the clutch release fork and move it aside.*

2. If the bell housing was not removed with the transmission, remove it.

3. Remove the clutch fork from the ball stud and the dust boot.

4. Using the Clutch Alignment tool No. J-33169 (V6) or J-33034 (4-cyl), insert it into the crankshaft pilot bearing to support the clutch assembly.

5. Check for an "X" or other painted mark

103. Brace
107. Wave Washer
108. Push Rod
109. Washer
110. Retainer
120. Nut
121. Reservoir Hose
122. Secondary Cylinder Hydraulic Line
123. Master Cylinder
124. Gasket
125. Bolt
126. Reservoir

Clutch pedal on hydraulic systems

FLYWHEEL

PRESSURE PLATE AND
COVER ASSEMBLY

ALIGNING TOOL

DRIVEN PLATE
ASSEMBLY

Clutch alignment tool is required to install the clutch assembly

on the pressure plate and flywheel. If there isn't a mark, mark the assembly for installation purposes.

6. Loosen the pressure plate-to-flywheel bolts, evenly and alternately, a little at a time, until the spring tension is released. Remove the pressure plate and the driven clutch plate.

7. Check the flywheel for cracks, wear, scoring or other damage. Check the pilot bearing for wear. Replace it by removing it with a slide-type bearing puller and driving in a new one with a wood or plastic hammer.

8. To install, use the clutch assembly alignment tool and reverse the removal procedures. The raised hub of the driven plate faces the transmission. Align the mating marks and torque the pressure plate-to-flywheel bolts (evenly and alternately) to 20 ft. lbs.

NOTE: *If equipped with a clutch cable (1982–83), install and/or adjust the clutch cable.*

Master Cylinder

The clutch master cylinder is located in the engine compartment, on the left-side of the firewall, above the steering column.

REMOVAL AND INSTALLATION

1. Disconnect negative battery terminal from the battery.

2. Remove hush panel from under the dash.

3. Disconnect push rod from clutch pedal.

4. Disconnect hydraulic line from the clutch master cylinder.

5. Remove the master cylinder-to-cowl brace nuts. Remove master cylinder and overhaul (if necessary).

6. Using a putty knife, clean the master cylinder and cowl mounting surfaces.

7. To install, reverse the removal procedures. Torque the master cylinder-to-cowl brace nuts to 10–15 ft. lbs. (14–20 Nm). Fill master cylinder with new hydraulic fluid conforming to DOT 3 specifications. Bleed and check the hydraulic clutch system for leaks.

OVERHAUL

1. Remove the filler cap and drain fluid from the master cylinder.

2. Remove the reservoir and seal from the master cylinder. Pull back the dust cover and remove the snapring.

3. Remove the push rod assembly. Using a block of wood, tap the master cylinder on it to eject the plunger assembly from the cylinder bore.

4. Remove the seal (carefully) from the

RESERVOIR
ADAPTER

ADAPTER
SEAL

MASTER
CYLINDER

SPRING

SEAL
SUPPORT

CIRCLIP

SHIM

DUST
COVER

PUSH
ROD

BACK
SEAL

PLUNGER

RECUPERATION
SEAL

Clutch master cylinder assembly

front of the plunger assembly, ensuring no damage occurs to the plunger surfaces.

5. From the rear of the plunger assembly, remove the spring, the support, the seal and the shim.

6. Using clean brake fluid, clean all of the parts.

7. Inspect the cylinder bore and the plunger for ridges, pitting and/or scratches, the dust cover for wear and cracking; replace the parts if any of the conditions exist.

8. To install, use new seals, lubricate all of the parts in clean brake fluid, fit the plunger seal to the plunger and reverse the removal procedures.

9. Insert the plunger assembly, valve end leading into the cylinder bore (easing the entrance of the plunger seal).

10. Position the push rod assembly into the cylinder bore, then install a new snapring to retain the push rod. Install dust cover onto the master cylinder. Lubricate the inside of the dust cover with Girling® Rubber Grease or equivalent.

NOTE: *Be careful not to use any lubricant that will deteriorate rubber dust covers or seals.*

Slave Cylinder

The slave cylinder is located on the left side of the bell housing and controls the clutch release fork operation.

REMOVAL AND INSTALLATION

1. Disconnect the negative battery cable.

2. Raise and safely support the front of the vehicle on jackstands.

3. Disconnect the hydraulic line from clutch master cylinder. Remove the hydraulic line-to-chassis screw and the clip from the chassis.

NOTE: *Be sure to plug the line opening to keep dirt and moisture out of the system.*

4. Remove the slave cylinder-to-bell housing nuts.

5. Remove the push rod and the slave cylin-

der from the vehicle, then overhaul it (if necessary).

6. To install, reverse the removal procedures. Lubricate leading end of the slave cylinder with Girling® Rubber Lube or equivalent. Torque the slave cylinder-to-bell housing nuts to 10–15 ft. lbs. (14–20 Nm). Fill the master cylinder with new brake fluid conforming to DOT 3 specifications. Bleed the hydraulic system.

OVERHAUL

1. Remove the shield, the pushrod and dust cover from the slave cylinder, then inspect the cover for damage or deterioration.

2. Remove the snapring from the end of the cylinder bore.

3. Using a block of wood, tap the slave cylinder on it to eject the plunger, then remove the seal and the spring.

4. Using clean brake fluid, clean all of the parts.

5. Inspect the cylinder bore and the plunger for ridges, pitting and/or scratches, the dust cover for wear and cracking; replace the parts if any of the conditions exist.

6. To install, use new seals and lubricate all of the parts in clean brake fluid. Install the spring, the plunger seal and the plunger into the cylinder bore, then install a new snapring.

7. Lubricate the inside of the dust cover with Girling® Rubber Grease or equivalent, then install it into the slave cylinder.

NOTE: *Be careful not to use any lubricant that will deteriorate the rubber dust covers or seals.*

BLEEDING THE HYDRAULIC CLUTCH

Bleeding air from the hydraulic clutch system is necessary whenever any part of the system has been disconnected or the fluid level (in the reservoir) has been allowed to fall so low, that air has been drawn into the master cylinder.

1. Fill master cylinder reservoir with new brake fluid conforming to Dot 3 specifications.

CAUTION: *Never, under any circumstances, use fluid which has been bled from a system to fill the reservoir as it may be aerated, have too much moisture content and possibly be contaminated.*

2. Raise and safely support the front of the vehicle on jackstands.

3. Remove the slave cylinder attaching bolts.

4. Hold slave cylinder at approximately 45° with the bleeder at highest point. Fully depress clutch pedal and open the bleeder screw.

5. Close the bleeder screw and release clutch pedal.

CLUTCH FORK

14-20 N·m
(10-15 FT. LBS.)

FRT

PUSH
ROD

SLAVE
CYLINDER

Clutch slave cylinder assembly

6. Repeat the procedure until all of the air is evacuated from the system. Check and refill master cylinder reservoir as required to prevent air from being drawn through the master cylinder.

NOTE: *Never release a depressed clutch pedal with the bleeder screw open or air will be drawn into the system.*

AUTOMATIC TRANSMISSION

Identification

The Turbo Hydra-Matic (THM) 180C and 200C transmission are fully automatic transmissions which provide 3 forward gears and a reverse gear.

The Turbo Hydra-Matic (THM) 700-R4 and 4L60 transmission is a fully automatic transmission which provides 4 forward gears and a reverse gear. The oil pressure and shifting points are controlled by the throttle opening, via a Throttle Valve (TV) cable.

Fluid Pan

REMOVAL AND INSTALLATION

NOTE: *The fluid should be drained when the transmission is warm.*

1. Raise and safely support the front of the vehicle with jackstands.
2. Place a drain catch pan under the transmission oil pan.
3. Remove the pan bolts from the front and sides of the pan, then loosen the rear bolts 4 turns.
4. Using a small pry bar, pry the oil pan loose and allow the pan to partially drain. Remove the remaining pan bolts and carefully lower the pan away from the transmission.

NOTE: *If the transmission fluid is dark or has a burnt smell, transmission damage is indicated. Have the transmission checked professionally.*

CAUTION: *If the pan sticks, carefully tap sideways on the pan with a rubber or plastic mallet to break it loose; DO NOT dent the pan.*

5. Empty and wash the pan in solvent, then blow dry with compressed air.
6. Using a putty knife, clean the gasket mounting surfaces.
7. To install, use a new filter, a new gasket and reverse the removal procedures. Torque the pan-to-transmission bolts to 12–14 ft. lbs. (in a criss-cross pattern). Recheck the bolt torque after all of the bolts have been tightened once. Add Dexron®II automatic transmission fluid through the filler tube.

CAUTION: *DO NOT OVERFILL the transmission; foaming of the fluid and subsequent transmission damage due to slippage will result.*

8. With the gear selector lever in the Park position, start the engine and let it idle; DO NOT race the engine.
9. Move the gear selector lever through each position, holding the brakes. Return the lever to Park and check the fluid level with the engine idling. The level should be between the two dimples on the dipstick, about $1/4$ in. (6mm) below the ADD mark. Add fluid, if necessary.
10. Check the fluid level after the vehicle has been driven enough to thoroughly warm the transmission. Details are given under "Fluid Level Checks" earlier in Chapter 1. If the transmission is overfilled, the excess must be drained off. Use a suction pump, if necessary.

FILTER SERVICE

1. Refer to the "Fluid Pan, Removal and Installation" procedures in this Chapter and remove the fluid pan.
2. Remove the transmission filter screws or clips and the filter from the valve body. The filter may have either a fibrous or screen filtering element and is retained by one or two fasteners.

NOTE: *If the transmission uses a filter having a fully exposed screen, it may be*

Four speed automatic transmission

Three speed automatic transmission

cleaned and reused.

3. To install, use a new filter, a new gasket and reverse the removal procedures. Torque the pan-to-transmission bolts to 12–14 ft. lbs. (in a criss-cross pattern). Recheck the bolt torque after all of the bolts have been tightened once. Add Dexron®II automatic transmission fluid through the filler tube.

Adjustments

SHIFT LINKAGE

The shift linkage should be adjusted so that the engine will start when the transmission is in the Park and Neutral positions only.

1. Firmly apply the parking brake and chock the rear wheels.

2. Raise and safely support the front of the vehicle on jackstands.

3. At the left-side of the transmission, loosen the shift rod swivel-to-equalizer lever nut.

4. Rotate the transmission shift lever clockwise (forward) to the last detent (Park) position, then turn it counterclockwise (rearward) to the rear of the 2nd detent (Neutral) position.

5. At the steering column, place the gear selector lever into the Neutral position.

NOTE: *When positioning the gear selector lever, DO NOT use the steering column indicator to find the Neutral position.*

6. Tightly, hold the shifting rod (swivel) against the equalizer lever, then torque the adjusting nut to 11 ft. lbs.

7. Using the gear selector lever (on the steering column), place it in the Park position and check the adjustment. Move the gear selector lever into the various positions; the engine must start in the Park and the Neutral positions.

NOTE: *If the engine will not start in the Neutral and/or Park positions, refer to Back-Up Light Switch adjustment procedures in Chapter 5 and adjust the switch.*

CAUTION: *With the gear selector lever in the Park position, the parking pawl should engage the rear internal gear lugs or output ring gear lugs to prevent the vehicle from rolling and causing personal injury.*

8. Align the gear selector lever indicator, if necessary. Lower the vehicle and release the parking brake.

THROTTLE VALVE (TV) CABLE

If the TV cable is broken, sticking, misadjusted or using an incorrect part for the model, the vehicle may exhibit various malfunctions, such as: delayed or full throttle shifts.

Preliminary Checks

1. Inspect and/or correct the transmission fluid level.

2. Make sure that the brakes are not dragging and that the engine is operating correctly.

3. Make sure that the cable is connected at both ends.

4. Make sure that the correct cable is installed.

Three speed and four speed transmission pans

Transmission shift linkage adjustment

Removal of automatic transmission

Throttle valve (TV) cable

Adjustment

1. If necessary, remove the air cleaner.

2. If the cable has been removed and installed, check to see that the cable slider is in the zero or the fully adjusted position; if not, perform the following procedures:

   a. Depress and hold the readjust tab.

   b. Move the slider back through the fitting (away from the throttle lever) until it stops against the fitting.

   c. Release the readjust tab.

3. Rotate the throttle lever to the Full Throttle Stop position to obtain a minimum of 1 click.

4. Release the throttle lever.

Neutral Safety Switch

The Neutral Safety Switch is a part of the Back-Up Light Switch. For the replacement or adjustment procedures, refer to the "Back-Up Light Switch, Removal and Installation" procedures in Chapter 6, Chassis Electrical.

Back-Up Light Switch

NOTE: *The back-up light switch is located on the steering column. To replace the back-up light switch, refer to the "Back-Up Light Switch, Removal and Installation" procedures in Chapter 6, Chassis Electrical.*

Transmission

REMOVAL AND INSTALLATION

NOTE: *The following procedure requires the use of the Torque Converter Holding Strap tool No. J-21366 or equivalent.*

1. Disconnect the negative battery terminal from the battery.

2. Remove the air cleaner assembly.

3. Disconnect the Throttle Valve (TV) cable from the throttle linkage.

NOTE: *If equipped with a 4-cyl engine, remove the upper starter bolt.*

4. Raise and safely support the truck on jackstands.

5. Remove the driveshaft-to-differential bolts, the slide the driveshaft from the transmission (2WD) or transfer case (4WD).

6. Disconnect the speedometer cable, the dipstick tube (and seal), the shift linkage and the electrical wiring connectors from the transmission.

7. Remove the transmission-to-catalytic converter support brackets and the engine–to–transmission support brackets, if equipped.

8. Remove the transmission-to-crossmember nuts/bolts, slide the crossmember rearward and remove it from the vehicle.

9. Remove the torque converter cover, then

match-mark the torque converter-to-flywheel.

10. Remove the torque converter-to-fly-wheel bolts. Using the Converter Holding Strap tool No. J-21366 or equivalent, secure the torque converter to the transmission.

11. Using a transmission jack, position and secure it to the underside of the transmission, then to take up its weight.

12. Remove the transmission-to-engine mount bolts and the mounts from the vehicle.

13. Lower the transmission slightly to gain access to the fluid cooler lines, then disconnect and cap the fluid lines.

14. Disconnect the Throttle Valve (TV) cable from the transmission.

15. Position a floor jack or jackstand under the engine and support it.

16. Remove the transmission-to-engine bolts and then the transmission from the engine; pull the transmission rearward to disengage it and lower it from the truck.

NOTE: *When removing the transmission, be careful not to allow the transmission to hang from the pilot shaft, for it could become bent.*

To install:

17. Carefully position the transmission behind the engine and push it forward to engage the pilot shaft.

18. Install the transmission–to–engine bolts. On 4–cylinder engines, torque the bolts to 25 ft. lbs. (30 Nm). On V6 engines, torque the bolts to 55 ft. lbs. (75 Nm).

19. Connect the fluid coolant lines and the TV cable.

20. Install the transmission mount bolts and torque to 25 ft. lbs. Make sure the torque converter turns freely by hand.

21. Install the crossmember bolts and torque to 25 ft. lbs. (35 Nm).

23. Install all the converter–to–flywheel bolts finger tight, then torque to 35 ft. lbs. (50 Nm). Install the converter cover.

24. Install the transmission–to–engine bracket bolts, if equipped and torque to 41 ft. lbs. (55 Nm) at the transmission end and 52 ft. lbs. (70 Nm) at the engine end.

25. Install the catalyst support bracket and torque to 50 Ft. lbs. (68 Nm).

26. Install the dipstick tube, speedometer cable and wiring.

27. Attach and adjust the shift linkage as required.

28. Install the driveshaft(s). Torque the shaft bearing cap retainer bolts on both 2WD and 4WD shafts to 17 ft. lbs. (23 Nm). On two piece shafts, torque the center bearing mount bolts to 25 ft. lbs. (39 Nm).

29. On 4 cylinder engines, install the starter bolt.

30. Lower the vehicle and connect the TV

TV cable adjustment

cable. Adjust as necessary.

31. Refill the transmission with fluid and check as described in Filter Service.

TRANSFER CASE

Identification

An identification tag, which is attached to the rear half of the case, gives the model number, low range reduction ratio and assembly number. The vehicles use two units: the New Process 207 and the New Process 231.

The Model 207 transfer case is an aluminum case, chain drive, 4 position unit providing 4WD High and Low ranges, a 2WD High range and a Neutral position. The 207 is a part-time 4WD unit. Range positions are selected by a floor mounted shift lever. Dexron® II automatic transmission fluid, or equivalent, is the recommended lubricant.

The Model 231 is a part-time transfer case with a built in low range gear reduction system. A front axle disconnect mechanism is used for 2-wheel drive operation. The 231 has three operating ranges — 2-wheel drive High and 4-wheel drive High and Low, plus Neutral. The 4-wheel drive operating ranges are undifferentiated. Dexron® II automatic transmission fluid, or equivalent, is used as a lubricant.

Adjustment

SHIFT LEVER

Model 207 and 231

1. Loosen the switch-to-transfer case bolt and the shift lever-to-transfer case pivot bolt.

2. Using the shift lever, shift the transfer case to the 4WD High position.

3. Remove the console and slide the upper boot Up the shift lever.

4. Loosen the lower transfer case shift lever-to-transfer case lock bolt.

5. Using a $\frac{5}{16}$ in. (8mm) drill bit, insert it through the shift lever and into the switch bracket.

A. Gasket Tab
120. Gasket
121. Adapter
122. Seal
123. Bolt
124. Gasket
125. Bolt
126. Gasket

MANUAL TRANSMISSION

Removing transfer case from manual and automatic transmission

6. Install the lower transfer case shift lever-to-transfer case lock bolt to lock the lever into position; this will lock the transfer case into 4WD High position.

7. Torque the switch bracket bolt to 30 ft. lbs. and the shifter pivot bolt to 96 ft. lbs.

8. Remove the lower transfer case shift lever-to-transfer case lock bolt, which was installed to lock the lever.

9. Remove the drill bit and check the shifting action.

Transfer Case

REMOVAL AND INSTALLATION

1. Disconnect the negative battery cable from the battery.

2. Shift the transfer case into the 4WD High range.

3. Raise and safely support the vehicle on jackstands.

4. From under the transmission/transfer case assembly, remove the skid plate bolts and the skid plate.

5. Remove the front/rear driveshaft-to-transfer case nuts/bolts and lower the driveshafts from the transfer case.

6. Remove the speedometer cable, the vacuum harness and/or the electrical connectors from the transmission.

7. Remove console cover from the console; slide the upper boot up the shift lever and remove the shift boot.

8. Remove the shift lever-to-transfer case bolt and shift lever from the case.

9. Remove the catalytic converter hanger-to-catalytic converter bolts.

10. Remove the transmission/transfer case assembly mount-to-crossmember bolts.

11. Using a transmission jack, secure it to the transmission/transfer case assembly, then raise the assembly.

12. Remove the crossmember-to-chassis bolts and the crossmember from the vehicle.

13. Lower the transmission/transfer case assembly, then remove transfer case-to-transmission bolts, the transfer case from the adapter (A/T) or extension housing (M/T).

To install:

14. Use a new transfer case-to-transmission

gasket and mount the unit to the transmission. Torque the bolts to 23 ft. lbs. (31 Nm).

15. Lower the transmission enough to install the shift lever bracket bolts, if removed.

16. Raise the transmission to install the catalytic converter hanger and crossmember. Torque the crossmember and the converter hanger–to–transmission bolts to 22 ft. lbs. (30 Nm). Torque the converter bolts to 40 ft. lbs. (53 Nm).

17. Install the driveshafts and torque the bearing cap retainer bolts to 15 ft. lbs. (20 Nm).

18. Connect the speedometer cable and shift linkage. Adjust as required.

19. Install the skid plate if equipped, fill the transfer case with Dexron®II transmission fluid and road test the vehicle.

DRIVELINE

On all models, conventional, open type driveshafts are used. Located at either end of the driveshaft is a universal joint (U-joint), which allows the driveshaft to move up and down to match the motion of the rear axle.

Since the truck can be obtained in 2WD and 4WD, three types of driveshafts may be employed. On the 2WD model, a one-piece driveshaft is used. On some 4WD models is a two-piece rear driveshaft with a center bearing, and the front shaft is a two piece telescope type with internal splines.

On the front of the one-piece driveshaft (2WD) or the two-piece driveshaft (4WD), the U-joints connect the driveshaft to a slip-jointed yoke. This yoke is internally splined and allows the driveshaft to move in and out on the transmission splines.

On the rear of the one-piece driveshaft (2WD) or the two-piece driveshaft (4WD), the U-joint is clamped to the rear axle pinion. It is attached to the rear axle pinion by use of bolted straps.

On the front driveshaft (4WD), the U-joints are secured to the transfer case and the front differential by the use of bolted straps. Located in the center of the driveshaft is a slip-joint, which allows the driveshaft to move in and out on its own splines.

On production U-joints, nylon is injected through a small hole in the yoke during manufacture and flows along a circular groove between the U-joint and the yoke, creating a nonmetallic snapring.

Bad U-joints, requiring replacement, will produce a clunking sound when the vehicle is put into gear and when the transmission shifts from gear-to-gear. This is due to worn needle

Shift lever adjustment on Model 207 and 231 transfer case

bearings or scored trunnion ends. U-joints require no periodic maintenance and therefore have no lubrication fittings.

Front driveshaft and U-Joints

REMOVAL AND INSTALLATION

NOTE: *DO NOT pound on the original driveshaft ears or the injected nylon U-joints may fracture.*

1. Raise and safely support the front of the truck on jackstands.

2. Mark the relationship of the driveshaft to the front axle and the transfer case flanges.

3. Remove the driveshaft-to-retainer bolts and the retainers.

4. Collapse the driveshaft so it may be disengaged from the transfer case flange.

5. Move the driveshaft rearward (between the transfer case and the chassis) to disengage it from the front axle.

NOTE: *Use care when handling the driveshaft to avoid dropping the U-joint cap assemblies.*

6. Using tape, wrap it around the loose caps (if necessary) to hold them in place.

7. To install, use the alignment marks and reverse the removal procedures. Torque the retainer-to-transfer case/front axle bolts to 12 – 17 ft. lbs.

U-JOINT OVERHAUL

A universal type U-joint is used: it uses an internal snapring (production is plastic injected).

NOTE: *The following procedure requires the use of an Arbor Press, the GM Cross Press tool No. J-9522-3 or equivalent, the GM*

Pressing out the old U-joint

Spacer tool used to push the cup out all the way

Spacer tool No. J-9522-5 or equivalent, and a 1¹/₈ in. (29mm) socket.

1. While supporting the driveshaft, in the horizontal position, position it so that the lower ear of the front universal joint's shaft yoke is supported on a 1¹/₈ in. (29mm) socket.

NOTE: *DO NOT clamp the driveshaft tube in a vise, for the tube may become damaged.*

2. Using the GM Cross Press tool No. J-9522-3 or equivalent, place it on the horizontal bearing cups and press the lower bearing cup out of the yoke ear; the pressing action will shear the plastic retaining ring from the lower bearing cup. If the bearing cup was not completely removed, insert the GM Spacer tool No. J-9522-5 or equivalent, onto the universal joint, then complete the pressing procedure to remove the joint.

3. Rotate the driveshaft and shear the plastic retainer from the opposite side of the yoke.

4. Disengage the slip yoke from the driveshaft.

5. To remove the universal joint from the slip yoke, perform the procedures used in Steps 1–4.

NOTE: *When the front universal joint has been disassembled, it must be discarded and replaced with a service kit joint, for the production joint is not equipped with bearing retainer grooves on the bearing cups.*

6. Clean (remove any remaining plastic particles) and inspect the slip yoke and driveshaft for damage, wear or burrs.

NOTE: *The universal joint service kit includes: A pregreased cross assembly, four bearing cups with seals, needle rollers, washers, four bearing retainers and grease. Make sure that the bearing cup seals are installed to hold the needle bearings in place for handling.*

7. To install, position one bearing cup assembly part way into the yoke ear (turn the ear to the bottom), insert the bearing cross (into the yoke) so that the trunnion seats freely into

Front drive shaft assembly on Blazer and Jimmy; Bravada similar

Internal snapring U-joint assembly

Installing the snapring

the bearing cup. Turn the yoke 180° and install the other bearing cup assembly.

NOTE: *When installing the bearing cup assemblies, make sure the trunnions are started straight and true into the bearing cups.*

8. Using the arbor press, press the bearing cups onto the cross trunnion, until they seat.

NOTE: *While installing the bearing cups, twist the cross trunnion to work it into the bearings. If there seems to be a hangup, stop the pressing and recheck the needle roller alignment.*

9. Once the bearing cup retainer grooves have cleared the inside of the yoke, stop the pressing and install the snaprings.

10. If the other bearing cup retainer groove has not cleared the inside of the yoke, use a hammer to aid in the seating procedure.

11. To install the yoke/universal assembly to the driveshaft, perform the Steps 7–10 of this procedure.

Rear Driveshaft and U-Joints

REMOVAL AND INSTALLATION

NOTE: *DO NOT pound on the original propeller shaft yoke ears for the injected nylon joints may fracture.*

1. Raise and safely support the rear of the vehicle on jackstands.

2. Mark relationship of the driveshaft-to-pinion flange and disconnect the rear universal joint by removing retainers. If the bearing cups are loose, tape them together to prevent dropping and loss of bearing rollers.

3. If equipped with a one-piece driveshaft, perform the following procedures:

a. Slide the driveshaft forward to disengage it from the rear axle flange.

b. Move the driveshaft rearward to disengage it from the transmission slip-joint, passing it under the axle housing.

4. If equipped with a two-piece driveshaft, perform the following procedures:

a. Slide the driveshaft forward to disengage it from the rear axle flange.

b. Slide the driveshaft rearward to disen-

gage it from slip-joint of the front half-shaft, passing it under the axle housing.

c. Remove the center bearing-to-support nuts and bolts.

d. Slide the front half-shaft rearward to disengage it from the transfer case slip-joint.

NOTE: *DO NOT allow the driveshaft to drop or allow the universal joints to bend to extreme angles, as this might fracture injected joint internally. Support propeller shaft during removal.*

5. Inspect the slip-joint splines for damage, burrs or wear, for this will damage the transmission seal. Apply engine oil to all splined propeller shaft yokes.

6. DO NOT use a hammer to force the driveshaft into place. Check for burrs on transmission output shaft spline, twisted slip yoke splines or possibly the wrong U-joint. Make sure the splines agree in number and fit. To prevent trunnion seal damage, DO NOT place any tool between yoke and splines.

7. If installing a one-piece driveshaft, perform the following procedures:

a. Slide driveshaft into the transmission.

b. Align the rear universal joint-to-rear axle pinion flange, make sure the bearings are properly seated in the pinion flange yoke.

c. Install the rear driveshaft-to-pinion fasteners. Torque the fasteners to 15 ft. lbs. (20 Nm).

8. If installing a two-piece driveshaft, perform the following procedures:

Seating the snapring

Two-piece rear drive shaft

a. Install the front half-shaft into the transmission and bolt the center bearing-to-support. Torque the center bearing to support nuts and bolts to 25 ft. lbs. (34 Nm).

NOTE: *The front half-shaft yoke must be bottomed out in the transmission (fully forward) before installation to the support.*

b. Rotate the shaft so that the front U-joint trunnion is in the correct position.

NOTE: *Before installing the rear driveshaft, align the U-joint trunnions (a "key" in the output spline of the front half-shaft will align with a missing spline in the rear yoke).*

c. Attach the rear U-joint to axle. Torque the retainers to 15 ft. lbs. (20 Nm).

9. Road test the vehicle.

Center Support Bearing

REMOVAL AND INSTALLATION

1. Refer to the "Rear Driveshaft, Removal and Installation" procedures in this Chapter and remove the driveshaft.

2. Remove the strap retaining the rubber cushion from the bearing support.

3. Pull the support bracket from the rubber cushion and the cushion from the bearing.

Single piece rear drive shaft

4. Press the bearing assembly from half-shaft.

5. To assemble the bearing support, perform the following procedures:

a. If removed, install the inner deflector onto the half-shaft and prick punch the deflector at 2 opposite points to make sure it is tight on the shaft.

b. Fill the space between the inner dust shield and bearing with lithium soap grease.

c. Start the bearing and slinger assembly straight onto the shaft journal. Support the half-shaft and using a length of pipe over the splined end of the shaft, press the bearing and inner slinger against the shoulder of the half-shaft.

d. Install the bearing retainer, the rubber cushion onto bearing, the bracket onto the cushion and the retaining strap.

6. To install driveshaft, reverse the removal procedures. Torque the center bearing-to-support nuts/bolts to 20–30 ft. lbs. and the driveshaft-to-pinion retainer bolts to 12–17 ft. lbs.

REAR AXLE

Identification

The rear axle identification code and manufacturer's code must be known before attempting to adjust or repair axle shafts or rear axle case assembly. Rear axle ratio, differential type, manufacturer, and build date information is stamped on the right axle tube on the forward side. Any reports made on rear axle assemblies must include the full code letters and build date numbers.

Determining Axle Ratio

An axle ratio is obtained by dividing the number of teeth on the drive pinion gear into the number of teeth on the ring gear. For instance, on a 4.11:1 ratio, the driveshaft will turn 4.11 times for every turn of the rear wheels.

The most accurate way to determine the axle ratio is to drain the differential, remove the cover and count the number of teeth on the ring and the pinion.

An easier method is raise and safely support the rear of the vehicle on jackstands. Make a chalk mark on the rear wheel and the driveshaft. Block the front wheels and put the transmission in Neutral. Turn the rear wheel one complete revolution and count the number of turns made by the driveshaft. The number of driveshaft rotations is the axle ratio. More ac-

Axle data on the rear axle housing

curacy can be obtained by going more than one tire revolution and dividing the result by the number of tire rotations.

The axle ratio is also identified by the axle serial number prefix on the axle; the axle ratios are listed in the dealer's parts books according to the prefix number.

Axle Shaft, Bearing and Seal

REMOVAL AND INSTALLATION

NOTE: *The following procedures requires the use of the GM Slide Hammer tool No. J-2619 or equivalent, the GM Adapter tool No. J-2619-4 or equivalent, the GM Axle Bearing Puller tool No. J-22813-01 or equivalent, the GM Axle Shaft Seal Installer tool No. J-33782, J-23771 or equivalent and the Axle Shaft Bearing Installer tool No. J-34974, J-23765 or equivalent.*

1. Raise and support the rear of the vehicle on jackstands.

2. Remove the rear wheel assemblies and the brake drums.

CAUTION: *Brake shoes contain asbestos, which has been determined to be a cancer causing agent. Never clean the brake surfaces with compressed air! Avoid inhaling any dust from any brake surface! When cleaning brake surfaces, use a commercially available brake cleaning fluid.*

Removing the axle shaft C-lock

Installing the axle seal

Removing the axle bearing

Axle bearing and seal

3. Using a wire brush, clean the dirt/rust from around the rear axle cover.

4. Place a catch pan under the differential, then remove the drain plug (if equipped) or rear axle cover and drain the oil.

5. At the differential, remove the rear pinion shaft lock bolt and the pinion shaft.

6. Push the axle shaft inward and remove the C-lock from the button end of the axle shaft.

7. Remove the axle shaft from the axle housing, be careful not to damage the oil seal.

8. Using a putty knife, clean the gasket mounting surfaces.

NOTE: *It is recommended, when the axle shaft is removed, to replace the oil seal.*

9. To replace the oil seal, perform the following procedures:

a. Using a medium pry bar, pry the oil seal from the end of the rear axle housing; DO NOT damage the housing oil seal surface.

b. Clean and inspect the axle tube housing.

c. Using the GM Axle Shaft Seal Installer tool No. J-33782, J-23771 or equivalent, drive the new seal into the housing until it is flush with the axle tube.

d. Using gear oil, lubricate the new seal lips.

10. If replacing the wheel bearing, perform the following procedures:

a. Using the GM Slide Hammer tool No. J-2619 or equivalent, the GM Adapter tool

No. J-2619-4 or equivalent and the GM Axle Bearing Puller tool No. J-22813-01 or equivalent, install the tool assembly so that the tangs engage the outer race of the bearing.

b. Using the action of the slide hammer, pull the wheel bearing from the axle housing.

c. Using solvent, thoroughly clean the wheel bearing, then blow dry with compressed air. Inspect the wheel bearing for excessive wear or damage. If it feels rough, replace it.

d. With a new or the reused bearing, place a blob of heavy grease in the palm of your hand, then work the bearing into the grease until it is thoroughly lubricated.

e. Using the Axle Shaft Bearing Installer tool No. J-34974, J-23765 or equivalent, drive the bearing into the axle housing until it bottoms against the seat. Install a new seal.

11. To install, slide the axle shaft into the rear axle housing and engage the splines of the axle shaft with the splines of the rear axle side gear,

Installing the axle bearing

then install the C-lock retainer on the axle shaft button end. After the C-lock is installed, pull the axle shaft outward to seat the C-lock retainer in the counterbore of the side gears.

NOTE: *When installing the axle shaft(s), be careful not to cut the oil seal lips.*

12. Install the pinion shaft through the case and the pinions, then install a new pinion shaft lock bolt. Torque the new lock bolt to 25 ft. lbs. (34 Nm).

13. To complete the installation, use a new rear axle cover gasket and reverse the removal procedures. Torque the carrier cover-to-rear axle housing bolts to 20 ft. lbs. (27 Nm). Refill the housing with SAE-80W or SAE-80W-90 GL-5 oil to a level $3/8$ in. (10mm) below the filler plug hole.

NOTE: *When adding oil to the rear axle, be aware that some locking differentials require the use of a special gear lubricant additive GM No. Seal Replacement*

Pinion Oil Seal Replacement

REMOVAL AND INSTALLATION

NOTE: *The following procedure requires the use of the Pinion Holding tool No. J-8614-10 or equivalent, the Pinion Flange Removal tool No. J-8614-1, J-8614-2, J-8614-3 or equivalent, and the Pinion Oil Seal Installation tool No. J-23911 or equivalent.*

1. Mark the driveshaft and pinion flange so they can be reassembled in the same position.

2. Disconnect the driveshaft from rear axle pinion flange and support the shaft up in body tunnel by wiring the driveshaft to the exhaust pipe. If the U-joint bearings are not retained by a retainer strap, use a piece of tape to hold bearings on their journals.

3. Mark the position of the pinion flange, the pinion shaft and nut so the proper pinion bearing pre-load can be maintained.

4. Using the Pinion Holding tool No. J-8614-10 or equivalent, the Pinion Flange Removal tool No. J-8614-1, J-8614-2, J-8614-3 or equivalent, remove the pinion flange nut and washer.

5. With suitable container in place to hold any fluid that may drain from rear axle, remove the pinion flange.

6. Remove the oil seal by driving it out of the differential with a blunt chisel; DO NOT damage the carrier.

7. Examine the seal surface of pinion flange for tool marks, nicks or damage, such as a groove worn by the seal. If damaged, replace flange as outlined under PINION FLANGE RE-PLACEMENT.

8. Examine the carrier bore and remove any burrs that might cause leaks around the O.D. of the seal.

9. To install a new seal, apply GM Seal Lubricant No. 1050169 or equivalent, to the outside diameter of the pinion flange and sealing lip of new seal. Drive the new seal into place with the correct size tool.

10. Install the pinion flange and tighten nut to the same position as marked in Step 4. While holding the pinion flange tighten the nut $1/16$ in. (1.6mm) beyond the alignment marks.

Pinion Flange Replacement

REMOVAL AND INSTALLATION

1. Raise and safely support the rear of the truck on jackstands. Remove both rear wheels and drums.

2. Mark the driveshaft and pinion flange, then disconnect the rear U-joint and support the driveshaft out of the way. If the U-joint bearings are not retained by a retainer strap, use a piece of tape to hold bearing caps on their journals.

3. The pinion rides against a tapered roller bearing. Check the pre-load by reading how much torque is required to turn the pinion. Use an inch pound torque wrench on the pinion flange nut and record the reading. This will give combined pinion bearing, carrier bearing, axle bearing and seal pre-load.

4. Remove pinion flange nut and washer.

5. With a suitable container in place to hold

Puller used to remove pinion flange

Special tools used to remove the pinion nut

J-23911 INSTALLER
7-1/2" (190 MM) AXLES

PINION OIL
SEAL

Installing pinion oil seal

any fluid that may drain from the rear axle, remove the pinion flange.

6. Apply the GM Seal lubricant No. 1050169 or equivalent, to the outside diameter of the new pinion flange, then install the pinion flange, washer and pinion flange nut finger tight.

7. While holding the pinion flange, tighten the nut a little at a time and turn the drive pinion several revolutions after each tightening to set the rollers. Check the pre-load of bearings each time with an inch pound torque wrench until pre-load is 3–5 inch lbs. more than the reading obtained in Step 3.

8. Install the driveshaft-to-rear axle pinion flange and torque the retainer bolts to 15 ft. lbs. (20 Nm).

9. To complete the installation, reverse the removal procedures. Check and/or add correct lubricant as necessary.

Axle Housing

REMOVAL AND INSTALLATION

1. Refer to the "Driveshaft, Removal and Installation" procedures in this Chapter and disconnect the driveshaft from the rear axle housing; the driveshaft may either be removed or supported on a wire. Using a floor jack, position it under and support the rear axle housing.

NOTE: *When supporting the rear of the vehicle, be sure to place the jackstands under the frame.*

2. Remove the rear wheel assemblies.

3. Remove the shock absorber-to-axle housing nuts/bolts, then swing the shock absorbers away from the axle housing.

4. Disconnect the brake lines from the axle housing clips and the backing plates (wheel cylinders).

NOTE: *When disconnecting the brake lines from the wheel cylinders, be sure to plug the lines to keep dirt from entering the lines.*

5. Disconnect the axle housing-to-spring U-bolt nuts, the U-bolts and the anchor plates.

6. Remove the vent hose from the top of the axle housing.

7. The axle can either be moved to the side to clear the leaf spring or, if desired, the leaf springs can be disconnected from the frame at the rear end to lower the axle down and back.

8. When installing the axle, be sure the housing is properly positioned on the leaf spring. Tighten the U-bolt nuts in a cross pattern to 18 ft. lbs. (25 Nm) to made sure everything is evenly seated. Then torque the nuts in steps to 41 ft. lbs. (55 Nm), then to 85 ft. lbs. (115 Nm).

9. Torque the lower shock mount nuts to 74 ft. lbs. (100 Nm) and the U-joint–to–pinion flange retainer bolts to 15 ft. lbs. (20 Nm).

10. Reconnect the rear brake lines and bleed the system as described in the Chapter 9. Check the fluid level in the axle before test driving: it should be almost even with the filler plug hole.

1. Nut
2. Shock absorber
3. Bolt
4. Retainer
5. Pinion flange
6. U-bolts
7. Vent hose
8. Nut
10. Axle housing

Removing the rear axle

Remove the drive axle bolts

Thrust washer

FRONT DRIVE AXLE

Axle Tube and Shaft Assembly

REMOVAL AND INSTALLATION

Identification

The front axle assembly, used on the 4WD models, utilizes a central disconnect type front axle/transfer case system which allows shifting in and out of 4WD when the vehicle is moving under most driving conditions. The axle has an aluminum carrier which includes a vacuum activated center lock feature.

The drive axles employ completely flexible assemblies which consist of inner and outer constant velocity (CV) joints connected by an axle shaft. The inner CV joint is a "tri-pot" design, which is completely flexible and can move in and out. The outer CV joint is a "Rzeppa" design which is also flexible but cannot move in or out.

NOTE: *The following procedure requires the use of the Shift Cable Housing Seal Installer tool No. J-33799 or equivalent.*

1. Disconnect the negative battery terminal from the battery.

2. Disconnect the shift cable from the vacuum actuator by disengaging the locking spring. Then push the actuator diaphragm in to release the cable.

3. Unlock the steering wheel at steering column so the linkage is free to move.

4. Raise and safely support the front of the truck on jackstands.

NOTE: *If a twin post hoist is used, place the jackstands under frame and lower front post hoist.*

Disconnect the vacuum actuator

11. Shift cable housing

Checking the shift mechanism on the front axle

FRAME ASSEMBLY

BOLT

TUBE AND
SHAFT ASSEMBLY

NUT
60-80 N·m
(45-60 FT. LBS.)

Tube-to-frame attachment

5. Remove the front wheel assemblies, the engine drive belt shield and the front axle skid plate (if equipped).

6. Place a support under right-side lower control arm and disconnect right-side upper ball joint, then remove the support so the control arm will hang free.

NOTE: *To keep the axle from turning, insert a drift through the opening in the top of the brake caliper, into the corresponding vane of the brake rotor.*

7. Remove the right-side drive axle shaft-to-tube assembly bolts and separate the drive axle from the tube assembly, then remove the drift from the brake caliper and rotor.

8. Disconnect the four wheel drive indicator lamp electrical connector from the switch.

9. Remove the three bolts securing the cable and switch housing-to-carrier and pull the housing away to gain access to the cable locking spring. DO NOT unscrew the cable coupling nut unless the cable is being replaced.

10. Disconnect the cable from the shift fork shaft by lifting spring over slot in shift fork.

11. Remove the two bolts securing the tube bracket to the frame.

12. Remove the remaining upper bolts securing the tube assembly to the carrier.

13. Remove the tube assembly by working around the drive axle. Be careful not to allow the sleeve, thrust washers, connector and output shaft to fall out of carrier or be damaged when removing the tube.

To install:

14. Install the sleeve, thrust washers, connector and output shaft in carrier. Apply Sealant No. 1052357, Loctite® 514 or equivalent, on the tube-to-carrier surface. Be sure to install the thrust washer. Apply grease to the washer to hold it in place during assembly.

15. Install the tube and shaft assembly-to-carrier and install a bolt at one o'clock position

but DO NOT torque. Pull the assembly down, then install the cable/switch housing and the remaining bolts. Torque the bolts to 55 ft. lbs. (75 Nm).

16. Install the tube-to-frame nuts/bolts and torque to the bolts to 36 ft. lbs. (48 Nm) and the nuts to 55 ft. lbs. (75 Nm).

17. Using the Shift Cable Housing Seal Installer tool No. J-33799 or equivalent, check the operation of the 4WD mechanism. Insert tool into the shift fork and check for the rotation of the axle shaft.

18. Remove the Shift Cable Housing Seal Installer tool No. J-33799 or equivalent, and install the shift cable switch housing by pushing the cable through into fork shaft hole. The cable will automatically snap into place (Refer to Shift Cable Replacement).

19. Connect 4WD indicator light electrical connector to the switch.

20. Install the support under the right-side lower control arm to raise arm and connect upper ball joint.

21. Install right-side drive axle-to-axle tube by installing one bolt first, then, rotate the axle to install remaining bolts. Torque the bolts to 60 ft. lbs. (80 Nm).

NOTE: *To hold the axle from turning, insert a drift through the opening in the top of the brake caliper into the corresponding vane of the brake rotor.*

22. To complete the installation, reverse the removal procedures. Connect the shift cable-to-vacuum actuator by pushing the cable end into the vacuum actuator shaft hole. The cable will snap into place, automatically; Refer to the Shift Cable Replacement.

1. Shaft	15. Seal
2. Deflector	16. Spring
3. Seal	17. Shift shaft and fork
4. Bearing	18. Bolt
5. Tube	19. Tab washer
6. Bolt	20. Thrust washer
7. Thrust washer	21. Differential pilot bearing
8. Retaining ring	22. Sleeve
9. Carrier connector	23. Output shaft
10. Shift cable	24. Washer
11. Shift cable housing	25. Plug
12. Gasket	26. Washer
13. Indicator switch	27. Pin
14. Spring	28. Bolt
	29. Carrier case
	30. Bearing
	31. Insert
	32. Sleeve

33. Side bearing
34. Differential case
36. Screw
37. Pinion
38. Shim
39. Bearing
40. Spacer
41. Bearing
42. Seal
43. Deflector
44. Flange
45. Washer
46. Nut
47. Plug
48. Bushing
49. Vent hose
50. Vent
51. Fitting
52. Shaft
53. Thrust washer
54. Side gear
55. Thrust washer
56. Differential pinion gear
57. Cover
58. Bolt
59. Shaft

Exploded view of front drive axle

Removing the right side axle tube seal and bearing

Differential Output Shaft Pilot Bearing

REMOVAL AND INSTALLATION

NOTE: *The following procedures requires the use of the Pilot Bearing Remover tool No. J-34011 or equivalent, and the Pilot Bearing Installer tool No. J-33842 or equivalent.*

1. Refer to the "Tube and Shaft Assembly, Removal and Installation" procedures in this Chapter and remove the tube and shaft.

2. Using the Pilot Bearing Remover tool No. J-34011 or equivalent, remove the pilot bearing.

3. Using axle fluid, lubricate the new bearing.

4. Using the Pilot Bearing Installer tool No.

J-33842 or equivalent, install the new pilot bearing.

Differential Carrier

REMOVAL AND INSTALLATION

1. Raise and safely support the front of the truck on jackstands.

NOTE: *If a twin post hoist is used, place jackstands under the frame and lower front post.*

2. Refer to the "Tube and Shaft Assembly, Removal and Installation" procedures in this Chapter and remove the tube and shaft assembly.

3. Remove the stabilizer-to-frame bolts.

4. Using a scribing tool, mark the location of the steering idler arm-to-frame, then remove the steering arm-to-frame bolts.

5. Push the steering linkage towards the front of the truck.

6. Remove the axle vent hose from the carrier fitting.

7. Remove the left-side drive axle shaft-to-carrier bolts and the drive axle shaft.

NOTE: *To keep the axle from turning, insert a drift through top opening of the brake caliper, then through the corresponding vane of the brake rotor.*

8. Disconnect the front driveshaft.

9. Remove the differential carrier-to-frame bolts; use an 18mm combination wrench to hold the upper nut from turning, by holding it through the frame.

10. To remove the differential carrier, tip it counterclockwise while lifting it up to gain clearance from the mounting ears.

11. To install, reverse the removal procedures. Torque the left-side drive axle shaft-to-differential carrier bolts to 60 ft. lbs. (80 Nm). Check and/or add axle lubricant, fill to level of fill plug hole. Lower vehicle, test drive and recheck the lubricant.

Shift Cable

REMOVAL AND INSTALLATION

1. Disengage the shift cable from the vacuum actuator by disengaging the locking spring, then, push the actuator diaphragm in to release the cable. Using a pair of pliers, squeeze the two cable locking fingers, then pull the cable out of the bracket hole.

2. Raise and safely support the front of the truck on jackstands, then remove cable/switch housing-to-carrier bolts and pull housing away to gain access to the cable locking spring. Disconnect the cable from the shift fork shaft by lifting the spring over shift fork slot.

3. Unscrew the cable from the housing.

4. Remove the cable from the truck.

5. To install the cable, observe the proper routing.

6. Install the cable/switch housing-to-carrier bolts. Torque the bolts to 36 ft. lbs. (48 Nm).

7. Guide the cable through the switch housing into the fork shaft hole and push the cable inward; the cable will automatically snap into place. Start turning the coupling nut by hand, to avoid cross threading, then torque the nut to 71–106 inch lbs. DO NOT overtorque the nut as this will cause thread damage to the plastic housing.

8. Lower the vehicle.

9. Connect the shift cable-to-vacuum actuator by pressing the cable into the bracket hole. The cable and housing will snap into place, automatically.

10. Check the cable operation.

WHEELS

2- and 4-Wheel Drive

REMOVAL AND INSTALLATION

These vehicles use a variety of wheel styles, but from the factory they are all one piece rims with 5 bolt holes in a 4.75 in. (120.6mm) bolt circle. Standard sizes are 14 × 6 in. (355.6mm × 152.4mm) and 15 × 7 in. (381mm × 177.8mm). A space saver spare for emergency use only comes in a 16 × 4 in. (406.4mm × 101.6mm) size.

1. When removing a wheel, loosen all the lug nuts with the wheel on the ground, then raise and safely support the vehicle.

2. If the wheel is stuck or rusted on the hub, make all the lug nuts finger tight, then back each one off 2 turns. Put the truck back on the ground and rock it side to side. Get another person to help if necessary. This is far safer than hitting a stuck wheel with the vehicle on a jack or lift.

3. When installing a wheel, tighten the lug nuts in a rotation, skipping every other one. If the nuts are numbered 1 through 5 in a circle, the tightening sequence will be 1-3-5-2-4.

4. Always use a torque wrench to avoid uneven tightening, which will distort the brake drum or disc. On steel wheels, torque the nuts to 73 ft. lbs. (100Nm). On aluminum alloy wheels, torque the nuts to 90 ft. lbs. (120Nm).

INSPECTION

Wheels can be distorted or bent and not effect dry road handling to a noticeable degree. Out of round wheels will show up as uneven tire wear, or will make it difficult to balance the tire. Runout can be checked with the wheel on or off the truck, with the tire on or off the rim, but off is better.

1. If the tire is on the wheel, set a dial indicator to touch the wheel in position "A" in the illustration to measure lateral runout.

2. To measure radial runout, set the dial indicator to position "B".

3. If the tire is not on the wheel, use the same positions on the inside of the rim. This is usually more accurate and easier to get a clean surface for the indicator stem.

4. For steel wheels, the radial runout limit is 0.040 in. (1mm), the lateral runout limit is 0.045 in. (1.1mm).

5. For aluminum alloy wheels, the limit for both runout directions is 0.030 in. (0.8mm).

Wheel Lug Studs

REMOVAL AND INSTALLATION

2-Wheel Drive Front Wheels

1. Raise and safely support the vehicle and remove the wheel.

2. Remove the brake pads and caliper. Refer to the Chapter 9.

3. Remove the outer wheel bearing and lift the rotor off the axle. Refer to **Front Wheel Bearings** later in this Chapter, if necessary.

4. Properly support the rotor and press the stud out.

5. Clean the stud hole with a wire brush and start the new stud with a hammer and drift pin. Do not use any lubricant or thread sealer.

6. Finish installing the stud with the press.

7. Install the rotor, adjust the wheel bearing and install the brake caliper and pads.

Use a dial indicator to measure radial and lateral runout with or without the tire on the rim

Pressing the old stud off

4-Wheel Drive Front and
2- and 4-Wheel Drive Rear

1. Raise and safely support the vehicle and remove the wheel.

2. On front wheels, remove the brake, caliper and rotor. On rear wheels, remove the brake drum. Refer to the Chapter 9.

3. Do not hammer the wheel stud to remove it. This will ruin the wheel bearing. Use the stud press tool J6627A or equivalent to press the stud out of the hub.

4. Clean the hole with a wire brush and start the new stud into the hole. Do not use any lubricant or thread sealer.

5. Stack 4 or 5 washers onto the stud and then put the nut on. Tighten the nut to draw the stud into place.It should be easy to feel when the stud is seated.

6. Reinstall the rotor and caliper or drum and use a torque wrench when installing the wheel.

FRONT SUSPENSION

Coil Spring — 2WD

REMOVAL

NOTE: *The following procedure requires the use of the Coil Spring Removal and Installation tool No. J-23028 or equivalent.*

1. Raise and safely support the front of the vehicle so that the front wheels hang free.

2. Remove the shock absorber-to-lower control arm bolts, then push the shock up through the control arm and into the spring.

3. Using the Coil Spring Removal and Installation tool No. J-23028 or equivalent, secured to the end of a jack, cradle the inner control arm bushings.

4. Remove the stabilizer bar link from the lower control arm.

5. To remove the lower control arm pivot bolts, perform the following procedures:

    a. Raise the jack to remove the tension from the lower control arm pivot bolts.

    b. Install a chain around the spring and through the control arm as a safety measure.

    c. Remove the lower control arm-to-frame pivot nuts and bolts—remove the rear pivot bolt first.

    d. Lower the control arm by slowly lowering the jack.

6. When all of the compression is removed from the spring, remove the safety chain and the spring.

NOTE: *DO NOT apply force to the lower control arm and/or ball joint to remove the spring. Proper maneuvering of the spring will allow for easy removal.*

7. To install, properly position the spring on the control arm, make sure the spring insulator is in place.

8. Using the Coil Spring Removal and Installation tool No. J-23028 or equivalent, raise the control arm and spring assembly into position.

9. To complete the installation, align the control arm with the frame and install the pivot bolts (front bolt first) and nuts, then reverse the removal procedures. Torque the lower control arm-to-frame pivot nuts/bolts to 45 ft. lbs., the stabilizer bar-to-lower control arm link to 13 ft. lbs. and the shock absorber-to-lower control arm bolts to 20 ft. lbs. Road test the vehicle.

SPRING TO BE INSTALLED WITH TAPE AT LOWEST POSITION. BOTTOM OF SPRING IS COILED HELICAL, AND THE TOP IS COILED FLAT WITH A GRIPPER NOTCH NEAR END OF SPRING COIL.

AFTER ASSEMBLY, END OF SPRING COIL MUST COVER ALL OR PART OF ONE INSPECTION DRAIN HOLE. THE OTHER HOLE MUST BE PARTLY EXPOSED OR COM-

With the spring compressor secured to the jack, lift the control arm to take the tension off the spring

Front control arms and components on 2WD

Torsion Bar — 4WD

REMOVAL AND INSTALLATION

NOTE: *The following procedure requires the use of the Torsion Bar Unloader tool No. J-22517-C or equivalent.*

1. Raise and safely support the front of the vehicle on jackstands.
2. Using the Torsion Bar Unloader tool No. J-22517-C or equivalent, attach it and apply pressure (to relax the tension) to the torsion bar adjusting arm screw; remove the adjusting screw by counting the number of turns necessary to remove the screw.
3. Remove the torsion support-to-insulator nut/bolt, the support insulator-to-frame nuts/bolts, the insulator retainer and the insulator from the support.

4. Slide the torsion bar(s) forward into the control arm(s) to clear the support.
5. Remove the adjusting arm, the adjusting arm screw and the nut from the support.
6. Remove the torsion bar from the control arm and the support.
7. To install the support insulator, reverse the removal procedures. Torque the insulator-to-frame nuts/bolts to 26 ft. lbs. and the torsion support-to-insulator nut/bolt to 25 ft. lbs.
8. To install the torsion bar, perform the following procedures:
   a. Slide the torsion bar into the lower control arm.
   b. Raise and slide the torsion bar into the adjusting arm.
NOTE: *Be sure the torsion bar clearance at the support is 0.236 in. (6mm).*

J-22517-C

A. Nut
B. Torsion bar adjusting bolt
C. Apply lubricant at points to ease installation
D. Torsion bar

Using the torsion bar unloader tool

175. Support	182. Torsion bar(s)
176. Nut	183. Lower control arm
177. Nut	184. Adjusting bolt
178. Bolt/screw	185. Nut
179. Nut	186. Adjusting arm
180. Bolt	187. Insulator
181. Bolt	188. Retainer

Torsion bar front suspension on 4WD

c. Using the Torsion Bar Unloader tool No. J-22517-C or equivalent, install it to the adjusting arm, then turn the adjusting arm screw the same number of turns which were necessary to remove it.

d. After the adjustment is complete, remove the Torsion Bar Unloader tool No. J-22517-C or equivalent.

9. Lower the truck. Refer to the "Front End Alignment" in this Chapter and adjust the final "Z" trim height.

Shock Absorbers

REMOVAL AND INSTALLATION

2WD Models

1. Raise and safely support the front of the truck.

2. Using an open end wrench, hold the shock absorber upper stem from turning, then remove the upper stem retaining nut, the retainer and rubber grommet.

3. Remove the shock absorber-to-lower control arm bolts and lower the shock absorber assembly from the bottom of the control arm.

4. Inspect and test the shock absorber; replace it, if necessary.

5. To install the shock absorber, fully extend the shock absorber stem, then push it up through the lower control arm and spring, so that the upper stem passes through the mounting hole in the upper control arm frame bracket.

6. Torque the upper shock absorber nut to 8 ft. lbs. If desired, use the old nut as a jam nut. Be careful not to crush the rubber bushing.

7. Torque the shock absorber-to-lower control arm bolts to 20 ft. lbs.

4WD Models

1. Raise and safely support the front of the truck.

2. Remove the shock absorber-to-lower control arm nut and bolt, then collapse the shock absorber.

3. Remove the upper shock absorber-to-frame nut and bolt.

4. Inspect and test the shock absorber; replace it, if necessary.

5. To install, reverse the removal procedures. Torque the upper and lower mounting bolts to 54 ft. lbs.

TESTING

Visually inspect the shock absorber. If there is evidence of leakage and the shock absorber is covered with oil, the shock is defective and should be replaced.

If there is no sign of excessive leakage (a small amount of weeping is normal) bounce the truck at one corner by pressing down on the bumper and releasing it. When you have the truck bouncing as much as you can, release the bumper. The truck should stop bouncing after the first rebound. If the bouncing continues past the center point of the bounce more than once, the shock absorbers are worn and should be replaced.

Upper Ball Joint

INSPECTION

NOTE: *Before performing this inspection, make sure that the wheel bearings are adjusted correctly and that the control arm bushings are in good condition.*

1. Raise and safely support the front of the vehicle by placing jackstands under each lower control arm as close as possible to each lower ball joint. Make sure that the vehicle is stable and the control arm bumpers are not contacting the frame.

2. Using a dial indicator, position it so that it contacts the wheel rim.

3. To measure the horizontal deflection, perform the following procedures:

a. Grasp the tire (top and bottom), then pull outward on the top and push inward on the bottom; record the reading on the dial indicator.

b. Grasp the tire (top and bottom), then pull outward on the bottom and push inward on the top; record the reading on the dial indicator.

c. If the difference in the dial indicator reading is more than 0.125 in. (3mm), or if the rubber seal is cut or appears damaged, the ball joint must be replaced.

A. Dial Indicator

Using a dial indicator to determine ball joint ware

Use a ball joint removal tool to press the ball joint out of the steering knuckle

REMOVAL AND INSTALLATION

NOTE: *The following procedure requires the use of the GM Ball Joint Remover tool No. J-23742 or equivalent.*

1. Raise and safely support the front of the vehicle by placing jackstands under the frame, not the lower control arms.

2. Place the floor jack under the lower control arm spring seat and raise it slightly to retain the spring and the lower control arm in position.

CAUTION: *With the ball joint nut removed, the floor jack is holding the lower control arm in place against the coil spring. Make sure the jack is firmly engaged with the spring seat and cannot move, or personal injury could result.*

3. Remove the wheel and brake caliper. Without disconnecting the hydraulic line, hang the caliper from the body with wire so it does not hang on the line.

5. From the upper ball joint, remove the cotter pin, the nut and the grease fitting.

6. Using the GM Ball Joint Remover tool

No. J-23742 or equivalent, separate the upper ball joint from the steering knuckle. Pull the steering knuckle free of the ball joint after removal.

NOTE: *After separating the steering knuckle from the upper ball joint, be sure to support the steering knuckle/hub assembly to prevent damaging the brake hose.*

7. To remove the upper ball joint from the upper control arm, perform the following procedures:

a. Using a $1/8$ in. (3mm) drill bit, drill a $1/4$ in. (6mm) deep hole into each rivet.

b. Using a $1/2$ in. (13mm) drill bit, drill off the rivet heads.

c. Using a pin punch and the hammer, drive the rivets from the upper ball joint-to-upper control arm assembly and remove the upper ball joint.

8. Clean and inspect the steering knuckle hole. Replace the steering knuckle if the hole is out of round.

To install:

9. When installing the new joint, put the bolts up through the control arm and install

Punch the rivets out to remove the ball joint

Drill the upper ball joint rivets

Drill the rivet heads

Install the new joint down onto the bolts, nuts touching the joint

the joint down onto the bolts. Torque the nuts to 17 ft. lbs.

10. To complete the installation, seat the upper ball joint into the steering knuckle and install the nut. Torque the upper ball joint-to-steering knuckle nut to 65 ft. lbs. and install a new cotter pin.

NOTE: *When installing the cotter pin, never loosen the castle nut to expose the cotter pin hole.*

11. Use a grease gun to lubricate the upper ball joint.

12. Install the brake caliper and pads and the wheel. When a ball joint is replaced, a front end alignment is strongly recommended.

Lower Ball Joint

INSPECTION

NOTE: *Before performing this inspection, make sure that the wheel bearings are adjusted correctly and that the control arm bushings are in good condition.*

Visually check the wear indicator, the small nub that the grease fitting screws into. If it is flush or inside the ball joint cover surface, replace the ball joint. If the rubber grease seal is broken, the ball joint must be replaced.

WORN

NEW

SINTERED IRON BEARING

WEAR SURFACES

HOUSING SOCKET

RUBBER PRESSURE RING

1.27mm (.050″)

WEAR INDICATOR (OUT WHEN NEW)

WHEN BALL JOINT WEAR CAUSES THIS SHOULDER TO RETREAT BELOW THE SURFACE, REPLACEMENT IS REQUIRED.

The grease fitting mounting is also the wear indicator

Installing the new ball joint

Pressing the lower ball joint out of the control arm

REMOVAL AND INSTALLATION

NOTE: *The following procedure requires the use of the GM Ball Joint Separator tool No. J-23742 or equivalent, the GM Front and Rear Lower Control Arm Bushing Installer tool No. J-21474-13 or equivalent, the GM Ball Joint Installer tool No. J-9519-9 or equivalent, the GM Ball Joint Installer tool No. J-9519-16 or equivalent, and the GM Ball Joint Fixture tool No. J-9519-10 (1982-85) or J-9519-30 (1986-91) or equivalent.*

1. Raise and safely support the front of the vehicle on jackstands. Remove the wheel and brake caliper.

2. Using a floor jack, place it under the spring seat of the lower control arm, then raise the jack to support the arm.

NOTE: *The floor jack MUST remain under the lower control arm, during the removal and installation procedures, to retain the arm and spring positions.*

3. Remove the cotter pin (discard it) and the ball joint nut.

4. Using the GM Ball Joint Separator tool No. J-23742 or equivalent, disconnect the lower ball joint from the steering knuckle. Pull the steering knuckle away from the lower control arm, place a block of wood between the frame and the upper control arm; make sure that the brake hose is free of tension.

5. From the lower ball joint, remove the rubber grease seal and the grease fitting.

6. Using the GM Ball Joint Installer tool No. J-9519-16 or equivalent, the GM Front and Rear Lower Control Arm Bushing Installer tool No. J-21474-13 or equivalent, and the GM Ball Joint Fixture tool No. J-9519-10 (1982-85) or J-9519-30 (1986-91) or equivalent, remove the lower ball joint from the lower control arm.

7. To install, position the new lower ball joint into the lower control arm. Using the GM Ball Joint Installer tool No. J-9519-9 or equivalent, and the GM Ball Joint Fixture tool No. J-9519-10 (1982-85) or J-9519-30 (1986-91) or equivalent, press the new lower ball joint into the lower control arm.

8. Install the grease fitting and the grease seal onto the lower ball joint; the grease seal MUST BE fully seated on the ball joint and the grease purge hole MUST face inboard.

9. To complete the installation, reverse the removal procedures. Torque the ball joint-to-steering knuckle nut to 90 ft. lbs.

10. Install a new cotter pin to the lower ball joint stud.

NOTE: *When installing the cotter pin, never loosen the castle nut to expose the cotter pin hole.*

11. Use a grease gun to lubricate the ball joint.

12. Install the brake caliper and pads and the wheel. When a ball joint is replaced, a front end alignment is strongly recommended.

Stabilizer Bar

REMOVAL AND INSTALLATION

1. Raise and safely support the front of the vehicle on jackstands. Remove the wheels.

2. Disconnect the stabilizer bar link nuts from the lower control arms.

3. Remove the stabilizer bar-to-frame clamps.

100. Frame
101. Lower control arm
103. Weld nut
104. Clamp
105. Bolts
106. Insulator
107. Stabilizer shaft
108. Clamp
109. Bolt
110. Insulator
111. Nut

Front stabilizer bar mounting on 2WD

Front stabilizer bar mounting on 4WD

4. Remove the stabilizer bar from the vehicle.

5. To install, reverse the removal procedures. Torque the stabilizer bar link-to-lower control arm nuts/bolts to 13 ft. lbs. (2WD) or 24 ft. lbs. (4WD) and the stabilizer retainer-to-frame nuts/bolts to 24 ft. lbs. (2WD) or 35 ft. lbs. (4WD).

Upper Control Arm

REMOVAL AND INSTALLATION

NOTE: *The following procedure requires the use of the GM Ball Joint Remover tool No. J-23742 or equivalent.*

1. Raise and safely support the front of the vehicle by placing jackstands under the frame.

NOTE: *Allow the floor jack to remain under the lower control arm seat, to retain the spring and the lower control arm position.*

2. Remove the wheels and brake caliper. Hang the caliper from the body with wire to avoid straining the hydraulic line.

3. From the upper ball joint, remove the cotter pin and the ball joint-to-upper control arm nut.

4. Using the GM Ball Joint Remover tool No. J-23742 or equivalent, separate the upper ball joint from the steering knuckle/hub assembly. Pull the steering knuckle free of the ball joint after removal.

Upper control arm removal

SUGGESTED ASSEMBLY SEQUENCE
INSTALL THE FRONT LEG OF THE LOWER CONTROL ARM INTO THE CROSSMEMBER PRIOR TO INSTALLING THE REAR LEG IN THE FRAME BRACKET

Pivot bolt installation

Upper control arm components

NOTE: *After separating the steering knuckle from the upper ball joint, be sure to support steering knuckle/hub assembly to prevent damaging the brake hose.*

5. Remove the upper control arm-to-frame nuts and bolts, then lift and remove the upper control arm from the vehicle.

NOTE: *On 2WD, tape the shims together and identify them so that they can be re-installed in the same place*

6. Clean and inspect the steering knuckle hole. Replace the steering knuckle, if any out of roundness is noted.

To install

7. Attach the upper control arm to the frame, insert the shims in their proper positions, and torque the upper control arm bolts to 45 ft. lbs. (2WD) or 70 ft. lbs. (4WD).

8. Seat the upper ball joint into the steering knuckle, install the nut and torque it to 61 ft. lbs.

9. Install a new cotter pin to the upper ball joint stud.

NOTE: *When installing the cotter pin, never loosen the castle nut to expose the cotter pin hole.*

10. Use a grease gun to lubricate the upper ball joint.

11. Install the brake caliper and pads and the wheel. On 4WD, when a control arm is removed, a front end alignment is essential.

Lower Control Arm

REMOVAL AND INSTALLATION

2WD Models

NOTE: *The following procedure requires the use of the GM Ball Joint Remover tool No. J-23742 or equivalent.*

1. Refer to the "Coil Spring, Removal and Installation" procedures in this Chapter and remove the coil spring.

2. Remove the cotter pin (discard it) and the ball joint nut.

3. Using the GM Ball Joint Remover tool No. J-23742 or equivalent, disconnect the

116. Upper ball joint
117. Nut
118. Pin
119. Hub and knuckle assembly
140. Bolt
141. Bolt
142. Cam
143. Cam
144. Frame
145. Nut
146. Bushing
147. Nut
148. Upper control arm
149. Bumper
153. Bushing
154. Nut
155. Cam
156. Cam

Upper control arm assembly on 4WD vehicles

lower ball joint from the steering knuckle and the lower control arm from the vehicle.

NOTE: *Place a block of wood between the frame and the upper control arm; make sure that the brake hose is free of tension.*

4. To install, position the lower ball joint stud into the steering knuckle and finger tighten it for now.

5. Install the control arm bolts, making sure the bolt goes in from the front of the vehicle. Torque the front nut and bolt to 94 ft. lbs., and the rear nut and bolt to 66 ft. lbs. Torque the ball joint-to-steering knuckle nut to 81 ft. lbs.

6. Install a new cotter pin to the lower ball joint stud.

NOTE: *When installing the cotter pin, never loosen the castle nut to expose the cotter pin hole.*

7. Pull the shock absorber down, then install the shock absorber-to-lower control arm nuts/bolts. Torque the nuts and bolts to 20 ft. lbs.

8. Remove the lower control arm support and lower the vehicle.

4WD Models

1. Refer to the "Torsion Bar, Removal and Installation" procedures in this Chapter, then remove the torsion bar and support assembly.

2. Remove the stabilizer bar-to-lower control arm nuts/bolts.

3. Remove the shock absorber-to-lower control arm nuts/bolts and push the shock absorber upward.

4. Remove the lower control arm-to-frame

125 N·m
(92 FT. LBS.)

200 N·m
(148 FT. LBS.)

3   2

FRT

200 N·m
(148 FT. LBS.)

4

5   1

125 N·m
(92 FT. LBS.)

1. Lower control arm
2. Frame
3. Crossmember
4. Frame bracket
5. Bushing

Lower control arm installation on 2WD

BOLT/SCREW
MUST BE INSTALLED
IN DIRECTION SHOWN.

FRT

BOLT/SCREW
MUST BE INSTALLED
IN DIRECTION SHOWN.

SUGGESTED ASSEMBLY SEQUENCE
INSTALL THE FRONT LEG OF THE LOWER CONTROL
ARM INTO THE CROSSMEMBER PRIOR TO
INSTALLING THE REAR LEG IN THE FRAME
BRACKET.

Lower control arm on 4WD

nuts/bolts and the lower control arm from the truck.

5. To install, reverse the removal procedures. Torque the lower control arm-to-frame bolts to 148 ft. lbs., the lower control arm-to-frame nuts to 92 ft. lbs., the shock absorber-to-lower control arm nut/bolt to 54 ft. lbs., the stabilizer bar-to-lower control arm nuts/bolts to 24 ft. lbs. and the lower control arm ball joint-to-steering knuckle nut to 83 ft. lbs.

Steering Knuckle and Spindle

REMOVAL AND INSTALLATION

2WD Model

NOTE: *The following procedure requires the use of the GM Tie Rod End Puller tool J-6627 or equivalent, and the GM Ball Joint Remover tool No. J-23742 or equivalent.*

1. Siphon some brake fluid from the brake master cylinder.

2. Raise and safely support the front of the vehicle on jackstands. Remove the wheels.

NOTE: *When supporting the vehicle on jackstands, DO NOT place the jackstands under the lower control arms. Place them under the frame.*

3. Remove the brake caliper from the steering knuckle and hang it from the body on a wire.

4. Remove the grease cup, the cotter pin, the castle nut and the hub-and-rotor assembly.

5. Remove the splash shield-to-steering knuckle bolts and the shield.

6. At the tie rod end-to-steering knuckle stud, remove the cotter pin and the nut. Using the GM Tie Rod End Puller tool J-6627 or equivalent, separate the tie rod end from the steering knuckle.

7. Using a floor jack, place it under the

spring seat of the lower control arm and support the arm.

8. From the upper and lower ball joint studs, remove the cotter pins and the nuts.

9. Using the GM Ball Joint Remover tool No. J-23742 or equivalent, separate the upper ball joint from the steering knuckle.

10. Raise the upper control arm to separate it from the steering knuckle.

11. Using the GM Ball Joint Remover tool No. J-23742 or equivalent, separate the lower ball joint from the steering knuckle, then lift the steering knuckle from the lower control arm.

12. Clean and inspect the steering knuckle and spindle for signs of wear or damage; if necessary, replace the steering knuckle.

13. To install the steering knuckle, position

J-6627

Removing the tie rod end from the steering knuckle

it onto the lower ball joint stud, then lift the upper control arm to insert the upper ball joint stud into the steering knuckle. Torque the upper ball joint-to-steering knuckle nut to 65 ft. lbs. and the lower ball joint-to-steering knuckle nut to 90 ft. lbs. Remove the floor jack from under the lower control arm.

14. Install a new cotter pin into the upper and lower ball joint studs.

NOTE: *When installing the cotter pin, never loosen the castle nut to expose the cotter pin hole.*

15. To complete the installation, reverse the removal procedures. Torque the tie rod end-to-steering knuckle nut to 40 ft. lbs., the splash shield-to-steering knuckle bolts to 10 ft. lbs. Check and/or adjust the wheel bearing and the front end alignment.

16. Remove the jackstands and lower the vehicle. Refill the brake master cylinder.

4WD Model

NOTE: *The following procedure requires the use of the Universal Steering Linkage Puller tool No. J-24319-01 or equivalent, the Axle Shaft Boot Seal Protector tool No. J-28712 or equivalent, the Ball Joint Separator tool No. J-34026 or equivalent, and the Steering Knuckle Seal Installation tool No. J-28574 or equivalent.*

1. Refer to the "Torsion Bar, Removal and Installation" procedures in this Chapter and relieve the torsion bar pressure.

2. Raise and support the front of the truck on jackstands; place the jackstands under the frame.

3. Remove the wheel and tire.

4. Using the Axle Shaft Boot Seal Protector tool No. J-28712 or equivalent, attach it to the tripot axle joint.

5. Remove the disc brake caliper-to-steering knuckle bolts, lift the brake caliper and support it (out of the way) on a wire.

6. Remove the brake disc from the wheel hub.

7. At the wheel hub, remove the cotter pin, the retainer, the castle nut, the thrust washer.

8. From the tie-rod-to-steering knuckle assembly, remove the cotter pin and the castle nut.

9. Using the Universal Steering Linkage Puller tool No. J-24319-01 or equivalent, tie-rod from the steering knuckle.

10. Remove the hub/bearing assembly-to-steering knuckle bolts and the hub/bearing assembly from the steering knuckle.

11. From the upper and lower ball joints, remove the cotter pin(s) and back off the castle nut(s).

12. Using the Ball Joint Separator tool No.

J-34026 or equivalent, disconnect the ball joints from the steering knuckle. Remove the ball joint nut(s) and separate the ball joint(s) from the steering knuckle.

NOTE: *When removing the steering knuckle from the wheel hub, be careful not to damage the splined surface of the half shaft.*

13. Remove the spacer and the seal from the steering knuckle.

14. Clean and inspect the parts for nicks, scores and/or damage, then replace them as necessary.

15. Using the Steering Knuckle Seal Installation tool No. J-28574 or equivalent, install a new seal into the steering knuckle.

16. Install the spacer, then the upper and lower ball joints to the steering knuckle. Torque the upper ball joint-to-steering knuckle

115. Bolt
116. Upper control arm ball joint
117. Nut
118. Pin
119. Knuckle
121. Hub and bearing assembly
122. Washer
123. Nut
124. Retainer
125. Pin
127. Pin
128. Nut
129. Pin
130. Nut
131. Lower control arm ball joint
132. Tie rod end
133. Seal

Steering knuckle and hub assembly on 4WD

A. Hammer
B. Knuckle

Installing the new steering knuckle seal on 4WD

nut to 61 ft. lbs. and the lower ball joint-to-steering knuckle nut to 83 ft. lbs. DO NOT loosen the nut for the cotter pin installation, simply turn the nut a $\frac{1}{6}$ turn further; bend the pin ends against the nut flats.

17. Install the wheel hub/bearing assembly-to-steering knuckle, be careful to align the threads and splines carefully. Torque the hub/bearing assembly-to-steering knuckle bolts to 86 ft. lbs.

18. Install the tie-rod end-to-steering knuckle, then torque the tie-rod end nut to 35 ft. lbs. Install the cotter pin and bend the ends against the nut flats.

19. To complete the installation, reverse the removal procedures. Before torquing the wheel hub/bearing, put the vehicle on the ground. The torque is high enough to cause the truck to fall off the jack stands. Torque the wheel hub/bearing assembly-to-half shaft nut to 181 ft. lbs. Check and/or adjust the front end alignment.

Front Wheel Bearings

The proper functioning of the front suspension cannot be maintained unless the front wheel taper roller bearings are correctly adjusted. The cones must be a slip fit on the spindle and the inside diameter should be lubricated to insure that the cones will creep. The spindle nut must be a free-running fit on threads.

2-WHEEL DRIVE ADJUSTMENT

1. Raise and support the front of the vehicle on jackstands, then remove the grease cap from the hub.

2. Remove the cotter pin from axle spindle and spindle nut.

3. Tighten the spindle nut to 12 ft. lbs. while turning the wheel assembly forward by hand to fully seat the bearings. This will remove any grease or burrs which could cause excessive wheel bearing play later.

4. Back off the nut to "just loose" position.

5. Hand tighten the spindle nut. Loosen the spindle nut until either hole in the spindle aligns with a slot in the nut; not more than $\frac{1}{2}$ flat.

6. Install a new cotter pin; bend the ends against nut flat, cut off extra length to ensure ends will not interfere with the grease cap.

7. Measure the looseness in the wheel hub assembly. There will be from 0.001-0.005 in. (0.03-0.13mm) end play when properly adjusted.

8. Install the grease cap onto the wheel hub.

REMOVAL AND INSTALLATION

2WD Models

NOTE: *The following procedure requires the use of the Wheel Bearing Removal tool No. J-29117 or equivalent, the Wheel Bearing Installation tools No. J-8092 and J-8850 or equivalent.*

1. Remove to the "Disc Brake Caliper, Removal and Installation" procedures in the Chapter 9 and remove the disc brake caliper.

CAUTION: *Brake shoes and pads contain asbestos, which has been determined to be a cancer causing agent. Never clean the brake surfaces with compressed air! Avoid inhaling any dust from any brake surface! When cleaning brake surfaces, use a commercially available brake cleaning fluid.*

2. Remove the grease cup from wheel hub.

3. Remove the cotter pin, the castle nut and the thrust washer from the spindle.

4. Carefully pull wheel hub assembly from the spindle.

5. Remove the outer wheel bearing from the wheel hub. The inner wheel bearing will remain in the hub and may be removed after prying out the inner wheel bearing grease seal; discard the seal.

6. Using the Wheel Bearing Removal tool No. J-29117 or equivalent, remove the inner

Front rotor and wheel bearings, 2WD

and outer wheel bearing races from the wheel hub.

7. Clean all of the parts in clean solvent and air dry.

8. Inspect the bearings for cracks, worn or pitted rollers.

9. Inspect the bearing races for cracks, scores or a brinelled condition.

10. If the outer races were removed, use the Wheel Bearing Installation tools No. J-8092 and J-8850 or equivalent, drive or press the races into the hub.

11. Clean off any grease in the hub/spindle and thoroughly clean out any grease in the bearings. Use clean solvent and a small brush, with no loose bristles, to clean out all old grease. DO NOT spin the bearing with compressed air while drying it or the bearing may be damaged.

12. Use an approved high temperature front wheel bearing grease.

NOTE: *DO NOT mix greases as mixing may change the grease properties and result in poor performance.*

13. Apply a thin film of grease to the spindle at the outer bearing seat and at the inner bearing seat, the shoulder and the seal seat.

14. Put a small quantity of grease inboard of each bearing cup in the hub. This can be applied with your finger, forming a dam to provide extra grease availability to the bearing and to keep thinned grease from flowing out of the bearing.

15. Fill the bearing cone and roller assemblies full of grease.

NOTE: *A preferred method for doing this is with a cone type grease machine that forces grease into the bearing. If a cone greaser is not available, the bearings can be packed by hand. If hand packing is used, it is extremely important to work the grease thoroughly into*

J-8092

J-8850

Installing inner bearing race

the bearings between the rollers, cone and the cage. Failure to do this could result in premature bearing failure.

16. Place the inner bearing cone and roller assembly in the hub. Then using your finger, put an additional quantity of grease outboard of the bearing.

17. Install a new grease seal using a flat plate until the seal is flush with the hub. Lubricate the seal lip with a thin layer of grease.

18. Carefully install the hub and rotor assembly. Place the outer bearing cone and roller assembly in the outer bearing cup. Install the washer and nut and initially tighten the nut to 12 ft. lbs. while turning the wheel assembly forward by hand. Put an additional quantity of grease outboard the bearing. This provides extra grease availability to the bearing.

19. Check and/or adjust the wheel bearing.

4WD Models

NOTE: *The wheel bearing is installed in the wheel hub assembly and is serviced by replacement only.*

CAUTION: *Brake shoes and pads contain asbestos, which has been determined to be a cancer causing agent. Never clean the brake surfaces with compressed air! Avoid inhaling any dust from any brake surface! When cleaning brake surfaces, use a commercially available brake cleaning fluid.*

Refer to the "Steering Knuckle, Removal and Installation" procedures in this Chapter and replace the wheel hub assembly.

PACKING

Clean the wheel bearings thoroughly with solvent and check their condition before installation.

NOTE: *If blow drying the wheel bearings with compressed air, DO NOT spin them, for damage may occur to the bearings.*

Apply a sizable daub of lubricant to the palm of one hand. Using your other hand, work the bearing into the lubricant so that the grease is pushed through the rollers and out the other side. Keep rotating the bearing while continuing to push the lubricant through it.

Front End Alignment

CASTER

Caster is the tilting of the front steering axis either forward or backward from the vertical. A backward tilt is said to be positive (+) and a forward tilt is said to be negative (–).

CAMBER

Camber is the inward or outward tilting of the front wheels from the vertical. When the

Camber, caster and toe are adjusted in degrees

wheels tilt outward at the top, the camber is said to be positive (+). When the wheels tilt inward at the top, the camber is said to be negative (–). The amount of tilt is measured in degrees from the vertical and this measurement is called the camber angle.

TOE-IN

Toe-in is the turning in of the front wheels. The actual amount of toe-in is normally only a fraction of a degree. The purpose of toe-in is to ensure parallel rolling of the front wheels. Excessive toe-in or toe-out will cause tire wear.

REAR SUSPENSION

The rear suspension system consists of several major components: The double acting shock absorbers, variable rate multi-leaf springs and various attachment parts. The multi-leaf springs are connected to the frame by a hanger assembly with integral bushings in the front and a shackle assembly with integral bushings in the rear. The shackle assembly, in response to different road and payload conditions, allows the leaf spring to "change its length". The rear axle is connected to both the leaf springs and the shock absorbers by various attaching parts.

Leaf Springs

REMOVAL AND INSTALLATION

NOTE: *The following procedure requires the use of two sets of jackstands.*

1. Raise and safely support the rear frame of the vehicle on jackstands. support the rear axle with the second set of jackstands.

NOTE: *When supporting the rear of the vehicle, support the axle and the body separately to relieve the load on the rear spring.*

2. Remove the wheel and tire assembly.
3. At the rear of the spring, loosen (DO NOT remove) the shackle-to-frame bolt and the shackle-to-spring bolt.
4. Remove the shock absorber.
5. Remove the axle U-bolt-to-anchor plate nuts, the lower plate-to-anchor plate nuts, the U-bolts and the lower plate, then jack up the axle on that side only just enough to lift off of the spring.
6. At the front of the spring, remove the retainer-to-hanger assembly nuts, the washers and the retainer(s).
7. At the rear of the spring, remove the spring-to-shackle nut, washer and bolt. Remove the spring from the vehicle.

To install:

8. When installing a new spring, it is usually easier to put the rear end up first. Put the bolts through one of the shackle plates, hang the shackle on the frame, hang the spring on

WHEEL ALIGNMENT SPECIFICATIONS

Toe-in		Camber		Caster	
Range (in.)	Preferred (in.)	Range (deg.)	Preferred (deg.)	Range (deg.)	Preferred (deg.)
1/16P–1/4P	1/8P	0–1 5/8P	13/16P	1P–3P	2P

FRT

BUSHING

BUMPER

U-BOLT

SHACKLE

LEAF
SPRING

ANCHOR
PLATE

FRAME
HANGER

Rear leaf spring and axle attachment

the shackle and put on the other shackle plate. Install the nuts finger tight.

9. It should be possible to move the spring enough on the shackle to line up the holes for the front mounting bolt. Install the washers and nut finger tight.

10. Lower the axle to rest on the spring and install the U-bolts and anchor plates. Torque the nuts in a cross pattern first to 18 ft. lbs., then to 85 ft. lbs. It is important that the U-bolts are tightened evenly.

11. Raise the axle so there is about 6.75 in. (170mm) between the axle housing and the frame of the truck. Measure from the housing between the U-bolts to the metal part of the rubber bump stop on the frame.

12. Torque the front spring mounting bolt and the rear shackle bolts to 92 ft. lbs. Install the shock absorber and wheel.

Shock Absorbers

REMOVAL AND INSTALLATION

1. Raise and support the rear of the truck on jackstands; support the rear axle.

2. At the upper mounting location, disconnect shock absorber bolts.

3. At the lower mounting location, remove the nut and washer.

4. Remove the shock absorber(s) from the vehicle.

5. To install the shock absorber, place it into position and reattach at upper mounting location.

6. Align the lower-end of the shock absorber with the anchor plate stud and install the washer and nut.

7. Torque the shock absorber-to-body bolts to 15 ft. lbs. and the shock absorber-to-axle nut to 50 ft. lbs.

8. Lower vehicle and remove from hoist.

TESTING

Visually inspect the shock absorber. If there is evidence of leakage and the shock absorber is covered with oil, the shock is defective and should be replaced.

If there is no sign of excessive leakage (a small amount of weeping is normal) bounce the truck at one corner by pressing down on the bumper and releasing it. When you have the truck bouncing as much as you can, release the bumper. The truck should stop bouncing after the first rebound. If the bouncing continues past the center point of the bounce more than once, the shock absorbers are worn and should be replaced.

STEERING

The steering box (manual or power) consists of a recirculating balls, which transmits force from the worm gear to the sector gear. A relay type steering linkage is used with a pitman arm connected to one end of the relay rod. The relay rod is supported by two idler arms; the idler arms pivot on a support which is attached to the frame. The relay rod is connected to the steering arms by two adjustable tie rods. The trucks are equipped with a collapsible steering column designed to collapse on impact, thereby reducing possible chest injuries during accidents. When making any repairs to the steering column or steering wheel, excessive pressure or force capable of collapsing the column must be avoided. The ignition lock, ignition switch and an anti theft system are built into each column.

On the automatic transmission, the ignition key cannot be removed unless the shift lever is in the Park position and the ignition switch in the Lock position. Placing the key in the Lock position activates a rod within the column which locks the steering wheel and shift lever.

Steering Wheel

REMOVAL AND INSTALLATION

NOTE: *The following procedure requires the use of the GM Steering Wheel Puller tool No. J-1859-03 or equivalent.*

1. Disconnect the negative battery cable from the battery.

2. Position the steering wheel so that it is in the horizontal position and the front wheel are straight.

3. If equipped with a horn cap, pry the cap from the center of the steering wheel. If equipped with a steering wheel shroud, remove the screw from the rear of the steering wheel and remove the shroud.

NOTE: *If the horn cap or shroud is equipped with an electrical connector, disconnect it.*

4. Remove the steering wheel-to-steering shaft retainer (snapring) and nut.

NOTE: *Since the steering column is designed to collapse upon impact, it is recommended NEVER to hammer on it!*

5. Matchmark the relationship of the steering wheel to the steering shaft.

6. Using the GM Steering Wheel Puller tool No. J-1859-03 or equivalent, press the steering wheel from the steering column.

NOTE: *Before installing the steering wheel, be sure that the turn signal switch is in the Neutral position. DO NOT misalign the steering wheel more than 1 in. (25mm) from the horizontal centerline.*

7. To install the steering wheel, align the matchmarks and push it onto the steering shaft splines, torque the steering wheel-to-steering shaft nut to 30 ft. lbs. Install the horn cap or pad.

Combination Switch

The combination switch is a combination of the turn signal, the windshield wiper/washer, the dimmer and the cruise control switches.

REMOVAL AND INSTALLATION

NOTE: *The following procedure requires the use of the GM Lock Plate Compressor tool No. J-23653 or equivalent.*

1. Disconnect the negative battery cable. Refer to the "Steering Wheel, Removal and Installation" procedures in this Chapter and remove the steering wheel.

2. If necessary, remove the steering column-to-lower instrument panel cover. Disconnect the electrical harness connector from the steering column jacket (under the dash).

3. Using a screwdriver, insert into the slots

J-1859-03

Using a steering wheel puller

Make sure the wheel is properly aligned when installing it

Removing the steering column lock plate with the compressor tool installed

Removing the wire protector

between the steering shaft lock plate cover and the steering column housing, then pry upward to remove the cover from the lock plate.

4. Using the GM Lock Plate Compressor tool No. J-23653-A or equivalent, screw the center shaft onto the steering shaft (as far as it will go), then screw the center post nut clockwise until the lock plate is compressed.

5. Pry the snapring from the steering shaft slot.

NOTE: *If the steering column is being disassembled on a bench, the steering shaft will slide out of the mast jacket when the snapring is removed.*

6. Remove the GM Lock Plate Compressor tool No. J-23653 or equivalent, and the lock plate.

7. Remove the multi-function lever-to-switch screw and the lever.

8. To remove the hazard warning switch, press the knob inward and unscrew it.

9. Remove the combination switch assembly-to-steering column screws.

10. Lift the combination switch assembly from the steering column, then slide the electrical connector through the column housing and the protector.

NOTE: *If the steering column is the tilting type, position the steering housing into the Low position.*

11. To remove the harness cover, pull it toward the lower end of the column; be careful not to damage the wires.

12. To remove the wire protector, grab the protector's tab with a pair of pliers, then pull the protector downward, out of the steering column.

NOTE: *When assembling the steering column, use only fasteners of the correct length; overlength fasteners could prevent a portion of the assembly from compressing under impact.*

To install:

13. To install the combination switch electri-

cal connector, perform the following procedures:

a. On the non-tilt columns, be sure that the electrical connector is on the protector, then feed it and the cover down through the housing and under the mounting bracket.

b. On the tilt columns, feed the electrical connector down through the housing and under the mounting bracket, then install the cover onto the housing.

14. Install the clip on the electrical connector to the clip on the jacket, the combination switch-to-steering column mounting screws, the lower instrument trim panel, the turn signal lever/screws and the hazard warning knob.

NOTE: *With the multi-function lever installed, place it into the Neutral position. With the hazard warning knob installed, pull it Outward.*

15. Onto the upper end of the steering shaft, install the washer, the upper bearing preload spring, the canceling cam, the lock plate and a new retaining ring (snapring). Using the GM Lock Plate Compressor tool No. J-23653 or equivalent, compress the lock plate and slide the new retaining ring into the steering shaft groove.

16. To complete the installation, reverse the removal procedures. Torque the multi-function switch-to-steering column screws to 35 inch lbs. and the steering wheel nut to 30 ft. lbs.

Ignition Switch

The ignition switch, for anti-theft reasons, is located inside the channel section of the brake pedal support and is completely inaccessible without first lowering the steering column. The switch is actuated by a rod and rack assembly. A gear on the end of the lock cylinder engages the toothed upper end of the actuator rod.

REMOVAL AND INSTALLATION

1. Remove the lower instrument panel-to-steering column cover. Remove the steering column-to-dash bolts and lower the steering column; be sure to properly support it.

2. Place the ignition switch in the Locked position.

NOTE: *If the lock cylinder was removed, the actuating rod should be pulled up until it stops, then moved down one detent; the switch is now in the Lock position.*

3. Remove the two ignition switch-to-steering column screws and the switch assembly.

4. Before installing the ignition switch, place it in the Locked position, then make sure that the lock cylinder and actuating rod are in the Locked position (1st detent from the top).

5. Install the activating rod into the ignition switch and assemble the switch onto the steering column. Torque the ignition switch-to-steering column screws to 35 inch lbs.

NOTE: *When installing the ignition switch, use only the specified screws since overlength screws could impair the collapsibility of the column.*

6. To complete the installation, install the steering column and the lower instrument panel cover. Torque the steering column-to-instrument bolts to 22 ft. lbs.

Ignition Lock Cylinder

REMOVAL AND INSTALLATION

1. Disconnect the negative battery cable. Refer to the "Combination Switch, Removal and Installation" procedures in this Chapter and remove the combination switch.

2. Place the lock cylinder in the **Run** position.

1. Retainer	21. Bushing, bearing retaining
2. Nut, hexagon	22. Contact, horn circuit
3. Cover, shaft lock	23. Retainer, upper bearing
4. Ring, retaining	24. Switch assy, pivot &
5. Lock, steering shaft	25. Bolt assy, spring &
6. Cam assy, turn signal cancelling	26. Spring, rack preload
7. Spring, upper bearing	27. Rack assy, switch actuator rod &
8. Screw, binding head cross recess	28. Cover, housing
9. Screw, round washer head	29. Screw, binding head cross recess
10. Arm assy, switch actuator	30. Screw, flat head cross recess
11. Switch assy, turn signal	31. Gate, shift lever
12. Screw, hex washer head tapping	32. Washer, spring thrust
13. Washer, thrust	33. Pin, switch actuator pivot
16. Screw, lock retaining	34. Protector, wiring
17. Housing, steering column	35. Switch assy, ignition
18. Sector assy, switch actuator	36. Stud, dimmer & ignition switch mounting
19. Lock cylinder set, steering column	37. Screw, washer head
20. Bearing assy	38. Spring, upper shift lever

39. Bowl, gearshift lever
40. Shroud, gearshift bowl
41. Bearing, bowl lower
42. Jacket assy, steering column
43. Rod, dimmer switch actuator
44. Switch assy, dimmer
45. Nut, hexagon
46. Ring, retaining
47. Shaft assy, steering
48. Tube assy, shift
54. Seal, dash
55. Washer spring thrust
56. Spring shift tube return
57. Adapter, lower bearing
58. Bearing assembly
59. Retainer bearing adapter
60. Clip, lower bearing adapter

Standard steering column components

Ignition lock cylinder replacement

3. Remove the buzzer switch, the lock cylinder screw and the lock cylinder.

CAUTION: *If the screw is dropped upon removal, it could fall into the steering column, requiring complete disassembly to retrieve the screw.*

4. To install, rotate the lock cylinder clockwise to align the cylinder key with the keyway in the housing.

5. Push the lock cylinder all the way in.

6. Install the cylinder lock-to-housing screw. Tighten the screw to 14 inch lbs.

1. Retainer
2. Nut, hexagon jam
3. Cover, shaft lock
4. Ring, retaining
5. Lock, steering shaft
6. Cam assy, turn signal cancelling
7. Spring, upper bearing
8. Screw, binding head cross recess
9. Screw, round washer head
10. Arm assy, switch actuator
11. Switch assy, turn signal
12. Screw, hex washer head tapping
13. Washer, thrust
16. Screw, lock retaining
17. Housing, steering column
18. Sector assy, switch actuator
19. Lock cylinder set, steering column
20. Bearing assy
21. Bushing, bearing retaining
22. Retainer, upper bearing
23. Switch assy, pivot &
24. Bolt assy, spring &
25. Spring, rack preload
26. Rack, switch actuator

27. Rod, switch actuator
28. Washer, spring thrust
29. Pin, switch actuator pivot
30. Washer, wave
31. Lever, key release
32. Spring, key release
33. Protector, wiring
34. Stud, dimmer and ignition switch mounting
35. Screw, washer head
36. Switch assy, ignition
37. Bowl, floor shift
38. Shroud, shift bowl
39. Screw, binding head cross recess
40. Rod, dimmer switch actuator
41. Switch assy, dimmer
42. Nut, hexagon
43. Jacket assy, steering column
47. Ring, retaining
48. Shaft assy, steering
49. Bushing assy. steering shaft
50. Retainer, bearing adapter
51. Clip, lower bearing adapter
54. Bracket assy, column dash

Key release standard steering column components

1. Bearing assy
2. Lever, shoe release
3. Pin, release lever
4. Spring, release lever
5. Spring, shoe
6. Pin, pivot
7. Pin, dowel
8. Shaft, drive
9. Shoe, steering wheel lock
10. Shoe, steering wheel lock
11. Bolt, lock
12. Bearing assy
14. Actuator, dimmer switch rod
15. Lock cylinder set, strg column
16. Cover, lock housing
17. Screw, lock retaining
20. Screw, pan head cross recess
21. Race, inner
22. Seat, upper bearing inner race
23. Switch assy, turn signal
24. Arm assy, signal switch
25. Screw, round washer head
26. Retainer
27. Nut, hex jam
28. Cover, shaft lock
29. Ring, retaining
30. Lock, shaft
31. Cam assy, turn signal cancelling
32. Spring, upper bearing
33. Screw, binding head cross recess
34. Protector, wiring
35. Spring, pin preload
36. Switch assy, pivot &
37. Pin, switch actuator pivot
38. Cap, column housing cover end
39. Retainer, spring
40. Spring, wheel tilt
41. Guide, spring
42. Spring, lock bolt
43. Screw, hex washer head
44. Sector, switch actuator
45. Housing, steering column
46. Spring, rack preload
47. Rack, switch actuator
48. Actuator assy, ignition switch
49. Bowl, gearshift lever
50. Spring, shift lever
51. Washer, wave
52. Plate, lock
53. Washer, thrust
54. Ring, shift tube retaining
55. Screw, oval head cross recess
56. Gate, shift lever
57. Support, strg column housing
58. Screw, support
59. Pin, dowel
60. Shaft assy, lower steering
61. Sphere, centering
62. Spring, joint preload
63. Shaft assy, race & upper
64. Screw, washer head
65. Stud, dimmer & ignition switch mounting
66. Switch assy, ignition
67. Rod, dimmer switch
68. Switch assy, dimmer
69. Jacket assy, steering column
70. Tube assy, shift
74. Nut, hexagon
75. Shroud, gearshift bowl
76. Seal, dash
77. Bushing assy, steering shaft
78. Retainer, bearing adapter
79. Clip, lower bearing adapter

Tilt steering column components

36. Rack, switch actuator
37. Spring, rack preload
38. Housing, steering column
39. Sector, switch actuator
40. Screw, hex washer head
41. Guide, spring
42. Spring, wheel tilt
43. Retainer, spring
44. Cap, column housing cover end
45. Pin, switch actuator pivot
46. Switch assy, pivot &
47. Spring, pin preload
48. Switch assy, ignition
49. Stud, dimmer & ignition switch mounting
50. Screw, washer head
51. Plate, shroud retaining
52. Screw, oval head cross recess
53. Pin, dowel
54. Protector, wiring
55. Shaft assy, race & upper
56. Sphere, centering
57. Spring, joint preload
58. Shaft assy, lower steering
59. Screw, support
60. Support, steering column housing
61. Plate, lock
62. Finger pad, release lever
63. Lever, key release
64. Spring, key release
65. Shroud, steering column housing
66. Rod, dimmer switch
67. Switch assy, dimmer
68. Nut, hexagon
69. Jacket assy, steering column
73. Bushing assy, steering shaft
74. Retainer, bearing adapter
75. Clip, lower bearing adapter
80. Bracket assy, column dash

1. Retainer
2. Nut, hexagon jam
3. Cover, shaft lock
4. Ring, retaining
5. Lock, shaft
6. Cam assy, turn signal cancelling
7. Spring, upper bearing
8. Screw, binding head cross recess
9. Screw, round washer head
10. Arm assy, signal switch
11. Switch assy, turn signal
12. Seat, upper bearing inner race
13. Race, inner
14. Screw, pan head cross recess
17. Screw, lock retaining
18. Cover, lock housing
19. Lock cylinder set, steering column
20. Actuator, dimmer switch rod
22. Bearing assy
23. Bolt, lock
24. Spring, lock bolt
25. Shoe, steering wheel lock
26. Shoe, steering wheel lock
27. Shaft, drive
28. Pin, dowel
29. Pin, pivot
30. Spring, shoe
31. Spring, release lever
32. Pin, release lever
33. Lever, shoe release
34. Bearing assy
35. Actuator assy, ignition switch

Tilt steering column with key release components

1. Steering column
2. Support bracket
3. Seal
4. Nut
5. Bolt
6. Screws

Steering column removal

Pot joint angle not to exceed 12.5 degrees

Steering Linkage

The steering linkage consists of: a forward mounted linkage, crimp nuts at the inner pivots, castellated nuts at the steering knuckle arm, an idler arm, a steering gear pitman arm, a relay rod and a steering damper (manual steering). Grease fittings are equipped with each joint, for durability.

REMOVAL AND INSTALLATION

Pitman Arm

NOTE: *The following procedure requires the use of the GM Steering Linkage Puller tool No. J-24319-01 or equivalent, the GM Pitman Arm Remover tool No. J-6632 or equivalent, and the GM Steering Linkage Installer tool No. J-29193 (12mm) or J-29194 (14mm) or equivalent.*

1. Raise and safely support the front frame of the vehicle on jackstands.
2. Disconnect the nut from the pitman arm ball joint stud.
3. Using the GM Steering Linkage Puller tool No. J-24319-01 or equivalent, separate the relay rod from the pitman arm. Pull down on the relay rod and separate it from the stud.
4. Remove the pitman arm-to-pitman shaft nut, mark the relationship the arm to the shaft. Using the GM Pitman Arm Remover tool No. J-6632 or equivalent, separate the pitman arm from the pitman shaft.

NOTE: *When separating the pitman arm from the shaft, DO NOT use a hammer or apply heat to the arm.*

Steering linkage

5. To install, align the pitman arm-to-pitman shaft matchmark and the pitman shaft nut; torque the pitman arm-to-pitman shaft nut to 185 ft. lbs.
6. Connect the pitman arm to the relay rod ball stud (make sure that the seal is on the stud). Using the GM Steering Linkage Installer tool No. J-29193 (12mm) or J-29194 (14mm) or equivalent, install the correct one onto the ball stud and torque it to 40 ft. lbs. to seat the taper.
7. After seating, remove the tool, install the lock washer and nut and torque to 60 ft. lbs.

Idler Arm

NOTE: *The following procedure requires the use of the GM Steering Linkage Puller tool No. J-24319-01 or equivalent, the GM Steering Linkage Installer tool No. J-29193 (12mm) or J-29194 (14mm) or equivalent, and a spring scale.*

1. Raise and safely support the front frame of the vehicle on jackstands.

NOTE: *Jerking the right wheel assembly back and forth is not an acceptable testing procedure; there is no control on the amount of force being applied to the idler arm. Before suspecting idler arm shimmying complaints, check the wheels for imbalance, runout, force variation and/or road surface irregularities.*

2. To inspect for a defective idler arm, perform the following procedures:

   a. Position the wheels in the straight ahead position.

   b. Using a spring scale, position it near the relay rod end of the idler arm, then exert 25 lbs. of force upward and then downward.

   c. Measure the distance between the upward and downward directions that the idler arm moves. The allowable deflection is $1/8$ in. (3mm) for each direction; a total difference of $1/4$ in. (6mm); if the idler arm deflection is beyond the allowable limits, replace it.

3. Remove the idler arm-to-frame bolts and the idler arm-to-relay rod ball joint nut.

4. Using the GM Steering Linkage Puller tool No. J-24319-01 or equivalent, separate the relay rod from the ball joint stud.

5. Inspect and/or replace (if necessary) the idler arm.

6. Install the idler arm-to-frame bolts and torque them to 60 ft. lbs.

7. Connect the relay rod to the idler arm ball joint stud. Using the GM Steering Linkage Installer tool No. J-29193 (12mm) or J-29194 (14mm) or equivalent, seat (torque) the relay rod-to-idler arm ball joint stud to 40 ft. lbs., then remove the tool.

8. Install the idler arm-to-relay rod stud nut and torque it to 35 ft. lbs. (2WD) or 60 ft. lbs. (4WD).

9. Lower the vehicle. Check and/or adjust the toe-in.

Relay Rod

NOTE: *The following procedure requires the use of the GM Steering Linkage Puller tool No. J-24319-01 or equivalent, and the GM Steering Linkage Installer tool No. J-29193 (12mm) or J-29194 (14mm) or equivalent.*

1. Refer to the "Tie Rod, Removal and Installation" procedures in this Chapter and disconnect the inner tie rod ends from the relay rod.

2. Remove the idler arm stud-to-relay rod nut.

3. Using the GM Steering Linkage Puller tool No. J-24319-01 or equivalent, disconnect the relay rod from the idler arm, then remove the relay rod from the vehicle.

4. Clean and inspect the threads on the tie rod, the tie rod ends and the ball joints for damage, and replace them (if necessary). Inspect the ball joint seals for excessive wear, and replace them (if necessary).

5. To install, position the relay rod onto the idler arm (no mounting nut). Using the GM Steering Linkage Installer tool No. J-29193 (12mm) or J-29194 (14mm) or equivalent, install it onto the idler arm stud and torque the idler arm-to-relay rod stud nut to 35 ft. lbs. (to seat the taper). Remove the installer tool, then install the mounting nuts and torque the idler arm-to-relay arm stud nut to 35 ft. lbs. (2WD) or 60 ft. lbs. (4WD).

6. Position the inner tie rod ball joints onto the relay rod. Install the mounting nuts and torque the tie rod-to-relay rod stud nuts to 35 ft. lbs.

7. Lower the vehicle and check the steering linkage performance.

Tie Rod

NOTE: *The following procedure requires the use of the Steering Linkage Installer tool No. J-29193 (12mm) or J-29194 (14mm) or equivalent, and the GM Wheel Stud and Tie Rod Remover tool No. J-6627-A or equivalent.*

1. Raise and safely support the front frame of the vehicle on jackstands.

2. Remove the cotter pin from the tie rod-to-steering knuckle stud.

Pitman arm removal using the proper tool

Disconnecting the tie rod end with the proper tool

TIE ROD-INNER

RELAY ROD

CAUTION Clamp must be between & clear of dimples before torquing nut.

TIE ROD-OUTER

NOTE Equal within three threads, must be visible at inner and outer ends of adjuster sleeve when assembled to steering knuckle.

FWD

HORIZONTAL LINE

ADJUSTER SLEEVE SLOT

50°

FWD

10°

REARWARD ROTATION

NOTE Slot in adjuster sleeve must not be within this area of clamp jaws.

NOTE Locate clamps within tolerance shown.

.005" MIN. (.127 mm)

TIGHT

CAUTION Clamp ends may touch when nuts are torqued to specifications, but gap adjacent to adjuster sleeve must not be less than minimum dimension shown.

VIEW A

VIEW B

Tie rod clamp and sleeve positioning

S/ T-Model

1. Inner tie rod
2. Adjuster tube
3. Outer tie rod
4. Nut
5. Cotter pin
6. Nut
7. Bolts
9. Idler arm
10. Relay rod
12. Steering dampner
13. Pitman arm
14. Washer
15. Nut

Steering linkage with damper

3. Remove the tie rod-to-relay rod stud nut and the tie rod-to-steering knuckle stud nut.

NOTE: *DO NOT attempt to separate the tie rod-to-steering knuckle joint using a wedge type tool for seal damage could result.*

4. Using the GM Wheel Stud Remover tool No. J-6627-A or equivalent, separate the outer tie rod stud from the steering knuckle and the inner tie rod stud from the relay rod. Remove the tie rod from the vehicle.

5. If removing ONLY the tie rod end, perform the following procedures:

　a. Disconnect the defective ball joint end of the tie rod.

　b. Loosen the adjuster tube clamp bolt.

　c. Unscrew the tie rod end from the adjuster tube; count the number of turns necessary to remove the tie rod end.

　d. Clean, inspect and lubricate the adjuster tube threads.

　e. To install a new tie rod end, screw it into the adjuster tube using the same number of turns necessary to remove it.

　f. Position the clamp bolts between the adjuster tube dimples (located at each end) and in the proper location (see illustration). Torque the adjuster tube clamp bolt 13 ft. lbs.

6. To install, position the tie rod onto the steering knuckle and the relay rod. Using the Steering Linkage Installer tool No. J-29193 (12mm) or J-29194 (14mm) or equivalent, install them onto the studs and torque them to 35 ft. lbs. (to seat the tapers). After seating the tapers, remove the tool.

7. At the tie rod-to-steering knuckle stud, tighten the nut until the castle nut slot aligns with the hole in the stud, then install a new cotter pin.

8. Lower the vehicle and check the steering linkage performance.

Damper Assembly

The damper assembly is used to the remove steering wheel vibration and vehicle wonder; not all vehicles are equipped with it.

NOTE: *The following procedure requires the use of the Steering Linkage Puller tool No. J-24319-01 or equivalent.*

1. Raise and safely support the front frame of the vehicle on jackstands.

2. Remove the damper assembly-to-relay rod cotter pin and nut.

3. Using the Steering Linkage Puller tool No. J-24319-01 or equivalent, separate the damper assembly from the relay rod.

4. Remove the damper assembly-to-bracket nut/bolt and the damper assembly from the vehicle.

5. If necessary, use a new damper assembly and reverse the removal procedures. Torque the damper assembly-to-bracket nut/bolt to 26 ft. lbs. and the damper assembly-to-relay rod nut to 45 ft. lbs. Align the castle nut slot with the hole in the ball joint stud and install a new cotter pin.

Manual Steering Gear

The recirculating ball type manual steering gear is manufactured by Saginaw and is equipped with a mechanical ratio of 24:1.

ADJUSTMENTS

NOTE: *The following procedure requires the use the GM Steering Linkage Puller tool No. J-6632 or equivalent, and a 0-50 inch lbs. torque wrench.*

1. Disconnect the negative battery cable from the battery.

2. Raise and safely support the front frame of the vehicle on jackstands.

NOTE: *Before adjustments are made to the steering gear, be sure to check the front end alignment, the shock absorbers, the wheel balance and the tire pressure.*

3. Remove the pitman arm-to-pitman shaft nut and matchmark the pitman arm to the pitman shaft. Using the GM Steering Linkage Puller tool No. J-6632 or equivalent, remove the pitman arm from the pitman shaft.

4. Loosen the steering gear adjuster plug locknut and back-off the adjuster plug 1/4 turn.

5. From the steering wheel, remove the horn cap or cover.

6. Gently, turn the steering wheel (in one direction) to the stop; then, turn it back 1/2 turn.

NOTE: *When the steering linkage is disconnected from the steering gear, DO NOT turn the steering wheel hard against the stops for damage to the ball guides may result.*

7. Using a torque wrench (0-50 inch lbs.), position it onto the steering wheel nut, then measure and record the bearing drag. To meas-

Manual steering gear adjustment points

Measure steering wheel rotation effort

ure the bearing drag, use the torque wrench to rotate the steering wheel 90°.

8. Using a torque wrench (0-50 inch lbs.), tighten the adjuster plug (on the steering gear) to obtain a thrust bearing preload of 5-8 inch lbs. After the thrust bearing preload is obtained, torque the adjuster plug locknut to 25 ft. lbs.

NOTE: *If the steering gear feels lumpy (after adjustment), suspect damage to the bearings, probably due to the improper adjustment or severe impact.*

9. To adjust the overcenter preload, perform the following procedures:

a. Turn the steering wheel, from one stop all the way to the other stop, counting the number of turns. Turn the steering wheel back exactly 1/2 way, to the center position.

b. Turn the overcenter adjusting screw clockwise, until the lash is removed between the ball nut and the pitman shaft sector teeth, then tighten the locknut.

c. Using a torque wrench (0-50 inch lbs.), check the highest force necessary to turn the steering wheel through the center position; the usable torque is 4-10 inch lbs.

Steering gear mounting

d. If necessary, loosen the locknut and readjust the overcenter adjusting screw to obtain the proper torque. Retorque the locknut to 25 ft. lbs. and recheck the steering wheel torque through the center of travel.

NOTE: *If the maximum is too high, turn the overcenter adjuster screw counterclockwise, then torque the adjuster lock nut in the clockwise motion to achieve the proper torque.*

10. To install, realign the pitman arm-to-pitman shaft, torque the pitman shaft nut to 185 ft. lbs.

REMOVAL AND INSTALLATION

NOTE: *The following procedure requires the use of the GM Pitman Arm Remover tool No. J-6632 or equivalent.*

1. Disconnect the negative battery cable from the battery.

2. Raise and safely support the front frame of the vehicle on jackstands. Position the wheel in the straight ahead direction.

3. Remove the intermediate shaft-to-steering gear pinch bolt.

4. Remove the pitman arm-to-pitman shaft nut, mark the relationship the arm to the shaft. Using the GM Pitman Arm Remover tool No. J-6632 or equivalent, separate the pitman arm from the pitman shaft.

NOTE: *When separating the pitman arm from the shaft, DO NOT use a hammer or apply heat to the arm.*

5. Remove the steering gear-to-frame bolts and the gear from the vehicle.

NOTE: *When installing the steering gear, be sure that the intermediate shaft bottoms on the worm shaft, so that the pinch bolt passes through the undercut on the worm shaft. Check and/or adjust the alignment of the pitman arm-to-pitman shaft.*

6. To install, align the matchmarks and reverse the removal procedures. Torque the steering gear-to-frame bolts to 60 ft. lbs., the pitman arm-to-pitman shaft nut to 185 ft. lbs. and the intermediate steering shaft-to-steering gear bolt to 30 ft. lbs.

Power Steering Gear

The recirculating ball type power steering gear is basically the same as the manual steering gear, except that it uses a hydraulic assist on the rack piston.

The power steering gear control valve directs the power steering fluid to either side of the rack piston, which rides up and down the worm shaft. The steering rack converts the hydraulic pressure into mechanical force. Should the vehicle loose the hydraulic pressure, it can still be controlled mechanically.

Removing the adjuster plug lock nut from the power steering gear

A. Index mark

Marking the housing with the adjuster plug hole

ADJUSTMENTS

NOTE: *To perform adjustments to the power steering gear, it is recommended to remove the power steering gear from the vehicle and place it in a vise. Before adjustments are performed to the system, be sure to check problems relating to hydraulic pressures and performance.*

Worm Bearing Preload

NOTE: *The following procedure requires the use of the GM Adjustable Spanner Wrench tool No. J-7624 or equivalent.*

1. Refer to the "Power Steering Gear, Removal and Installation" procedures in this Chapter, remove the steering gear from the vehicle and position it in a vise.

2. Using a hammer and a brass punch, drive the adjuster plug lock nut counterclockwise and remove it from the end of the steering gear.

3. Using the GM Adjustable Spanner Wrench tool No. J-7624 or equivalent, turn the adjuster plug inward, until it firmly bottoms in the housing with a torque of 20 ft. lbs.

4. Using a scribing tool, place a matchmark (on the housing) next to the one of the spanner wrench holes in the adjuster plug.

5. Using a ruler, measure $1/2$ in. (12.7mm) counterclockwise from the scribed mark (on the housing) and place another mark.

6. Using the GM Adjustable Spanner Wrench tool No. J-7624 or equivalent, turn the adjuster plug (counterclockwise) until the hole in the adjuster plug aligns with the 2nd scribed mark.

7. While holding the adjuster plug in alignment, install and tighten the adjuster plug lock nut.

8. Perform the overcenter preload adjustment.

Overcenter Preload

1. Refer to the "Power Steering Gear, Removal and Installation" procedures in this Chapter, remove the steering gear from the vehicle and position it in a vise.

A. First index mark
B. Second index mark

Using the spanner to align the adjuster plug with the second mark

B. Second index mark

Make the second index mark

C. Adjuster screw
D. Master spline on the Pitman shaft

Align the pitman arm shaft master spline

A. Stub shaft flat
B. Side cover

Alining the stub shaft with the side cover

2. Rotate the stud shaft from stop-to-stop and count the number of turns necessary.

3. Starting from one stop, turn the stub shaft back $1/2$ the number of turns (center of the gear).

NOTE: *With the stub gear centered, the flat on top of the shaft should face upward and be parallel with the side cover; the master spline on the pitman shaft should be in line with the adjuster screw.*

4. Loosen the pitman shaft adjuster screw locknut and turn the adjuster screw counterclockwise until it is fully extended, then turn it clockwise one full turn.

5. Using a torque wrench (0-50 inch lbs.), position it onto the stub shaft, rotate it 45° (to each side) and record the highest drag measured near or on the center.

6. Turn the adjuster screw inward until the torque on the stub shaft is 6-10 inch lbs. greater than the initial reading.

7. Install the adjuster screw jam nut and torque it to 20 ft. lbs. Reinstall the power steering gear into the vehicle.

REMOVAL AND INSTALLATION

1. Refer to the "Pitman Arm, Removal and Installation" procedures in this Chapter and disconnect the pitman arm from the power steering gear.

2. Position a fluid catch pan under the power steering gear.

3. At the power steering gear, disconnect and plug the pressure hoses; any excess fluid will be caught by the catch pan.

NOTE: *Be sure to plug the pressure hoses and the openings of the power steering pump to keep dirt out of the system.*

4. Remove the intermediate shaft-to-steering gear bolt. Matchmark the intermediate shaft-to-power steering gear and separate the shaft from the gear.

A. Center line

Reading over center rotation torque

5. Remove the power steering gear-to-frame bolts, washers and the steering gear from the vehicle.

6. To install, reverse the removal procedures. Torque the power steering gear-to-frame bolts to 55 ft. lbs., the intermediate shaft-to-power steering gear bolt to 30 ft. lbs. and the pitman arm-to-pitman shaft nut to 185 ft. lbs.

7. Connect the pressure hoses to the power steering gear, refill the power steering reservoir and bleed the power steering system.

8. Road test the vehicle.

Power Steering Pump

Two types of power steering pumps are offered, they are: The submerged and the non-submerged. The submerged pump has a housing and internal parts which are inside the res-

NONSUBMERGED   SUBMERGED

Two pumps are in production

Removing the power steering pump pulley

ervoir and operate submerged in oil. The non-submerged pump functions the same as the submerged pump except the reservoir is separate from the housing and internal parts.

REMOVAL AND INSTALLATION

NOTE: *The following procedure requires the use of the GM Puller tool No. J-29785-A or equivalent, and the GM Pulley Installer tool No. J-25033-B or equivalent.*

1. Position a fluid catch pan under the power steering pump.

2. Remove the pressure hoses from the power steering pump and drain the excess fluid into the catch pan.

NOTE: *On models equipped with a remote fluid reservoir, disconnect and plug the hose(s).*

3. Loosen the power steering pump adjusting bolt, the washer and the pivot bolt, then remove the drive belt.

4. Using the GM Puller tool No. J-29785-A or equivalent, install it onto the power steering pump pulley. While holding the tool body, turn the pilot bolt counterclockwise to press the drive pulley from the pump.

NOTE: *When installing the puller tool onto the power steering pump pulley, be sure that the pilot bolt bottoms in the pump shaft by turning the head of the pilot bolt.*

5. Remove the power steering pump-to-bracket bolts and the pump from the vehicle.

6. To install, reverse the removal proce-

dures. Torque the power steering pump-to-bracket bolts to 18 ft. lbs.

7. Using the GM Pulley Installer tool No. J-25033-B or equivalent, press the drive pulley onto the power steering pump. While holding the tool body, turn the pilot bolt clockwise to press the drive pulley onto the pump.

NOTE: *When installing the installer tool onto the power steering pump pulley, be sure that the pilot bolt bottoms in the pump shaft by turning the head of the pilot bolt.*

8. Hand tighten the pivot bolt, the adjusting bolt and the washer.

9. Install the drive belt and adjust the drive belt tension. Torque the mounting bolts and nut to 36 ft. lbs. (submerged type) or 20 ft. lbs. (nonsubmerged type). Install the pressure hoses (to the pump), refill the power steering reservoir and bleed the system.

NOTE: *Be sure to secure any hoses which may get in the way or rub other components.*

10. Test drive the vehicle.

SYSTEM BLEEDING

1. Run the engine until the power steering fluid reaches normal operating temperature, approximately 170°F (76°C), then shut the engine Off. Remove the reservoir filler cap and check the oil level.

2. If the oil level is low, add power steering fluid to proper level and replace the filler cap. When adding or making a complete fluid

Installing the pulley

TOOL MUST BOTTOM IN PUMP SHAFT

Installing pilot bolt

change, always use GM No. 1050017 or equivalent, power steering fluid. DO NOT use transmission fluid.

3. Start the engine and turn the wheels in both directions (to the stops) several times. Stop the engine and add power steering fluid to the level indicated on the reservoir.

NOTE: *Maintain the fluid level just above the internal pump casting. Fluid with air in it will have a light tan or milky appearance. This air must be eliminated from the fluid before normal steering action can be obtained.*

4. Return the wheels to the center position and continue to run it for 2-3 minutes, then shut the engine Off.

5. Road test the vehicle to make sure the

Installing the puller

steering functions normally and is free from noise.

6. Allow the vehicle to stand for 2-3 hours, then recheck the power steering fluid.

9

BRAKE SYSTEM

These trucks are equipped with independent front and rear brake systems. The systems consist of a power booster, a master cylinder, a combination valve, front disc and rear drum assemblies.

The master cylinder, mounted on the left-firewall or power booster, consists of two fluid reservoirs, a primary (rear) cylinder, a secondary (front) cylinder and springs. The reservoirs, being independent of one another, are contained within the same housing; fluid cannot pass from one to the other. The rear reservoir supplies fluid to the front brakes while the front reservoir supplies fluid to the rear brakes.

During operation, fluid drains from the reservoirs to the master cylinder. When the brake pedal is applied, fluid from the master cylinder is sent to the combination valve (mounted on a bracket, directly under the master cylinder), here it is monitored and proportionally distributed to the front or rear brake systems. Should a loss of pressure occur in one system, the other system will provide enough braking pressure to stop the vehicle. Also, should a loss of pressure in one system occur, the differential warning switch (located on the combination valve) will turn ON the brake warning light (located on the dash board).

As the fluid enters each brake caliper or wheel cylinder, the pistons are forced outward. The outward movement of the pistons force the brake pads against a round flat disc or the brake shoes against a round metal drum. The brake lining attached to the pads or shoes comes in contact with the revolving disc or drum, causing friction, which brings the wheel to a stop.

In time, the brake linings wear down. If not replaced, their metal support plates (bonded type) or rivet heads (riveted type) will come in contact with the disc or drum; damage to the disc or drum will occur. Never use brake pads or shoes with a lining thickness less than $\frac{1}{32}$ in. (0.8mm).

Most manufacturers provide a wear sensor, a piece of spring steel, attached to the rear edge of the inner brake pad. When the pad wears to the replacement thickness, the sensor will contact the disc and produce a high pitched squeal.

Adjustments

FRONT DISC BRAKES

Disc brakes are not adjustable. They are, in effect, self adjusting.

ADJUSTMENT OF REAR BRAKES

Normal adjustments of the rear drum brakes are automatic and are made during the reverse applications of the brakes. ONLY, if the lining has been renewed, should the following procedure be performed.

NOTE: *The following procedure requires the use of the GM Brake Adjustment tool No. J-4735 or equivalent.*

INSERT SMALL SCREWDRIVER OR AWL THROUGH BACKING PLATE SLOT AND HOLD ADJUSTER LEVER AWAY FROM SPROCKET BEFORE BACKING OFF BRAKE SHOE ADJUSTMENT

Adjusting the rear brake star wheel

1. Raise and support the vehicle safely.

2. Using a punch and a hammer, at the rear of the backing plate, knock out the lanced metal area near the starwheel assembly.

NOTE: *When knocking out the lanced metal area from the backing plate, the wheels must be removed and all of the metal pieces discarded.*

3. Using the GM Brake Adjustment tool No. J-4735 or equivalent, insert it into the slot and engage the lowest possible tooth on the starwheel. Move the end of the brake tool downward to move the starwheel upward and expand the adjusting screw. Repeat this operation until the brakes just lock the wheel.

4. Insert a small screwdriver or piece of firm wire (coat hanger wire) into the adjusting slot and push the automatic adjuster lever out and free of the starwheel on the adjusting screw.

5. While holding the adjusting lever out of the way, engage the top-most tooth possible on the starwheel (with the brake tool). Move the end of the adjusting tool upward to move the adjusting screw starwheel downward and contact the adjusting screw. Back off the adjusting screw starwheel until the wheel spins freely with a minimum of drag. Keep track of the number of turns the starwheel is backed off.

6. Repeat this operation for the other side. When backing off the brakes on the other side, the adjusting lever must be backed off the same number of turns to prevent side-to-side brake pull.

NOTE: *Backing off the starwheel 12 notches (clicks) is usually enough to eliminate brake drag.*

7. Repeat this operation on the other side of the rear brake system.

8. After the brakes are adjusted, install a rubber hole cover into the backing plate slot. To complete the brake adjustment operation, make several stops while backing the truck to equalize the adjustment.

9. Road test the vehicle.

BRAKE PEDAL TRAVEL

The brake pedal travel is the distance the pedal moves toward the floor from the fully released position. Inspection should be made with 100 lbs. pressure on the brake pedal, when the brake system is Cold. The brake pedal travel should be $4^3/4$ in. (120mm) for manual, or $2^1/2$ in. (61mm) for power.

NOTE: *If equipped with power brakes, be sure to pump the brake pedal at least 3 times with the engine Off, before making the brake pedal check.*

1. From under the dash, remove the pushrod-to-pedal clevis pin and separate the

311. Urethane adhesive
333. Window frame pinchweld
334. Glass assembly
335. Clip

Adjusting the brake light switch

pushrod from the brake pedal.

2. Loosen the pushrod adjuster lock nut, then adjust the pushrod.

3. After the correct travel is established, reverse the removal procedure.

Brake Light Switch

REMOVAL AND INSTALLATION

1. Remove the negative battery cable.

2. Disconnect the electrical connector from the brake light switch.

3. Turn the brake light switch retainer (to align the key with the bracket slot), then remove the switch with the retainer.

4. Installation is the reverse of removal. Adjust the brake light switch.

ADJUSTMENT

1. Depress the brake pedal and press the brake light switch inward until it seats firmly against the clip.

NOTE: *As the switch is being pushed into the clip, audible clicks can be heard.*

2. Release the brake pedal, then pull it back against the pedal stop until the audible click can no longer be heard.

3. The brake light switch will operate when the pedal is depressed 0.53 in. (13mm) from the fully released position.

Master Cylinder

REMOVAL AND INSTALLATION

1. Apply the parking brakes and block the wheels.

2. Use a line wrench to disconnect the hydraulic lines from the master cylinder. Plug the lines to prevent contamination.

RESERVOIR COVER

RESERVOIR DIAPHRAGM

RESERVOIR

RESERVOIR GROMMET

QUICK TAKE-UP VALVE (NOT SERVICEABLE)

SPRING RETAINER

PRIMARY SEAL

SECONDARY PISTON

SECONDARY SEAL

MASTER CYLINDER BODY

SPRING

SECONDARY PISTON ASSEMBLY

PRIMARY PISTON ASSEMBLY

LOCK RING

Master cylinder exploded view

3. If equipped with non-power brakes, disconnect the pushrod from the brake pedal.

4. Remove the master cylinder attachment nuts, then separate the combination valve/bracket from the master cylinder.

5. Remove the master cylinder, the gasket and the rubber boot from the vehicle.

To install:

6. Fill the master cylinder with new brake fluid and operate the pushrod to bench bleed the master cylinder.

7. Install the master cylinder and torque the mounting nuts to 20 ft. lbs.

8. Install the combination valve and connect the brake lines. Torque the line nuts to 120 in. lbs. (13.5 Nm).

9. Refill the master cylinder with clean brake fluid, bleed the brake system and check the brake pedal travel.

PUSH ROD   SEAL

COVER

WITHOUT J-50

NUT
14-34 N•m

NUTS

POWER BOOSTER

MASTER CYLINDER

NUT
20-34 N•m

WITH J-50

Master cylinder attachment

NOTE: *If equipped with manual brakes, be sure to reconnect the pushrod to the brake pedal.*

OVERHAUL

1. Remove the master cylinder from the vehicle.

2. At the rear of the master cylinder, depress the primary piston and remove the lock ring.

3. Block the rear outlet hole on the master cylinder. Using compressed air, gently direct it into the front outlet hole to remove the primary and secondary pistons from the master cylinder. If compressed air is not available, use a hooked wire to pull out the secondary piston.

CAUTION: *If using compressed air to remove the pistons from the master cylinder, DO NOT stand in front of the pistons, for too much air will cause the pistons to be fired from the master cylinder, causing bodily harm.*

4. From the secondary piston, remove the spring retainer and the seals.

5. Using the mounting flange (ear) on the master cylinder, clamp it into a vise.

6. Using a medium pry bar, pry the reservoirs from the master cylinder. Remove the reservoir grommets.

NOTE: *DO NOT attempt to remove the quick take-up valve from the master cylinder body; the valve is not serviceable separately.*

7. Using denatured alcohol, clean and blow dry all of the master cylinder parts.

8. Inspect the master cylinder bore for corrosion or scratches; if damaged, replace the master cylinder with a new one.

To install:

9. Use new reservoir grommets (lubricated with brake fluid) and press them into the master cylinder body. Install new seals onto the primary and secondary pistons.

10. Position the reservoirs on flat, hard surfaces (block of wood), then press the master cylinder onto the reservoirs, using a rocking motion.

11. Using heavy duty brake fluid, meeting DOT 3 specifications, lubricate the primary and secondary pistons, then install them into the master cylinder. While depressing the primary piston, install the lock ring.

12. Install new diaphragms onto the reservoir covers.

13. Install the master cylinder on the vehicle, fill with new brake fluid and bleed the brakes.

Power Brake Booster

The power brake booster is a tandem vacuum suspended unit, equipped with a single or dual function vacuum switch that activates a brake warning light should low booster vacuum be present. Under normal operation, vacuum is present on both sides of the diaphragms. When the brakes are applied, atmospheric air is admitted to one side of the diaphragms to provide power assistance.

REMOVAL AND INSTALLATION

1. Apply the parking brake and block the wheels.

2. Remove the master cylinder-to-power brake booster nuts and move the master cylinder out of the way; if necessary, support the master cylinder on a wire.

NOTE: *When removing the master cylinder from the power brake booster, it is not necessary to disconnect the hydraulic lines.*

3. Disconnect the vacuum hose from the power brake booster.

4. From under the dash, disconnect the pushrod from the brake pedal.

5. From under the dash, remove the power brake booster-to-cowl nuts.

4-cylinder engine vacuum lines

Power brake booster attachment

6-cylinder engine vacuum lines

6. From the engine compartment, remove the power brake booster and the gasket from the vehicle.

To install:

7. Install the booster to the firewall with a new gasket and torque the nuts to 15 ft. lbs. (20 Nm).

8. Connect the pedal pushrod.

9. Install the master cylinder, connect the vacuum hose and run the engine to test the system.

Combination Valve

The combination valve is located in the engine compartment, directly under the master cylinder. It consists of three sections: the metering valve, the warning switch and the proportioning valve.

The metering section limits the pressure to the front disc brakes until a predetermined

front input pressure is reached, enough to overcome the rear shoe retractor springs. Under 3 psi, there is no restriction of the inlet pressures; the pressures are allowed to equalize during the no brake period.

The proportioning section controls the outlet pressure to the rear brakes after a predetermined rear input pressure has been reached; this feature is provided for vehicles with light loads, to help prevent rear wheel lock-up. The by-pass feature of this valve assures full system pressure to the rear brakes in the event of a front brake system malfunction. Also, full front pressure is retained if the rear system malfunctions.

The pressure differential warning switch is designed to constantly compare the front and the rear brake pressures; if one should malfunc-

Combination valve

tion, the warning light (on the dash) will turn On. The valve and switch are designed to lock On the warning position once the malfunction has occurred. The only way the light can be turned Off is to repair the malfunction and apply a brake line force of 450 psi.

REMOVAL AND INSTALLATION

1. Disconnect and plug the hydraulic lines from the combination valve to prevent the loss of brake fluid or dirt from entering the system.

2. Disconnect the electrical connector from the combination valve.

3. Remove the combination valve-to-bracket nuts and the combination valve from the vehicle.

NOTE: *The combination valve is not repairable and must be replaced as a complete assembly.*

4. Using a new combination valve (if defective), torque the combination valve-to-bracket

nuts to 12 ft. lbs. Reconnect the electrical connector to the combination valve.

5. Bleed the brake system.

Brake Pipes and Hoses

REMOVAL AND INSTALLATION

Flexible Hoses

Flexible hoses are installed between the frame-to-front calipers and the frame-to-rear differential.

1. Using a wire brush, clean the dirt and/or grease from both ends of the hose fittings.

2. Disconnect the steel pipes from the flexible hose.

3. To remove the brake hose from the front brake caliper or the rear differential, perform the following procedures:

  a. Remove the brake hose-to-frame bracket retaining clip.

Rear brake hoses

Front brake hoses

A. Single flare
B. Double flare
Single and double flare tube ends

  b. Remove the brake hose-to-brake caliper or differential junction block bolt.

  c. Remove the brake hose and the gaskets from the vehicle.

NOTE: *After disconnecting the brake hose(s) from the fittings, be sure to plug the fittings to keep the fluid from discharging or dirt from entering the system.*

  5. Clean and inspect the brake hose(s) for cracking, chafing or road damage; replace the hose(s) if any signs are observed.

  6. When installing the flexible hose, and torque the hose–to–steel pipe fitting to 13 ft. lbs.

  7. Use new copper gaskets to install the hose to the front caliper and torque the fitting to 32 ft. lbs.

  8. Install the line retaining clips and bleed the brake system.

NOTE: *Be sure that the hoses do not make contact with any of the suspension components.*

Steel Pipes

When replacing the steel brake pipes, always use steel piping which is designed to withstand high pressure, resist corrosion and is of the same size.

CAUTION: *Never use copper tubing. It is subject to fatigue, cracking, and/or corrosion, which will result in brake line failure.*

NOTE: *The following procedure requires the use of the GM Tube Cutter tool No. J-23533 or equivalent, and the GM Flaring tool No. J-23530 or equivalent.*

  1. Disconnect the steel brake pipe(s) from the flexible hose connections or the rear wheel cylinders; be sure to remove any retaining clips.

  2. Remove the steel brake pipe from the vehicle.

  3. Using new steel pipe (same size) and the GM Tube Cutter tool No. J-23533 or equivalent, cut the pipe to length; be sure to add $1/8$ in. (3mm) for each flare.

NOTE: *Be sure to install the correct pipe fittings onto the tube before forming any flares.*

  4. Using the Flaring tool No. J-23530 or equivalent, follow the instructions equipped with the tool to form double flares on the ends of the pipes.

  5. Using the small pipe bending tool, bend the pipe to match the contour of the pipe which was removed.

  6. Install the pipe and torque the fittings to 13 ft. lbs. Make sure the pipe is in the same place as the original and will not contact any suspension or other moving parts.

  7. Bleed the brake system.

Bleeding

WITHOUT ABS

The hydraulic brake system must be bled any time one of the lines is disconnected or any time air enters the system. If the brake pedal feels spongy upon application, and goes almost to the floor but regains height when pumped, air has entered the system. It must be bled out. Check for leaks that would have allowed the entry of air and repair them before bleeding the system. The correct bleeding sequence is; right-rear, left-rear, right-front and left-front.

CAUTION: *If the vehicle has rear wheel or 4 wheel anti–lock braking, do not use this procedure. Improper service procedures on anti–lock braking systems can cause serious personal injury. Refer to the ABS service procedures.*

MANUAL

This method of bleeding requires two people, one to depress the brake pedal and the other to open the bleeder screws.

NOTE: *The following procedure requires the use of a clear vinyl hose, a glass jar and*

BLEEDER WRENCH

BLEEDER TUBE J-7779-2

TUBE MUST BE SUBMERGED IN BRAKE FLUID

Brake bleeding

Pressure bleeding the brake system

Depressing the combination valve

clean brake fluid.

1. Clean the top of the master cylinder, remove the cover and fill the reservoirs with clean fluid. To prevent squirting fluid, replace the cover.

NOTE: *On vehicles equipped with front disc brakes, it will be necessary to hold in the metering valve pin during the bleeding procedure. The metering valve is located beneath the master cylinder and the pin is situated under the rubber boot on the end of the valve housing. This may be tapped in or held by an assistant.*

2. Fill the master cylinder with clean brake fluid.

3. Install a box end wrench onto the bleeder screw on the right rear wheel.

4. Attach a length of small diameter, clear vinyl tubing to the bleeder screw. Submerge the other end of the tubing in a glass jar partially filled with clean brake fluid. Make sure the tube fits on the bleeder screw snugly or you may be squirted with brake fluid when the bleeder screw is opened.

5. Have your assistant slowly depress the brake pedal. As this is done, open the bleeder screw ½ turn and allow the fluid to run through the tube. Close the bleeder screw, then return the brake pedal to its fully released position.

6. Repeat this procedure until no bubbles appear in the jar. Refill the master cylinder.

7. Repeat this procedure on the left-rear, right-front and the left-front wheels, in that order. Periodically, refill the master cylinder so that it does not run dry.

8. If the brake warning light is On, depress the brake pedal firmly. If there is no air in the system, the dash light will turn Off.

PRESSURE

NOTE: *The following procedure requires the use of the GM Brake Bleeder Adapter tool No. J-29567 or equivalent, and the GM Combination Valve Depressor tool No. J-23709 or equivalent.*

1. Using the GM Brake Bleeder Adapter tool No. J-29567 or equivalent, fill the pressure tank to at least ⅓ full of brake fluid. Using compressed air, charge the pressure tank to 20–25 psi., then install it onto the master cylinder.

2. Using the GM Combination Valve Depressor tool No. J-35856 or equivalent, install it onto the combination valve to hold the valve open during the bleeding operation.

3. Bleed each wheel cylinder or caliper in the following sequence: right-rear, left-rear, right-front and left-front.

4. Connect a hose from the bleeder tank to the adapter at the master cylinder, then open the tank valve.

5. Attach a clear vinyl hose to the brake bleeder screw, then immerse the opposite end into a container partially filled with clean brake fluid.

6. Open the bleeder screw ¾ turn and allow the fluid to flow until no air bubbles are seen in the fluid, then close the bleeder screw.

7. Repeat the bleeding process to each wheel.

8. Inspect the brake pedal for sponginess and if necessary, repeat the entire bleeding procedure.

9. Remove the depressor tool from the combination valve and the bleeder adapter from the master cylinder.

10. Refill the master cylinder to the proper level with brake fluid.

FRONT DISC BRAKES

CAUTION: *Brake shoes contain asbestos, which has been determined to be a cancer causing agent. Never clean the brake surfaces with compressed air! Avoid inhaling any dust from any brake surface! When cleaning brake surfaces, use a commercially available brake cleaning fluid.*

Brake Pads

INSPECTION

Brake pads should be inspected once a year or at 7,500 miles, which ever occurs first. Check both ends of the outboard shoe, looking in at each end of the caliper; then check the lining thickness on the inboard shoe, looking down through the inspection hole. The lining should be more than 0.032 in. (0.8mm) thick above the rivet (so that the lining is thicker than the metal backing). Keep in mind that any applicable state inspection standards that are more stringent, take precedence. All four pads must be replaced if one shows excessive wear.

NOTE: *All models have a wear indicator that makes a noise when the linings wear to a degree where replacement is necessary. The spring clip is an integral part of the inboard shoe and lining. When the brake pad reaches a certain degree of wear, the clip will contact the rotor and produce a warning noise.*

REMOVAL AND INSTALLATION

NOTE: *The following procedure requires the use of a C-clamp and channel lock pliers.*

1. If the fluid reservoir is full, siphon off about 2/3 of the brake fluid from the master cylinder reservoirs.

CAUTION: *The insertion of thicker replacement pads will push the piston back into its bore and will cause a full master cylinder reservoir to overflow, possibly causing paint damage. In addition to siphoning off fluid, it would be wise to keep the reservoir cover on during pad replacement.*

2. Raise and safely support the front of the vehicle on jackstands. Remove the wheels.

NEW SHOE & LINING   READY
                          FOR REPLACEMENT

New and worn brake pads

WEAR INDICATOR

NEW   WORN

Disk brake pad wear indicator operation

NOTE: *When replacing the pads on just one wheel, uneven braking will result; always replace the pads on both wheels.*

3. Install a C-clamp on the caliper so that the frame side of the clamp rests against the back of the caliper and so the screw end rests against the metal part (shoe) of the outboard pad.

4. Tighten the clamp until the caliper moves enough to bottom the piston in its bore. Remove the clamp.

5. Remove the two Allen head caliper mount-

Inspecting the front brake pads

Removing the pads from the caliper

Checking caliper-to-bracket stop clearance

Using a C-clamp to bottom the brake caliper piston

Suspending the caliper out of the way during brake servicing

Caliper mounting

ing bolts enough to allow the caliper to be pulled off the disc.

6. Remove the inboard pad and loosen the outboard pad. Place the caliper where it will not strain the brake hose; hang it from the suspension with wire.

7. Remove the pad support spring clip from the piston.

8. Remove the two bolt ear sleeves and the four rubber bushings from the ears.

9. Brake pads should be replaced when they are worn to within $\frac{1}{32}$ in. (0.8mm) of the rivet heads.

To install:

10. Check the inside of the caliper for leakage and the condition of the piston dust boot.

11. Lubricate the two new sleeves and four bushings with a silicone spray.

12. Install the bushings in each caliper ear. Install the two sleeves in the two inboard ears.

13. Install the pad support spring clip and the old pad into the center of the piston. You will then push this pad down to get the piston flat against the caliper. This part of the job is a hassle and requires an assistant. While the assistant holds the caliper and loosens the bleeder valve to relieve the pressure, obtain a medium pry bar and try to force the old pad inward, making the piston flush with the cali-

per surface. When it is flush, close the bleeder valve so that no air gets into the system.

NOTE: *Make sure that the wear sensor is facing toward the rear of the caliper.*

14. Place the outboard pad in the caliper with its top ears over the caliper ears and the bottom tab engaged in the caliper cutout.

15. After both pads are installed, lift the caliper and place the bottom edge of the outboard pad on the outer edge of the disc to make sure that there is no clearance between the tab on the bottom of the shoes and the caliper abutment.

16. Place the caliper over the disc, lining up the hole in the caliper ears with the hole in the

CALIPER HOUSING

SHOE RETAINER SPRING

Installing the pads in the caliper

SHOE RETAINER SPRING

INBOARD SHOE AND LINING

Installing the shoe retainer spring

mounting bracket. Make sure that the brake hose is not kinked.

17. Start the caliper-to-mounting bracket bolts through the sleeves in the inboard caliper ears and through the mounting bracket, making sure that the ends of the bolts pass under the retaining ears of the inboard shoe.

18. Push the mounting bolts through to engage the holes in the outboard shoes and the outboard caliper ears and then thread them into the mounting bracket.

19. Torque the mounting bolts to 37 ft. lbs. Pump the brake pedal to seat the linings against the rotors.

20. Using a pair of channel lock pliers, place them on the notch on the caliper housing, bend the caliper upper ears until no clearance exists between the shoe and the caliper housing.

21. Install the wheels, lower the vehicle and refill the master cylinder reservoirs with brake fluid. Pump the brake pedal to make sure that it is firm. If it is not, bleed the brakes.

Brake Caliper

REMOVAL AND INSTALLATION

1. Remove the brake caliper from the steering knuckle.

2. Disconnect the flexible brake hose-to-caliper bolt, discard the pressure fitting washers, then remove the brake caliper from the vehicle and place it on a work bench.

CHANNEL LOCK PLIERS

Seating the caliper

3. To inspect the caliper assembly, perform the following procedures:

a. Check the inside of the caliper assembly for signs of leakage; if necessary, replace or rebuild the caliper.

b. Check the mounting bolts and sleeves for signs of corrosion; if necessary, replace the bolts.

NOTE: *If the mounting bolts have signs of corrosion, DO NOT attempt to polish away the corrosion.*

4. Using new caliper bushings and sleeves, apply Delco® Silicone Lube or equivalent to lubricate the mounting bolts and new brake pads (if necessary).

5. After both pads are installed, lift the caliper and place the bottom edge of the outboard pad on the outer edge of the disc to make sure that there is no clearance between the tab on the bottom of the shoes and the caliper abutment.

6. Place the caliper over the disc, lining up the hole in the caliper ears with the hole in the mounting bracket.

7. Start the caliper-to-mounting bracket bolts through the sleeves in the inboard caliper ears and through the mounting bracket, making sure that the ends of the bolts pass under the retaining ears of the inboard shoe.

8. Push the mounting bolts through to engage the holes in the outboard shoes and the outboard caliper ears, then thread them into the mounting bracket.

9. To complete the installation, use new flexible brake hose-to-caliper washers and reverse the removal procedures. Torque the caliper-to-steering knuckle bolts to 37 ft. lbs. and the flexible brake hose-to-caliper bolt to 32 ft. lbs. Refill the master cylinder reservoirs and bleed

CALIPER HOUSING

OUTBOARD SHOE AND LINING

Positioning the shoe in the caliper

Place a clean rag as shown to catch the caliper piston when using compressed air to remove the piston from the bore

Removing the dust boot

the brake system. Pump the brake pedal to seat the linings against the rotors.

10. Using a pair of channel lock pliers, place them on the caliper housing notch, bend the caliper upper ears until no clearance exists between the shoe and the caliper housing.

11. Install the wheels, lower the vehicle. Pump the brake pedal to make sure that it is firm. Road test the vehicle.

OVERHAUL

1. Remove the brake caliper from the vehicle.

2. Remove the inlet fitting from the brake caliper.

3. Position the caliper on a work bench and place clean shop cloths in the caliper opening. Using compressed air, force the piston from it's bore.

CAUTION: *DO NOT apply too much air pressure to the bore, for the piston may jump out,*

causing damage to the piston and/or the operator.

4. Remove and discard the piston boot and seal. Be careful not to scratch the bore.

5. Clean all of the parts with non-mineral based solvent and blow dry with compressed air. Replace the rubber parts with those in the brake service kit.

6. Inspect the piston and the caliper bore for damage or corrosion. Replace the caliper and/or the piston (if necessary).

7. Remove the bleeder screw and it's rubber cap.

8. Inspect the guide pins for corrosion, replace them (if necessary). When installing the guide pins, coat them with silicone grease.

9. To install, perform the following procedures:

　　a. Lubricate the piston, caliper and seal with clean brake fluid.

Caliper and pad assembly

Installing the caliper seal

NOTE: *When positioning the piston seal on the piston, it goes in the groove nearest the piston's flat end with the lap facing the largest end. If placement is correct, the seal lips will be in the groove and not extend over the groove's step.*

b. Replace the caliper-to-steering knuckle bolts and torque the bolts to 37 ft. lbs.

10. To complete the installation, reverse the removal procedures. Bleed the brake system after installation.

Brake Disc (Rotor)

REMOVAL AND INSTALLATION

2WD Model

1. Siphon some brake fluid from the brake master cylinder.

2. Raise and safely support the front of the vehicle on jackstands. Remove the wheels.

3. Remove the brake caliper from the steering knuckle and hang it on a wire.

4. Remove the grease cup, the cotter pin, the castle nut and the hub assembly.

5. Inspect the brake discs for signs of wear or damage; if necessary, replace the brake disc.

6. If installing a new disc, drive the outer bearing race out of the disc hub and carefully install it into the new disc using a suitable installation tool. Refer to the Chapter 8.

7. Grease the inner and outer bearings, install the inner bearing and seal and place the disc onto the axle.

8. Install the outer bearing, thrust washer and nut. Torque the nut to 12 ft. lbs. while turn-

Use a dial indicator to determine the brake disc runout

Caliper piston assembly

ing the wheel. Loosen the nut again, then make it as tight as possible using just fingers, no other tools. Loosen the nut as required to install the cotter pin, no more than $1/2$ turn.

7. Install the wheel, refill the brake fluid and road test the vehicle.

4WD Model

1. Raise and safely support the front of the truck on jackstands; place the jackstands under the frame.

2. Remove the wheel and tire assembly.

3. Remove the disc brake caliper and hang it out of the way on a wire.

4. Remove the brake from the wheel hub.

5. Inspect the disc for nicks, scores and/or damage, then replace it if necessary.

6. When installing the caliper, spread the brake pads to slide the caliper into position over the disc. Torque the bolts to 35 ft. lbs.

7. Install the wheel, lower the vehicle and pump the brakes before road testing.

INSPECTION

1. Raise and safely support the front of the vehicle on jackstands. Remove the wheels.

2. To check the disc runout, perform the following procedures:

　a. Using a dial indicator, secure and position it so that the button contacts the disc about 1 in. (25.4mm) from the outer edge.

　b. Rotate the disc. The lateral reading should not exceed 0.004 in. (0.1mm). If the reading is excessive, recondition or replace the disc.

3. To check the disc parallelism, perform the following procedures:

　a. Using a micrometer, check the disc thickness at 4 locations around the disc, at the same distance from the edge.

　b. The thickness should not vary more than 0.0005 in. (0.0127mm). If the readings are excessive, recondition or replace the disc.

4. The surface finish must be relatively smooth to avoid pulling and erratic performance, also, to extend the lining life. Light rotor surface scoring of up to 0.015 in. (0.38mm) in

depth, can be tolerated. If the scoring depths are excessive, refinish or replace the rotor.

REAR DRUM BRAKES

CAUTION: *Brake shoes contain asbestos, which has been determined to be a cancer causing agent. Never clean the brake surfaces with compressed air! Avoid inhaling any dust from any brake surface! When cleaning brake surfaces, use a commercially available brake cleaning fluid.*

Brake Drums

REMOVAL AND INSTALLATION

1. Raise and safely support the rear of the vehicle on jackstands.

2. Remove the wheel and tire assemblies.

3. Pull the brake drum off. It may by necessary to gently tap the rear edges of the drum to start it off the studs.

4. If the drum will not come off past the shoes, it will be necessary to retract the adjusting screw. Remove the access hole cover from

Rear brake assembly

the backing plate and turn the adjuster to retract the linings away from the drum.

5. Install a replacement hole cover before reinstalling the drum.

6. Install the drums in the same position on the hub as removed.

NOTE: *The rear wheel bearings are not adjustable, they are serviced by replacement ONLY. If necessary to replace the rear wheel bearings, refer to the Axle Shaft, Bearing and Seal, Removal and Installation procedures and follow the replacement procedures.*

INSPECTION

1. Check the drums for any cracks, scores, grooves or an out-of-round condition; if it is cracked, replace it. Slight scores can be removed with fine emery cloth while extensive scoring requires turning the drum on a lathe.

2. Never have a drum turned more than 0.060 in. (1.5mm) larger than the original inside diameter. The brake shoes will not make proper contact.

Brake Shoes

INSPECTION

Remove the drum and inspect the lining thickness of both brake shoes. The rear brake shoes should be replaced if the lining is less than $\frac{1}{16}$ in. (1.5mm) at the lowest point (bonded linings) or above the rivet heads (riveted linings) on the brake shoe. However, these lining thickness measurements may disagree with your state inspections laws.

NOTE: *Brake shoes should always be replaced in sets.*

REMOVAL AND INSTALLATION

NOTE: *The following procedure requires the use of the GM Brake Spring Pliers tool No. J-8057 or equivalent.*

1. Raise and safely support the rear of the vehicle on jackstands.

2. Slacken the parking brake cable.

3. Remove the rear wheels and the brake drum.

4. Using the GM Brake Spring Pliers tool No. J-8057 or equivalent, disconnect the brake shoe return springs, the actuator pullback spring, the holddown pins/springs and the actuator assembly.

NOTE: *Special brake spring tools are available from the auto supply stores, which will ease the replacement of the spring and anchor pin, but the job may still be performed with common hand tools.*

5. Disconnect the adjusting mechanism and spring, then remove the primary shoe. The pri-

mary shoe has a shorter lining than the secondary and is mounted at the front of the wheel.

6. Disconnect the parking brake lever from the secondary shoe and remove the shoe.

7. Clean and inspect all of the brake parts.

8. Check the wheel cylinders for seal condition and leaking.

9. Inspect the axle seal for leakage and replace, if necessary.

10. Inspect the replacement shoes for nicks or burrs, lightly lubricate the backing plate contact points, the brake cable, the levers and adjusting screws with brake grease, then reassemble them.

11. Make sure that the right and left hand adjusting screws are not mixed. You can prevent this by working on one side at a time. This will also provide you with a reference for reassembly. The star wheel should be nearest to the secondary shoe when correctly installed.

12. Install the parking brake lever to the secondary shoe.

13. Connect the parking brake cable to the lever and lightly lubricate the shoe contact areas of the back plate with brake grease.

14. Install the shoes to the backplate with the hold down springs.

15. Install the parking brake strut and spring, making sure the strut properly engages the parking brake lever.

16. Install the self adjusting screw, spring, actuating lever and spring.

17. Install the actuating link, lift up on the actuating lever and hook it to the link.

18. Install the return springs. Lightly sandpaper the shoes to make sure they are clean before installing the drum.

Wheel cylinder attachment

Wheel cylinder components

Installing the wheel cylinder retainer

Removing the wheel cylinder retainer

19. Adjust the brakes as previously described and road test the vehicle.

Wheel Cylinders

REMOVAL AND INSTALLATION

1. Remove the brake shoe assembly from the backing plate.

2. Clean away all of the dirt, crud and foreign material from around the wheel cylinder. It is important that dirt be kept away from the brake line when the cylinder is disconnected.

3. Disconnect and plug the hydraulic line at the wheel cylinder.

4. Remove the wheel cylinder-to-backing plate bolts and the wheel cylinder from the backing plate.

NOTE: *If the wheel cylinder is sticking, use a hammer and a punch to drive the wheel cylinder from the backing plate.*

5. When installing the new wheel cylinder, torque the bolts to 160 inch lbs. and the hydraulic line to 13 ft. lbs.

6. Install the brake shoes, adjust the brakes, then bleed the hydraulic system before road testing the vehicle.

OVERHAUL

1. Remove the boots, pistons, seals and spring.

2. Dry the bore and pistons, then check for wear, scoring, pitting or corrosion. GM does not recommend honing of the bore. If light corrosion exists it may be removed with crocus cloth. If crocus cloth does not do the job, replace the cylinder.

3. To assemble, use new seals/boots, coat all of the parts with clean silicone brake fluid and reverse the removal procedures.

PARKING BRAKE

Front Cable

REMOVAL AND INSTALLATION

1. Raise and safely support the front of the vehicle on jackstands.

2. Under the left-center of the vehicle, loosen the cable equalizer assembly.

3. Separate the front-cable connector from the equalizer cable.

4. Remove the front-cable retaining bolts and clips, then bend the retaining fingers.

5. Disconnect the front cable from the parking pedal assembly and the cable from the vehicle.

NOTE: *On some models, it may be necessary to remove the dash trim panels to gain access to the brake pedal.*

6. To install the front-cable, attach a piece of wire to the cable, fish it through the cowl and connect it to the pedal assembly.

7. Attach the cable to the equalizer and secure it to the frame before adjusting the parking brake.

Front parking brake cable

Intermediate rear parking brake cable

Rear Cable

REMOVAL AND INSTALLATION

Left and Right Rear Cables

1. Raise and safely support the rear of the vehicle on jackstands.

2. Under the left-center of the vehicle, loosen the cable equalizer assembly.

3. Separate the front-cable connector from the equalizer cable.

4. Refer to the "Brake Shoe, Removal and Installation" procedures in this Chapter and remove the brake shoes.

5. At the backing plate, bend the cable retaining fingers.

6. Disconnect the rear cable from the secondary brake shoe and the cable from the vehicle.

7. When installing the cable, attach it to the brake shoe levers and assemble the brakes. Before installing the drums, pull the cable by hand and watch the parking brake action for smooth operation.

8. Secure the cable retainers at the frame brackets and the clips to the cable housing.

Parking brake adjustment

9. Attach the cable to the equalizer and adjust the parking brake.

ADJUSTMENT

NOTE: *Before adjusting the parking brakes, check the condition of the service brakes; replace any necessary parts.*

1. Block the front wheels.
2. Raise and safely support the rear of the vehicle on jackstands.
3. Under the left-center of the vehicle, loosen the equalizer.
4. On the 2WD model, position the parking brake pedal (ratchet) on the 8th click (1982–84) or 2nd click (1985–91); on the 4WD model, position the parking brake pedal (ratchet) on the 10th click (1983–84) or the 3rd click (1985–91).
5. Turn the cable equalizer until the rear wheel drags (when turned by hand).
6. Tighten the equalizer lock nut.
7. Release the parking brake pedal, then test it; the correct adjustment to specifications.

REAR WHEEL ANTILOCK (RWAL)SYSTEM

SYSTEM FILLING

The master cylinder is filled in the usual manner with no special procedures being necessary. Only DOT 3 brake fluid must be used; silicone or DOT 5 fluid is specifically prohibited. Do not use any fluid which contains a petroleum base; these fluids will cause swelling and distortion of the rubber parts within the system. Do not use old or contaminated brake fluid.

SYSTEM BLEEDING

The brake system is bled in the usual manner with no special procedures required because of

the RWAL system. The use of a power bleeder is recommended but the system may also be bled manually. If a power bleeder is used, it must be of the diaphragm type and provide isolation of the fluid from air and moisture.

Do not pump the pedal rapidly when bleeding; this can make the circuits very difficult to bleed. Instead, press the brake pedal slowly 1 time and hold it down while bleeding takes place. Tighten the bleeder screw, release the pedal and wait 15 seconds before repeating the sequence. Because of the length of the brake lines and other factors, it may take 10 or more repetitions of the sequence to bleed each line properly. When necessary to bleed all 4 wheels, the correct order is right rear, left rear, right front and left front.

CAUTION: *Do not move the vehicle until a firm brake pedal is achieved. Failure to properly bleed the system may cause impaired braking and the possibility of injury and/or property damage*

RWAL Electronic Control Unit (ECU)

REMOVAL AND INSTALLATION

The RWAL ECU is a non–serviceable unit. It must be replaced when diagnosis indicates a malfunction.

1. Turn the ignition switch **OFF**.
2. Disconnect the wiring harness to the ECU.
3. Gently pry the tab at the rear of the ECU; remove the control unit toward the front of the vehicle.

NOTE: *Do not touch the electrical connectors or pins; do not allow them to contact brake fluid. If contaminated with brake fluid, clean them with water followed by isopropyl alcohol.*

4. Install the RWAL ECU by sliding it into the bracket until the tab locks into the hole.
5. Connect the wiring harness to the ECU.

Isolation/Dump Valve (Control Valve)

REMOVAL AND INSTALLATION

1. Disconnect the brake line fittings at the valve. Protect surrounding paint work from spillage.
2. Remove the bolts holding the valve to the bracket.

CHILTON'S
AUTO BODY REPAIR TIPS

Tools and Materials • Step-by-Step Illustrated Procedures
How To Repair Dents, Scratches and Rust Holes
Spray Painting and Refinishing Tips

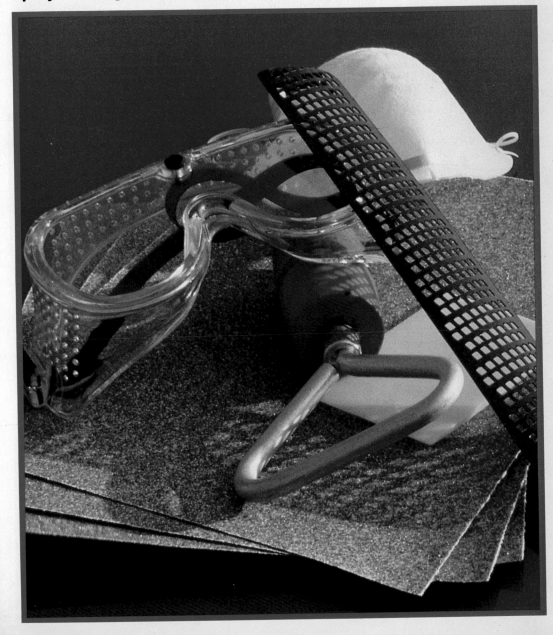

With a little practice, basic body repair procedures can be mastered by any do-it-yourself mechanic. The step-by-step repairs shown here can be applied to almost any type of auto body repair.

TOOLS & MATERIALS

You may already have basic tools, such as hammers and electric drills. Other tools unique to body repair — body hammers, grinding attachments, sanding blocks, dent puller, half-round plastic file and plastic spreaders — are relatively inexpensive and can be obtained wherever auto parts or auto body repair parts are sold. Portable air compressors and paint spray guns can be purchased or rented.

Auto Body Repair Kits

The best and most often used products are available to the do-it-yourselfer in kit form, from major manufacturers of auto body repair products. The same manufacturers also merchandise the individual products for use by pros.

Kits are available to make a wide variety of repairs, including holes, dents and scratches and fiberglass, and offer the advantage of buying the materials you'll need for the job. There is little waste or chance of materials going bad from not being used. Many kits may also contain basic body-working tools such as body files, sanding blocks and spreaders. Check the contents of the kit before buying your tools.

BODY REPAIR TIPS

Safety

Many of the products associated with auto body repair and refinishing contain toxic chemicals. Read all labels before opening containers and store them in a safe place and manner.

• Wear eye protection (safety goggles) when using power tools or when performing any operation that involves the removal of any type of material.

• Wear lung protection (disposable mask or respirator) when grinding, sanding or painting.

Sanding

1 Sand off paint before using a dent puller. When using a non-adhesive sanding disc, cover the back of the disc with an overlapping layer or two of masking tape and trim the edges. The disc will last considerably longer.

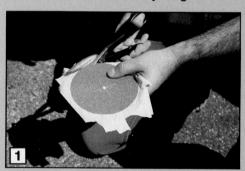

2 Use the circular motion of the sanding disc to grind *into* the edge of the repair. Grinding or sanding away from the jagged edge will only tear the sandpaper.

3 Use the palm of your hand flat on the panel to detect high and low spots. Do not use your fingertips. Slide your hand slowly back and forth.

WORKING WITH BODY FILLER

Mixing The Filler

Cleanliness and proper mixing and application are extremely important. Use a clean piece of plastic or glass or a disposable artist's palette to mix body filler.

1 Allow plenty of time and follow directions. No useful purpose will be served by adding more hardener to make it cure (set-up) faster. Less hardener means more curing time, but the mixture dries harder; more hardener means less curing time but a softer mixture.

2 Both the hardener and the filler should be thoroughly kneaded or stirred before mixing. Hardener should be a solid paste and dispense like thin toothpaste. Body filler should be smooth, and free of lumps or thick spots.

Getting the proper amount of hardener in the filler is the trickiest part of preparing the filler. Use the same amount of hardener in cold or warm weather. For contour filler (thick coats), a bead of hardener twice the diameter of the filler is about right. There's about a 15% margin on either side, but, if in doubt use less hardener.

3 Mix the body filler and hardener by wiping across the mixing surface, picking the mixture up and wiping it again. Colder weather requires longer mixing times. Do not mix in a circular motion; this will trap air bubbles which will become holes in the cured filler.

Applying The Filler

1 For best results, filler should not be applied over 1/4" thick.

Apply the filler in several coats. Build it up to above the level of the repair surface so that it can be sanded or grated down.

The first coat of filler must be pressed on with a firm wiping motion.

Apply the filler in one direction only. Working the filler back and forth will either pull it off the metal or trap air bubbles.

REPAIRING DENTS

Before you start, take a few minutes to study the damaged area. Try to visualize the shape of the panel before it was damaged. If the damage is on the left fender, look at the right fender and use it as a guide. If there is access to the panel from behind, you can reshape it with a body hammer. If not, you'll have to use a dent puller. Go slowly and work the metal a little at a time. Get the panel as straight as possible before applying filler.

1 This dent is typical of one that can be pulled out or hammered out from behind. Remove the headlight cover, headlight assembly and turn signal housing.

2 Drill a series of holes ½ the size of the end of the dent puller along the stress line. Make some trial pulls and assess the results. If necessary, drill more holes and try again. Do not hurry.

3 If possible, use a body hammer and block to shape the metal back to its original contours. Get the metal back as close to its original shape as possible. Don't depend on body filler to fill dents.

4 Using an 80-grit grinding disc on an electric drill, grind the paint from the surrounding area down to bare metal. Use a new grinding pad to prevent heat buildup that will warp metal.

5 The area should look like this when you're finished grinding. Knock the drill holes in and tape over small openings to keep plastic filler out.

6 Mix the body filler (see Body Repair Tips). Spread the body filler evenly over the entire area (see Body Repair Tips). Be sure to cover the area completely.

7 Let the body filler dry until the surface can just be scratched with your fingernail. Knock the high spots from the body filler with a body file ("Cheese-grater"). Check frequently with the palm of your hand for high and low spots.

8 Check to be sure that trim pieces that will be installed later will fit exactly. Sand the area with 40-grit paper.

9 If you wind up with low spots, you may have to apply another layer of filler.

10 Knock the high spots off with 40-grit paper. When you are satisfied with the contours of the repair, apply a thin coat of filler to cover pin holes and scratches.

11 Block sand the area with 40-grit paper to a smooth finish. Pay particular attention to body lines and ridges that must be well-defined.

12 Sand the area with 400 paper and then finish with a scuff pad. The finished repair is ready for priming and painting (see Painting Tips).

Materials and photos courtesy of Ritt Jones Auto Body, Prospect Park, PA.

REPAIRING RUST HOLES

There are many ways to repair rust holes. The fiberglass cloth kit shown here is one of the most cost efficient for the owner because it provides a strong repair that resists cracking and moisture and is relatively easy to use. It can be used on large and small holes (with or without backing) and can be applied over contoured areas. Remember, however, that short of replacing an entire panel, no repair is a guarantee that the rust will not return.

1 Remove any trim that will be in the way. Clean away all loose debris. Cut away all the rusted metal. But be sure to leave enough metal to retain the contour or body shape.

2 Grind away all traces of rust with a 24-grit grinding disc. Be sure to grind back 3-4 inches from the edge of the hole down to bare metal and be sure all traces of paint, primer and rust are removed.

3 Block sand the area with 80 or 100 grit sandpaper to get a clear, shiny surface and feathered paint edge. Tap the edges of the hole inward with a ball peen hammer.

4 If you are going to use release film, cut a piece about 2-3″ larger than the area you have sanded. Place the film over the repair and mark the sanded area on the film. Avoid any unnecessary wrinkling of the film.

5 Cut 2 pieces of fiberglass matte to match the shape of the repair. One piece should be about 1″ smaller than the sanded area and the second piece should be 1″ smaller than the first. Mix enough filler and hardener to saturate the fiberglass material (see Body Repair Tips).

6 Lay the release sheet on a flat surface and spread an even layer of filler, large enough to cover the repair. Lay the smaller piece of fiberglass cloth in the center of the sheet and spread another layer of filler over the fiberglass cloth. Repeat the operation for the larger piece of cloth.

7 Place the repair material over the repair area, with the release film facing outward. Use a spreader and work from the center outward to smooth the material, following the body contours. Be sure to remove all air bubbles.

8 Wait until the repair has dried tack-free and peel off the release sheet. The ideal working temperature is 60°-90° F. Cooler or warmer temperatures or high humidity may require additional curing time. Wait longer, if in doubt.

9 Sand and feather-edge the entire area. The initial sanding can be done with a sanding disc on an electric drill if care is used. Finish the sanding with a block sander. Low spots can be filled with body filler; this may require several applications.

10 When the filler can just be scratched with a fingernail, knock the high spots down with a body file and smooth the entire area with 80-grit. Feather the filled areas into the surrounding areas.

11 When the area is sanded smooth, mix some topcoat and hardener and apply it directly with a spreader. This will give a smooth finish and prevent the glass matte from showing through the paint.

12 Block sand the topcoat smooth with finishing sandpaper (200 grit), and 400 grit. The repair is ready for masking, priming and painting (see Painting Tips).

Materials and photos courtesy Marson Corporation, Chelsea, Massachusetts

PAINTING TIPS

Preparation

1 SANDING — Use a 400 or 600 grit wet or dry sandpaper. Wet-sand the area with a 1/4 sheet of sandpaper soaked in clean water. Keep the paper wet while sanding. Sand the area until the repaired area tapers into the original finish.

2 CLEANING — Wash the area to be painted thoroughly with water and a clean rag. Rinse it thoroughly and wipe the surface dry until you're sure it's completely free of dirt, dust, fingerprints, wax, detergent or other foreign matter.

3 MASKING — Protect any areas you don't want to overspray by covering them with masking tape and newspaper. Be careful not get fingerprints on the area to be painted.

4 PRIMING — All exposed metal should be primed before painting. Primer protects the metal and provides an excellent surface for paint adhesion. When the primer is dry, wet-sand the area again with 600 grit wet-sandpaper. Clean the area again after sanding.

Painting Techniques

P aint applied from either a spray gun or a spray can (for small areas) will provide good results. Experiment on an old piece of metal to get the right combination before you begin painting.

SPRAYING VISCOSITY (SPRAY GUN ONLY) — Paint should be thinned to spraying viscosity according to the directions on the can. Use only the recommended thinner or reducer and the same amount of reduction regardless of temperature.

AIR PRESSURE (SPRAY GUN ONLY) — This is extremely important. Be sure you are using the proper recommended pressure.

TEMPERATURE — The surface to be painted should be approximately the same temperature as the surrounding air. Applying warm paint to a cold surface, or vice versa, will completely upset the paint characteristics.

THICKNESS — Spray with smooth strokes. In general, the thicker the coat of paint, the longer the drying time. Apply several thin coats about 30 seconds apart. The paint should remain wet long enough to flow out and no longer; heavier coats will only produce sags or wrinkles. Spray a light (fog) coat, followed by heavier color coats.

DISTANCE — The ideal spraying distance is 8"-12" from the gun or can to the surface. Shorter distances will produce ripples, while greater distances will result in orange peel, dry film and poor color match and loss of material due to overspray.

OVERLAPPING — The gun or can should be kept at right angles to the surface at all times. Work to a wet edge at an even speed, using a 50% overlap and direct the center of the spray at the lower or nearest edge of the previous stroke.

RUBBING OUT (BLENDING) FRESH PAINT — Let the paint dry thoroughly. Runs or imperfections can be sanded out, primed and repainted.

Don't be in too big a hurry to remove the masking. This only produces paint ridges. When the finish has dried for at least a week, apply a small amount of fine grade rubbing compound with a clean, wet cloth. Use lots of water and blend the new paint with the surrounding area.

WRONG

Thin coat. Stroke too fast, not enough overlap, gun too far away.

CORRECT

Medium coat. Proper distance, good stroke, proper overlap.

WRONG

Heavy coat. Stroke too slow, too much overlap, gun too close.

1. Master cylinder
7. Isolation/dump valve
8. RWAL control unit

Rear wheel anti-lock ECU and isolation/dump valve

3. Disconnect the bottom connector from the RWAL ECU. Do not allow the isolation/dump valve to hang by the wiring.

NOTE: *Do not touch the electrical connectors or pins; do not allow them to contact brake fluid. If contaminated with brake fluid, clean them with water followed by isopropyl alcohol.*

4. Remove the valve from the vehicle.
To install:
5. Place the valve in position and install the retaining bolts. Tighten the bolts to 21 ft. lbs. (29 Nm).
6. Connect the electrical connector to the RWAL ECU.
7. Install the brake lines; tighten the fittings to 18 ft. lbs. (24 Nm)
8. Bleed the brake system at all 4 wheels.

Speed Sensor

REMOVAL AND INSTALLATION

The speed sensor is not serviceable and must replaced if malfunctioning. The sensor is located in the left rear of the transmission case on 2wd vehicles and on the transfer case of 4wd vehicles.

The speed sensor may be tested with an ohmmeter; the correct resistance is 900–2000 ohms. To remove the speed sensor:
1. Disconnect the electrical connector from the speed sensor.
2. Remove the sensor retaining bolt if one is used.
3. Remove the speed sensor; have a container handy to catch transmission fluid when the sensor is removed.
4. Recover the O-ring used to seal the sensor; inspect it for damage or deterioration.

●----- ELECTRIC
●━━━ HYDRAULIC

A. To front brakes
1. Master Cylinder
2. Brake light switch
3. Instrument cluster
4. Digital ratio adapter (within inst. cluster)
5. Speed sensor (2wd shown)
6. Transmission
7. Isolation/dump valve
8. RWAL ECU
9. BRAKE warning light
10. Combination valve

Rear wheel anti-lock system schematic

To install:

5. When installing, coat the new O-ring with a thin film of transmission fluid.

6. Install the O-ring and speed sensor.

7. If a retaining bolt is used, tighten the bolt to 8 ft. lbs. (11 Nm) in automatic transmissions or 9 ft. lbs. (12 Nm) for all other transmissions.

8. If the sensor is a screw-in unit, tighten it to 32 ft. lbs. (43 Nm).

9. Connect the wire harness to the sensor.

BRAKE SPECIFICATIONS

(All measurements are given in inches)

| Master Cylinder Bore | Drum Brakes | | | Disc Brakes | | |
	Standard Drum Diameter	Maximum Drum Diameter	Minimum Lining Thickness	Minimum Rotor Thickness	Maximum Rotor Runout	Minimum Lining Thickness
0.945	9.500	9.560	0.062	0.980 ①	0.004	0.030

① Discard at 0.965

1. Harness connector
2. O-ring
3. Speed sensor

Speed sensor locations and installation

Door hinge pins — exploded view

Using a spring compressor to replace the door hinge pins

EXTERIOR

Doors

REMOVAL AND INSTALLATION

NOTE: *The following procedure requires the use of the GM Door Hinge Spring Compressor tool No. J-28625-A or equivalent.*

1. If equipped with power door components, perform the following procedures:

    a. Disconnect the negative battery cable from the battery.

    b. Remove the door trim panel.

    c. Disconnect the electrical harness connector from the power door lock motor and/or the power window regulator.

    d. Remove the electrical harness from the door.

CAUTION: *Before removing the hinge spring from the door, cover the spring with a towel to prevent the spring from flying and possibly causing personal injury.*

2. Using the GM Door Hinge Spring Compressor tool No. J-28625-A or equivalent, compress the door hinge spring and remove it.

3. To remove the door hinge pin clips, spread the clips and move them above the

recess on the pin; when the pin is removed, the clip will ride on the pin and fall free of it.

4. Using a soft-head hammer and a pair of locking pliers, remove the lower pin from the door hinge; then, install a bolt (in the lower pin hole) to hold the door in place until the upper hinge pin is removed.

5. Remove the upper door hinge pin and support the door, then remove the bolt from the lower hinge pin hole and the door from the truck.

6. To install the door, position it on the hinges and insert a bolt through the lower hinge pin hole.

7. Using a new hinge pin clip, install the upper hinge pin.

8. Remove the bolt from the lower hinge pin hole. Using a new hinge pin, install it into the lower hinge pin holes.

9. Using the GM Door Hinge Spring Compressor tool No. J-28625-A or equivalent, compress the door hinge spring and install it into the door hinge.

10. If equipped with power door components, reconnect the electrical harness connector(s), install the door panel and the reconnect the negative battery terminal.

ADJUSTMENTS

Factory installed hinges are welded in place, so no adjustment of the system is necessary or recommended.

Door Hinges

NOTE: *The following procedure requires the use of an $1/8$ in. (3mm) drill bit, $1/2$ in. (13mm) drill bit, a center punch, a cold chisel, a portable body grinder, a putty knife and a scribing tool.*

REMOVAL AND INSTALLATION

1. Remove the door(s), then place the door on a padded workbench.

2. Using a putty knife, remove the sealant from the around the edge of the hinge.

3. Using a scribing tool, outline the position of the hinge(s) on the door and the body pillar.

4. Using a center punch, mark the center position of the hinge-to-door and the hinge-to-body pillar welds.

5. Using a $1/8$ in. (3mm) drill bit, drill a pilot hole completely through each weld.

LEFT DOOR

CENTER PUNCH UPPER AND LOWER INBOARD CORNER OF HINGE

SCRIBE LOCATION OF HINGE ON DOOR HINGE PILLAR

Marking the door hinges for replacement

46
40
44
43
445

40. Upper door side hinge
43. Lower door side hinge
44. Lower body side hinge
46. Upper body side hinge
445. Backing plate

Exploded view of the door hinge

Using a cold chisel to open the door pillar pinch weld

Opening the door pillar to insert the tapped anchor plate

Using a drill to remove the door hinge welds

NOTE: *When drilling the holes through the hinge welds, DO NOT drill through the door or the body pillar.*

6. Using a $1/2$ in. (13mm) drill bit, drill a hole through the hinge base, following the $1/8$ in. (3mm) pilot hole.

7. Using a cold chisel and a hammer, separate the hinge from the door and/or the body pillar. Using a portable grinder, clean off any welds remaining on the door or the body pillar.

8. To fasten the replacement hinge(s) to the door and/or body pillar, perform the following procedures:

a. Align the replacement hinge, with the scribe lines, previously made.

b. Using a center punch and the new hinge as a template, mark the location of each bolt hole.

c. Using a $1/2$ in. (13mm) drill bit, drill holes (using the center marks) through the door and body pillar.

d. If the upper body-side hinge is to be replaced, remove the instrument panel fasteners, pull the panel outwards and support it. Using a cold chisel, open the door pillar pinch weld to install the tapped anchor plate.

9. To install, use medium body sealant (apply it to the hinge-to-door or body pillar surface), the hinge-to-door/body pillar bolts and tapped anchor plate. Torque the hinge-to-door/body pillar bolts to 14–26 ft. lbs. Apply paint to the hinge and the surrounding area.

NOTE: *If the instrument panel was removed, replace it.*

ADJUSTMENT

NOTE: *The $1/2$ in. (13mm) drill hinge holes provide for some adjustment.*

1. Loosen, adjust, then tighten the hinge-to-door/body pillar bolts; close the door, then check the door gap, it should be 0.157–0.235 in. (4–6mm) between the door and the door frame.

2. With the door closed, it should be flush ($\pm$ 0.039 in. [$\pm$ 1.0mm]) with the body; if not, enlarge the striker hole.

3. Make sure that the striker properly engages the lock fork bolt.

Hood

REMOVAL AND INSTALLATION

1. Using protective covers, place them on the fenders.

2. Disconnect the electrical wiring connector from the underhood light.

3. Using a scribing tool, mark the area around the hinges to make the installation easier.

4. Support the hood and remove the hinge-to-hood bolts.

5. Remove the hood from the truck.

6. Installation is the reverse of removal.

ALIGNMENT

Align the hood so that the gaps between all of the components are equal; it must be flush with the fender and the cowl vent grille. Center the hood in the opening between the fenders, the cowl and the radiator grille. If it is difficult to center the hood or if the hood appears to be out of square, the front end sheet metal may need to be adjusted.

Tailgate

REMOVAL AND INSTALLATION

1. Lower and support the tailgate on a table or equivalent support.
2. Remove the left and right-side tailgate-to-fender striker bolts.
3. Remove the left and right-side tailgate hinge bolts and the tailgate from the truck.
4. To install, reverse the removal procedures. Torque the tailgate hinge bolts to 20 ft. lbs. and the striker plate-to-fender bolts to 20 ft. lbs. Check the operation of the tailgate.

ALIGNMENT

Align the tailgate so the gaps between all of the components are equal; it must be flush with the fenders. Center the tailgate in the opening between the fenders by adjusting the hinges and/or the striker bolts.

Outside Mirrors

Removal of outside mirrors is accomplished by removing the attaching screws from the anchoring plate and removing the mirror. Installation is the reverse of removal.

Outside mirror — standard

160
162   161
164   158
164
156   159
158
163
157
156

155. End gate
156. Bolt
157. Hinge
158. Screw
159. Bumper
160. Bolt
161. Striker plate bolt
162. Striker plate
163. End gate hinge
164. Bumper

Exploded view of the tailgate assembly

Outside mirror — fold-in type

Antenna

REMOVAL AND INSTALLATION

1. Remove the negative battery cable.
2. Remove the mast retaining nut, mast and bezel.
3. Remove the antenna cable from the receiver cable.
4. Remove the screw and star washer attaching the antenna to the fender.
5. Remove the antenna.
6. Installation is the reverse of removal.

Spare Tire Carrier

REPLACEMENT

1. Lower the spare tire and remove it.
2. Remove the cotter pin and bolts attaching the spare tire hoist to the frame.
3. Remove the spare tire hoist.
4. Installation is the reverse of removal. Tighten bolts to 11 ft. lbs.

INTERIOR

Door Trim Panel

REMOVAL AND INSTALLATION

NOTE: *The following procedure requires the use of the Trim Pad Removal tool No. J-24595 or equivalent, and the Window Regulator Clip Removal tool No. J-9886-01 or equivalent.*

1. Remove the door handle bezel-to-door screws and the bezel.
2. Remove the armrest-to-door screws and the armrest.
3. Using the Window Regulator Clip Re-

55. Antenna Cable, Receiver
58. Antenna
59. Nut
60. Bezel
61. Heater Vent Pipe
62. Clamp
63. Antenna Cable
64. Strap
65. Antenna Cable
A. Heater Hoses
B. Right Fender

Radio antenna components

moval tool No. J-9886-01 or equivalent, remove the window regulator clip and the handle from the door.

4. Using the Trim Pad Removal tool No. J-24595 or equivalent, remove the nylon fasteners from the inner door panel.

5. If equipped with power windows, disconnect the electrical connector.

6. Installation is the reverse of removal.

Door Locks

REMOVAL AND INSTALLATION

Door Lock Assembly

1. Remove the door trim panel from the door.
2. Remove the water deflector.
3. Remove the lock rod and the lever rod from the inner door handle housing.
4. Remove the outside handle lock rod from the lock assembly.
5. Remove the lock cylinder rod from the lock cylinder.
6. Remove the lock assembly-to-door screws and the assembly from the door.

7. Installation is the reverse of removal. Check the operation of the lock assembly.

Lock Cylinder Assembly

1. Remove the door panel.
2. Remove the armrest bracket-to-door screws and the bracket from the door.
3. Remove the water deflector and roll up the window.
4. Disconnect the actuator rod from the lock cylinder.
5. Remove the lock cylinder-to-door retainer, then remove the lock cylinder and seal from the door.
6. Installation is the reverse of removal. Check the operation of the lock cylinder.

Inner door handle and lock assembly — exploded view

Outside door handle and cylinder lock assembly — exploded view

Door Glass and Regulator

REMOVAL AND INSTALLATION

CAUTION: *Always wear heavy gloves when handling glass to minimize the risk of injury.*

Door Glass

NOTE: *The following procedure requires the use of the Trim Pad Removal tool No. J-24595 or equivalent, the Water Deflector Removal tool No. J-21104 or equivalent, and the Window Regulator Clip Removal tool No. J-9886-01 or equivalent.*

1. Remove the door trim panel.
2. Remove the armrest bracket-to-door screws and the bracket.
3. Using the Water Deflector Removal tool No. J-21104 or equivalent, remove the water deflector from the door.
4. Lower the window until it and the sash channel can be seen in the door panel opening, then remove the sash assembly-to-window bolts.
5. Remove the sash assembly and the window from the door.
6. Installation is the reverse of removal.

Removing the window regulator handle retaining spring

Door Regulator

NOTE: *The following procedure requires the use of the Trim Pad Removal tool No. J-24595 or equivalent, the Water Deflector Removal tool No. J-21104 or equivalent, and the Window Regulator Clip Removal tool No. J-9886-01 or equivalent.*

1. Remove the door trim panel.
2. Remove the armrest bracket-to-door screws and the bracket.
3. Using the Water Deflector Removal tool No. J-21104 or equivalent, remove the water deflector from the door.
4. Raise the window to the Full Up position. Using cloth backed tape, tape the glass to the door frame.
5. Remove the regulator-to-door bolts and separate the regulator lift arm roller from the window sash, then remove the regulator from the door.

50. Door garnish molding	58. Screw	25. Window handle
51. Screw	59. Arm rest	64. Door pocket
52. Adhesive strip	60. Cover	65. Window handle spacer
53. Inner panel water deflector	61. Bolt	67. Arm rest bracket
54. Door insulator	62. Plate	68. Trim panel
55. Retainer	63. Screw	69. Trim panel retaining plate
56. Trim panel insert	26. Window handle bearing plate	70. Trim panel fastener
57. Trim panel	24. Window handle spring	71. Trim panel retainer

Door panel removal

7. Door handle rod
9. Lock handle rod
10. Outside handle rod
12. Lock cylinder rod
13. Lock mechanism
14. Screw

Door lock assembly — exploded view

34. Key
35. Door lock cylinder
36. Lock cylinder retainer
37. Lock cylinder gasket
39. Outside door handle

Lock Cylinder assembly — exploded view

LOCK CONNECTING ROD

LOCK LEVER

INSERT AWL TO
DISENGAGE TANG   CLIP ENGAGED

CLIP DISENGAGED

Disengaging and engaging the connecting rod retaining clip

6. Installation is the reverse of removal.

Electric Window Motor

REMOVAL AND INSTALLATION

NOTE: *The following procedure requires the use of the Trim Pad Removal tool No. J-24595 or equivalent, the Water Deflector Removal tool No. J-21104 or equivalent, the Rivet Installation tool No. J-29022 or equiv-*

alent, the Window Regulator Clip Removal tool No. J-9886-01 or equivalent, and $\frac{3}{16}$ in. (5mm) rivets.

1. Remove the door trim panel.
2. Disconnect the negative battery terminal from the battery.
3. Remove the armrest bracket-to-door screws and the bracket.
4. Using the Water Deflector Removal tool No. J-21104 or equivalent, remove the water deflector from the door.
5. Raise the window to the Full Up position. Using cloth backed tape, tape the glass to the door frame.
6. Disconnect the electrical wiring connector from the window regulator motor.
7. Separate the regulator lift arm roller from the window sash.
8. If removing the window regulator motor

REGULATOR

BOLT
8-11 N·m

FRT

Electric window regulator

1. Door
18. Glass
19. Window glass mount washer
20. Window mount bushing
21. Bolt
22. Window mount sash
23. Side window retainer
29. Window mount sash
74. Nut

Window sash components

18. Glass
27. Bolt
28. Window Regulator
29. Window Mount Sash

Standard window regulator

from the door, perform the following procedure:

a. Drill a hole through the regulator sector gear and backplate, then install a bolt/nut to lock the sector gear in position.

b. Using a $\frac{3}{16}$ in. (5mm) drill bit, drill out the motor-to-door rivets.

c. Remove the motor from the door.

9. Using the Rivet Installation tool No. J-29022 or equivalent, rivet the window regulator motor to the door.

10. After the motor is riveted to the door, remove the nut/bolt from the sector gear.

11. Installation is the reverse of removal.

Windshield

NOTE: *Bonded windshields require special tools and special removal procedures to be performed to ensure the windshield will be removed without being broken. For this reason we recommend that you refer all removal and installation to a qualified technician.*

Side Window — Extended Cab

REMOVAL AND INSTALLATION

Stationary

NOTE: *The following procedure requires the use of the Urethane Glass Sealant Remover (hot knife) tool No. J-24709-1 or equivalent, and the Glass Sealant Remover Knife tool No. J-24402-A or equivalent.*

1. Remove the upper quarter trim molding.
2. Remove the retaining clips.

NOTE: *If the glass is cracked, it should be crisscrossed with masking tape to reduce the risk of damage to the vehicle. If a crack extends to the edge of the glass, mark the cab with a piece of chalk at the point where the crack meets the cab; this will aid the inspection later.*

3. Working from inside the vehicle, use the Urethane Glass Sealant Remover (hot knife) tool No. J-24709-1 or equivalent, or the Glass Sealant Remover Knife tool No. J-24402-A or equivalent, separate the window glass and molding.

4. Remove the molding and the glass from the window frame.

5. Using a scraper or a chisel, remove the adhesive from the pinchweld flange; be sure to remove all of the mounds or loose adhesive.

6. Using alcohol and a clean cloth, clean the pinchweld flange. Allow the alcohol to air dry.

7. Using the pinchweld primer, found in the service kit, apply it to the pinchweld area. DO NOT let any of the primer touch the exposed paint for damage to the finish may occur; allow five minutes for the primer to dry.

8. Apply a smooth continuous bead of adhesive around the molding edge. Be sure that the adhesive contacts the entire edge of the molding and extends to fill the gap between the glass and the primed sheet metal.

9. Using hand pressure, press the glass/molding assembly onto the pinchweld flange. Using retaining clips, secure the glass/molding assembly to the pinchweld.

10. Spray a mist of warm or hot water onto the urethane. Water will assist in the curing process. Dry the area where the reveal molding will contact the body and glass.

Latched

NOTE: *The following procedure requires the use of a pin punch and a mallet.*

1. Using a pin punch and a mallet, drive the pin from the latch assembly.

2. Remove the glass-to-hinge retaining screws and the glass from the vehicle.

3. Installation is the reverse of removal.

Rear Window Glass

REMOVAL AND INSTALLATION

NOTE: *The following procedure requires the use of a $^1/_4$ in. (6mm) cord, a putty knife and an assistant.*

1. Using a putty knife, run it between the weatherstrip and the flange on both sides.

2. Position an assistant on the outside of the cab by the window, to catch the window.

3. Using a putty knife, on the inside of the rear window, force the weatherstrip/glass assembly, from the flange.

4. Separate the glass from the weatherstrip.

NOTE: *To ease the weatherstrip installation, heat it with a non-flame source heater; at higher temperatures the weatherstrip is more pliable. DO NOT heat it above 125°F (52°C) or for more than $1^1/_2$ hours.*

5. To install, position the rear window glass in the weatherstrip.

6. Using a $^1/_4$ in. (6mm) cord, place it in the weatherstrip groove; the ends should overlap 6 in. (152mm) at the bottom of the window.

7. Using soapy water, lubricate the flange and the weatherstrip.

8. Position an assistant inside the cab, install the weatherstrip/glass assembly and have the assistant pull the cord to seat the weatherstrip on the window flange.

9. Apply a light mist of water to the window to check for leaks. If leak(s) are present, use urethane sealant to remedy the problem(s).

Inside Rear View Mirror

REPLACEMENT

1. Determine the location of the rear view mirror and using a wax pencil, draw a centerline on the outside of the glass from the roof panel to the windshield base.

2. Draw a line intersecting the centerline 23 in. (584mm) from the base of the glass. THe

A. Overlap

Using a cord to install the rear window

base of the support will be located at the intersection of these lines.

3. Clean the inside glass within 3 in. (76mm) of the intersecting lines. Using a glass cleaning solution rub the area until completely dry. Reclean with a towel saturated with alcohol.

4. Sand the bonding surface of the rear view mirror support with 320 grit sandpaper. Remove all traces of the factory adhesive if reusing the old support. Wipe the mirror support with alcohol and allow to dry.

5. Apply Loctite® Minute Bond Adhesive 312, or equivalent to the mirror support bonding surfaces.

6. Place the bottom of the support at the pre-marked line. The rounded edge of the support should face upward.

7. Press the support against the glass for 30–60 seconds with a steady pressure. Allow the adhesive to dry 5 minutes to dry before cleaning.

8. Clean all traces of adhesive and wax from the windshield with alcohol.

Seats

REMOVAL AND INSTALLATION

To remove the front bench seat, simply remove the seat retaining nuts and lift the seat assembly from the body. Installation is the reverse of removal. Tighten the seat retaining nuts to 24 ft. lbs.

336. Hinge
337. Rivet
338. Seal
339. Bolt
340. Screw
341. Pin
342. Latch
343. Retainer
344. Glass
345. Bearing
346. Bushing
347. Nut
348. Shim

Latched side window on the extended cab model — exploded view

21. Clip
22. Switch (with cruise control)
23. Switch (without cruise control)

Stationary side window on the extended cab model — exploded view

A. 587mm (23 1/8")

Locating the mirror support

VIEW I

VIEW II

VIEW III

VIEW IV

1. SEAT CUSHION ASSEMBLY
2. SPRING WASHER
3. PIVOT BUSHING
4. SEAT LAP BELT
5. SEAT MOUNTING SUPPORT BRACKET
6. SEAT BACK LOCK-ASSEMBLY
7. SEAT BACK ASSEMBLY
8. TENSIONER SPRING
9. FRONT SEAT BELT ASSEMBLY
10. PLUG
11. SEAT CUSHION BOTTOM TRIM PANEL
12. BODY SIDE LOWER TRIM PANEL

Folding jump seat components

Front bench seat and adjuster assembly

11

General Conversion Table

Multiply By	To Convert	To	
		LENGTH	
2.54	Inches	Centimeters	.3937
25.4	Inches	Millimeters	.03937
30.48	Feet	Centimeters	.0328
.304	Feet	Meters	3.28
.914	Yards	Meters	1.094
1.609	Miles	Kilometers	.621
		VOLUME	
.473	Pints	Liters	2.11
.946	Quarts	Liters	1.06
3.785	Gallons	Liters	.264
.164	Cubic inches	Liters	61.02
16.39	Cubic inches	Cubic cms.	.061
28.32	Cubic feet	Liters	.0353
		MASS (Weight)	
28.35	Ounces	Grams	.035
.4536	Pounds	Kilograms	2.20
—	To obtain	From	Multiply by

Multiply By	To Convert	To	
		AREA	
6.45	Square inches	Square cms.	.155
.836	Square yds.	Square meters	1.196
		FORCE	
4.448	Pounds	Newtons	.225
.138	Ft. lbs.	Kilogram/meters	7.23
1.356	Ft. lbs.	Newton-meters	.737
.113	In. lbs.	Newton-meters	8.844
		PRESSURE	
.068	Psi	Atmospheres	14.7
6.89	Psi	Kilopascals	.145
		OTHER	
1.104	Horsepower (DIN)	Horsepower (SAE)	.9861
.746	Horsepower (SAE)	Kilowatts (KW)	1.34
1.609	Mph	Km/h	.621
.425	Mpg	Km/L	2.35
—	To obtain	From	Multiply by

Tap Drill Sizes

National Coarse or U.S.S.

Screw & Tap Size	Threads Per Inch	Use Drill Number
No. 5	40	.39
No. 6	32	.36
No. 8	32	.29
No. 10	24	.25
No. 12	24	.17
1/4	20	8
5/16	18	F
3/8	16	5/16
7/16	14	U
1/2	13	27/64
9/16	12	31/64
5/8	11	17/32
3/4	10	21/32
7/8	9	49/64

National Coarse or U.S.S.

Screw & Tap Size	Threads Per Inch	Use Drill Number
1	8	7/8
1 1/8	7	63/64
1 1/4	7	1 7/64
1 1/2	6	1 11/32

National Fine or S.A.E.

Screw & Tap Size	Threads Per Inch	Use Drill Number
No. 5	44	.37
No. 6	40	.33
No. 8	36	.29
No. 10	32	.21

National Fine or S.A.E.

Screw & Tap Size	Threads Per Inch	Use Drill Number
No. 12	28	.15
1/4	28	3
6/16	24	1
3/8	28	Q
7/16	20	W
1/2	20	29/64
9/16	18	33/64
5/8	18	37/64
3/4	16	11/16
7/8	14	13/16
1 1/8	12	1 3/64
1 1/4	12	1 11/64
1 1/2	12	1 27/64

Drill Sizes In Decimal Equivalents

Inch	Decimal	Wire	mm
1/64	.0156		.39
	.0157		.4
	.0160	78	
	.0165		.42
	.0173		.44
	.0177		.45
	.0180	77	
	.0181		.46
	.0189		.48
	.0197		.5
	.0200	76	
	.0210	75	
	.0217		.55
	.0225	74	
	.0236		.6
	.0240	73	
	.0250	72	
	.0256		.65
	.0260	71	
	.0276		.7
	.0280	70	
	.0292	69	
	.0295		.75
	.0310	68	
1/32	.0312		.79
	.0315		.8
	.0320	67	
	.0330	66	
	.0335		.85
	.0350	65	
	.0354		.9
	.0360	64	
	.0370	63	
	.0374		.95
	.0380	62	
	.0390	61	
	.0394		1.0
	.0400	60	
	.0410	59	
	.0413		1.05
	.0420	58	
	.0430	57	
	.0433		1.1
	.0453		1.15
3/64	.0465	56	
	.0469		1.19
	.0472		1.2
	.0492		1.25
	.0512		1.3
	.0520	55	
	.0531		1.35
	.0550	54	
	.0551		1.4
	.0571		1.45
	.0591		1.5
	.0595	53	
	.0610		1.55
1/16	.0625		1.59
	.0630		1.6
	.0635	52	
	.0650		1.65
	.0669		1.7
	.0670	51	
	.0689		1.75
	.0700	50	
	.0709		1.8
	.0728		1.85

Inch	Decimal	Wire	mm
	.0730	49	
	.0748		1.9
	.0760	48	
	.0768		1.95
5/64	.0781		1.98
	.0785	47	
	.0787		2.0
	.0807		2.05
	.0810	46	
	.0820	45	
	.0827		2.1
	.0846		2.15
	.0860	44	
	.0866		2.2
	.0886		2.25
	.0890	43	
	.0906		2.3
	.0925		2.35
	.0935	42	
3/32	.0938		2.38
	.0945		2.4
	.0960	41	
	.0965		2.45
	.0980	40	
	.0981		2.5
	.0995	39	
	.1015	38	
	.1024		2.6
	.1040	37	
	.1063		2.7
	.1065	36	
	.1083		2.75
7/64	.1094		2.77
	.1100	35	
	.1102		2.8
	.1110	34	
	.1130	33	
	.1142		2.9
	.1160	32	
	.1181		3.0
	.1200	31	
	.1220		3.1
1/8	.1250		3.17
	.1260		3.2
	.1280		3.25
	.1285	30	
	.1299		3.3
	.1339		3.4
	.1360	29	
	.1378		3.5
	.1405	28	
9/64	.1406		3.57
	.1417		3.6
	.1440	27	
	.1457		3.7
	.1470	26	
	.1476		3.75
	.1495	25	
	.1496		3.8
	.1520	24	
	.1535		3.9
	.1540	23	
5/32	.1562		3.96
	.1570	22	
	.1575		4.0
	.1590	21	
	.1610	20	

Inch	Decimal	Wire & Letter	mm
	.1614		4.1
	.1654		4.2
	.1660	19	
	.1673		4.25
	.1693		4.3
	.1695	18	
11/64	.1719		4.36
	.1730	17	
	.1732		4.4
	.1770	16	
	.1772		4.5
	.1800	15	
	.1811		4.6
	.1820	14	
	.1850	13	
	.1850		4.7
	.1870		4.75
3/16	.1875		4.76
	.1890		4.8
	.1890	12	
	.1910	11	
	.1929		4.9
	.1935	10	
	.1960	9	
	.1969		5.0
	.1990	8	
	.2008		5.1
	.2010	7	
13/64	.2031		5.16
	.2040	6	
	.2047		5.2
	.2055	5	
	.2067		5.25
	.2087		5.3
	.2090	4	
	.2126		5.4
	.2130	3	
7/32	.2165		5.5
	.2188		5.55
	.2205		5.6
	.2210	2	
	.2244		5.7
	.2264		5.75
	.2280	1	
	.2283		5.8
	.2323		5.9
	.2340	A	
15/64	.2344		5.95
	.2362		6.0
	.2380	B	
	.2402		6.1
	.2420	C	
	.2441		6.2
	.2460	D	
	.2461		6.25
	.2480		6.3
1/4	.2500	E	6.35
	.2520		6.
	.2559		6.5
	.2570	F	
	.2598		6.6
	.2610	G	
	.2638		6.7
17/64	.2656		6.74
	.2657		6.75
	.2660	H	
	.2677		6.8

Inch	Decimal	Letter	mm
	.2717		6.9
	.2720	I	
	.2756		7.0
	.2770	J	
	.2795		7.1
	.2810	K	
9/32	.2812		7.14
	.2835		7.2
	.2854		7.25
	.2874		7.3
	.2900	L	
	.2913		7.4
	.2950	M	
	.2953		7.5
19/64	.2969		7.54
	.2992		7.6
	.3020	N	
	.3031		7.7
	.3051		7.75
	.3071		7.8
	.3110		7.9
5/16	.3125		7.93
	.3150		8.0
	.3160	O	
	.3189		8.1
	.3228		8.2
	.3230	P	
	.3248		8.25
	.3268		8.3
21/64	.3281		8.33
	.3307		8.4
	.3320	Q	
	.3346		8.5
	.3386		8.6
	.3390	R	
11/32	.3425		8.7
	.3438		8.73
	.3445		8.75
	.3465		8.8
	.3480	S	
	.3504		8.9
	.3543		9.0
	.3580	T	
	.3583		9.1
23/64	.3594		9.12
	.3622		9.2
	.3642		9.25
	.3661		9.3
	.3680	U	
	.3701		9.4
	.3740		9.5
3/8	.3750		9.52
	.3770	V	
	.3780		9.6
	.3819		9.7
	.3839		9.75
	.3858		9.8
	.3860	W	
	.3898		9.9
25/64	.3906		9.92
	.3937		10.0
	.3970	X	
	.4040	Y	
13/32	.4062		10.31
	.4130	Z	
	.4134		10.5
27/64	.4219		10.71

Inch	Decimal	mm
7/16	.4331	11.0
	.4375	11.11
	.4528	11.5
29/64	.4531	11.51
15/32	.4688	11.90
	.4724	12.0
31/64	.4844	12.30
	.4921	12.5
1/2	.5000	12.70
	.5118	13.0
33/64	.5156	13.09
17/32	.5312	13.49
	.5315	13.5
35/64	.5469	13.89
	.5512	14.0
9/16	.5625	14.28
	.5709	14.5
37/64	.5781	14.68
	.5906	15.0
19/32	.5938	15.08
39/64	.6094	15.47
	.6102	15.5
5/8	.6250	15.87
	.6299	16.0
41/64	.6406	16.27
	.6496	16.5
21/32	.6562	16.66
	.6693	17.0
43/64	.6719	17.06
11/16	.6875	17.46
	.6890	17.5
	.7031	17.85
	.7087	18.0
23/32	.7188	18.25
	.7283	18.5
47/64	.7344	18.65
	.7480	19.0
3/4	.7500	19.05
49/64	.7656	19.44
	.7677	19.5
25/32	.7812	19.84
	.7874	20.0
51/64	.7969	20.24
	.8071	20.5
13/16	.8125	20.63
	.8268	21.0
53/64	.8281	21.03
27/32	.8438	21.43
	.8465	21.5
55/64	.8594	21.82
	.8661	22.0
7/8	.8750	22.22
	.8858	22.5
57/64	.8906	22.62
	.9055	23.0
29/32	.9062	23.01
59/64	.9219	23.41
	.9252	23.5
15/16	.9375	23.81
	.9449	24.0
61/64	.9531	24.2
	.9646	24.5
31/32	.9688	24.6
	.9843	25.0
63/64	.9844	25.0
1	1.0000	25.4

AIR/FUEL RATIO: The ratio of air to gasoline by weight in the fuel mixture drawn into the engine.

AIR INJECTION: One method of reducing harmful exhaust emissions by injecting air into each of the exhaust ports of an engine. The fresh air entering the hot exhaust manifold causes any remaining fuel to be burned before it can exit the tailpipe.

ALTERNATOR: A device used for converting mechanical energy into electrical energy.

AMMETER: An instrument, calibrated in amperes, used to measure the flow of an electrical current in a circuit. Ammeters are always connected in series with the circuit being tested.

AMPERE: The rate of flow of electrical current present when one volt of electrical pressure is applied against one ohm of electrical resistance.

ANALOG COMPUTER: Any microprocessor that uses similar (analogous) electrical signals to make its calculations.

ARMATURE: A laminated, soft iron core wrapped by a wire that converts electrical energy to mechanical energy as in a motor or relay. When rotated in a magnetic field, it changes mechanical energy into electrical energy as in a generator.

ATMOSPHERIC PRESSURE: The pressure on the Earth's surface caused by the weight of the air in the atmosphere. At sea level, this pressure is 14.7 psi at 32°F (101 kPa at 0°C).

ATOMIZATION: The breaking down of a liquid into a fine mist that can be suspended in air.

AXIAL PLAY: Movement parallel to a shaft or bearing bore.

BACKFIRE: The sudden combustion of gases in the intake or exhaust system that results in a loud explosion.

BACKLASH: The clearance or play between two parts, such as meshed gears.

BACKPRESSURE: Restrictions in the exhaust system that slow the exit of exhaust gases from the combustion chamber.

BAKELITE: A heat resistant, plastic insulator material commonly used in printed circuit boards and transistorized components.

BALL BEARING: A bearing made up of hardened inner and outer races between which hardened steel balls roll.

BALLAST RESISTOR: A resistor in the primary ignition circuit that lowers voltage after the engine is started to reduce wear on ignition components.

BEARING: A friction reducing, supportive device usually located between a stationary part and a moving part.

BIMETAL TEMPERATURE SENSOR: Any sensor or switch made of two dissimilar types of metal that bend when heated or cooled due to the different expansion rates of the alloys. These types of sensors usually function as an on/off switch.

BLOWBY: Combustion gases, composed of water vapor and unburned fuel, that leak past the piston rings into the crankcase during normal engine operation. These gases are removed by the PCV system to prevent the buildup of harmful acids in the crankcase.

BRAKE PAD: A brake shoe and lining assembly used with disc brakes.

BRAKE SHOE: The backing for the brake lining. The term is, however, usually applied to the assembly of the brake backing and lining.

BUSHING: A liner, usually removable, for a bearing; an anti-friction liner used in place of a bearing.

BYPASS: System used to bypass ballast resistor during engine cranking to increase voltage supplied to the coil.

CALIPER: A hydraulically activated device in a disc brake system, which is mounted straddling the brake rotor (disc). The caliper contains at least one piston and two brake pads. Hydraulic pressure on the piston(s) forces the pads against the rotor.

CAMSHAFT: A shaft in the engine on which are the lobes (cams) which operate the valves. The camshaft is driven by the crankshaft, via a belt, chain or gears, at one half the crankshaft speed.

CAPACITOR: A device which stores an electrical charge.

CARBON MONOXIDE (CO): A colorless, odorless gas given off as a normal byproduct of combustion. It is poisonous and extremely dangerous in confined areas, building up slowly to toxic levels without warning if adequate ventilation is not available.

CARBURETOR: A device, usually mounted on the intake manifold of an engine, which mixes the air and fuel in the proper proportion to allow even combustion.

CATALYTIC CONVERTER: A device installed in the exhaust system, like a muffler, that converts harmful byproducts of combustion into carbon dioxide and water vapor by means of a heat-producing chemical reaction.

CENTRIFUGAL ADVANCE: A mechanical method of advancing the spark timing by using fly weights in the distributor that react to centrifugal force generated by the distributor shaft rotation.

CHECK VALVE: Any one-way valve installed to permit the flow of air, fuel or vacuum in one direction only.

CHOKE: A device, usually a movable valve, placed in the intake path of a carburetor to restrict the flow of air.

CIRCUIT: Any unbroken path through which an electrical current can flow. Also used to describe fuel flow in some instances.

CIRCUIT BREAKER: A switch which protects an electrical circuit from overload by opening the circuit when the current flow exceeds a predetermined level. Some circuit breakers must be reset manually, while most reset automatically

COIL (IGNITION): A transformer in the ignition circuit which steps up the voltage provided to the spark plugs.

COMBINATION MANIFOLD: An assembly which includes both the intake and exhaust manifolds in one casting.

COMBINATION VALVE: A device used in some fuel systems that routes fuel vapors to a charcoal storage canister instead of venting them into the atmosphere. The valve relieves fuel tank pressure and allows fresh air into the tank as the fuel level drops to prevent a vapor lock situation.

COMPRESSION RATIO: The comparison of the total volume of the cylinder and combustion chamber with the piston at BDC and the piston at TDC.

CONDENSER: 1. An electrical device which acts to store an electrical charge, preventing voltage surges.
2. A radiator-like device in the air conditioning system in which refrigerant gas condenses into a liquid, giving off heat.

CONDUCTOR: Any material through which an electrical current can be transmitted easily.

CONTINUITY: Continuous or complete circuit. Can be checked with an ohmmeter.

COUNTERSHAFT: An intermediate shaft which is rotated by a mainshaft and transmits, in turn, that rotation to a working part.

CRANKCASE: The lower part of an engine in which the crankshaft and related parts operate.

CRANKSHAFT: The main driving shaft of an engine which receives reciprocating motion from the pistons and converts it to rotary motion.

CYLINDER: In an engine, the round hole in the engine block in which the piston(s) ride.

CYLINDER BLOCK: The main structural member of an engine in which is found the cylinders, crankshaft and other principal parts.

CYLINDER HEAD: The detachable portion of the engine, fastened, usually, to the top of the cylinder block, containing all or most of the combustion chambers. On overhead valve engines, it contains the valves and their operating parts. On overhead cam engines, it contains the camshaft as well.

DEAD CENTER: The extreme top or bottom of the piston stroke.

DETONATION: An unwanted explosion of the air/fuel mixture in the combustion chamber caused by excess heat and compression, advanced timing, or an overly lean mixture. Also referred to as "ping".

DIAPHRAGM: A thin, flexible wall separating two cavities, such as in a vacuum advance unit.

DIESELING: A condition in which hot spots in the combustion chamber cause the engine to run on after the key is turned off.

DIFFERENTIAL: A geared assembly which allows the transmission of motion between drive axles, giving one axle the ability to turn faster than the other.

DIODE: An electrical device that will allow current to flow in one direction only.

DISC BRAKE: A hydraulic braking assembly consisting of a brake disc, or rotor, mounted on an axle, and a caliper assembly containing, usually two brake pads which are activated by hydraulic pressure. The pads are forced against the sides of the disc, creating friction which slows the vehicle.

DISTRIBUTOR: A mechanically driven device on an engine which is responsible for electrically firing the spark plug at a predetermined point of the piston stroke.

DOWEL PIN: A pin, inserted in mating holes in two different parts allowing those parts to maintain a fixed relationship.

DRUM BRAKE: A braking system which consists of two brake shoes and one or two wheel cylinders, mounted on a fixed backing plate, and a brake drum, mounted on an axle, which revolves around the assembly. Hydraulic action applied to the wheel cylinders forces the shoes outward against the drum, creating friction, slowing the vehicle.

DWELL: The rate, measured in degrees of shaft rotation, at which an electrical circuit cycles on and off.

ELECTRONIC CONTROL UNIT (ECU): Ignition module, amplifier or igniter. See Module for definition.

ELECTRONIC IGNITION: A system in which the timing and firing of the spark plugs is controlled by an electronic control unit, usually called a module. These systems have no points or condenser.

ENDPLAY: The measured amount of axial movement in a shaft.

ENGINE: A device that converts heat into mechanical energy.

EXHAUST MANIFOLD: A set of cast passages or pipes which conduct exhaust gases from the engine.

FEELER GAUGE: A blade, usually metal, of precisely predetermined thickness, used to measure the clearance between two parts. These blades usually are available in sets of assorted thicknesses.

F-HEAD: An engine configuration in which the intake valves are in the cylinder head, while the camshaft and exhaust valves are located in the cylinder block. The camshaft operates the intake valves via lifters and pushrods, while it operates the exhaust valves directly.

FIRING ORDER: The order in which combustion occurs in the cylinders of an engine. Also the order in which spark is distributed to the plugs by the distributor.

FLATHEAD: An engine configuration in which the camshaft and all the valves are located in the cylinder block.

FLOODING: The presence of too much fuel in the intake manifold and combustion chamber which prevents the air/fuel mixture from firing, thereby causing a no-start situation.

FLYWHEEL: A disc shaped part bolted to the rear end of the crankshaft. Around the outer perimeter is affixed the ring gear. The starter drive engages the ring gear, turning the flywheel, which rotates the crankshaft, imparting the initial starting motion to the engine.

FOOT POUND (ft.lb. or sometimes, ft. lbs.): The amount of energy or work needed to raise an item weighing one pound, a distance of one foot.

FUSE: A protective device in a circuit which prevents circuit overload by breaking the circuit when a specific amperage is present. The device is constructed around a strip or wire of a lower amperage rating than the circuit it is designed to protect. When an amperage higher than that stamped on the fuse is present in the circuit, the strip or wire melts, opening the circuit.

GEAR RATIO: The ratio between the number of teeth on meshing gears.

GENERATOR: A device which converts mechanical energy into electrical energy.

HEAT RANGE: The measure of a spark plug's ability to dissipate heat from its firing end. The higher the heat range, the hotter the plug fires. **HUB:** The center part of a wheel or gear.

HYDROCARBON (HC): Any chemical compound made up of hydrogen and carbon. A major pollutant formed by the engine as a byproduct of combustion.

HYDROMETER: An instrument used to measure the specific gravity of a solution.

INCH POUND (in.lb. or sometimes, in. lbs.): One twelfth of a foot pound.

INDUCTION: A means of transferring electrical energy in the form of a magnetic field. Principle used in the ignition coil to increase voltage.

INJECTION PUMP: A device, usually mechanically operated, which meters and delivers fuel under pressure to the fuel injector.

INJECTOR: A device which receives metered fuel under relatively low pressure and is activated to inject the fuel into the engine under relatively high pressure at a predetermined time.

INPUT SHAFT: The shaft to which torque is applied, usually carrying the driving gear or gears.

INTAKE MANIFOLD: A casting of passages or pipes used to conduct air or a fuel/air mixture to the cylinders.

JOURNAL: The bearing surface within which a shaft operates.

KEY: A small block usually fitted in a notch between a shaft and a hub to prevent slippage of the two parts.

MANIFOLD: A casting of passages or set of pipes which connect the cylinders to an inlet or outlet source.

MANIFOLD VACUUM: Low pressure in an engine intake manifold formed just below the throttle plates. Manifold vacuum is highest at idle and drops under acceleration.

MASTER CYLINDER: The primary fluid pressurizing device in a hydraulic system. In automotive use, it is found in brake and hydraulic clutch systems and is pedal activated, either directly or, in a power brake system, through the power booster.

MODULE: Electronic control unit, amplifier or igniter of solid state or integrated design which controls the current flow in the ignition primary circuit based on input from the pickup coil. When the module opens the primary circuit, the high secondary voltage is induced in the coil.

NEEDLE BEARING: A bearing which consists of a number (usually a large number) of long, thin rollers.

OHM:(Ω) The unit used to measure the resistance of conductor to electrical flow. One ohm is the amount of resistance that limits current flow to one ampere in a circuit with one volt of pressure.

OHMMETER: An instrument used for measuring the resistance, in ohms, in an electrical circuit.

OUTPUT SHAFT: The shaft which transmits torque from a device, such as a transmission.

OVERDRIVE: A gear assembly which produces more shaft revolutions than that transmitted to it.

OVERHEAD CAMSHAFT (OHC): An engine configuration in which the camshaft is mounted on top of the cylinder head and operates the valves either directly or by means of rocker arms.

OVERHEAD VALVE (OHV): An engine configuration in which all of the valves are located in the cylinder head and the camshaft is located in the cylinder block. The camshaft operates the valves via lifters and pushrods.

OXIDES OF NITROGEN (NOx): Chemical compounds of nitrogen produced as a byproduct of combustion. They combine with hydrocarbons to produce smog.

OXYGEN SENSOR: Used with the feedback system to sense the presence of oxygen in the exhaust gas and signal the computer which can reference the voltage signal to an air/fuel ratio.

PINION: The smaller of two meshing gears.

PISTON RING: An open ended ring which fits into a groove on the outer diameter of the piston. Its chief function is to form a seal between the piston and cylinder wall. Most automotive pistons have three rings: two for compression sealing; one for oil sealing.

PRELOAD: A predetermined load placed on a bearing during assembly or by adjustment.

PRIMARY CIRCUIT: Is the low voltage side of the ignition system which consists of the ignition switch, ballast resistor or resistance wire, bypass, coil, electronic control unit and pick-up coil as well as the connecting wires and harnesses.

PRESS FIT: The mating of two parts under pressure, due to the inner diameter of one being smaller than the outer diameter of the other, or vice versa; an interference fit.

RACE: The surface on the inner or outer ring of a bearing on which the balls, needles or rollers move.

REGULATOR: A device which maintains the amperage and/or voltage levels of a circuit at predetermined values.

RELAY: A switch which automatically opens and/or closes a circuit.

RESISTANCE: The opposition to the flow of current through a circuit or electrical device, and is measured in ohms. Resistance is equal to the voltage divided by the amperage.

RESISTOR: A device, usually made of wire, which offers a preset amount of resistance in an electrical circuit.

RING GEAR: The name given to a ring-shaped gear attached to a differential case, or affixed to a flywheel or as part a planetary gear set.

ROLLER BEARING: A bearing made up of hardened inner and outer races between which hardened steel rollers move.

ROTOR: 1. The disc-shaped part of a disc brake assembly, upon which the brake pads bear; also called, brake disc.
2. The device mounted atop the distributor shaft, which passes current to the distributor cap tower contacts.

SECONDARY CIRCUIT: The high voltage side of the ignition system, usually above 20,000 volts. The secondary includes the ignition coil, coil wire, distributor cap and rotor, spark plug wires and spark plugs.

SENDING UNIT: A mechanical, electrical, hydraulic or electromagnetic device which transmits information to a gauge.

SENSOR: Any device designed to measure engine operating conditions or ambient pressures and temperatures. Usually electronic in nature and designed to send a voltage signal to an on-board computer, some sensors may operate as a simple on/off switch or they may provide a variable voltage signal (like a potentiometer) as conditions or measured parameters change.

SHIM: Spacers of precise, predetermined thickness used between parts to establish a proper working relationship.

SLAVE CYLINDER: In automotive use, a device in the hydraulic clutch system which is activated by hydraulic force, disengaging the clutch.

SOLENOID: A coil used to produce a magnetic field, the effect of which is to produce work.

SPARK PLUG: A device screwed into the combustion chamber of a spark ignition engine. The basic construction is a conductive core inside of a ceramic insulator, mounted in an outer conductive base. An electrical charge from the spark plug wire travels along the conductive core and jumps a preset air gap to a grounding point or points at the end of the conductive base. The resultant spark ignites the fuel/air mixture in the combustion chamber.

SPLINES: Ridges machined or cast onto the outer diameter of a shaft or inner diameter of a bore to enable parts to mate without rotation.

TACHOMETER: A device used to measure the rotary speed of an engine, shaft, gear, etc., usually in rotations per minute.

THERMOSTAT: A valve, located in the cooling system of an engine, which is closed when cold and opens gradually in response to engine heating, controlling the temperature of the coolant and rate of coolant flow.

TOP DEAD CENTER (TDC): The point at which the piston reaches the top of its travel on the compression stroke.

TORQUE: The twisting force applied to an object.

TORQUE CONVERTER: A turbine used to transmit power from a driving member to a driven member via hydraulic action, providing changes in drive ratio and torque. In automotive use, it links the driveplate at the rear of the engine to the automatic transmission.

TRANSDUCER: A device used to change a force into an electrical signal.

TRANSISTOR: A semi-conductor component which can be actuated by a small voltage to perform an electrical switching function.

TUNE-UP: A regular maintenance function, usually associated with the replacement and adjustment of parts and components in the electrical and fuel systems of a vehicle for the purpose of attaining optimum performance.

TURBOCHARGER: An exhaust driven pump which compresses intake air and forces it into the combustion chambers at higher than atmospheric pressures. The increased air pressure allows more fuel to be burned and results in increased horsepower being produced.

VACUUM ADVANCE: A device which advances the ignition timing in response to increased engine vacuum.

VACUUM GAUGE: An instrument used to measure the presence of vacuum in a chamber.

VALVE: A device which control the pressure, direction of flow or rate of flow of a liquid or gas.

VALVE CLEARANCE: The measured gap between the end of the valve stem and the rocker arm, cam lobe or follower that activates the valve.

VISCOSITY: The rating of a liquid's internal resistance to flow.

VOLTMETER: An instrument used for measuring electrical force in units called volts. Voltmeters are always connected parallel with the circuit being tested.

WHEEL CYLINDER: Found in the automotive drum brake assembly, it is a device, actuated by hydraulic pressure, which, through internal pistons, pushes the brake shoes outward against the drums.

A: Ampere

AC: Alternating current

A/C: Air conditioning

A-h: Amper hour

AT: Automatic transmission

ATDC: After top dead center

μA: Microampere

bbl: Barrel

BDC: Bottom dead center

bhp: Brake horsepower

BTDC: Before top dead center

BTU: British thermal unit

C: Celsius (Centigrade)

CCA: Cold cranking amps

cd: Candela

cm^2: Square centimeter

cm^3, cc: Cubic centimeter

CO: Carbon monoxide

CO_2: Carbon dioxide

cu.in., in^3: Cubic inch

CV: Constant velocity

Cyl.: Cylinder

DC: Direct current

ECM: Electronic control module

EFE: Early fuel evaporation

EFI: Electronic fuel injection

EGR: Exhaust gas recirculation

Exh.: Exhaust

F: Farenheit

F: Farad

pF: Picofarad

μF: Microfarad

FI: Fuel injection

ft.lb., ft. lb., ft. lbs.: foot pound(s)

gal: Gallon

g: Gram

HC: Hydrocarbon

HEI: High energy ignition

HO: High output

hp: Horsepower

Hyd: Hydraulic

Hz: Hertz

ID: Inside diameter

in.lb; in. lbs.; in. lbs.: inch pound(s)

Int: Intake

K: Kelvin

kg: Kilogram

kHz: Kilohertz

km: Kilometer

km/h: Kilometers per hour

kΩ: Kilohm

kPa: Kilopascal

kV: Kilovolt

kW: Kilowatt

l: Liter

l/s: Liters per second

m: Meter

mA: Milliampere

mg: Milligram

mHz: Megahertz

mm: Millimeter

mm^2: Square millimeter

m^3: Cubic meter

$M\Omega$: Megohm

m/s: Meters per second

MT: Manual transmission

mV: Millivolt

μm: Micrometer

N: Newton

N–m: Newton meter

NOx: Nitrous oxide

OD: Outside diameter

OHC: Over head camshaft

OHV: Over head valve

Ω: Ohm

PCV: Positive crankcase ventilation

psi: Pounds per square inch

pts: Pints

qts: Quarts

rpm: Rotations per minute

rps: Rotations per second

R–12: refrigerant gas (Freon)

SAE: Society of Automotive Engineers

SO_2: Sulfur dioxide

T: Ton

t: Megagram

TBI: Throttle Body Injection

TPS: Throttle Position Sensor

V: 1. Volt; 2. Venturi

μV: Microvolt

W: Watt

∞: Infinity

<: Less than

>: Greater than

Chilton's Repair & Tune-Up Guides

The Complete line covers domestic cars, imports, trucks, vans, RV's and 4-wheel drive vehicles.

RTUG Title	Part No.
AMC 1975-82	7199
Covers all U.S. and Canadian models	
Aspen/Volare 1976-80	6637
Covers all U.S. and Canadian models	
Audi 1970-73	5902
Covers all U.S. and Canadian models.	
Audi 4000/5000 1978-81	7028
Covers all U.S. and Canadian models including turbocharged and diesel engines	
Barracuda/Challenger 1965-72	5807
Covers all U.S. and Canadian models	
Blazer/Jimmy 1969-82	6931
Covers all U.S. and Canadian 2- and 4-wheel drive models, including diesel engines	
BMW 1970-82	6844
Covers U.S. and Canadian models	
Buick/Olds/Pontiac 1975-85	7308
Covers all U.S. and Canadian full size rear wheel drive models	
Cadillac 1967-84	7462
Covers all U.S. and Canadian rear wheel drive models	
Camaro 1967-81	6735
Covers all U.S. and Canadian models	
Camaro 1982-85	7317
Covers all U.S. and Canadian models	
Capri 1970-77	6695
Covers all U.S. and Canadian models	
Caravan/Voyager 1984-85	7482
Covers all U.S. and Canadian models	
Century/Regal 1975-85	7307
Covers all U.S. and Canadian rear wheel drive models, including turbocharged engines	
Champ/Arrow/Sapporo 1978-83	7041
Covers all U.S. and Canadian models	
Chevette/1000 1976-86	6836
Covers all U.S. and Canadian models	
Chevrolet 1968-85	7135
Covers all U.S. and Canadian models	
Chevrolet 1968-79 Spanish	7082
Chevrolet/GMC Pick-Ups 1970-82 Spanish	7468
Chevrolet/GMC Pick-Ups and Suburban 1970-86	6936
Covers all U.S. and Canadian $\frac{1}{2}$, $\frac{3}{4}$ and 1 ton models, including 4-wheel drive and diesel engines	
Chevrolet LUV 1972-81	6815
Covers all U.S. and Canadian models	
Chevrolet Mid-Size 1964-86	6840
Covers all U.S. and Canadian models of 1964-77 Chevelle, Malibu and Malibu SS; 1974-77 Laguna; 1978-85 Malibu; 1970-86 Monte Carlo; 1964-84 El Camino, including diesel engines	
Chevrolet Nova 1986	7658
Covers all U.S. and Canadian models	
Chevy/GMC Vans 1967-84	6930
Covers all U.S. and Canadian models of $\frac{1}{2}$, $\frac{3}{4}$, and 1 ton vans, cutaways, and motor home chassis, including diesel engines	
Chevy S-10 Blazer/GMC S-15 Jimmy 1982-85	7383
Covers all U.S. and Canadian models	
Chevy S-10/GMC S-15 Pick-Ups 1982-85	7310
Covers all U.S. and Canadian models	
Chevy II/Nova 1962-79	6841
Covers all U.S. and Canadian models	
Chrysler K- and E-Car 1981-85	7163
Covers all U.S. and Canadian front wheel drive models	
Colt/Challenger/Vista/Conquest 1971-85	7037
Covers all U.S. and Canadian models	
Corolla/Carina/Tercel/Starlet 1970-85	7036
Covers all U.S. and Canadian models	
Corona/Cressida/Crown/Mk.II/Camry/Van 1970-84	7044
Covers all U.S. and Canadian models	

RTUG Title	Part No.
Corvair 1960-69	6691
Covers all U.S. and Canadian models	
Corvette 1953-62	6576
Covers all U.S. and Canadian models	
Corvette 1963-84	6843
Covers all U.S. and Canadian models	
Cutlass 1970-85	6933
Covers all U.S. and Canadian models	
Dart/Demon 1968-76	6324
Covers all U.S. and Canadian models	
Datsun 1961-72	5790
Covers all U.S. and Canadian models of Nissan Patrol; 1500, 1600 and 2000 sports cars; Pick-Ups; 410, 411, 510, 1200 and 240Z	
Datsun 1973-80 Spanish	7083
Datsun/Nissan F-10, 310, Stanza, Pulsar 1977-86	7196
Covers all U.S. and Canadian models	
Datsun/Nissan Pick-Ups 1970-84	6816
Covers all U.S. and Canadian models	
Datsun/Nissan Z & ZX 1970-86	6932
Covers all U.S. and Canadian models	
Datsun/Nissan 1200, 210, Sentra 1973-86	7197
Covers all U.S. and Canadian models	
Datsun/Nissan 200SX, 510, 610, 710, 810, Maxima 1973-84	7170
Covers all U.S. and Canadian models	
Dodge 1968-77	6554
Covers all U.S. and Canadian models	
Dodge Charger 1967-70	6486
Covers all U.S. and Canadian models	
Dodge/Plymouth Trucks 1967-84	7459
Covers all $\frac{1}{2}$, $\frac{3}{4}$, and 1 ton 2- and 4-wheel drive U.S. and Canadian models, including diesel engines	
Dodge/Plymouth Vans 1967-84	6934
Covers all $\frac{1}{2}$, $\frac{3}{4}$, and 1 ton U.S. and Canadian models of vans, cutaways and motor home chassis	
D-50/Arrow Pick-Up 1979-81	7032
Covers all U.S. and Canadian models	
Fairlane/Torino 1962-75	6320
Covers all U.S. and Canadian models	
Fairmont/Zephyr 1978-83	6965
Covers all U.S. and Canadian models	
Fiat 1969-81	7042
Covers all U.S. and Canadian models	
Fiesta 1978-80	6846
Covers all U.S. and Canadian models	
Firebird 1967-81	5996
Covers all U.S. and Canadian models	
Firebird 1982-85	7345
Covers all U.S. and Canadian models	
Ford 1968-79 Spanish	7084
Ford Bronco 1966-83	7140
Covers all U.S. and Canadian models	
Ford Bronco II 1984	7408
Covers all U.S. and Canadian models	
Ford Courier 1972-82	6983
Covers all U.S. and Canadian models	
Ford/Mercury Front Wheel Drive 1981-85	7055
Covers all U.S. and Canadian models Escort, EXP, Tempo, Lynx, LN-7 and Topaz	
Ford/Mercury/Lincoln 1968-85	6842
Covers all U.S. and Canadian models of FORD Country Sedan, Country Squire, Crown Victoria, Custom, Custom 500, Galaxie 500, LTD through 1982, Ranch Wagon, and XL; MERCURY Colony Park, Commuter, Marquis through 1982, Gran Marquis, Monterey and Park Lane; LINCOLN Continental and Towne Car	
Ford/Mercury/Lincoln Mid-Size 1971-85	6696
Covers all U.S. and Canadian models of FORD Elite, 1983-85 LTD, 1977-79 LTD II, Ranchero, Torino, Gran Torino, 1977-85 Thunderbird; MERCURY 1972-85 Cougar,	

continued on next page

RTUG Title	Part No.	RTUG Title	Part No.
1983-85 Marquis, Montego, 1980-85 XR-7; LINCOLN 1982-85 Continental, 1984-85 Mark VII, 1978-80 Versailles		Mercedes-Benz 1974-84 Covers all U.S. and Canadian models	6809
Ford Pick-Ups 1965-86 Covers all 1/2, 3/4 and 1 ton, 2- and 4-wheel drive U.S. and Canadian pick-up, chassis cab and camper models, including diesel engines	6913	Mitsubishi, Cordia, Tredia, Starion, Galant 1983-85 Covers all U.S. and Canadian models	7583
		MG 1961-81 Covers all U.S. and Canadian models	6780
Ford Pick-Ups 1965-82 Spanish	7469	Mustang/Capri/Merkur 1979-85	6963
Ford Ranger 1983-84 Covers all U.S. and Canadian models	7338	Mustang/Cougar 1965-73 Covers all U.S. and Canadian models	6542
Ford Vans 1961-86 Covers all U.S. and Canadian 1/2, 3/4 and 1 ton van and cutaway chassis models, including diesel engines	6849	Mustang II 1974-78 Covers all U.S. and Canadian models	6812
		Omni/Horizon/Rampage 1978-84 Covers all U.S. and Canadian models of DODGE omni, Miser, 024, Charger 2.2; PLYMOUTH Horizon, Miser, TC3, TC3 Tourismo; Rampage	6845
GM A-Body 1982-85 Covers all front wheel drive U.S. and Canadian models of BUICK Century, CHEVROLET Celebrity, OLDSMOBILE Cutlass Ciera and PONTIAC 6000	7309		
		Opel 1971-75 Covers all U.S. and Canadian models	6575
GM C-Body 1985 Covers all front wheel drive U.S. and Canadian models of BUICK Electra Park Avenue and Electra T-Type, CADILLAC Fleetwood and deVille, OLDSMOBILE 98 Regency and Regency Brougham	7587	Peugeot 1970-74 Covers all U.S. and Canadian models	5982
		Pinto/Bobcat 1971-80 Covers all U.S. and Canadian models	7027
		Plymouth 1968-76 Covers all U.S. and Canadian models	6552
GM J-Car 1982-85 Covers all U.S. and Canadian models of BUICK Skyhawk, CHEVROLET Cavalier, CADILLAC Cimarron, OLDSMOBILE Firenza and PONTIAC 2000 and Sunbird	7059	Pontiac Fiero 1984-85 Covers all U.S. and Canadian models	7571
		Pontiac Mid-Size 1974-83 Covers all U.S. and Canadian models of Ventura, Grand Am, LeMans, Grand LeMans, GTO, Phoenix, and Grand Prix	7346
GM N-Body 1985-86 Covers all U.S. and Canadian models of front wheel drive BUICK Somerset and Skylark, OLDSMOBILE Calais, and PONTIAC Grand Am	7657		
		Porsche 924/928 1976-81 Covers all U.S. and Canadian models	7048
		Renault 1975-85 Covers all U.S. and Canadian models	7165
GM X-Body 1980-85 Covers all U.S. and Canadian models of BUICK Skylark, CHEVROLET Citation, OLDSMOBILE Omega and PONTIAC Phoenix	7049	Roadrunner/Satellite/Belvedere/GTX 1968-73 Covers all U.S. and Canadian models	5821
		RX-7 1979-81 Covers all U.S. and Canadian models	7031
GM Subcompact 1971-80 Covers all U.S. and Canadian models of BUICK Skyhawk (1975-80), CHEVROLET Vega and Monza, OLDSMOBILE Starfire, and PONTIAC Astre and 1975-80 Sunbird	6935	SAAB 99 1969-75 Covers all U.S. and Canadian models	5988
		SAAB 900 1979-85 Covers all U.S. and Canadian models	7572
		Snowmobiles 1976-80 Covers Arctic Cat, John Deere, Kawasaki, Polaris, Ski-Doo and Yamaha	6978
Granada/Monarch 1975-82 Covers all U.S. and Canadian models	6937		
Honda 1973-84 Covers all U.S. and Canadian models	6980	Subaru 1970-84 Covers all U.S. and Canadian models	6982
International Scout 1967-73 Covers all U.S. and Canadian models	5912	Tempest/GTO/LeMans 1968-73 Covers all U.S. and Canadian models	5905
Jeep 1945-87 Covers all U.S. and Canadian CJ-2A, CJ-3A, CJ-3B, CJ-5, CJ-6, CJ-7, Scrambler and Wrangler models	6817	Toyota 1966-70 Covers all U.S. and Canadian models of Corona, MkII, Corolla, Crown, Land Cruiser, Stout and Hi-Lux	5795
		Toyota 1970-79 Spanish	7467
Jeep Wagoneer, Commando, Cherokee, Truck 1957-86 Covers all U.S. and Canadian models of Wagoneer, Cherokee, Grand Wagoneer, Jeepster, Jeepster Commando, J-100, J-200, J-300, J-10, J20, FC-150 and FC-170	6739	Toyota Celica/Supra 1971-85 Covers all U.S. and Canadian models	7043
		Toyota Trucks 1970-85 Covers all U.S. and Canadian models of pick-ups, Land Cruiser and 4Runner	7035
		Valiant/Duster 1968-76 Covers all U.S. and Canadian models	6326
Laser/Daytona 1984-85 Covers all U.S. and Canadian models	7563	Volvo 1956-69 Covers all U.S. and Canadian models	6529
Maverick/Comet 1970-77 Covers all U.S. and Canadian models	6634	Volvo 1970-83 Covers all U.S. and Canadian models	7040
Mazda 1971-84 Covers all U.S. and Canadian models of RX-2, RX-3, RX-4, 808, 1300, 1600, Cosmo, GLC and 626	6981	VW Front Wheel Drive 1974-85 Covers all U.S. and Canadian models	6962
		VW 1949-71 Covers all U.S. and Canadian models	5796
Mazda Pick-Ups 1972-86 Covers all U.S. and Canadian models	7659	VW 1970-79 Spanish	7081
Mercedes-Benz 1959-70 Covers all U.S. and Canadian models	6065	VW 1970-81 Covers all U.S. and Canadian Beetles, Karmann Ghia, Fastback, Squareback, Vans, 411 and 412	6837
Merecds-Benz 1968-73 Covers all U.S. and Canadian models	5907		

Chilton's Repair Manuals are available at your local retailer or by mailing a check or money order for **$14.95** per book plus **$3.50** for 1st book and **$.50** for each additional book to cover postage and handling to:

Chilton Book Company
Dept. DM
Radnor, PA 19089

NOTE: When ordering be sure to include your name & address, book part No. & title.